Capital, Interest, and Waiting

"For an intertemporal view of the price system, a better understanding of monetary policy, and an in-depth analysis of the 'economics of waiting,' there is no better book than *Capital, Interest, and Waiting*."

—James A. Dorn, *Senior Fellow Emeritus at the Cato Institute and editor of* Populism and the Future of the Fed

"*Capital, Interest, and Waiting* takes a deep dive into the nature of the interest rate understood as the price paid for waiting. Authors Leland Yeager and Steve Hanke place waiting into the working of the price system and, as it turns out, the interest rate is a much more complicated phenomenon than just the interest one pays on credit card balances. For example, as a relative price, it is part of the real economy controlling market exchanges. Yet central banks set it as an instrument for implementing monetary policy. How, then, can central banks control a real price when they control something so nominal: money creation? Yeager and Hanke offer no cut-and-dried answers. Instead, they take the reader on a voyage through the insights of the most brilliant economists over the ages. One should come to this book prepared to think critically."

—Robert L. Hetzel, *Senior Affiliated Scholar, Mercatus Center, George Mason University; Fellow, Institute for Applied Economics, Johns Hopkins University; and author of* The Federal Reserve

"Yeager and Hanke add substantial clarity to the complexity of capital theory by depicting interest as a payment for waiting. Their approach to capital theory clarifies past controversies and offers a theory consistent with well-established concepts in price theory. Economists will find the analysis both easy to follow and insightful."

—Randall G. Holcombe, *DeVoe Moore Professor of Economics, Florida State University and author of* Coordination, Cooperation, and Control

"At the centenary of Leland Yeager's birth, here is a welcome surprise: his final magnum opus. Co-author Steve Hanke has performed an impressive feat by taking Yeager's tangled mess of a manuscript (I saw it for myself), filling in many gaps, and producing a book that preserves Yeager's distinctive writing style. The style is marked by clarity, polish, and a concern with everyday experience, not just for economists' models—though Yeager has a superb grasp of what his predecessors thought. Among the thousands of books and articles on the theory of capital, there is little else that has all those qualities."

—Kurt Schuler, *Senior Fellow, Center for Financial Stability*

"Read this respected examination of the economic function of waiting in human economic betterment."

—Vernon L. Smith,*Chapman University, author of* Adam Smith's Theory of Society, and 2002 Nobel Laureate in Economics

"Yeager and Hanke created a masterful book that weaves together both intellectual history and solid economic theory. This book breaks down interest theory and the role prices play in coordinating all manner of economic activity. Students and professionals alike will find value in this thorough analysis."

—Meg Tuszynski, *Bridwell Institute for Economic Freedom, Cox School of Business, Southern Methodist University and coauthor of* Reason, Ideology, and Democracy

"The passage of time imposes costs on human activity; Yeager and Hanke provide a transformative account of the implications of this. A great work by two giant interpreters of monetary phenomena."

—Richard Vedder, *Distinguished Emeritus Professor of Economics, Ohio University and Senior Fellow, Independent Institute*

"Capital theory has long presented an impenetrable morass to economists. Many economists have entered that morass, invariably failing to chart a clear path through it despite the prolixity of their efforts. In the 19th century, Eugen von Böhm-Bawerk devoted over a thousand pages to creating *The Theory of Capital and Interest*. About a century later, Don Patinkin invested over 700 pages in seeking to integrate a theory of *Money, Interest, and Prices*. And numerous other economists contributed their thoughts without any sense of conceptual coherence coming into existence. Now, the authors have shown how the elemental concept of waiting can, when deftly employed by theorists, provide coherence to cover nearly all past tergiversations over capital theory. To be sure, Yeager died in April 2018 his manuscript considerably unfinished, I can testify from a conversation with Yeager a few years before his death. Steve Hanke assembled the final manuscript, for which he deserves applause from all economists with interest in capital theory because the Yeager-Hanke volume is a graceful and compelling read."

—Richard E. Wagner, *Holbert Harris Professor of Economics, Emeritus, George Mason University and author of* Macroeconomics as Systems Theory

Leland B. Yeager · Steve H. Hanke

Capital, Interest, and Waiting

Controversies, Puzzles, and New Additions to Capital Theory

palgrave
macmillan

Leland B. Yeager
Ludwig von Mises Distinguished
Professor Emeritus of Economics
Auburn University
Auburn, AL, USA

Paul Goodloe McIntire Professor
of Economics Emeritus
University of Virginia
Charlottesville, VA, USA

Steve H. Hanke
Professor of Applied Economics
Johns Hopkins University
Baltimore, MD, USA

ISBN 978-3-031-63397-3 ISBN 978-3-031-63398-0 (eBook)
https://doi.org/10.1007/978-3-031-63398-0

This Palgrave Macmillan imprint is published by the registered company Springer Nature Switzerland AG
The registered company address is: Gewerbestrasse 11, 6330 Cham, Switzerland

Preface

I am, unfortunately, obliged to write the preface to this Yeager-Hanke volume alone, without my good friend, mentor, and collaborator Leland Yeager, who met the grim reaper on Monday morning, April 23, 2018.

I first met Leland in the summer of 1967, when I attended a summer program at the University of Virginia. The program was offered to young faculty with an interest in free-market economics. I qualified because I had recently joined the faculty of the Colorado School of Mines. What a program it was. The "Big Guns" lectured. They included: Armen Alchian, Bill Allen, Bill Breit, Jim Buchanan, Warren Nutter, Gordon Tullock, and Leland Yeager. Leland presented the lectures on international trade. I can still recall them. He arrived fully prepared and ready to go—armed with a yardstick. Yes, a yardstick, which Leland used to draw complicated trade diagrams. And, typical of Leland, he did so with great precision. Indeed, Leland is the only professor I have ever observed who could, and did, draw picture-perfect diagrams on a chalkboard. Even while lecturing, Leland was an ever-careful and precise scholar.

For over 50 years, Leland and I remained in contact. Since around 1976, we engaged in what became a rather intense collaboration on capital and interest theory, with an emphasis on the importance of "waiting" as a factor of production and "interest" as its price. I primarily served as Leland's sounding board and reviewed his notes and manuscript drafts. As time passed, our interactions on this research program became more intense. Leland regularly complained about his age and a growing number of ailments. These complaints were always made in the context of Leland's worries that he would not be able to finish this book. And, they always ended with Leland's request that I finish the manuscript if he did not make it to the finish line.

These complaints were such regular refrains that I brushed them off and told Leland to stop worrying, that he was going to finish the book manuscript, and that, yes, I would finish things if need be.

However, in his last email (April 5, 2018), Leland alarmingly went way beyond his usual grumblings about his age and ill health. He wrote, "At age 93 and suffering from weakness, fatigue, various ailments, and severe pains (most recently from osteoporosis), I must admit that I am in no condition to contribute much more to the MS." Leland's shot across the bow shocked me because he remained as sharp as a tack. Indeed, in his last email, Leland did what he had always done: he never stopped turning over ideas and fretting about the quality of his work. Until his dying day, Leland remained to me that precise professor who lectured with a yardstick—a master of rhetoric, blackboard economics, and much, much more.

In that email, Leland also stated: "According to my trust and will, as I said before, you as coauthor will have complete discretion about format (ranging from the whole book to one or more articles) and about how to list our names."

After Leland went to the other side, Luis Dopico, a former student of Leland's and a trustee of Leland's estate, and myself immediately set out to put Leland's affairs in order. This was a big task, but it was made easier because Leland left detailed instructions on how he wanted us to proceed. Eventually, I received large boxes of materials and computer disks, which contained an array of additional notes, draft material, and reference books.

As it turned out, the materials, which had been produced over some 40 years, were in disorder. To organize things, my chief of staff Christopher Arena spent weeks sorting and organizing materials so that we could assess whether a book manuscript could be produced. After Christopher's painstaking work was completed, it was determined that a book manuscript would be possible, but that an enormous amount of work would be required to put the materials Leland had drafted into shape. Fortunately, Spencer Ryan, one of my most senior assistants, was willing to assist in my final push to produce a book-length manuscript. It required a good bit of effort, but, fortunately, it turned out to be a labor of love. We wish to also thank Kurt Schuler and Matt Sekerke for their valuable comments and suggestions on an earlier draft of our manuscript. In the end, the final product is one that I am pleased with and certainly think that Leland would be pleased with, too.

****

In "Is Interest the Price of a Factor of Production?" (1979), John Hicks defined a factor as any input that, if removed, would result in diminished production. Hicks then concluded that "waiting," or as he called it, "Intertemporal Switch in Output," is a factor of production, and "interest" is its price. Hicks was, of course, not the first to grapple with this problem.

Interest on a loan and the ratio of annual net rental payments to an asset's price are forms of an interest rate pervading the entire economy; so, equivalently, there is a pervasive "agio" or price premium of present over future goods. All are forms of the price received for "waiting"—for tying up wealth over time instead of using it for consumption or other current purpose. An amount of waiting is expressed in dollar-years. Its price is the explicit or implicit return on wealth tied up for a period, say a year. Since monetary values appear in both the numerator and the denominator of a ratio, they conveniently cancel out, leaving the percent per year as the dimension of the interest rate.

Many economists have taken positions on whether this rate is the price of a distinct factor of production. Nassau Senior (1790–1864) identified that factor early (1965, pp. 58–60). He called it "abstinence," recognizing that the term is inadequate (and "capital" worse) but unable to think of a better one. Anyway, Senior defined abstinence as "the conduct of a person who either abstains from the unproductive use of what he can command, or designedly prefers the production of remote to that of immediate results" (p. 58).

Silas Marcus MacVane (1887/1890/1892), introduced the term "waiting," and David Green (1894) offered an early but brief objection. Alfred Marshall (1947, 232–34) accepted the term "waiting." Eugene von Böhm-Bawerk (1959, 1:379) recognized MacVane's use of the term but rejected the concept. Gustav Cassel used the term "waiting" throughout his book of 1903, although saying that MacVane's formulation was not clear enough (Cassel 1956, pp. 41–42). Already, in 1766, Anne Robert Jacques Turgot noted that the interest rate—in the broad sense of the term—is "the price given for the use of a certain quantity of value during a certain time" (quoted in Cassel 1956, pp. 20–21). He put this use on a par with other factors of production. Turgot's formulation, said Cassel, has "never afterwards [been] surpassed in clearness and definiteness."

Cassel considered it settled, "once and for all, that interest is the price paid for an independent and elementary factor of production which may be called either waiting or use of capital, according to the point of view from which it is looked at... It is... an independent or primary factor in this sense, that it cannot be reduced to more elementary factors" (1956, pp. 67, 89). Hubert Henderson called "waiting... the essential reality underlying the phenomena of capital and interest. It is really this which constitutes an independent factor of production, distinct from labour and nature, and equally necessary" (1958, p. 98). Robert Dorfman "reaffirmed the reality of waiting as one of the primary factors of production, coordinate with labor, land, etc... waiting is a genuine scarce factor of production... The unit of waiting [may be taken as] one unit of consumption deferred for one unit of time" (Dorfman 1959, pp. 367, 370; compare Blaug 1962, pp. 471–475).

Capital goods—factories, machinery, and so forth—are evidence that waiting is taking place, but they are not themselves waiting. They embody waiting already performed and being continued, yes, but also labor and land use. In a world without wealth carried through time, labor and other ordinary factors would convert themselves instantly into capital goods and semi-finished goods, which in turn would convert themselves into houses, refrigerators, food, and so forth, all of which would render all of their ultimate consumer satisfaction instantly and in full.

To call waiting a factor of production in no way implies that reality embraces a specific small number of distinct factors and that it, like labor, is one of them. Waiting is performed in many ways, with different durations and degrees of risk and so forth, just as labor comes in different kinds and is performed in different conditions and paid at different rates. All this is a similarity, not a difference, among factors. Just what to treat as a factor is a question of convenience in each particular context. The same is true of production functions. Should a firm's production function count machinery used as an input, or should machinery be resolved into the land use, labor, and waiting that went into making it? Either choice could be legitimate, but not both at the same time. Again, reality does not dictate the answer; the choice depends on context and convenience.

The theory that regards waiting as a factor of production and its price as a measure of opportunity cost need not be presented as a challenge to more familiar versions like those inspired by Böhm-Bawerk. Rather, it completes those versions and unites them with standard price theory by recognizing waiting as a factor and its price as a means of allocating it among rival demands in view of opportunity cost.

This volume rests on the history of the controversies and debates that have swirled around capital and interest theory. We simplify capital and interest theory, tie it in better with general micro theory, and clear up certain puzzles by resurrecting the view that the interest rate is the price of "waiting," a factor of production. Waiting is the service performed by holding financial and physical assets instead of selling them and devoting the proceeds to current consumption or to other current exercise of command over resources. Waiting has the dimension of value over time.

Baltimore, MD, USA
November 2023

Prof. Steve H. Hanke

Contents

Table of Contents

List of Figures

List of Tables

CHAPTER 1

Introduction

1.1 A Challenge

Why does interest exist? Why does the value of output usually exceed the total cost of all obvious ultimate ingredients, including labor and land services? Why doesn't competition erode this discrepancy? The theory of competition says that the price of a good or service in long-run equilibrium tends to equal the values contributed by the factors producing it; the value of output should equal the total incomes of those original or ultimate factors. Capital and interest theory tackles such questions as part of general price theory and is a test of fully understanding it.

Time is indispensable for production and consumption. Try to imagine a world in which labor and other factors of production converted themselves instantly into machinery and semi-finished goods, which in turn converted themselves into final consumer goods and their services—all instantly. In the real world, some people must be willing to tie up wealth over time, forgoing immediate consumption. If building a house is to be worthwhile, the contractor must tie up resources while building it and must expect someone to buy it and wait for its services in a stream extending years into the future. If the prospective owner or occupant is unwilling or unable to tie up wealth of his own, he must find someone to take over that burden from him, by lending him money or by renting the property to him. An airline unable to tie up its own wealth in airplanes

L. B. Yeager and S. H. Hanke, *Capital, Interest, and Waiting*, https://doi.org/10.1007/978-3-031-63398-0_1

may rent them or borrow money to purchase them. Both the production and use of a house, plane, car, or refrigerator require waiting.

Capital goods—factories, machinery, and so forth—embody the original factors of production and are not themselves independent factors; so, counting them in addition to the original factors would be double counting.[1] Since they are intermediate stages between the original factors and final goods, the theory seems to suggest that the contribution of capital goods to the value of final products should exactly equal the payments made for the land and labor services embodied in them. How, then, could any income remain for the owner of capital goods beyond payment for embodied labor and land use? Citing roundabout, time-consuming methods of production is not enough of an answer. No income beyond compensation of original factors would flow from merely repeating roundabout methods incorporated into the circular flow of long-run competitive equilibrium—or so Joseph Schumpeter argued (1911/1934/1983, Chapter V).

Schumpeter saw three possible answers to this puzzle[2]: (1) A third ultimate factor of production, perhaps somehow related to capital goods, exists along with land and labor. (2) The theory that competition channels all value of output to the productive factors is flawed. Maybe Karl Marx, with his theory of exploitation, was onto something; Hubert Henderson summarizes Marx's argument.[3] (3) Interest as a return on capital would

[1] Saying so does not reject treating capital goods and other intermediate goods as factors of production; rather, it warns against *double* counting, as factors, both these and also the more nearly original or ultimate inputs that they embody. Just what to count as factors—how to handle intermediate goods and their own inputs—is simply a question of convenience in each piece of analysis. To ask what the factors of production *really* are is worse than pointless; what counts is analytical convenience. More on this follows in the section "Factors of Production and Production Functions."

[2] The following paragraphs summarize Schumpeter's argument and Conard's exposition (1959, pp. 20–21, 109–111).

[3] The factories and machinery which are admittedly essential to production were themselves produced in the same way as consumable goods. They were produced by labor, working with the assistance of nature, and, again, if you choose, of capital in the form of further factories, machinery, etc. But these further capital goods can in their turn be regarded as the product of labor, nature, and capital: and so, we can proceed until it seems as though the element of capital must disappear in the last analysis, as though labor and nature were the sole ultimate agents of production, and the reward of capital represented no more than the exercise of the exploiter's power. (Henderson 1921/1958, pp. 96–97).

indeed disappear in full competitive equilibrium. Anyway, it would not exist as something related to production and distinct from interest on consumer loans. It exists as a permanent flow of income in the real world only because competition is imperfect or because continuous innovation blocks static equilibrium.

Restating the puzzle may help. Interest on business loans relates to the fact that a user of capital goods or intermediate (semi-finished) goods can buy them, if all goes as expected, for less than they contribute to revenue from selling the final products. If all factors are paid what they contribute to the values of the final products, why are the full values of those products not swept back to original labor and land services? Why can capital goods yield net revenues beyond payments for the original factors that went into making them? Most briefly, why isn't the value of using capital goods fully equal to their contributions to the value of their ultimate product? How can any surplus emerge?

Of his three conjectured explanations, Schumpeter chose the third: interest would not exist in the circular flow of perfectly competitive equilibrium. It exists because innovative entrepreneurs keep creating profit opportunities (and arguably because consumers borrow). The economy never reaches the long-run competitive and static equilibrium of zero interest.

But is this answer satisfactory? Even static or repetitious production requires time. Interest would in all probability persist even in an economy without continuing innovation. Profit is a kind of income distinct from interest, perhaps the reward in disequilibrium for risk-bearing or entrepreneurship or both. Still, Schumpeter's puzzle and versions of it remain a challenge worthy of much of the literature devoted to it.

Hubert Henderson's own answer recognizes a third independent factor of production, which is not capital in the sense of capital goods like factories and machinery but something more abstract, as we endeavor to explain.

1.2 Scope of the Book

Capital and interest theory, or its "real" as distinct from the monetary side, receives less attention in courses and textbooks nowadays than it deserves. Yet, understanding it is important not only in itself but also for consolidating and testing one's grasp of opportunity cost and the logic of a price system. This book aims to analyze interest as a factor price on par with the wages of labor and rent on land.

Like other prices, the interest rate rations something useful but scarce, motivates supply, and conveys information. Yet it looks like a peculiar price. What sorts of supply and demand interact in determining it? How might it be related both to a preference for early over later satisfactions and to what Eugen von Böhm-Bawerk (1851–1914)[4] called the greater productivity of wisely chosen—repeat, wisely chosen—roundabout methods of production?

What should we call the factor whose price is the interest rate? Several suggestions will be reviewed later in passing. The word "patience" might have some appeal, but "waiting" has a better claim because of some use in the literature, and it is adopted here. It means tying up wealth or resources over time rather than using them for current consumption. It has the two dimensions of value tied up and length of time, thus "dollar-years." It is priced in dollars per dollar-year, which conveniently simplifies into "percent."

The very existence of machinery and other instruments of production and consumer durables shows that waiting is taking place. Someone who makes a loan performs waiting, while the borrower gets advanced command over resources by paying the lender to do the waiting for him.

Waiting is not the same as saving. Saving, the nonconsumption of income, adds to the stock of waiting; dissaving subtracts from it, for example, by running down productive equipment without repair or replacement. "Waiting" implies duration more clearly than "saving" does. When net saving is zero, the volume of waiting continues unchanged. Sometimes it is stylistically convenient to speak interchangeably of influences on saving and on the volume of waiting. Influences that promote saving promote waiting and vice versa.

Böhm-Bawerk was the leading theorist of capital and interest in the Austrian school of economists, who are intellectual heirs of Carl Menger (1840–1921). Menger (1871/1950, Chapter I) had introduced the concept of lower and higher stages of production and "orders" of goods.

Although widely, if regrettably, seen as a rival of mainstream economics, the Austrian school now flourishes at several institutions in the United States. The term no longer refers to Austria in particular. Austrian

[4] His full name, with title, is Eugen Böhm Ritter von Bawerk, commonly shortened to Böhm-Bawerk (or von Böhm-Bawerk) and sometimes just Böhm.

ideas recur occasionally in the following pages. The valid ideas of early and contemporary Austrians, along with criticism of questionable ones, contribute to a correct and comprehensive theory.

Still, this book is not an Austrian work. Nor does it claim much originality, for all sound strands of the theory have already appeared somewhere in a vast literature. Probably the works most instructive for us have been Böhm-Bawerk (1884–1912/1959), Wicksell (1898/1936/1965), Cassel (1903/1956 and 1932/1967), Fisher (1930/1955), Allais (1947), and Eucken (1954). If those names are not already household words, they will become so for the reader. Although the book includes some history of thought, it is not a comprehensive history organized around great thinkers. Here the history aims merely to give credit for important ideas and felicitous formulations and to learn from provocative errors.

Despite an abundance of errors, contradictions, and quibbles, the purpose here is not polemics. It is to pick out the valid points, contrast them with errors, and mesh them with broader economic theory. That is one reason for pushing analogies between different factors and factor prices as far as they will comfortably go.

Explaining interest does not alone *justify* it. Understanding some policy or institution belongs before judging its desirability, and that judgment must involve both objective facts and values going beyond them (Yeager 2001, esp. pp. 11–12, 238–241).

1.3 Narrow and Broad Senses of the "Interest Rate"

Definitions of the interest rate are traditionally imprecise. In equilibrium, it is the rate at which desired net saving, governed by the time preferences of savers and borrowers, equals desired net investment, influenced by prospective return on investments. Equivalently, it is the rate that equilibrates the total demand for and supply of waiting. But is it a long-run or short-run equilibrium rate? For explaining the essentials, the long-run equilibrium seems more relevant. Sometimes, however, a writer (e.g., Hetzel 2012) uses Wicksell's term "natural rate of interest" (1898/1936/1965) even for a short-run equilibrium, perhaps one influenced by the phase of the business cycle and associated optimism or pessimism.

In the narrowest sense, interest rates are the prices of money loans. More broadly, the interest rate is a fundamentally "real"—nonmonetary—phenomenon pervading the whole economy. Interest rates do, however, also respond to changes in the quantity of money and the demand to hold it, which can affect the supply of and demand for loans. This monetary response works mainly in the short run, although the demand to hold money has some influence in principle, however slight, even in the long run.

In contexts of money and inflation, although not everywhere, the "real rate" means a rate adjusted for price inflation (or deflation), while the quoted "nominal" rate does reflect the influence of inflation or expectations of it. Outside those contexts, the "interest rate" mostly considered here is the "fundamental" or "real" rate or Wicksell's "natural" rate.

Many different market rates of interest exist, along with implicit rates not explicitly quoted. Often, "*the* interest rate" is a convenient shorthand for the general level or range of these many different forms of interest. Theorizing about "the" interest rate can be as convenient and legitimate as theorizing about "the" wage of labor and "the" rent on land. Given stable money, the various interest rates tend to gravitate, although widely, around an equilibrium rate governed by the real factors sloganized as "productivity and thrift."

1.4 Productivity and Thrift

That slogan refers to the greater productivity of well-chosen time-consuming methods of production than of direct and quick methods and to people's preferences about *when* they consume. "Productivity" means transformation of goods potentially available now into more goods in the future. "Thrift" or "time preference" means the degree of willingness to save or, seen the other way around, impatience to enjoy goods now rather than later. Far from being exclusively physical or objective data, both productivity and thrift have subjective aspects. That is obviously true of time preference. The transformation of goods over time, or the yield on investment, is likewise more than physical reality; it also involves people's assessments and predictions. Keynes, for example, wrote about "animal spirits." What concerns people is not just transformation of physical things but of present into future values or satisfactions.

Optimism about greater future abundance and so the lower marginal utility[5] of future than of present goods makes people less inclined to save and perhaps more inclined to borrow for early consumption. This effect, by itself, works toward a high interest rate. Pessimism about the future and a prospective scarcity of future goods, on the other hand, discourages consumption and promotes saving.

Time preference is not an all-or-nothing matter. As so often in economics, the margin counts. A person entitled to much consumption in the present and little in the future would want to postpone having some of it: at the margin his time preference is negative. Someone in the opposite situation would want to shift some of his prospectively great future consumption into the present: his marginal time preference is positive. A person with equal entitlements to consumption in the present and future and who is indifferent, moreover, to marginally shifting consumption between the two periods, unless given an inducement, has *neutral* time preference at the margin. Where the margin occurs depends on inducements like the interest rate, which in turn depends partly on the productivity of thrift devoted to investment. Thrift, the willingness to save, suggests slight time preference, while high time preference means impatience or even spend thriftiness.

As for "productivity," both Austrian and mainstream economists recognize that the terms on which production can be shifted in time are likewise not an objectively given magnitude. Marginal productivity or marginal efficiency of capital or investment hinges partly on *subjective expectations* of both physical results and prospective profitability. Business pessimism depresses both the demand for investable funds and the interest rate.

Much of what is true of the real interest rate also holds for the wage rate of labor and for rent on land. Many specific rates prevail. Still, the concepts of labor in general and its wage rate and land services and

[5] The term "marginal utility" is too convenient to sacrifice, even though it may seem to imply that utility is cardinally measurable. Here, it expresses the amount of other goods, perhaps measured in dollars, that people would just willingly give up or acquire in exchange for a small gain or loss of the good or combination of goods in question. "Diminishing marginal utility" means that the more of one good (or a combination of goods) people have, the less of other goods, say dollars-worths, they would give up to have more of it. Ordinarily, increased or reduced relative marginal utility of something accompanies increased or reduced scarcity of it. Léon Walras (1874/1926/1954) used the word "*rareté*" to mean marginal utility.

their rent make sense. Concepts like labor's contribution to production and its irksomeness (or workers' leisure preference) enter into explaining the wage rate. Explanations of different wage rates for different types and conditions of labor build on this theory. Workers' preferences between labor and leisure are obviously subjective. Employers cannot know precisely how much using more or less labor will affect physical output, and their expectations about the sales value of output are even more subjective.

None of this means that subjective assessments totally control economic life (although a few Austrian economists have seemed to say so). Of course, business firms and individuals must recognize objective reality. Otherwise, they would perish.

1.5 "The Chief Problem of Capital Theory"

For individual entrepreneurs, interest is no puzzle. They pay or earn it and react to its rate. Capital, in one accountants' sense or another, appears in their balance sheets, but individual firms need not understand how capital accounting helps guide the economy. As Walter Eucken argues (1954, p. 221), economics should not stop at the horizon of the individual entrepreneur. Its task is to show economywide linkages. Why is there interest? What is the function of capital, somehow conceived? What is the logic of capital accounting? If economics shoves these questions aside and confines itself to an exact description of what goes on within the individual firm, "it remains stuck in pointless observation and loses its very purpose."

Economics describes how different needs or wants—for bread, meat, housing, and so forth—compete for productive factors. It explains how this allocational struggle is decided. But another struggle intertwines with this intersectoral one. Wants arising today, tomorrow, in a few months, and in several years, all compete for the productive forces available *today*. Some uses tie up productive factors for relatively brief periods until they "ripen" into final consumer goods and services; other uses require long ripening times. How is this intertemporal struggle decided? Eucken identifies those questions as "the chief problem of capital theory" (Eucken 1954, p. 197).

This theory deals more with the economic system as a whole than with managing a business firm or investment portfolio, although those topics require some attention. It exploits parallels between capital and interest and more familiar microeconomic topics. It portrays decisions about saving and investment as decisions about production and resource allocation. The interest rate appears as a particular factor price performing the familiar informational, incentive, and rationing functions. It comes within the purview of ordinary theories of supply and demand and functional income distribution, which show how the principle of derived demand applies to determining it, as well as other factor prices, and what sort of opportunity cost the interest-rate measures.

Whether something—here called "waiting"—properly counts as a factor of production is further considered throughout the book. Meanwhile, something's being a factor does not rule out it also being something else. Something can be a factor and a consumer good, like labor in domestic service or land kept as wilderness. The distinction between what is a factor and what is not is fuzzy and unnecessary.

So is any sharp distinction between capital goods—machinery and so forth—and durable consumer goods; both kinds of goods embody waiting. Undeniably, though, some investments, as in machinery and research, contribute more to economic growth than spending on items of conspicuous consumption. But economics itself does not condemn consumer's choices. The ultimate purpose of economic activity is people's satisfaction.

A focus on essentials postpones fringe complications and qualifications. Until Chapter 9, this book usually refers to "the" rate of interest as if there were only one. It does not distinguish between the rates at which one can borrow and can lend. Provisionally, it mostly ignores upward distortions from a "pure" rate of interest that allows for risks, trouble, and expense of lending and downward distortions like the implicit nonpecuniary yields from quasi-liquid claims. It collapses the whole range of time periods into only "the present" or "this year" and "the future" or "next year." Dropping these simplifications later will not upset but extend the essential theory.

1.6 Capital and Waiting

The many different meanings of the word "capital" almost recommend avoiding it altogether. Exceptions are excusable where a particular meaning is unmistakable or where precision is unnecessary or premature (as in this book's title).

"Capital" is especially unsatisfactory as the name of a factor of production in a theoretical production function. Sometimes the word is contaminated by conceptual realism or reification, the fallacy of supposing, if only tacitly, that a word implies the actual existence of a definite thing or condition so labeled. We should not emulate Socrates, who reputedly went around asking people what "courage," "virtue," and so forth actually *are*. We should not expect a definite answer to what "capital" actually *is*.[6] Often the word means "capital *goods*"–buildings, machinery, and other instruments used in production, and even purchased semi-finished goods. The word appears in "interest on capital," "land, labor, and capital," "the cost of capital," "the capital market," "human capital," shortage of capital," "international capital movements," "capital" as a balance sheet item or an amount defined by other entries on a balance sheet, and "capital-intensive" (like "labor-intensive") products and production methods.

1.7 Interdependence and Opportunity Cost

Gustav Cassel (1932, Chapter 4) presents a radically simplified general equilibrium equation system, adding realism step by step. It shows how consumers of various goods and services compete for the factors producing them. It shows how prices and quantities are established that enable consumers, workers, suppliers of other factors, and producers of all kinds to make informed choices. If some market does not yet clear or if a product price is greater or less than the cost, pressures operate toward market-clearing at price equaling cost. Consumers, facing prices, choose consumption patterns offering them the greatest expected satisfaction. Factor prices inform producers and product prices inform consumers of how much their choices of factors and goods cost the sacrifice of value to themselves and in other parts of the economy. Guided by prices, producers choose an overall pattern of production meshing with the choices of consumers.

The coefficients in Cassel's simplest equations fall into two main groups. The objective ones are the quantities of factors available, and the amount of each factor technically required per unit of each product.

[6] Menger (1888) is an example of agonizing at length over just what the word properly labels. Perhaps, excusably, he felt obliged to deal with the unsatisfactory state of the literature.

Subjective coefficients describe demand functions. Prices are determined neither from utilities alone nor from costs alone but from the scarcity of factors of production relative to consumers' derived demands for them. All the coefficients and what they represent are essential. "An 'objective' or 'subjective' theory of value, in the sense of a theory that would attribute the settlement of prices to objective or subjective factors alone, is therefore absurd; and the whole of the controversy between these theories of value, which has occupied such a disproportionately large place in economic literature, is a pure waste of energy" (1932, p. 146).

A consumer is considering whether to buy a $1000 refrigerator, and if yes, will he pay with cash or obtain a loan. Taking into account the $1000 as well as the interest rate and prices of other things that might also tempt him, he considers whether that purchase might crowd out some alternative use of productive factors offering greater value. He can estimate the *opportunity cost* of owning the fridge.

Opportunity cost is defined too narrowly as the individual chooser's sacrifice of his own next best option. Rather, it measures what anyone's choice of a product or a factor costs at the margin in sacrifice of other sources of value for himself and other persons. It inevitably follows from scarcity of goods and ultimately of factors.

An airline company is considering whether to buy a jet plane for $300 million. What alternative opportunities would buying the plane rule out? If the company already had the money, in what other ways might it invest it? If it got a loan to buy the plane, it would still *directly* bear the burden of tying up wealth in it as it rendered its services over time, but it would offload this burden by paying the lender to assume it. Or it might rent the plane. Or it might find the opportunity cost of an additional plane too high in view of other demands on its budget.

1.8 Interest as the Price of Waiting

Interest on a loan granted or obtained and the ratio of annual net rental payments to an asset's price are forms of an interest rate that pervades the entire economy; so also, is a pervasive "agio" or price premium of present over future goods. All are forms of the price received for "waiting"–for tying up wealth over time and delaying consumption. Its price is the explicit or implicit return for tying up a value for a period, say a year. Since monetary values appear in both the numerator and denominator of a ratio, they conveniently cancel out, leaving percent per year as the dimension of that price.

Many economists have taken positions on whether this service whose price is the interest rate is a distinct factor of production. Nassau Senior recognized that factor early (1836/1965, pp. 58–60) and called it "abstinence." He considered that term inadequate (and "capital" worse) but could not think of a better one. One trouble is that the term suggests perpetual deprivation and invites quips about the great wealth of the abstinent Rothschilds (Lassalle 1864/1918, p. 28). Anyway, Senior defined abstinence as "the conduct of a person who either abstains from the unproductive use of what he can command, or designedly prefers the production of remote to that of immediate results" (p. 58).

Silas M. MacVane (1887, 1890, 1892) introduced the term "waiting," which Alfred Marshall preferred (Marshall 1920/1947, p. 232–234). Böhm-Bawerk (1959, I, p. 379) recognized MacVane's use of the term but rejected the concept. Gustav Cassel used the term "waiting" throughout his book of 1903, although saying (pp. 41–42) that MacVane's formulation was not clear enough. "Patience" might be an equally good term—patience in keeping wealth tied up while waiting for a payoff—but "waiting" is entrenched.

Already two and a half centuries ago, A. R. J. Turgot noted that the interest rate—in the broad sense of the term—is "the price given for the use of a certain quantity of value during a certain time." He put this use on a par with other factors of production (Turgot 1766, p. 78, quoted in Cassel 1903, pp. 20–21). Turgot's formulation, said Cassel, has "never afterwards [been] surpassed in clearness and definiteness."

Cassel considered it settled "once and for all, that interest is the price paid for an *independent and elementary factor of production* which may be called either waiting or use of capital, according to the point of view from which it is looked at.[7] ... It is ... an independent or primary factor in this sense, that it cannot be reduced to more elementary factors" (1903, pp. 67, 89). Hubert Henderson called "waiting ... the essential reality underlying the phenomena of capital and interest. It is really this which

[7] The distinction is inessential. It is as if a new term had been invented for labor from the employer's point of view, reserving "labor" for the point of view of the worker performing it. Another inessential distinction lies between a factor of production and a direct consumer service, as between factory labor and household help or between productive waiting and consumer credit.

constitutes an independent factor of production, distinct from labour and nature, and equally necessary" (1921/1958, p. 98; Henderson's Chapter VIII is an excellent discussion). Robert Dorfman "reaffirmed the reality of waiting as one of the primary factors of production, coordinate with labor, land, etc. ... waiting is a genuine scarce factor of production. ... The unit of waiting [may be taken as] one unit of consumption deferred for one unit of time" (Dorfman 1959, pp. 367, 370; cf. Blaug 1962, pp. 471–475). Just what specific goods are being waited for is a diversionary question (Böhm-Bawerk clowned around with such questions; 1959, especially I, 379, 388ff., and some of his endnotes). Waiting means postponing the exercise of command over real resources. It also means extending the structure of production, a concept that has been a perennial theme of Austrian capital theory (see Skousen 2015 for an in-depth treatment of the structure of production).

In his 1932/1967 book, Chapter VI, Cassel, or his translator, more often uses "capital-disposal" to mean the same thing. He occasionally notes that "waiting" suggests the point of view of the supplier of the service, while "capital-disposal" suggests the buyer's (e.g., borrower's) point of view. "'Waiting' emphasises the negative aspect ..., the foregoing, for a certain time, of the consumption of an existing capital. 'Capital-disposal' is the positive command of capital, during the same period, which is thus provided" (p. 199).

The question might arise whether waiting should be measured in present goods or future goods. If we give up 100 potential consumption goods this year for 105 next year, holding wealth or a claim on wealth in the meanwhile, are we waiting for 100 goods, 105 goods, or for some intermediate amount? The question is misleading; for waiting is postponing the exercise of claims to goods that could have been received at the time of the postponing *or the continued postponing*. If a project grows in value as it continues toward completion, then so does the waiting performed by continuing to own it.

In Fig. 1.1, labor, land use, and even waiting went into creating the project at what counts as its initial value; but this is ancient history. Thereafter, only waiting and no other factors are devoted to the project. An example might be a tree growing with no further outlay for cultivation. The dotted curve rises at a percentage rate from the initial value invested in the project to its value at the end. The area between these lines represents the total waiting (time multiplied by value tied up) devoted to increasing the project's value between its beginning and end. The price of this waiting is the percentage rate of rise of the curved line, roughly the interest rate.

Without using the term and perhaps uncharacteristically for him, Frank Knight implicitly endorsed the concept of waiting by saying that "[w]hat is really invested is always consumption income, which has the dimensions of intensity and time" ("consumption" here meaning consumption abstained from for a while; Knight, 1936, pp. 441–442). Abba Lerner came close to endorsing the concept by suggesting "the postponement of one dollar for one year" as an "atom" related to capital or investment. "Probably annual postponement is the most convenient as an elementary unit out of which more durable investments may be considered to be built up" (1944/1947, p. 330). J. R. Hicks (1979) discussed waiting as a factor, but rather whimsically.

The Austrian economist Murray Rothbard neither clearly accepted nor rejected waiting as an independent factor. He did say, however, that "interest income ... is *not* derived from the concrete, heterogeneous capital *goods*, but from the generalized investment of time." The interest rate is the form in which capitalists receive payment for a "service—an advance of time" (1962, 319).

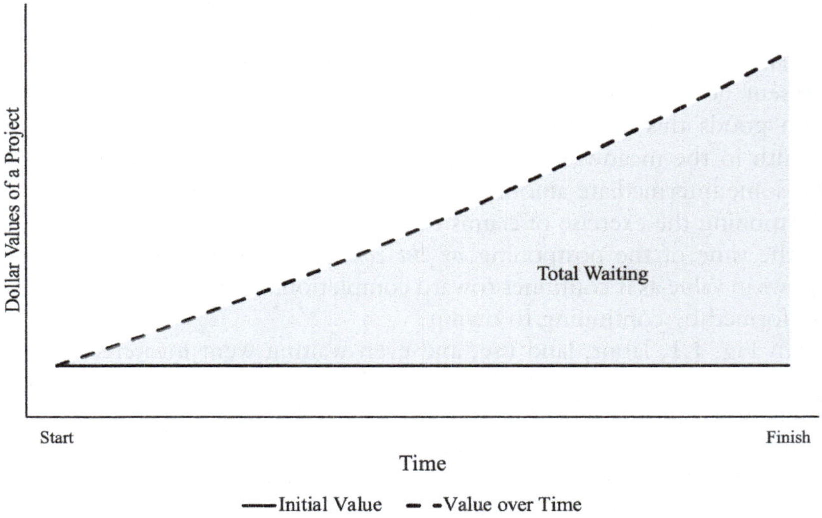

Fig. 1.1 Project values over time

But payment cannot be for time pure and simple. What is the price of an hour–not of an hour of something but just of an hour? As a percentage per time period, it must be a percentage of something, namely, of value tied up through time. But that is what waiting means. In recognizing interest as the price of a "service," then, Rothbard implicitly acquiesces in the concept of waiting.[8]

The word "waiting" does not describe the service bought and sold equally well from both points of view. It tends to focus attention on the supplier, who, while holding a claim or other asset, is indeed waiting to exercise command over resources that he could have devoted to his own current purposes. The buyer of the service (the borrower) does not perform waiting, however, but avoids it, paying someone else to do it for him. Anyway, "the rate of interest is the price of earlier rather than later availability." "Rigorously speaking, interest is the price of earlier availability of rights to use goods rather than later availability" (Alchian and Allen 1967, p. 203).

To call the interest rate "the price of time" is sloppy phrasing. We should not ask someone the price at which he would sell us a minute or hour or week or year, not further specified. A meaningful question must specify a week or whatever *of something*, like consulting services or use of a house, car, or borrowed money. Interest in either the narrow sense or the stretched sense of a general rate of return is paid or charged for advance or delay—depending on point of view—of use for a time of a specified amount of funds or resources.

Although the interest rate is often called "the price of money" and the market for short-term loans "the money market," this usage, too, invites confusion. The waiting of which interest is the price is *not* money. The price of money, if one insists on that term, is either money's purchasing power or its exchange rate quoted in another country's currency.

Besides the difference in viewpoints, another trouble with the term "waiting" is that it may bring Nassau Senior's "abstinence" to mind (Schumpeter 1954, pp. 638–642). Cassel (1932/1967, pp. 190, 199) saw the two terms pretty much as synonyms, as did Böhm-Bawerk. When identified with "abstinence," "waiting" may invite quibbles. Waiting may be the opposite of a sacrifice in some circumstances. Even when irksome at the margin, it may not be irksome on the whole.

[8] He even occasionally uses the word in a sense similar to that of this book, even if not explicitly as the name of a productive factor—e.g., in his 1962, I, 295, 298, 307.

Instead of two names for the same factor, depending on the point of view, it would be convenient to have a neutral, nonjudgmental term designating equally well what a lender supplies and a borrower obtains. To avoid twisting some familiar word into a technical term, we might imitate the natural sciences and coin a term from Greek roots, perhaps coming up with *chronaxia* or *anamoni* for value through time or waiting. But we fear that the Greek solution would not catch on.

Lacking a better term, then, we might as well *force* the neutral and symmetrical meaning we want onto "waiting." Several precedents recommend this solution. Equally uncompelling objections might be made to the term "labor:" the buyer is not performing labor but paying someone else to perform it, and "labor" also conveys a sometimes unwarranted implication of irksomeness. Labor, like waiting, may be irksome at the margin but not overall: a worker might prefer a shorter work week yet value being productive as well as being paid.

1.9 Factors of Production and Production Functions

Several concepts apply to waiting as to other factors of production. These include its productivity and diminishing marginal productivity, its being embodied in goods produced with its aid, its being employed along with other factors in proportions influenced by its own and their prices, and its price being influenced by changes in its supply and in tastes or technology affecting the derived demand for it.

Whether waiting *really is* a factor of production is not an ontological issue but one of convenience only. In some contexts, it is convenient to regard capital goods (machines, buildings, semi-finished goods, and so forth) or their services as factors of production and not theorize about waiting. In investigating an individual factory making a particular product, we would probably find it convenient to count purchased equipment, parts, and materials as inputs. In investigating the whole industry making the product, we might count as inputs not the things traded among firms in the industry but rather the labor and other more nearly ultimate factors of production already embodied in those things. We should, of course, avoid double counting both purchased inputs and inputs to those inputs, as distinct factors in the same production function.

What accounts for people's readiness to perform the waiting necessary for the existence, maintenance, and growth of the accumulated stock of capital, intermediate goods, and intangible capital necessary for the economy's functioning and growth? Investment in intangible capital, by the way, outstrips investment in tangible plants and equipment in the United States today. It "includes scientific and other R&D, brand equity, customer lists and reputation, worker training, and management and human resource systems" (Hulten 2015, p. 5; investment in software should also be counted). A notable subcategory is human capital—acquired and maintained abilities and experience. Business firms and individuals alike tie up wealth over time to acquire knowledge, reputations, and so forth. College students tie up tuition payments, and the earnings are forgone by not entering the labor force sooner. All are in effect trading wealth now in expectation of more wealth later.

Several questions beset the very concept of a production function, and additional difficulties beset the concept of a production function for a country's whole economy and its inputs. How does a statistician calculate a physical aggregate of heterogeneous capital and intermediate goods and intangibles, as well as its total and marginal physical product? Who, if anyone, uses such an aggregate so that its marginal net yield of revenue, expressed as a percentage of its own value, tends to equal the prevailing interest rate?

Even so, an aggregate production function, with the stock of tangible and intangible capital goods somehow represented, may be usable in some statistical or theoretical work. In any case, whether considering a firm or industry or whole economy, we must avoid double counting. If we treat all capital and semi-finished goods employed as distinct factors and probe no more deeply, we must not count labor and waiting embodied in them as distinct and additional factors. But if we resolve capital goods into the labor, land use, and waiting that they embody and do count the price of waiting among the costs of the goods produced, then we must not at the same time double count the capital goods themselves.

What inputs to production properly count as factors? What distinguishes them from everything else? Can a single factor have variants, and if so, what distinguishes them from one another? Entrepreneurship and risk-bearing are vitally important to the real world, but does that make them factors? These are conceptual questions worth some attention in later chapters; they cannot be answered by investigations of the real world alone.

Similarly, do production functions, with their specific mathematical forms and parameters, objectively exist? Not really, not like recipes in a cookbook. Entrepreneurs try to learn by doing, combining and recombining inputs to make products in ways that seem efficient, taking into account prices. A production function is just an analytical and expository tool to be used simply for convenience.

The same point holds for utility functions. They do not exist in reality, even before trial and error and experience. The consumer comes to the market with general preferences and perceived needs, yes, but with nothing like the graphical and mathematical formulations found in textbooks. Even less does the consumer have a utility function for a whole lifetime. Likewise, cost and supply and demand curves do not objectively exist with detailed properties to be pinned down by research. In a sense, they are created by producers and consumers as they follow and revise conjectures about the technologies and market conditions facing them. Economists use such curves, however, to help organize and teach the conditions and activities that determine market prices.

Defining factors and modeling production so that the rewards of the factors add up to exactly the whole product in full long-run equilibrium, if they do, can be an exercise ground for using and sharpening analytical and expository abilities and tools. Such work is not to be disparaged. The ultimate purpose of theory and models, however, is to understand and describe how the real world works. Not always, but sometimes, elegance must give way to reality.

The upshot of this discussion is not nihilistic, not a taboo on the very concepts of production functions, factors of production, cost, utility, and supply and demand. These are tools to be used as effective and convenient in each context. We are warning against supposing that concepts correspond to things objectively existing out in the real world. Reminders of these points recur throughout this book.

We maintain that it is often convenient to regard the interest rate as a factor price and to investigate its properties. Facts are not at issue here. Controversy over issues such as whether interest is the price of a productive factor, like the whole body of Böhm-Bawerk's work, illustrates, however, a general methodological point: many or most of the main advances in economic theory have not hinged on detailed investigation of empirical reality. Controversialists over capital and interest have agreed about features of reality observable even from the proverbial armchair. Disagreement concerns concepts and emphasis.

1.10 Saving and Savings

Waiting and saving are related but not identical. Saving (without a final *s*) means withholding part of current disposable income from consumption to acquire some asset or claim as a form of wealth to hold. Saving normally adds to savings (with the final *s*). Savings being assets or claims accumulated by past and current saving. Waiting is a broader concept than saving; it is the withholding from consumption not only of wealth newly saved from current income but also of wealth already accumulated and still withheld from consumption. The volume of value carried through time—waiting—is much greater than the volume of current saving.

What does a person do with non-consumed income? Does it simply fatten his wallet or bank account? Does he buy stocks and bonds? Does he buy capital goods or consumer durables that might count as capital goods? Does he invest in "human capital?" Giving income away shifts to the recipient the decision of how to consume it or what assets to acquire with it. The only remaining alternative would be destroying wealth. Burning up currency would amount to giving its value to the issuer or to whoever gains from price deflation.

Saving from current income implies a decision, then, if only passive, to acquire some assets or claims. Any analysis of supposed "oversaving" requires attention to those assets. A macroeconomic disequilibrium blamed on "oversaving" must involve an excess demand for the vehicles of saving, very probably including money held.

When gains in productivity let people choose more present and more future consumption, are they waiting more or less than before? People are stinting less on current consumption while postponing still more consumption that they could have enjoyed currently. What earns interest is the postponed potential present consumption. Trivially, bigger incomes allow more savings without requiring any cutback on current consumption. Even if it has become less of a sacrifice, more postponing is more waiting.

1.11 Concluding Questions

While this book's title, *Capital, Interest, and Waiting*, is a bit of a throwback into the custom and practice of professional economists, it is, in fact, a book simply about the economics of waiting. Throughout, a number of questions on the topic are raised and hopefully answered. These include:

how can waiting be used efficiently, does a rise in its price make its quantity supplied increase or decrease, does the interest rate perform its rationing function effectively even in the latter case, how can we estimate how much waiting goes on through holding existing wealth, and how much more is required to cover government deficits of the sizes experienced nowadays?

CHAPTER 2

Waiting as a Factor and Interest as Its Price

2.1 Complementary Frameworks

Arguing over what is or is not really a factor of production is as idle as arguing over just where to draw the line between capital goods and consumer goods or arguing over the mathematical form of a production function and what its inputs are. These are matters of convenience in each context.

In describing the whole economic system and the coordinating role of prices, it is convenient to treat waiting as a factor of production. Materials, capital goods, and even human capital resolve into the waiting they embody, along with labor, land services, risk-bearing, and entrepreneurship. Waiting is essential for time-consuming production using capital goods and stocks of semi-finished goods, as well as human training and experience. Someone must be willing to keep resources tied up in these processes and wait for their fruits; otherwise, production would shrivel. Capital consumption—using up capital goods and inventories without full replacement—is quite possible, as happened in Europe during World War II. During the war, people could reap the output emerging from the late stages of productive processes without initiating the early stages on the same scale as before.

This view does not claim exclusive validity. In several fields, alternative conceptual frameworks are useful. As Niels Bohr emphasized, his Principle of Complementarity applies far beyond the area of physics in which

L. B. Yeager and S. H. Hanke, *Capital, Interest, and Waiting*,
https://doi.org/10.1007/978-3-031-63398-0_2

he introduced it.[1] In some contexts, it is useful to focus on the wave nature of light, in others, on its particle nature; in some contexts, on human free will, in others, on causally determined behavior. Economists employ both the income-expenditure and money supply and demand approaches to total spending analysis, at least three approaches to balance of payments analysis, both stock and flow theories of exchange rates, both interest-parity and expectations theories of the relation between spot and forward exchange rates, and both the general equilibrium and Austrian market-process perspectives in microeconomics. Superficially contradictory approaches, even if only not yet fully reconciled, may all be useful in their own contexts.

2.2 Interest Rate, Agio, and Relative Prices

Conceiving of the interest rate as the price of waiting reconciles with its conception, preferred by some Austrian economists, as an "agio" in value of present goods over future goods (a price premium of some goods over others that is typically but not necessarily positive). The term "agio" brings to mind the pervasiveness of interest, showing itself in many forms besides the price of a money loan.

This "agio" doctrine is a merely superficial rival of interpreting interest as a factor price. A related non-rival is the concept of the ratio of the value of an asset's services to the value of the asset itself. While readily reconciled with the factor price interpretation, the agio is seen less as a straightforward price than as a pervasive phenomenon requiring a special and profound explanation. As a pervasive real phenomenon, interest is not especially connected with money, loans of money, or the demand for cash balances. But focusing on the price of waiting likewise stresses how pervasive interest is in its many manifestations.

An increased agio on present goods can be explained as a rise in their scarcity value relative to future goods; their subjective relative marginal utility rises. Perhaps a rise in the agio and interest rate reflects the principle of diminishing marginal utility operating when some other underlying change makes future goods relatively more abundant. Perhaps the change

[1] Bohr 1958 and 1963, *passim*; Teller 1980, pp. 93, 105–106, 138–140; Rucker 1987, pp. 6–8, 185; Theimer 1973, pp. 143, 245–246, 248, 274; Capra 1991, chapter 11, with a picture, p.144, of Bohr's coat of arms bearing the motto CONTRARIA SUNT COMPLEMENTA.

directly reflects a change in tastes. A decline in thrift means that people attribute reduced marginal utility of future goods relative to present goods.

The Austrian school's agio theory treats interest as a typically positive price premium of present over future goods or, almost equivalently, a premium of consumption goods over factors of production being transformed into them through time. As Alchian and Allen say (1972, p. 479), interest expresses the exchange rate between rights to present consumption and rights to future consumption. Present goods are future goods coupled with avoidance of waiting for them; future goods ordinarily bear lower money prices than present goods because part of their total price takes the form of the waiting necessary to obtain them. Ultimate factors of production are prototypical future goods, requiring time to ripen into final consumer goods and services.

In other words, present goods ordinarily carry an agio because they embody more waiting than future goods, in the sense that their waiting content has already been supplied. Future goods carry a discount because the waiting content necessary for them has yet to be fully supplied.

Carl Menger introduced the classification of goods into lower and higher orders (1871/1950, Chapter I and p. 157n.). Lowest-order goods are the ones closest to consumption, like food on the stove or dinner table. Flour and other ingredients belong to higher orders. Inputs to those ingredients, such as crops, machinery, and other capital goods, are of higher orders still. It is hard to specify goods of the highest order of all (other than land, labor, and whatever else might count as ultimate factors), but near-examples might be equipment for constructing an electric power station and a factory making machines to bore tunnels through mountains. Such things and their services require much waiting before emerging in final consumer goods.

Final consumer goods and services count as present goods, while the ingredients and factors entering into their production count as future goods, since they will have been transformed into present goods only after the lapse of time. Present goods ready to be consumed now are worth more than claims on the future goods of the same kind that will be ready only after their factors of production are transformed into them over time.[2]

[2] Classifications are useful in some contexts but not in others and more appealing to some theorists than to others. What is the relation between classifying goods by

Classifying goods by their Mengerian orders, while not wrong, appears less straightforward and useful than classifying them by their waiting contents. Furthermore, the total use of waiting in producing a final consumer good does not depend on how its production might be classified into the various stages of intermediate and capital goods. Of course, a firm specialized in one of those stages is interested in its own waiting requirement and the interest rate paid.

A thing's waiting content largely governs how interest-rate sensitive its production and the consumption of its services are (think of housing). It seems doubtful that a thing's waiting content, small or large, corresponds closely to any of the Austrian classifications. A durable consumer good, say a house or refrigerator, requires waiting, on top of waiting used in its production, while it gradually renders its services, and this waiting is an input complementary to the factors used in producing the good itself.

Analogies hold between waiting and labor. A good's production is relatively sensitive or insensitive to the wage rate according to its labor content. Also relevant to wage rate sensitivity is the further labor required, as a complementary factor, in the good's use or consumption. It may have low labor content in its own production yet require much additional labor as a complementary factor in its further transformation or use (think of housing, again, or of machines requiring expensive maintenance), and that fact would contribute to the wage rate sensitivity of the good's production and use.

A further analogy between waiting and labor is that international trade in goods and services amounts to trade in factors embodied in them (see Sect. 4.7).

In summary, the waiting content (like the labor content) of a good itself and the further waiting (like labor) required in its processing or consumption is more fundamental than its classification by Mengerian order or as a capital good or consumer good.

their orders or stages in the production process and distinguishing between capital and consumer goods? Such distinctions are fuzzy, as Chapter 3 further argues. Musings about classification are parallel to remarks about production functions and the factors of production entering into them: the issue is not one of reality but of analytical convenience in each case.

2.3 Pervasive Transactions in Waiting

Although incomplete, the agio theory recognizes that an aspect of the interest rate pervades the entire economy in the relative prices of all sorts of goods. This does not imply a definite and unambiguous price relation between capital and intermediate goods on the one hand and consumer goods on the other. Carpet cleaning might seem to be a service embodying relatively much labor and little waiting—plausibly but not necessarily, the service might employ elaborate waiting-intensive and durable equipment whose own cost and the value of whose services include sizable elements of interest. Carpet cleaning also is not only a service for final consumers; it can be remote from them, performed in business offices. On the other hand, relatively large amounts of capital goods used in producing some other consumer good or service might themselves be quick to produce, use, and have slight interest costs. Fireworks might be an example of a presumably low-waiting-intensive good used in producing a short but spectacular display.

Simple examples of unambiguous price relations, as between new and matured wine or growing trees and harvested timber, are instructive. They are exceptional, however, in having a final product unequivocally of a lower order, nearer to the consumer, than the intermediate good. Putting aside cases of direct consumption of a factor (as of labor in domestic service), a rise in the interest rate[3] plausibly raises the price of a final good or service relative to the prices of its nonwaiting factors of production. A fall in the interest rate tends to reduce this ratio of product price to prices of factors other than waiting.

In such examples, consumer goods are present goods, while factors are not-yet-ripened future consumption goods. In terms of our other discussed formulation, a rise in the interest rate does spell a rise in the agio of present goods over future goods.

Price relations among different goods and factors reflect waiting being performed in many ways besides saving and lending money, and these relations show interest in a broader sense than payment for loans. Böhm-Bawerk's desert island stories of fishnets, cabins, and pipelines exemplify waiting for the enhanced results of labor employed in roundabout

[3] Here this means a rise in the "individual experiment" sense, a rise taken as exogenous to the industry or decision maker concerned.

production. One can perform waiting by postponing current consumption to acquire a machine, an apartment house, or a piece of land that will yield its services only gradually over time.

Transactions in waiting may be quite direct, as when a saver lends command over resources to a consumer-borrower. On the other hand, a chain of intermediation may intervene between the ultimate suppliers of waiting, who postpone their own consumption, and the ultimate demanders, who acquire early command over resources. Financial intermediaries that borrow to relend are an obvious example. Less obviously, the ultimate demander of waiting, who pays someone else to perform waiting on his behalf, may be the consumer of a good or service produced by a roundabout, waiting-intensive process. The manufacturer is then an intermediary in waiting: he may buy waiting (i.e., waiting-avoidance) by borrowing money to buy a machine. Barring disappointment of expectations, the price paid for the machine covers the prices times quantities of the labor, waiting, and other factors embodied in it. On the other hand, the manufacturer provides the consumer of the final product with the services of the waiting and other factors already embodied in the machine and the further waiting required as the machine yields its productive services gradually over time. If all goes as expected, the manufacturer sells the final product at a price that at least covers all its costs. In paying that price, the consumer buys the waiting along with the other factor services embodied in the product.

Just as transactions in waiting may be quite indirect, so its price, the interest rate, may show itself less directly than as interest on a money loan. The price of a consumer good exceeds the sum of the quantities of the labor and other ordinary factor services embodied in it multiplied by their prices. This excess represents remuneration of the waiting also embodied in the good (increased or diminished, perhaps, by entrepreneurial profit or loss).

In another example (adapted from Fetter 1977, pp. 282–283), two capital goods yield the same amount of productive services over their entire useful lives, and their services have the same prices when they emerge. The two goods differ only in *when* they render their equal services. The one doing so sooner commands the higher current price. The reason is that the buyer of the capital good whose services come later will have to wait longer, for which the lower price of the good serves as compensation.

Far from appearing only in the explicit money rate of interest, then, the price of waiting pervades the price system and takes many hidden forms.

2.4 Arbitrage Among Prices and Yields

Credit rationing is common. By the very nature of waiting, and obviously of lending money or renting out property, waiting cannot be rationed by price alone. A prudent person engaging in a transaction stretching out over time must assess how willing and able his trading partner will be to perform his part of the bargain when the time comes. Also, in buying and selling other factors, like labor, nonprice considerations operate. Since facts of reality require nonprice rationing along with price rationing, calling it a "market imperfection" is an inaccurate term. Only for securities essentially free of default risk is credit rationing absent. In what follows, however, it will be convenient and legitimate to treat the interest rate as a proxy for the entire price of waiting, including both its explicit and nonpecuniary components.

Waiting and its productivity are distinct from specific capital goods and their productivities. The annual percentage yield on a capital good kept in good repair and so yielding its services indefinitely, net of depreciation and other costs of holding and using it, is the ratio of the annual net dollar value of its services to its own dollar value. This rate tends to move toward equality with the economywide general rate of return and with interest on loans.[4] Anyway, a tendency for a good's yield to equal other percentages in equilibrium does not make them all conceptually identical. More generally, a tendency of two magnitudes to coincide under competitive pressures does not make them the very same thing.

The following measures are distinct: (1) the dollar price of the annual service of a capital good, both (a) before and (b) after the deduction of depreciation, maintenance, and operating expenses and similar allowances and adjustments; (2) the dollar price of the capital good itself; and (3) the ratio of (1 b) to (2) expressed as a percentage, which is the good's rate of net yield. The dollar price of the good's service tends to equal the marginal value productivity of the service. An asset's net yield as a

[4] Familiar qualifications to this tendency, further noted in Chapter 9, concern lumpiness, transactions costs, risk and uncertainty, timing, duration, liquidity or illiquidity, and other benefits and costs of holding various assets and claims.

percentage of its price is one expression of the productivity and price of waiting.

Competition, substitution, and arbitrage—their meanings overlap—tend to make waiting performed by lending money, by holding an investment in capital goods, land, or other assets, and in other ways, all bear the same price or net rate of return—again with the standard qualifications.

> Within a single economy ... there may at one and the same moment be a hundred different agios on present goods and hence a hundred different rates of interest. But those hundreds and thousands of partial markets are not hermetically sealed off from each other. There is intercommunication among them through lively and incessant arbitrage (Böhm-Bawerk 1959, II, 379).

Consider a business firm deciding whether to buy or rent cars. The higher the interest rate relative to the rental charge, the less inclined the firm will be to borrow money to buy cars and the more inclined it will be to rent them. Making this switch will tend, however slightly, to reduce interest rates on money loans and increase rates of yield on rental cars, narrowing the spread between them. Conversely, the lower the interest rate relative to rental charges, the greater the borrowing undertaken to buy cars and the less they are rented, again tending to equalize the loan-interest and car-rental rates.

A further analogy illustrates this tendency toward equal rates of return. The price of wheat of a specific class is indeed determined by circumstances reflected in its own supply and demand schedules. Those schedules strongly reflect, however, the prices of other grades of wheat. If changed supplies and demands for wheat of grades 1 through 4 were to raise their prices, while nothing else happened to directly affect the supply and demand for classes 5 through 8, then substitution and arbitrage would come into play. As long as the prices of classes 5–8 had not yet also risen, some users of wheat would have reason to switch from 1–4 to 5–8. Some growers, similarly, would switch from 5–8 into growing the more profitable classes 1–4. With their demands thus strengthened and supplies weakened, classes 5–8 would rise in price more or less in line with classes 1–4, whose own price increases would be moderated. Despite changes *directly* affecting only the supplies or demands of specific classes, the prices of all classes would thus be kept equal, except only for differentials like those among wages of different types of labor and interest rates on different types of loans and investments.

Arbitrage links the prices of waiting supplied and demanded in different ways much as it links the prices of different types of labor and classes of wheat. Consider the value of the services of a particular type of machine, net of attendant expenses and depreciation, expressed as a percent per year of the machine's capital value. Suppose that this percentage becomes higher than the interest rate on loans. Firms would have an incentive to buy the machine, even with borrowed funds, bidding up its price and spurring construction of more like it. Its increased stock and the increased flow of its services would reduce the marginal value productivity of those services. The machine's increased rate of construction would also tend to bid up its cost, partly through higher prices of the factors employed. Both through increases in its own production cost and price and through a decrease in the prices of its services, then, the percentage net yield on the machine would tend to fall into line with the yields on other assets and with the interest rate on loans (and that rate itself might tend to be increased by firms' borrowing to buy the machine).

If the loan interest rate should happen to be *above* the machine's percentage net yield, the foregoing story would go into reverse. Firms' incentives to rent it rather than borrow to buy it would tend to bid up its rental price and reduce the interest rate, tending toward an equality between the two percentages.

Arbitrage brings all variables into a process of mutual determination, not one way causation. Even the interest rate on bonds and loans adjusts. Suppose that the net rate of return on rental housing somehow rises relative to yields on other assets: rents on houses and apartment buildings have become high in relation to their prices and construction costs. Investors have an incentive to shift from bonds into buildings, incidentally motivating the construction of more of them. On the other hand, some occupants who had been renting their dwellings, thereby paying for housing services month by month instead of paying in advance through investment in homeownership, would now find it advantageous to buy homes, paying with mortgage loans. In so doing, they would divert their demands for other people's waiting out of the market for housing services and into the loan market. Waiting performed through investment in rental housing would increase in supply and decrease in demand, while waiting performed through lending money would decrease in supply and increase in demand. Yields on waiting performed in these ways would tend to come together. Reportedly, an initial discrepancy in the opposite direction brought an appropriate response by housing-seekers: "[r]ental housing demand surges as mortgage money tightens, construction costs soar" (*Wall Street Journal*, 16 June 1966, p. 1). As waiting avoidance by one method became more expensive, demand shifted to the other method.

The equalization illustrated here for only two forms of waiting extends to the entire range of assets and loans and their rates of return. What concerns us is the nature and direction of the effects in such examples, not their size.

2.5 More About Arbitrage

"Business demand for larger and longer-term financing has been met through new lending techniques .... Since 1963, banks have bought motor trailers, jet airline[r]s, executive aircraft, computers, machine tools, and other equipment for leasing to customers" (Meigs 1966, p. 168). Typically operating with borrowed money, firms that buy airliners from manufacturers and lease them to airlines have become a major industry (Biddle 1998; Lunsford and Pleven 2008; "Commercial Aircraft Sales and Leasing"). Rather than buy computers or distribution facilities with borrowed money, customers can lease them from the manufacturer or a bank or a specialized firm, depending on the costs of the two methods. From both parties' points of view, rental payments on leased equipment or buildings closely resemble interest and amortization payments on a loan. The lessor performs waiting on behalf of the lessee, much as a lender would. Arbitrage under competition would tend toward an equilibrium in which neither suppliers nor demanders of waiting saw either loans or leases to have any advantage at the margin over the other type of transaction. Advantages of leasing, when it is chosen, often include considerations of balance sheet appearance, credit standing, and access to credit.[5]

[5] Barbara Martinez (1999) reports examples of sale and lease-back of buildings as an alternative to borrowing money.

Jonathan Weil (2004) describes how "leases on everything from aircraft to retail stores to factory equipment" enable companies to keep off their balance sheets billions of dollars of obligations "that are just as real as financial commitments originating from bank loans and other borrowings."

Alchian and Allen had arbitrage in mind when writing: "[t]he interest rate [in the broad sense] reflects the demand for *all* types of goods capable of rendering services in the future. And since rights to present and future income can be traded in many ways in many markets, the interest rate will be implicit or manifest in many markets." The loanable funds market is noteworthy because "almost all exchange occurs via the medium of money rather than between goods directly [and] people seek to revise the time profile of their income or consumption streams not by trading this good now for that good later, but by trading money now for money later." Thus, almost all changes in investment and saving will affect the loan markets (Alchian and Allen 1967, pp. 436–437).

A central point deserves restatement. The interest rate is determined not by any distinct and isolated supply of and demand for loans of money but by supplies of and demands for waiting overall. Suppose that people become less willing than before to postpone consumption and their decline in thrift occurs in one way: homeowners become renters, selling their homes, and spending the proceeds on current consumption. Rents rise and house prices fall relatively: the percentage rate of return on rental housing rises. Investors demand more loans to buy rental properties. Although the decline in thrift did not affect the loan market initially and directly, the price of waiting rises as manifested (however slightly) in the interest rate on loans.

2.6 Misleading (If Defensible) Formulations

Only small portions of supplies of and demands for waiting confront each other specifically on the loan market. This fact, together with the tendency for percentage rates of net return on securities, land, and all sorts of capital goods to become equal (subject to standard qualifications about lumpiness, duration, risk, liquidity, and so forth), has tempted some economists to describe the interest rate quite inclusively. Fundamentally, they say, it is the ratio of income to capital or the relation between the value of services and the value of their sources (briefly, the services/assets ratio),

"GE [General Electric] ... finances purchases of medical equipment, power-generation gear and aeroplanes, or leases them to users." Would-be buyers of expensive equipment often lack the capital to buy it outright. (*Economist*, 6 June 2015, pp. 67–68).

the reciprocal of the price of a permanent income stream (like the yield on a perpetual bond), or the hire value of assets.[6]

Such formulations emphasize the hopeless superficiality of interest theories that consider only the loan market, monetary factors, or liquidity preference. They emphasize the pervasive and fundamentally real character of interest and related rates of return. Unfortunately, one does not make these points by stretching the definition of "interest rate" to cover all related rates of return, rates of time preference, and intertemporal exchange ratios implicit in prices. Rates equal at the margin in equilibrium are not conceptually identical. Including distinct concepts under a single label and treating various rates of return as identical risks suppresses questions of how markets for various claims, assets, and services intertwine and risks shoving aside the substitution and arbitrage that tend to *make* those different rates equal.

Insistence on terms like "services-to-sources ratio" or "agio of present goods over future goods" obscures the parallelism between the interest rate as the clearest form of the price of waiting and the prices of other factors. It obscures the sometimes-convenient distinction between demand price and supply price, which are equal when the market clears but are not conceptually the same.

We should be able to explain how specified changes in wants, resources, or technology affect both the loan interest rate narrowly defined and its broader sense as the price of waiting performed in innumerable different ways. Substitution and arbitrage are keys to the explanation.

Calling interest a pervasive services-to-sources ratio comes close to exaggeration. Waiting performed and avoided by consumption loans creates no obvious source of services. Straightforward language would hardly describe a promissory note as a source of services. Not all instances of postponing consumption to invest resources in roundabout production give rise to capital goods that can be straightforwardly described as sources of services. Investment of resources in research presumably yields larger or more valuable ultimate outputs than a more direct employment of those resources; otherwise, companies would not undertake the research. Yet it would strain the English language, even if forgivably, to

[6] Such formulations occur in Walras (1954); Fisher (1930/1955, esp. pp. 32, 332); Friedman (1976, chapter 17); Hutt (1963, p. 211); and unpublished memoranda by Hutt. The interest rate is not merely a loan rate but "also a means of expressing current prices of capital goods relative to current service prices" (Alchian and Allen 1972, p. 461).

describe the knowledge gained by research as a source of services, and especially as a source with a definite market value. Similarly, investment in education or training, whether financed by students themselves or by employers, may be quite worthwhile, but it still does not give rise to anything straightforwardly called capital goods. It stretches the language, if perhaps excusably, to regard investment in human capital as adding some sort of service-yielding asset onto what a person would otherwise be. It stretches the language, again excusably, to call a worker also a capitalist on the grounds that he is waiting for the future returns on himself considered as an asset. Furthermore, a worker's wage is not simply the yield on his training; it also includes compensation for the disutility of labor.

2.7 Interest as a Factor Price

Even in a money loan, sheer nominal dollars, apart from their purchasing power, are not what the borrower demands and the lender supplies. The loan transfers command, for a time, over what money will buy. This, incidentally, is the briefest explanation of why merely lending newly created money into circulation cannot substantially and permanently lower the interest rate. It cannot do so unless it can also somehow increase the volume of *real* resources over which transactions transfer command.

2.8 Dimensions and Measurement

Waiting has two dimensions, amount and time: a quantity of waiting is the amount of value waited for multiplied by the length of time that the value is tied up. This time dimension resembles that of labor and land use. For those factors, the combined dimensions of time and amount can be expressed in physical units like man-*hours* and acre-*weeks*. But the amount of goods or productive factors not consumed and instead waited for must be expressed in numéraire goods like money. Once the quantity of waiting is expressed as a money value tied up through time and its remuneration is also expressed in money, it is convenient (but nothing more) to express the price as a percentage per year. Ideally, perhaps, the amount of value waited for should be measured in dollars of constant purchasing power; yet, such a measurement still would not be in straightforward physical units.

Failure of total parallelism between waiting and other productive factors should not be disconcerting. Each factor has its own distinctive characteristics. Without being exact, a parallelism among them is illuminating.

Economists ought to improve the parallelism by devising a physical, nonmonetary measure of the amount or intensity of waiting or of its time dimension. They do introduce concepts like *period of production* of goods and services or *period of investment* of factors. For example, Böhm-Bawerk introduced such concepts without recognizing waiting as a distinct productive factor.

This book does not particularly endorse those concepts or insist on distinguishing between the two, although one term or the other may be stylistically more convenient in particular contexts. One concept focuses on the time required to produce final goods and the other on the time that inputs are tied up in the productive process. Detailed exposition and criticisms await in Chapter 7, but some preliminary remarks belong here.

The average period of production or investment is the average time elapsing between the application of original productive factors and their transformation into final consumer goods and services. Robinson Crusoe might chase fish with his bare hands. He invests his labor in a roundabout way when he constructs and uses a fishing net. A longer time elapses between his efforts and their increased results. This sort of homely example is what the concepts of period of production or investment seek to sharpen and quantify even for a complex money-using economy.

Ludwig von Mises, while noting Böhm-Bawerk's contributions to understanding time preference, scorned his "average period of production" as an "empty concept." Past time spent on producing today's capital goods counts for nothing toward "their usefulness for future want-satisfaction" (Mises 1966, p. 489). Yes, but decisions about investing in capital goods must be forward-looking *as informed by experience*. Mises is right if he is warning against confusing the productivity of capital goods themselves with the greater productivity available from wise choices of time-consuming methods of production.

It may be convenient in describing the production function of an individual firm to count the capital and intermediate goods employed, or their services, as an input. It would be double counting, however, to count as inputs both these goods themselves and also their own inputs, including waiting. The marginal product of these capital and intermediate goods or their services is expressed in units of output (not as a percentage), and their price is measured in dollars (again, not as a percentage).

To interpret the interest rate as the marginal productivity of "capital," conceived as some physical or value aggregate, is an error. Still, a correct idea does pertain to the employment of labor and other factors. Market processes tend to equalize the interest rate and the marginal productivity of *something*. A business firm tends to adjust how much waiting it employs so that its marginal value of productivity equals its marginal cost. This marginal cost may be an explicit interest cost or forgone alternative uses of self-owned wealth.

If devising a physical measure of waiting or roundaboutness is a problem worth worrying about, it is so only for some economists, like ones preoccupied with the Cambridge capital theory paradoxes. The individual household or firm needs no such measure. It need not distinguish between money amounts and real amounts of command over resources since its own behavior does not by itself alter the correspondence between them.

Economists may seek a physical measure of waiting or roundaboutness for several reasons: (a) to emphasize that the economic process takes time and that some activities and goods are relatively close to completion while others are relatively remote from yielding ultimate consumer satisfaction; (b) to furnish, in principle, a way of comparing the time-structures or waiting-intensities of different productive processes, of different sectors of an economy, and of economic systems in different countries and at different times; and (c) to distinguish the greater productivity of wisely chosen roundabout methods from the productivity of capital goods.

2.9 Objections to the Concept of Waiting as a Factor

Many eminent economists have denied that waiting is a distinct productive factor. Objectors include Frank Knight (e.g., 1938, pp. 73–74) and Joseph Conard (1959). Friedrich Hayek criticizes "mystical" notions of free capital or a capital fund but somewhat softens his criticisms of the concept of waiting itself (1936/1946, esp. p. 377 of the reprint, and 1941, pp. 5, 93–94, 266–267, and *passim*). Böhm-Bawerk denies waiting's status as a factor (1959, I, Chapters 8 and 9, II, 97ff., 117, 341, III, 194ff.). So does even Irving Fisher (1930/1955, pp. 485–487, 534–541), whose doctrines otherwise figure in this book's synthesis. Klaus

Hennings also doubts whether the terms "waiting" or "abstinence" are useful (1987, vol. 4, p. 848, a mostly history of thought rather than substantive argument).

Böhm-Bawerk objected to Cassel's formulation in particular (1959, III, 195–201 and endnotes). He called it "mysticism" to speak, as Cassel did, of "the use of a certain quantity of value for a certain period of time." Why speak of using the *value* of goods rather than the goods themselves? If Böhm sells his horse for 500 guilders, he is of course renouncing any further use of it; but it is the horse that he gets paid for, not any distinct renunciation or abstinence. Cassel allegedly left the relation unclear between the "use of value," for which the buyer pays pure interest, and the "use of goods" or their "use services," for which he pays the gross rate of interest, including the net rate, or else the goods' purchase price. But, of course, the prices of goods or services are distinct from the prices of loans or other forms of waiting. What is a form of interest in the *ratio* of the value of services to the value of the goods providing them?

Böhm further rejected treating abstinence, waiting, or capital use as "an independent factor that finds no remuneration in the price of the good" produced with its supposed aid. "[A]ll attempts at elaborating such an independent factor ... must result in an ambiguous double calculation or unreal mystical speculation" (III, 196; Hennings 1997, p. 115, paraphrases Böhm on the supposed double counting).

Böhm is open to reply. Someone who makes a money loan *is* advancing to the borrower the use of an amount of value through time–the value of goods in general but not specific goods themselves. Someone who rents out a machine is tying up value, unused by himself, while the renter has the use of that value without having saved it himself. The rental price is or includes what amounts to interest. As for what things should count as factors of production, the answer is a matter of convenience in analyzing the topic at hand. If we treat capital goods and intermediate goods employed as factors of production and probe no more deeply, then we must not also count the waiting—nor the labor—that they embody as separate and additional factors. But if we resolve those goods into the waiting and all other primary factors embodied in them and do count interest on that waiting among the costs of the output produced, then we must not at the same time also count the costs of the capital goods themselves; doing so would be double counting. As for whether waiting as "an independent factor… finds no remuneration in the price of the good" produced (Böhm's words in criticism of Cassel), well, the cost of the waiting—interest expense—does indeed enter into the cost of the product and is covered in the product's price if the entrepreneur's plans go right. Saying that capital goods are productive and that waiting is productive are different slants on the same reality, for capital goods embody waiting (along with other factors). One slant may be more convenient in some contexts, another in others. But we must avoid double counting the productivities both of waiting itself and of the capital goods embodying it and other factors.

As for not double counting, consider an example. A business owner refrains from consuming some of his income and uses this savings to buy equipment. In doing so, he exchanges the price paid, which equals the value of resources that he could have devoted to other purposes for a stream of future net revenues, that is, implicit returns on the equipment. If all goes as expected, the not-time-discounted sum of these future revenues will exceed his payment for the equipment; and this excess is his reward for waiting in the meanwhile. Alternatively, he might borrow money to buy the capital good, paying interest to have the lender perform waiting for him. He then, in effect, offsets the waiting that he himself does in owning the equipment by dis-waiting through borrowing. The loan reallocates the burden of waiting.

In a similar example, a firm makes or buys a capital good and then rents it out, receiving a stream of explicit rentals. In all such stories, it is necessary to distinguish among three things: the cost of construction or price of the capital good, the rental paid on it, and the implicit interest included for accepting delay between the initial outlay and the future returns (whose undiscounted total, if all goes as expected, exceeds that initial outlay). Making these distinctions guards against double counting.

Some of Böhm's objections are minor indeed. For example, Cassel's notion that waiting and the use of capital are the same thing seen from the two different sides of the receiver and the payer of the price. Böhm even accuses Cassel of supposing that the applicability of the same (unspecified) mathematical formula to both sides shows that they are the same. To speak of waiting and waiting avoidance gets around this terminological difficulty if it is one. The payer of interest avoids doing the waiting himself by paying someone else to do it for him. Someone necessarily has to do the waiting associated with capital goods, and, if it is not the firm itself or its owners, then it is the suppliers of what is capital-use from the firm's point of view. And, Cassel's identification of waiting and use of value does not depend on any mathematical formula.

Before Cassel, says Böhm, the abstinence theory and some sort of use theory were considered competitive and mutually exclusive (III, 198–200). But the "use theory" that Böhm considers incompatible with the abstinence or waiting theory must be something other than Cassel's theory. Böhm goes on to defend himself against Cassel's charges of making errors in the history of thought. But the issue of who, if either, correctly interprets earlier writers is separate from questions of substance.

Böhm sums up: Cassel naively expected us to return to old and justly abandoned lines of theorizing but made no perceptible attempt to clear up disputed points. His mere words, lacking explanatory force, "consist of rather dangerous expressions that play dialectically with difficult material and actually lead us deeper into aberrations instead of leading us out" (III, 200–201). Thus, Böhm offers quibbles, verbal maneuvers, and polite invective against a theory that he has not fully understood. Historians of thought mention Böhm's polemical bent. "With surprising regularity, Böhm-Bawerk's treatment is most unfair to those authors who come closest to his own approach" (Blaug 1985, p. 565). Even if Cassel might not have been as clear as he should have been (which is not our judgment), that lapse would not discredit his theory itself, particularly if a better exposition is available.

Yet, Conard agrees with Böhm-Bawerk's criticism, arguing that.

> a factor of production ... is an entity ... which is capable of providing productive services. Any use of these services in production implies abstinence from some other use: if I labor, I abstain from swimming or playing tennis. As Boehm-Bawerk pointed out, payment for labor already includes payment for abstention from other activities. Abstinence simply is not an independent factor, but is the act by which factors are permitted to perform their services in production.
>
> The view does not deny that abstinence from present consumption in order to enjoy a later benefit may not involve a sacrifice and hence require a reward in an economy permitting freedom of choice to those who own control over factors. Indeed, ... the existence of this supply price is an essential element in any adequate theory of interest, and in this sense [Nassau] Senior's contribution was a crucial one. But the very nature of a factor of production denies to abstinence the role of an independent "factor..." (Conard 1959, p. 32).

Despite Conard, the issue here is not whether abstinence from swimming or tennis is a productive factor distinct from labor performed. What is at issue is abstinence in the sense of waiting as command over resources deferred by its suppliers and advanced to its demanders.

Donald Dewey (1965, pp. 197–201) calls the concept of waiting as a separate productive factor one of "three unfortunate survivals" in capital theory (the other two are identified in the coming pages). He complains that Nassau Senior, John Stuart Mill, and Alfred Marshall tried to invoke the notion of abstinence or waiting as to justify interest as its reward.[7] Gustav Cassel, who offered the "most uncompromising" treatment of interest as the payment for waiting, merely observed, says Dewey, that

> a capital asset during its lifetime yields a surplus of services greater than its cost of construction.... This surplus, which Cassel calls interest, is another name for what [Dewey calls income]. [It] is the reward one receives for not consuming capital and an addition to income (or interest) is what one receives for not consuming income (or interest). Therefore, waiting is not a separate factor of production. It is only another name for production itself. The statement that interest is payment for waiting or abstinence is not so much wrong as tautological.

Dewey continues by stating that "a rate of interest will exist even though every act of investment yields a consumable product 'immediately.'" He alludes to Frank Knight's Crusonia model (1944). Creating capital assets or making loans enables the individual investor to increase his income by delaying consumption. Arbitrage keeps the interest rate equal to the marginal product of investment, provided that investment outcomes are known with certainty (Dewey 1965, p. 199, quoted and closely paraphrased).

Dewey does notice Robert Dorfman's two articles of 1959 recognizing interest as a factor price (pp. 199–201). Dorfman models consumable income per time period as depending on labor and length of the period of production. Paying labor at a rate equal to its marginal productivity leaves a surplus that Dorfman calls "payment for waiting." Dewey prefers to call it payment for the use of "unfinished consumption goods" or "variable capital" or simply "capital" (using that troublesome word).

[7] But as Chapter 1 insists, explaining interest does not by itself justify it.

> There is payment for waiting only because an increase in the stock of unfinished consumption goods can only be secured by lengthening the period of production. Whatever it is called, this second factor of production, which is created by investing consumption, earns a reward because it has a cost of production and, hence, is scarce. The fact that, by the terms of Dorfman's problem, an additional increment of this second factor cannot be obtained "immediately" is true but essentially irrelevant (p. 201).

But is such criticism other than superficial?

Dewey's second target is the concept of period of production (1965, pp. 201–205). His "decisive objection" is not that the period "is zero or infinity, as Knight contends, but rather that, whatever it is, it tells us nothing that we wish to know." Dewey's third "unfortunate survival" in capital theory is attention to zero and negative rates of interest, which, though logical possibilities, are neither probable nor desirable (1965, pp. 205–211). Though rare when Dewey wrote, zero and negative nominal rates of interest have become more common in recent years.

2.10 Interest as a Measure of Opportunity Cost

Because waiting has a price, each business firm restrains the amount of value that it ties up over time as it transforms productive factors into final consumer goods and services. Ordinary factor prices similarly restrain a firm's use of labor and land.

But why should the firm exercise this restraint if it could use additional waiting, labor, or land *productively*? The answer, *opportunity cost*, invokes the very logic of a price system as a device that transmits information and incentives and accomplishes coordination. Their prices indicate that factors are scarce. Employing units of them in any particular line of production costs losing what they could have contributed to output in other lines. The prices of factors and products force each business firm to act as if it were considering not merely whether additional factor units would add *something* to its output, but also whether they would add *enough* to the value of its output to warrant the necessary sacrifice of output elsewhere in the economy. Prices enable the firm, in effect, to compare consumers' evaluations of the additional output it could offer and its cost as measured by consumers' evaluations of other goods forgone.

When the interest rate restrains a firm from adopting a roundabout or waiting-intensive process on a larger scale or in a greater degree, the reason is that doing so would have foreclosed a more valuable employment of waiting elsewhere. This is true, anyway, of an economy functioning by the logic of a competitive price system. The signaling and rationing function of the interest rate is on all fours with that of other factor prices.

Constructing apartment buildings that will serve with little maintenance for many years is a more waiting-intensive method of providing housing services than constructing cheaper buildings with shorter lives or requiring more maintenance. Even though the more durable buildings require more labor and other inputs and take more time to build than the more maintenance-intensive alternative, their services over their entire lives will be greater in relation to inputs with which waiting is substitutable.

Since waiting has a cost, however, it is not necessarily true that the more durable buildings are unequivocally advantageous. The longer intervals between inputs of resources and outputs of services, as well as the fact that the economies in maintenance accrue not all at once but only over time, do pose opportunity costs. Those costs pertain to other projects and products ruled out because the scarce capacity to wait for the fruits of tied up resources has been devoted to the durable apartments. The market calls this cost to the attention of firms in the form of interest.

It and other prices call the attention of consumers to the opportunity costs of the waiting and other factors embodied in the goods and services from which they must choose. Consumers consult their preferences in the light of the terms of choice posed by reality.[8]

The waiting bought and sold in an ordinary loan transaction is seldom waiting for any specific thing. Of what does the lender postpone consumption? Böhm-Bawerk, as mentioned previously, toyed frivolously with such questions. We might as well ask what particular movie a hater of all movies is *not* watching. It is less unusual to know what the borrower avoids having to wait for, namely, what he buys with the borrowed money. Seldom would the lender be waiting for the same thing that the borrower gets in advance. "The 'use of capital,' for which interest is paid, is not the use of a piece of concrete capital, ... but is the use of a certain amount

[8] Evoking the task of socialist planners, Hubert Henderson gives an excellent discussion of the rationing function of interest; 1921/1958, pp. 11–13.

of 'goods in general.' ... [I]f the thing lent is not a concrete piece of capital, but 'the command of a certain amount of goods in general,' the command of the same amount must be paid back" (Cassel 1903/1956, pp. 166–167). "The pure and obvious service of waiting" commands a price.

Still, transactions in waiting may indeed be linked to specific goods. Waiting can be performed and avoided, sold and bought, in many ways other than through money loans—so this chapter argues in its sections on arbitrage. A landowner receiving an annual rent is deferring the command over resources in general that he could exercise by selling the land and spending the proceeds. Among economists recognizing this point is Rothbard (1962, 422–423). A manufacturer who leases a machine instead of buying it keeps funds of his own available for command over other resources, much as if he had borrowed money to buy the machine.

The opportunity cost of waiting bears on the question of loan guarantees. The fact that a borrower with a worthy project could not get a loan at the terms available on the market but could get a loan if it were guaranteed by some authority does not by itself mean that the loan should be guaranteed and granted. This point remains valid even if in fact the project is successful, and the loan repaid without the guarantor's having to pay anything. The reason is that the waiting allocated by the guaranteed loan, like any productive factor, has an opportunity cost. Allocating it to a favored project deprives other projects of it, ones attractive enough to receive loans without any guarantee. Many decades of U.S. government policies promoting homeownership and housing construction before the peak of the boom around 2006 had the opportunity cost associated with the encroachment on physical and human capital formation that would have elsewhere been more productive.

This thought applies as well to government-guaranteed loans to finance exports or project loans made or guaranteed by the World Bank. The fact that scarce capital or waiting might be employed productively in a particular way does not neutralize the possibility that it might be employed still more productively in some other way. Saying so is not a blanket condemnation of loan guarantees, but some argument is necessary beyond deeming a purpose worthy.

Speaking of loan guarantees again reminds us that waiting is not allocated by its price alone. Risk, and perhaps other nonpecuniary factors, also come into loan decisions. The nonprice rationing of loans is a pervasive reality. Bankers traditionally specialize in judging the creditworthiness of potential borrowers. But the same is true of labor and land also: how they are employed depends on considerations beyond the wage rate or the land rent.

Artificially encouraging or burdening particular uses of any factor will distort its own allocation and those of substitute and complementary factors alike away from the pattern that would otherwise result from voluntary transactions. If support of mortgage loans encourages house-building, it reduces credit for producing other things. The same is true of loan guarantees to favored companies. Even if they do not turn out to require direct government payments, they still, as intended, encourage more use of waiting and complementary factors in the guaranteed activities at the expense of production elsewhere. But waiting, however allocated, is not a free good. To cite job creation as justifying encouragements to renewable energy and supposedly environment-friendly activities, for example, neglects their drawing productive factors away from other industries, leaving the total number of jobs substantially unchanged–apart from macroeconomic unemployment, as in a recession. To say so is not to idealize the free-market allocation and condemn all government interventions. The point here is simply that distortions to the use of waiting stand on par with ones affecting any ordinary factor.

2.11 Capital Goods, Capital, and Waiting

Chapter 3 explores whether some interpretation of the term "capital goods" might be useful. Meanwhile, the usual loose meaning suffices—structures, machinery, and so forth. Such items must be distinguished from whatever it is that the interest rate is the price of. It is misleading to label that "whatever" as "capital," for that word turns up in many different senses. Yet muddling together capital goods and capital as waiting has understandable appeal. When devoted to production rather than to consumer loans, waiting generally, but not necessarily, shows itself in capital goods. The muddle breeds misunderstanding about whether the price of capital is the interest rate, the ordinary dollar prices of machines and other capital goods, or of their services. It coexists with tedious and pointless questions about whether and when specific items–like a pickup truck–count as capital goods and when as consumer goods.

We are no better off if we slide from conceiving of capital as heterogeneous physical capital goods into conceiving of it as a homogeneous fund—even as a "permanent" substance flowing from one set of capital goods into another, changing its specific embodiments but always enduring. That was the view of John Bates Clark and Frank Knight, conveniently summarized in Lutz 1967, Chapter 8, esp. pp. 99, 106–107; also see Laibman and Nell 1977.

We need not embrace this mystical notion of a homogeneous fund of value that shifts around in pursuit of the highest return. Waiting is not performed in an aggregate amount. People perform it in a decentralized fashion by holding a variety of assets and claims. These different performances of waiting tend, through arbitrage and substitution, however, to command roughly the same price (subject to qualifications about lumpiness, risk, and so forth). In appropriate contexts, then, we may speak of "the" interest rate as the price of waiting, treating what bears that price, as we often treat labor, as quasi-homogeneous.

CHAPTER 3

Capital Goods, Intermediate Goods, and Land

3.1 Pointless Distinctions

The approach to capital and interest theory suggested here avoids unnecessary distinctions. For example, what goods do and do not count as *capital* goods? As usually defined, capital goods include factories, machinery, and other instruments of production. They count among the innumerable kinds of intermediate goods, which are stages in the time-consuming transformation of original factors of production into ultimate consumer satisfaction. Cotton seed, textile machinery, and cotton cloth alike are intermediate stages of transforming the ultimate factors embodied in them into the services of shirts. The cloth itself might be considered a short-lived capital good, just as a solera for producing fine sherry might be called either sherry-in-process or a capital good itself. Textile machinery, usually called a capital good, might just as well be called an intermediate good gradually transforming itself into apparel. Nothing of substance hinges on such issues of terminology—on where or whether to draw a line between capital goods and other goods.

Does an automobile count as a capital good or a consumer good according to who owns it? What about a car used partly for business and partly for pleasure? These questions are unnecessary and diversionary. Its owner, whether a business firm or a consumer, waits for its services of transportation and availability, or their value, yielded gradually over time. A consumer-owner performs that waiting for himself. Although, if he has

L. B. Yeager and S. H. Hanke, *Capital, Interest, and Waiting*,
https://doi.org/10.1007/978-3-031-63398-0_3

borrowed money to buy the car, he offloads the burden of waiting to the lender. A consumer leasing a car avoids tying up wealth and avoids waiting by shifting that burden to the leasing company, which may in turn shift the burden to its creditors and stockholders. A refrigerator, similarly, and regardless of who owns it, represents tied up wealth yielding its services over time.

Rejecting the distinction between capital and other goods, Walter Eucken goes so far as to reject the very notion of durable consumer goods. Furniture, pianos, clothing, and so forth are tools for producing consumer services. They do not merely resemble durable means of production but count among them (Eucken 1954, pp. 77–79). Cassel (1903, pp. 87–89) argues that waiting during the gradual consumption of durable goods is the most important source of demand for waiting (ordinary production being another source). He suggests using the term capital (meaning capital goods) to embrace all produced goods except ones already in consumer hands. Rental houses, not owned by their occupants, thus count as capital, but not clothing owned by the wearer. Again, though, not much depends on such distinctions.

One might object, questionably, that an increased stock of capital goods in the narrow sense—factories, machines, and the like—does more to increase the output of goods and services as counted gross domestic product than an increased stock of consumer durables does. Still, an increase in consumer durables does increase production of their *services*, which, although not ordinarily counted in GDP, are real and contribute to human well-being. The issue, a minor one, concerns *types* of output and conventions of measurement.

True enough, the question arises of how resources saved from making current consumer goods are applied. Do they go into constructing factories and machines or into making consumer durables like refrigerators and cars that provide consumer satisfaction more directly? How well does the allocation of resources take into account people's preferences and technological possibilities? Why should mere measurement conventions, and perhaps tax laws, dictate a preference between the output of factories and the services of consumer durables? Eucken, remember, saw no point in trying to distinguish between consumer durables and capital goods narrowly defined.

Capital *goods*, whether narrowly or inclusively defined, are not the same thing as the "capital" whose price is supposedly the interest rate, especially in theoretical models. Capital goods are not merely stored up waiting but stored up labor and land services also. On the other hand, waiting goes into producing not only capital goods, narrowly defined, but practically everything else, including electric power, medical care, and haircuts, since their production involves channeling factors of production through capital and intermediate goods and human training.

People hardly desire capital goods in their own right. They are just technologically necessary stages in transforming original productive factors into ultimate consumer satisfaction. Both they and other durable goods require waiting in two directions. On the one hand, constructing them takes time. On the other hand, further time elapses before they yield their entire usefulness in aiding the production of consumer goods and services. The services of original factors of production are channeled *through* them, first into and then from them. Factories, equipment, and consumer durable goods all require waiting in both construction and use.

3.2 Fundamental and Derivative Magnitudes

Investment gives up some consumption now for more in the future. It is a fact of reality, no mere logical truism, that this process involves constructing capital goods as usually understood. What Jack Hirshleifer says about interest and investment applies all the more so to capital goods:

> derivative rather than fundamental magnitudes in the theory of intertemporal choice. The fundamental magnitudes are the quantities and prices of the objects of choice-dated consumptions. Investment is not a choice-object but is the process of conversion (or the amount converted) of current funds or consumption potential into future consumption (Hirshleifer 1970, p. 130).

Before pursuing this line of thought, we may acknowledge a qualification, which is one of Frank Knight's favorite points (Knight 1936, Conard 1959, p. 88). Savers do not always, and perhaps not even typically, forgo current consumption and accumulate wealth to liquidate it later and spend the proceeds on consumption. Accumulation can become an end in itself. The owners of a country's wealth or capital stock ordinarily (apart from possible disasters) intend it to be permanent or growing. For this reason, we might split hairs and speak of choice not between present and future *consumption* but between present and future consumption *options*. When the future rolls around, wealth owners may, and often do, choose to forgo fully exercising their consumption option and postpone some of their available consumption still longer. References to future consumption in the literature and in this book should therefore be understood with this qualification.

If capital or durable goods are not fundamental entities, why pay attention to them? First, they are facts of reality. They help explain the greater productivity of well-chosen roundabout productive processes (the topic of Chapter 6). They enter into the portfolio choices of wealth owners. In some contexts, it is convenient to count capital goods or their services, rather than their own inputs, as factors of production. As argued in Chapter 2, how we conceive of a production function and what we count as its inputs—how slightly or how far we go toward decomposing produced inputs into the elemental factors that they embody—is a matter of convenience in the piece of analysis at hand. Our sometimes-counting capital goods or their services as productive factors no more destroys the status of waiting as a productive factor than it destroys the status of the labor and land use also embodied in capital goods. Attention to capital goods can be instructive in understanding the consequences for the interest rate of their catastrophic destruction or of their magic appearance (see Chapter 8).

"Capital formation" or "capital accumulation" commonly means the construction of capital and intermediate goods in excess of maintenance or replacement. Its opposite is capital consumption—using capital goods up or wearing them out without full replacement. Such treatment constitutes un-waiting or dis-waiting, the disembodiment of the previously embodied waiting, labor, and land services. This reversal of capital accumulation adds to the consumer goods and services available in the short run at the expense of the longer run.

If calculations and expectations prove correct, a capital good is worth more than the total value (less depreciation) of the land use, labor, and other *ordinary* factor services that went into constructing it. It also embodies waiting. To say so is not, however, to adopt a cost theory of value, attributing the value of a capital good or of anything else solely to what went into making it. In the other direction, it is just as much a half-truth to say that the specific values of a capital good and of the factors it embodies derive only from the final consumer satisfactions to which they contribute. Market values emerge from a multidirectional process of general interdependence (Walras 1874/1926/1954; Cassel 1932/1967, Chapter IV).

Miscalculations are possible, and expectations can be disappointed not only by error or by the accidental destruction of a capital good but also by changes in demands or technology. Such an event would fully or partially destroy the waiting and other factor services embodied in the capital good involved.

3.3 Should Land Count as a Capital Good?

How to classify land depends on the purpose (and ordinarily, it serves no real purpose to worry about whether land is a capital good). For a business firm deciding whether to buy, sell, rent, or rent out a capital good or a plot of land, the fact that one has been manufactured while the other is a "free gift of nature" is irrelevant. The firm looks to the profits expected from the asset. When an economist tries to estimate the average period of production of an industry or a whole economy, counting land in or excluding it from the value of capital goods of course affects the calculated result. While these issues, discussed in Chapter 7, may hold academic interest, they are unimportant for business and consumer decisions.

Land resembles a capital good except that, defined very narrowly as nature-given space and location, it cannot be produced. Defined more broadly, land, or its fertility and resource content, may be discovered, created, depleted, destroyed, or replenished.

Land, narrowly defined, is in inelastic supply. But so are some manmade goods, including Old Masters and other collectibles; and even these are sometimes used for business purposes. Some natural resources are exhaustible beyond some fuzzy limit, but manmade capital goods can also be used up. Land is a form of wealth and a vehicle of saving, but so are manmade capital and other goods or securities issued to finance them.

Land, narrowly defined, can scarcely be reproduced. The same is nearly true of some manmade capital goods, say the tunnel through a particular mountain. Furthermore, substitutability can resemble reproducibility in practice. The land needed for some projects may be reduced by using more labor and manmade capital goods.

Cassell (1932, p. 226) elaborates on this point:

> Capital-disposal can be substituted not only for labour, but also for land and the raw materials of nature. If, for instance, land were so dear that it would be cheaper to construct an underground railway than to buy the more expensive land for one on the surface, there would be a real

> substitution of capital-disposal for the use of land. If we assume that the annual cost of maintenance and renewal is the same for both lines, then it is clear that the rent that would have to be paid by the surface railway is replaced by the interest which the underground line has to pay for the extra capital it needs, and so there is a substitution of a certain amount of capital-disposal for the use of land. If, on the other hand, in a mountain district where the cost of land is not important, the underground line is preferred because the costs of transport on this line are cheaper through the saving in coal and time, then, other things being equal, the choice of the underground line means a substitution of capital-disposal for all the other factors of production which have a part in the extra cost of the other line, such as coal, the labour of the staff, and so forth.

Producibility, exhaustibility, usefulness as a substitute or complement in production or consumption, elasticity of supply and demand, serviceability as a vehicle of saving—these and other features enter into business and personal decisions and economic analysis, but they do not categorically distinguish between land and other things. How to treat land or any other item of wealth depends on the decision or analytical purpose at hand. Trying to draw a context-free distinction is pointless. No one specific conception of land is always the most useful.[1] The concept of waiting helps bypass these pointless distinctions.

[1] Murray Rothbard (1962, I, 414–417) distinguishes between *economic land* and *geographic land*. The former comprises all nature-given bearers of value—natural resources, land in the popular sense, water, and air, so far as they are scarce rather than superabundant and free. Examples of economic land whose value traces largely to human effort include farms and dredged harbors; their usefulness would deteriorate without ongoing maintenance. Rothbard's geographical (or "basic") land, in contrast, consists of indestructible physical space or position. Yet any distinction between (a) indestructible pure gifts of nature and (b) nature's gifts indestructibly improved by human effort—say the tunnel bored through the mountain—is probably of historical interest only. Decisions about using them do not depend fundamentally on whether the indestructible resources happen to be purely nature-given or are partially manmade. These decisions contrast with questions about using, maintaining, or replacing resources, whether manmade or not, that might indeed deteriorate or be exhausted.

3.4 Land Rent and Interest

Land and capital goods alike yield streams of services stretching into the future. The prices of those services are determined by demand and supply. Demands for them derive mainly from their value productivities, like the demands for various kinds of labor.

"[C]apital goods earn quasi-rents,[2] not interest. This is not a mere semantic quibble. The forces determining the return on capital goods are those described in the theory of rents and quasi-rents, not those described in the theory of interest" (Conard 1959, p. 7). This distinction between the price of an asset's services and the factor price explained by interest theory holds for land also. Just as we distinguish between the price of the *services* of a capital good, the good's own price, and the relation between those prices expressed as an annual rate of yield on the good's own value, so we must make the same distinctions for land. Rent is the price of land use and tends to equal its marginal value productivity. For land and capital goods alike, what does fall within the domain of interest theory is the *relation* between the prices of a year's services and the prices of the assets that yield them.

The percentage yield on the value of land is the price of waiting through holding an investment in land, much as the interest rate on bonds is the price of waiting through investment in bonds. Arbitrage and substitution tend to equalize these rates of return, subject to standard qualifications about lumpiness, risk, liquidity, and other advantages and disadvantages of various investments.

For land most narrowly conceived, Murray Rothbard's "geographic" or "basic" land, neither its physical amount nor any nonexistent cost of producing it can enter into the process of equalizing rates of return. But its own price can adjust. Suppose that the percentage yield on land of a particular type or location exceeds the interest rate on loans and the prevailing rate of net yield on assets in general. Investors have an incentive to shift into owning this land. They curtail their supply of loans while perhaps demanding loans to finance purchases of land. The resulting rise in the price of land reduces its percentage yield, while the reduced supply

[2] In the short run, when capital goods are in fixed supply, capital earns quasi-rents, a term introduced by Alfred Marshall. The quasi-rents are equal to the excess earned over the variable cost of production.

of and increased demand for loans raises the rate of interest. Arbitrage operates.

In a familiar textbook account, the price of a plot of land is determined by capitalizing its rent at the going rate of interest. However, causation does not only run in one direction. Not only does the interest rate influence the price of land, but the supply of and demand for land influence the interest rate. Investing in land and receiving the value of its services only as they stretch out over time is one way of performing waiting. Changes in technology affecting the productivity of land use, changes in tastes for landownership, changes in land taxation, and other changes could affect land rents and prices, affecting land's percentage yield. Arbitrage would extend this influence even to the interest rate on loans. One way only causation is *not* true of the prices of assets and of their services. Chapter 8 pursues this point further.

3.5 Waiting Through Landownership

Some economists reject any sharp distinction between rent on land and interest on money loans and between the reasons for these payments.[3] An owner who collects rent on land is nearly in the same position as someone who collects interest on money lent. The parallel is clear in a repurchase agreement: the effective lender buys a piece of land, and the effective borrower agrees to buy it back later at a higher price. The price difference is interest on a loan collateralized by land.

A quibble about units is no more than just that. Rent in *dollars per acre* per year is not the same as a *percentage* yield on a dollar value. In general equilibrium, a percentage yield on land value does indeed equal the rate of interest (subject to standard qualifications). But different concepts are not identical just because they tend toward the same number in equilibrium. Labor's wage rate in competitive equilibrium tends to equal but is

[3] E.g., Knight (1944, pp. 33–34; 1936, pp. 438–440). Conard (1959, pp. 8–9, 20–21, 79, 111) reviews Knight's rejection of any essential distinction between capital goods and original factors of production and his skepticism even about the concept of factors of production themselves. Stigler (1941, p. 316), expounds J.-B. Clark's classification of land not as a separate factor but as a special type of capital good.

Cassel (1903/1956, p. 5) notes that in the ages when the Catholic Church was trying to discourage paying and receiving interest, "it was a common practice to sell and purchase *rent-charges* on land." In effect, loans could be made at interest. The German language adopted the word *Zins* (from *census*, rent) as the general word for interest.

not conceptually identical with its marginal revenue product. Explaining the tendency toward equality and the arbitrage involved is part of the economist's job, which is only impeded by making rent, or even the percentage yield on land, downright identical to the interest rate on loans. Thanks to arbitrage, however, yields on asset values, an agio on present over future goods, and the explicit interest rate all are forms of the price of waiting.

If people became more willing to postpone consumption, and even if their increased thrift was only directed toward investment in land, the general rate of interest would tend to fall. By holding land instead of selling it and spending the proceeds, landowners, like bondholders, perform the service of waiting. Instead of drawing resources into providing for their own current consumption, they release resources for other purposes, including the construction of capital goods. True enough, land would continue to exist and yield its services regardless of whether any private owners were willing to wait. But if landowners did sell and spend the proceeds on consumption, their doing so would lower the price of and raise the percentage yield on land. Arbitrage would communicate this rise to the interest rate. Fewer resources would be available for constructing capital goods.

Waiting is the social function, then, for which the landowner is "rewarded." Saying so is not meant by itself to justify private landownership and collection of rent; it merely notes a parallel with collecting interest. Indeed, Maurice Allais has even expressed a worry, which is examined soon, about private landownership and rent collection.

3.6 Possible Diversion of Thrift

Thrift is more attractive with more rather than fewer ways to hold wealth available. This is true of land. While the opportunity to own land does tend to encourage thrift, it may reduce the degree to which that thrift directs resources from current consumption into real capital formation. Although slight and of little relevance to policy, this effect is of theoretical interest; and we shall address a version of it in Chapter 10.

In contrast with manmade capital goods, the supply of land given by nature in fixed quantities is unresponsive to price. To some degree, then, the desire to accumulate wealth in the form of land—land value, not mere acreage—can be met through mere growth in the market value of a fixed amount of land. By contrast, accumulating wealth in the form of manmade goods ordinarily does involve increasing their wealth in physical quantities. The bid up additional value of land is genuine wealth for its private owners but is rather fictitious wealth from the social point of view. Maurice Allais finds this distinction important (1947, II, Chapter IX, and widely scattered passages).

If people's *overall* willingness to wait were somehow predetermined, their thrift would promote capital construction all the more if they did not have the option of waiting through landownership. Accumulation of wealth as land value partially gratifies the overall willingness to wait, leaving less of that thrift for capital construction and securities to finance it.

How could this happen? Wealth appears with a positive sign in the consumption function and a negative sign in the saving function; this is the Pigou or wealth effect (and, when applied to money, part of the real-balance effect). For private owners, a $10,000 increase in the value of their land is just that, whether coming from a rise in the price of land already held or from inheritance of acreage. For this reason, the amount of real resources saved from consumption and made available for capital formation depends on whether thrift is partly satisfied by an increase in wealth that is genuine from the private but not the social point of view.

A socially fictitious increase in wealth—in valuation but not in physical quantity—diminishes the effective economywide propensity to save and apply savings to real capital formation. Such considerations speak further in favor of the conception of waiting as a factor of production. And nothing said here denies the role of flexible land prices in allocating productive resources.

An analogy holds between the two-sided effect of landownership and the creation and destruction of trade analyzed by the theory of customs unions. A union opens some formerly blocked trade among member countries, but it diverts some trade with the outside world to within the union. Specific facts govern which dominates—benefits from inside trade creation or damage from outside trade diversion. Here, similarly, the opportunity for private ownership of land presumably both promotes waiting and also diverts some of it into socially fictitious accumulation. But it is not obvious which effect prevails.

Like land, collectibles—Old Masters, antique furniture and cars, rare coins and stamps, and the like—are in inelastic supply. A rise in their prices from a strengthened demand does indeed increase wealth from the private (but not social, not physical) point of view and so tends to satisfy and absorb the propensity to accumulate.

One more analogy between waiting and labor as factors of production is that the willingness to supply either may be wasted. Workers might be set to digging and refilling holes, perhaps in an attempt to stimulate the whole economy, but their labor is still wasted.

3.7 Foreign Purchase of Land

Placement of savings in land might affect the interest rate and real capital formation in another way. Might foreigners' purchase of land in our country do so, and if so, how? The transaction contributes toward a balance of payments surplus on capital account and a deficit on current account. During a period of adjustment, imports of goods and services exceed exports, and our people gain use of the real resources embodied in those net imports. Foreigners perform waiting for our country by currently surrendering these resources and waiting for the yields on their newly purchased land. The foreign purchase tends to bid up land prices, reducing percentage yields and, through arbitrage, reducing the general interest rate as well. In this way, waiting is applied to domestic capital formation. Capital inflow through foreign purchases of land, much as of securities, promotes domestic capital formation.

This example reinforces a point about domestic saving. Consuming less, even to buy land, does promote real capital formation. The availability of land as an outlet for savings deters capital formation, on the other hand, only insofar as landowners, being privately wealthier in the socially fictitious form of bid up land values, abstain less from current consumption than they would otherwise have done. The two effects work at cross-purposes.

3.8 Conservation of Resources

For issues of conservation, no sharp distinction holds between manmade structures and equipment and nature-given land and resources. Regardless of their origin, all valuable assets can yield streams of future services. Along with other factors, manmade capital goods help satisfy the economy's current wants, partially substituting for natural resources and enabling them to last longer. So argues Anthony Scott (1955, p. 10 and *passim*).

Being nature's gift has little economic significance. To the Swiss Family Robinson who just landed on their desert island, it matters little whether their initial endowment is items salvaged from their wrecked ship or is naturally available. Either way, it is available to help produce new goods and services (pp. 10–11).

Scott challenges the presumption in favor of conserving land and resources in their natural forms. Just as economic theory does not condemn wearing out capital goods and replacing them with different ones, neither does it condemn replacing natural with produced goods. Yet some economists[4] do suppose a difference between the economic principles applying to minerals and to reproducible goods. But whether an asset is reproducible has nothing to do with its use (p. 6). The Robinsons need not worry about replacing their wasting capital stock in its original form; what matters is its power to help produce a stream of income (p. 11).

Resource conservation analytically resembles investing in capital goods (p. viii). Postponing the exhaustion of a stock of natural resources, like renewing a renewable resource, is an investment much like building a factory; "all conservation is merely a particular form of investment" (p. 8). Given a total flow of investable savings, more conservation of natural resources leaves fewer buildings and less physical and human capital for posterity. Like any other investment, conservation has an opportunity cost. Having more of something in the future is desirable, but is it worth having less of something else? "[C]onservation will not necessarily increase the future's inheritance, but merely change its composition from 'capital goods' to natural products" (p. viii).

[4] Scott names three (p. 6). As an example of the view that he challenges, he quotes from H. R. Bowen (*Toward Social Economy*, 1948, p. 239): a "discrepancy between the individual and the social point of view can easily be explained by the fact that no individual has any material interest to be sparing in the use of natural resources, however seriously he may consider the interest of future generations, because his efforts to conserve will be negligible in effect." Bowen overlooked the role of private property and markets for assets.

Conservation has "a faintly moral flavour that it does not deserve," Scott continues. Without an increase in total savings, increased conservation can easily require reducing the output of capital goods. "Conservation then ... involves increased investment in particular industries, with or without a change in the total endowment going to posterity" (p. 22).[5]

Conservation of natural resources is only one of the uses of social savings. Decisions about each type of investment depend on tastes and technology. Investing more in a particular type of project requires cutting back either in other projects or in consumption. Individuals plan to "save," not to "conserve zinc" (Scott 1955, p. 11).

The price system, working normally, treats all valuable things as scarce relative to demands. But conserving forest lands in particular treats them as "the" scarce resource, other resources being treated as more plentiful. Such an arbitrary allocation impairs efficiency in providing human satisfaction (p. 21). Misconceptions come to mind about penalizing energy consumption and about recycling. The opposite of Scott's position is "to economize on human welfare in order to achieve maximum 'welfare' for resources" (p. 13).

Exploiting resources is first step in producing consumable goods and services and maintaining capital goods, perhaps in new and better forms. Scott rejects any sharp distinction between *renewable* and *unrenewable* resources. He notes that Gustav Cassel got the argument right (pp. 13, 153, citing Cassel 1932/1967, Chapter VII). Exhaustible resources do not suddenly run out; rather, their use gradually grows more expensive. Given certain conditions, including respect for property rights, prices convey information and incentives and facilitate rationing of scarce resources, with prices tending to rise ahead of expected increases in scarcity (Scott, pp. 13–14).

3.9 Market Imperfections Regarding Conservation

In some cases, private profit-seeking may allocate resources poorly, suggesting that intervention might bring improvement. People might fail even to maximize their own profits or wealth. Negative or positive

[5] F. A. Hayek (1941, p. 88) had already noticed the similarity between exhaustible natural resources and manmade capital goods. There is nothing necessarily imprudent about disinvesting in the one to invest in the other.

externalities might relate to problems of scale of ownership, delineation of property rights, and property tenure. The price system might fail to register needs correctly because of an unsatisfactory income distribution. A further reason may be already implicit in the others: so-called market imperfections (realities), particularly in the credit markets, may impede postponing or hastening consumption and financing asset holdings. Arguments centering on defense, employment, risk, and monopoly also appear on such a list. "Risk [however] is an ubiquitous force which affects all provision for the future; a monopoly if anything tends to overemphasize provision for the future" (p. 74; Cassel 1932/1967, esp. p. 293, had already made the point about monopoly's *exaggerating* resource conservation).

Many of the foregoing arguments do not challenge the very logic of private property and the price system but cite the sometimes unavoidably incomplete application and operation of those institutions. A critic should identify specific defects, specify where and how to apply remedies, and weigh potential benefits against unwanted side effects. Inadequately defined or guaranteed property rights may weaken incentives to conserve or stockpile exhaustible fuels or other products expected to become especially scarce (cf. Cassel 1932/1967, esp. p. 292). It is diversionary, instead, to sweepingly bewail neglect of the environment or of future generations, or shortsightedness, or the profit motive, or greed.

Although recognizing the tradeoff between natural resources and manmade capital goods, given the total volume of investable saving, one may coherently (if not conclusively) worry about too low a market-determined *overall* rate of saving and investment. Several economists have indeed argued that an excessive market rate of interest reflects and reinforces an inadequate degree of concern for the future (Scott, Chapter 8, "A Social Rate of Time Preference"). Maurice Allais notes that a person's choices between present and future consumption are made by the present person only, with the future person having no say. Allais concludes that the state might legitimately impose some forced saving through taxation (1947, I, 220n., 221–225, and *passim*).[6]

Generally inadequate foresight, then, impairs saving and investment overall, not investment in resource conservation particularly. Seeking remedies for inadequate foresight or other market imperfections should

[6] On individuals' "telescopic faculty" being "defective" or "perverted," compare Pigou 1932/1950, pp. 24–26.

take account of public-choice theory and of experience accumulated since Allais and Scott wrote. How coherently can government and the democratic process respond? Scott (p. 99), for one, quotes Henry Sidgwick as already expressing a related worry.

3.10 Conclusion

The central topic of capital and interest theory, as Jack Hirschleifer explained, is intertemporal choice. What opportunities and desires govern the choice between different quantities of desired things available at different times?

Economists used to worry about how to distinguish capital goods from other forms of wealth. All valuable things yield a flow of services over time. A machine, as it wears out, contributes to producing goods closer to the ultimate consumer. A refrigerator provides a flow of services; and things like collectibles yield a flow of pleasures, satisfaction of ownership, benefits of portfolio diversification, or expected gain in value. Walter Eucken denies any important distinction between consumer durables and other capital goods. Creation and ownership of either requires waiting for desired results to emerge. And no theoretically important distinction holds between capital goods in the narrowest sense, like factories and machines, and materials and semi-finished goods used or created in ongoing processes of production.

Businesses and consumers care about the mix of capital goods that they own. Capital is not some homogeneous thing. It consists of many kinds of machines and structures and even human abilities, training, and experience. The array of complementary and substitutable capital goods employed in a developed and well-functioning economy has a certain logic or coherence. Some existing capital goods provide scope for profitable investment in others (a fact that helps undermine worries about any inexorable deficiency of investment opportunities) (Lachmann 1956/1978, pp. 2–7).

Land narrowly defined, unlike manmade capital goods, is a sheer "gift of nature," but this difference has little importance for economic theory. Both types are held for their services; and their holders perform waiting and expect returns, which constitute an interest in the broadest sense of the term. Privately owned land, as a vehicle of saving, can even, through substitution and arbitrage, indirectly promote the construction of manmade capital goods. Allais, however, has described a theoretically instructive exception of slight practical importance.

Anthony Scott has drawn parallels between natural resources—even exhaustible ones—and manmade capital goods. Holding wealth in both forms requires waiting, and waiting has opportunity costs: devoting it to some purposes means withholding it from others. Investment in conserving natural resources withholds waiting from the replacement of and investment in manmade capital goods. Economic theory does not teach that exhaustible resources should never be exhausted or that their conservation is an especially noble choice. Market participants will take into account the future if property rights are clearly defined and well enforced and if various market "imperfections" are absent or corrected.

Discussion of the allocation of waiting between natural and manmade capital goods leaves aside the distinct question of whether society's overall propensity to save and wait is too great or too small.

CHAPTER 4

Advantages of the Recommended View of Waiting

4.1 Bypassing Pointless Distinctions

The concept of waiting avoids distracting questions. Sweeping discussions of "what is capital?", "what are capital goods?", and so forth (as in Lewin 1999) verge on what Karl Popper condemned as "essentialism."[1] That style of discussion supposes that words label the essences of things or circumstances objectively existing out there in reality and seeks knowledge about those realties by brooding over the words. Schumpeter (1954, p. 898) identifies "the deplorable 'method' of trying to solve problems by means of hunting for the meaning of words." The concept of "waiting" helps avoid worrying over what goods do and what ones do not count as capital or capital goods. Unless downright identified with waiting, capital

[1] Further examples of confusion between real issues and brooding over words are questions like: what, really, is "justice," "liberty," "freedom," "democracy," "equality of opportunity," and "right" (as in "right to life" or "right" to health care)? In controversy over abortion, essentialists take seriously questions like "When does life begin?" or "What is human life?".

Popper condemned the idea that scientific explanation means getting at the "essences" of things and phenomena, essences corresponding to words. Popper (1982, pp. 17–31; 1959; 1966, passim), O'Hear (1980, pp. 7–8). See also Champion (2010).

Although the essentialism condemned by Popper and the essentialism practiced or admired by Carl Menger and some later Austrian economists both partly derive from Aristotle, they are not quite the same (Barry Smith 1994).

L. B. Yeager and S. H. Hanke, *Capital, Interest, and Waiting*,
https://doi.org/10.1007/978-3-031-63398-0_4

in the sense of capital goods is a product of waiting *and* other factors of production.

4.2 Negative Interest

The concept of waiting serves more smoothly than that of "capital" in explaining the occasionally observed phenomenon of an interest rate below zero. Not just a negative real rate due to inflation but even a negative nominal rate has appeared in peculiar circumstances, as for years after the 2008 global financial crisis. The slightly negative rate paid on Swiss government bonds reflects not so much negative time preference as a policy of trying to repel inflows of funds seeking a safe haven in an uncertain world. A few foreign central banks have also experimented with negative interest on reserves deposited with them.

The interest rate, broadly conceived, is sometimes described as the ratio of the value of an asset's periodic services to its own value. This description hardly works for negative interest, apart from peculiar circumstances. As just mentioned, sheer arithmetic would require a negative value of either the numerator or the denominator.

Viewing the interest rate as the price of waiting can handle even this odd but instructive case. It also explains why waiting need not necessarily be irksome and time preference positive at whatever margin: people need not necessarily prefer a small increment of goods in the present to an equal increment in the future.

A discussion extending over 1958–1960 and 1966 among Paul A. Samuelson (1958), Abba P. Lerner (1959), W. H. Meckling (1960), and David Cass and Menahem E. Yaari (1966) imagines an isolated community where all goods are perishable, where no money and no investment securities exist, where land is either superabundant and free or else not privately owned, and where no collectively organized or family-centered social security system operates. How could anyone save for old age? Retired people could not live by borrowing because they could not credibly promise repayment. With accumulating wealth in other forms impossible, the only way to store up command over goods for one's old age is to acquire claims on borrowers. In the absence of money, values and loans are expressed in some other numéraire, namely commodities or a composite basket of commodities.

Retired persons can receive loan repayments only if younger persons had borrowed from them. If people of all generations are to accomplish their purposes, a person must borrow goods in his youth, both repay this borrowing and lend goods in his peak working years, and receive repayment when retired. In his youth he must consume in excess of his current income; and in his peak years he must consume an amount falling short of his current income by more than his earlier excess consumption. Consumption must fall that much short to allow for the required saving and lending. In retirement, the person consumes only the repayments of loans made in his peak working years.[2]

Since the marginal utility of consumption in a given period diminishes with its amount, the typical person would want a more nearly even lifetime distribution of consumption than the one just described. He would want to borrow less (if anything) in his youth and receive more repayments in retirement, which implies making both smaller repayments and larger loans in his peak years. This, anyway, is what he would desire at a zero-interest rate.

With all people having preferences of this sort, however, desired lending would exceed desired borrowing. Only a negative rate of interest could persuade people to depart from the otherwise preferred equal distribution of consumption over their adult lifetimes. Only a reward for borrowing would persuade people to consume more than they produce in their youth. People in their peak working years would be willing to pay young people to take loans from them so that they could live on the repayments in retirement.

A running theme in the discussion just summarized is the unsatisfactory welfare characteristics of the imagined economy.

All this is easy to say in terms of waiting. Prospects of old age make people want to postpone consuming part of their current incomes; yet, they can do so only if younger people accommodate them by doing the opposite, anticipating consumption out of incomes to be earned later. The desired performance of waiting exceeds the volume accommodated at a zero interest rate. Clearing the market requires a penalty on waiting and reward for accommodating it.

[2] For simplicity, this discussion assumes a stable population of uniform age distribution and disregards any differences in people's tastes, including time preferences, at corresponding periods of their lives. All are alike in total production, earnings, loans, and consumption over their entire lives. People differ only in belonging to different generations—in *when* they live. Not all such definite assumptions are necessary, but they make a clear-cut case for analysis.

In our imaginary economy lacking storable goods, money, scarce privately owned land, and organized intergenerational transfers, the perishability of all goods implies that waiting has negative marginal productivity. Furthermore, the marginal utility of consumable income diminishes with its size, a plausible assumption here. Therefore, a person would want to shift some consumable income from a high-income to a low-income period, even at a cost, and would require payment for an opposite shift. Overall, then, marginal time preference is negative.

These odd conditions for a negative nominal interest rate help us understand, by contrast, why the rate is normally positive in the real world.

The *real* rate, however, is negative when the nominal rate falls short of the inflation rate. Even slightly negative *nominal* rates had occasionally been observed even before the 2008 crisis, as sometimes in the 1930s, when local property taxes or other legal peculiarities made people want to shift wealth temporarily into tax-exempt Treasury bills (Cecchetti 1988). Since 2008, negative nominal interest rates have become more familiar.

Maurice Allais had already imagined a negative interest economy (1947, I, p. 48ff). So, still earlier, had Irving Fisher (1930/1955, pp. 186–194). Each of some sailors shipwrecked on a desert island has salvaged a stock of figs. The figs rot at the rate of 10 percent a year; no other storable goods exist; and no production is possible. No one is in a position to borrow at a rate less negative than 10 percent, and no one would have reason to lend at a more negative rate. Negative 10 percent is the only rate that clears the loan market—but with no transactions taking place. This parable of the figs, as well as Fisher's similar parables of perfectly storable hardtack and spontaneously breeding sheep, emphasizes that technological or other objective conditions do influence the rate of interest and people's marginal rates of time preference.

Just as a negative price of waiting is unusual but possible, so are a negative marginal productivity and wage rate of labor. At a zero wage, the supply of labor to a particular occupation (perhaps as apprentices) might still exceed the demand, possibly because the job afforded valuable training or experience or was intrinsically attractive to people with independent incomes. Leisure preference would be negative at the margin for someone with so much idle time on his hands that he would welcome some small amount of work without pay or would even pay for the opportunity. If cooking were immensely attractive work, many cooks, while spoiling the broth at the margin, might indeed subsidize restaurants to permit selling meals cheap enough to provide a market-clearing number of jobs in the kitchen. These odd cases show that supply and demand analysis of the prices of waiting and of labor apply to both, and in parallel ways.

4.3 Pure Time-Preference Theory

Sometimes an effective method of exposition examines an incorrect theory and contrasts it with another theory offered as correct. Some Austrian economists defend a "pure time-preference" theory (PTPT) of interest. Following Mises (1966), they seem to regard interest as solely the preference for present over future goods. They seem to deny that the productivity of waiting—of well-chosen time-consuming production processes—has anything to do with interest. Sophisticated defenders like Israel Kirzner try to "dispel the bewilderment" over it, although without necessarily urging it as the best theory. Whether to treat waiting as a productive factor is a "philosophical" question not to be settled by reasoning and empirical research alone, says Kirzner (1993, pp. 170–171/ 2011, p. 100).

The issue is better called *conceptual*. What conceptualizations and terminology best link observed realities together? A "philosophical" stance that practically rules out refuting some proposition by reasoning and evidence is what Karl Popper would call an "immunizing stratagem" (Caldwell 1991, pp. 4, 5, 7, 12, 13, 20, 25; Boudry 2010 also describes, as similar, "epistemic defense mechanisms").

Interest theory is part of general value theory, where both subjective and objective influences operate. The interest rate is a price. Something commands a price because it is both wanted and scarce. It is wanted because it yields consumer satisfactions either directly or by ultimately contributing to production of wanted goods. It is scarce because its quantity demanded would exceed quantity supplied at a zero price; nature does not supply it or everything needed to produce it in superabundance. However, if the price were negative, it would reflect a bothersome overabundance. These propositions extend to "waiting," which is necessary for the existence of capital goods and roundabout production.

A price has four overlapping functions: (1) to ration the item among competing uses; (2) to carry information about opportunity cost, about how much using the item in any particular way requires ultimately sacrificing values to consumers of otherwise using it or its inputs; (3)

to provide incentives to heed this cost in decisions about production and consumption; and (4) along with other prices, to integrate widely dispersed information and decisions into a coherent overall pattern of resource allocation and production.

Economics portrays the economywide pattern of mutually interacting quantities and prices as ultimately determined by "wants, resources, and technology." Wants are tastes and preferences, including time preferences. Resources and technology refer to production possibilities, including possibilities of postponing consumption to obtain more in the future.

Pure time-preference theorists sweepingly regard positive time preference as a fact of human nature—a preference for goods earlier rather than later. Actually, marginalism qualifies that supposed fact. A person never faces a choice between consuming all now and all at a future date, just as he need not choose between a diet of pizza only or of hamburgers only. Each case presents a marginal choice of giving up some of the one for more of the other. A person with an entitlement to abundant consumption now but only skimpy consumption in the future might gladly give up some consumption now for an increase in the future or, in the opposite case of the imaginary stories covered earlier, even accepting a smaller addition to future consumption than the loss from present consumption.

Tradeoffs occur at the margin; and where the margin occurs depends not only on the chooser's own tastes but also on opportunities, including market opportunities reflected in prices and ultimately determined by wants, resources, and technology. These opportunities include increased production by more roundabout methods.

A few Austrians defend the PTPT label by remarking that time preference is not only a necessary condition but even alone a sufficient condition for an interest rate. It is necessary because if everyone was indifferent *at all margins* about *when* all goods and services were available, there would be no reason for intertemporal transactions and for any interest rate. It is a sufficient condition in the sense that with time preference, interest-bearing consumer loans could occur even in the barely imaginable pure exchange economy, where miraculous endowments of all goods with no productive effort made productivity and intertemporal transformability irrelevant. Agreed, such far-fetched conditions are imaginable, but that hardly justifies a pure time-preference theory for the real world.

Any price, including the interest rate, integrates information about both objective and subjective circumstances. Suppose that in almost unimaginably far-fetched cases, *nothing* objective—nothing about resource availabilities and technology—influences some price. That would hardly justify leaving only subjective conditions as the *general* explanation of the price. That some far-fetched circumstances could provide both necessary and sufficient conditions for some phenomenon hardly justifies giving the sufficient condition top billing in a *general* theory.

Even for the imaginary production-free exchange economy, questions arise of how and how often the traded goods magically come into existence and are distributed, whether they can be used up, whether they are storable (with or without deterioration or cost), and so forth. Such conditions affect even subjectively motivated interest-bearing loans. Even for the imaginary pure exchange economy, then, interest theory cannot be a *pure* time-preference theory.

Yet diehard adherents say that the PTPT is meant to explain the existence of interest, not necessarily what determines its rate.[3] For our world, however, a complete theory is supposed to consider not only the nature of a price and its rationing and other functions *but also* what factors determine its level.

Paul Samuelson (1981, pp. 22–23) imagined a clear-cut case of physical productivity, uncomplicated by issues of valuation: 100 units of rice today automatically ripen into 110 identical units 1 year later. Not even neutral time preference[4] can block a positive interest rate in terms of rice. Rather, people adjust their present and future consumption so that, *at the margin*, present rice does indeed have a subjective agio over future rice. Productivity influences where the margin and agio occur.[5]

Why is the price of a perpetually maintained orchard not bid up to the sum of the future values of its fruits net of any noninterest costs? Why

[3] Kirzner insists that explaining the very existence of interest need not bring in everything affecting its level. PTPT theorists recognize, he says, that factors besides positive time preference, including physical productivity, may affect its rate. The timing of traffic lights may well affect traffic density in rush hours; nevertheless, rush-hour traffic is better described as "people getting to work" than as "the result of traffic-light timing." While such an analogy does not actually deny a role for the physical productivity of waiting, then, Kirzner still defends what he acknowledges as the methodological essentialism of PTPT (1993, pp. 183–187, 191–192).

[4] Remember the marginal character of indifference and the distinctions introduced in Chapter 1 among time preferences that are neutral, biased toward impatience or patience, and zero or absent at all margins.

[5] In different words, Kirzner (1993, p. 176) concedes as much.

doesn't its price rise so high that an investment in it cannot have any positive net yield? Such a question in effect asks why waiting has a price. It is similar to asking why the price of a product produced with labor and other factors is not bid down to the sum of its nonlabor costs only. Well, its price *would* be so bid down if labor were free in unlimited amounts. In reality, both of the orchard's inputs—labor and waiting alike—have positive prices because both are useful and scarce. Workers do have some leisure preference and will not labor for free without limit.

Just as formally defensible as PTPT while just as "essentialist" and obfuscatory would be a pure-leisure-preference theory of labor wage rates.[6] The very existence of interest or wages, as distinguished from the level of either, could be imagined apart from the factor's productivity in any ordinary business sense. Disregarding any employment in productive business, one could imagine that labor produces nothing beyond itself. Everything that hired workers do, say housekeeping, would otherwise be done, if at all, by their employers. But workers and employers alike have leisure preference, so a positive wage rate emerges. This proposition holds true at any margin ordinarily encountered, although people could be doing so little work that they would prefer a bit less leisure.

Apart from contributing to production, then, labor, like waiting, is irksome: at plausible margins people prefer leisure to labor and earlier to later consumption. At such a margin, compensation is required to obtain the labor or the waiting. The extreme formulation challenged here would explain the *essence* of wages by leisure preference and of interest by time preference. Productivity supposedly just supplements those explanations by helping to explain the particular *levels* of the wage and interest rates. An "essentialist" explanation deals with the very existence of wages and interest, leaving the particular market-determined levels of the two rates for a "functionalist" explanation. But insisting on that distinction is diversionary.

The interest rate is not so exceptional a price as to be uninfluenced by resources and technology and be determined instead purely by subjective

[6] Alfred Marshall (1920/1947, p. 232) already alluded vaguely to such an analogy, imagining circumstances in which the wage rate, like the interest rate, might even be negative. Besides citing Marshall, Garrison (2002, p. 352) notes that Ludwig von Mises (1966, p. 65) briefly considered and rejected a leisure-preference theory of wages.

time preference. Surely, defenders cannot mean a literally *Pure* Time-Preference Theory, and the maneuvers deployed to defend one must tend to undermine students' understanding of how a market economy works.

Ludwig von Mises's theory of "originary interest" is probably the most prominent and extreme recent version of the doctrine of a fundamental agio of present over future goods. According to Mises, the interest rate is not determined by supply and demand expressing interaction between investment opportunities and people's tastes for the timing of their consumption. For Mises and a few other subjectivist purists, general value theory is misleadingly presented with the prices of all goods and factors of production, instead of being determined by interaction between tastes and objective circumstances, being derived unidirectionally from marginal utilities. In that theory, accordingly, the interest rate derives in one direction only from a systematic and pervasive characteristic of human psychology and human action.[7] It is monistic, for an *anti*eclectic theory.

[7] Consider the following passages from Mises, *Human Action* (1966, pp. 526–527):

"Originary interest is not a price determined on the market by the interplay of the demand for and the supply of capital or capital goods. Its height does not depend on the extent of this demand and supply. It is rather the rate of originary interest that determines both the demand for and the supply of capital and capital goods. It determines how much of the *available supply* [emphasis added] of goods is to be devoted to consumption in the immediate future and how much to provision for remoter periods of the future."

"People do not save and accumulate capital because there is interest. Interest is neither the impetus to saving nor the reward or the compensation granted for abstaining from immediate consumption. It is the ratio in the mutual valuation of present goods as against future goods."

"The loan market does not determine the rate of interest. It adjusts the rate of interest on loans to the rate of originary interest as manifested in the discount of future goods."

P. 483: "Other things being equal, satisfaction in a nearer period of the future is preferred to satisfaction in a more distant period; disutility is seen in waiting."

P. 484: "Time preference is a categorial requisite of human action. No mode of action can be thought of in which satisfaction within a nearer period of the future is not—other things being equal—preferred to that in a later period." ... "Purposive striving after want-satisfaction must needs be guided by a preference for satisfaction in the nearer future over that in a remoter future."

P. 526 (omitting a footnote): "Originary interest is not 'the price paid for the services of capital.' The higher productivity of more time-consuming roundabout methods of production ... does not explain the phenomenon. It is, on the contrary, the phenomenon of originary interest that explains why less time-consuming methods of production are resorted to in spite of the fact that more time-consuming methods would render a higher output per unit of input."

Rothbard (1962, Chapter 6) presents another Austrian exposition of the pure time-preference theory. He also edits and contributes a sympathetic introduction to writings

It is almost an opposite of Frank Knight's theory, which comes close to being monistic at the other extreme. Knight stresses the productivity of roundaboutness (though not using that term) to the almost complete subordination of time preference (e.g., 1946 reprint, pp. 396–401).[8] Mises himself expresses doubt about any *general* psychological tendency toward undervaluing future relative to present goods. Curiously, he does so in a criticism of Böhm-Bawerk's theory in untranslated pp. 439–443 of his *Nationalökonomie* (1940), pages that he himself cites in *Human Action*, 1966, p. 488n.

Mises, furthermore, appears to recognize the productivity element in interest, if in a backdoor way (*Human Action*, Scholar's Edition, pp. 536–538). Market interest rates on loans are not pure interest in the sense of his term "originary interest." Instead, on the side of both lenders and borrowers, the "gross market rate" contains an "entrepreneurial component," which involves judgment and risk-bearing. Business firms borrow to exploit perceived profitable opportunities. Although Mises does not explicitly say so, borrowing (as well as equity finance) enables firms to choose among a widened range of lines and methods of production, including ones that are more productive than quicker ones. He himself recognizes "that more time-consuming methods would render a higher output per unit of input" (1966, p. 526, or p. 523 in Scholar's Edition). Thus, the productivity element does, after all, enter into the demand for loans and so into the determination of actual interest rates. Perhaps "originary interest" has so narrow and peculiar a meaning for Mises—not satisfactorily explained—that pure time-preference does after all explain it, although not actual interest rates.[9]

of an earlier American exponent of the theory (Fetter 1977). Significantly, on the other hand, as good an Austrian as F. A. Hayek finds time preference "a subordinate factor compared with the productivity of investment in determining the rate of interest" (1941, p. 413). Hayek criticizes Frank Fetter and even Irving Fisher for overemphasizing time preference (p. 420).

[8] Knight does not reject time preference, however, and even has some good words for eclecticism. Cf. Conard (1959, pp. 79–89, 115).

[9] Kirzner (1974/1976) points out that Mises, although not citing specific authors whom he disagreed with to any great extent, did disagree with Böhm-Bawerk on capital and interest. Mises preferred his own praxeological and subjectivist approach to what he considered a nonsubjective, technical, and empirical explanation. He thought that

"Eclectic" is hardly a pejorative term in price theory. No single causal factor explains any price. Each is determined by many factors alternatively classifiable under the headings of "wants" and "resources and technology" or "supply" and "demand." A monistic theory of price is simply wrong. Eclecticism recognizing reality is a merit.

4.4 Time Preference at the Margin

The rate of time preference or the subjective agio is as much an expression as a cause of the interest rate. Individuals pull their subjective marginal rates of substitution between present and future goods into line with the interest rate. An interest rate of 5 percent means that 100 units of goods in general available now trade for 105 units in 1 year. By borrowing or lending, a person arranges his command over present and future goods so as to be indifferent at the margin between 100 present and 105 future goods; his subjective agio on present goods becomes 5 percent. Among the simplifying assumptions already stated, we still assume that people can borrow and lend at the same interest rate. If at the margin, the person happens to prefer 100 present goods to 110 future goods—if his marginal subjective agio exceeds the market interest rate—then he increases his borrowing or reduces his saving and lending. In doing so, he increases his command over present goods and so reduces their relative marginal utility and reduces his command over future goods and so increases their relative marginal utility. In equilibrium at his new margin, 100 present goods and 105 future goods have the same importance to him. If, still at a 5 percent market interest rate, he starts in an opposite disequilibrium, valuing 100 present goods at only 102 future goods, he increases his saving and lending or reduces his borrowing. As a result, his subjectively appraised scarcity value rises for present goods and declines for future goods. At his new equilibrium, his marginal rate of time preference corresponds to the market interest rate after all. Of course, the preferences of persons in the aggregate *do* enter into supply and demand on the loan market, but the preferences of one individual alone have no appreciable power.

Böhm-Bawerk failed to do justice to the universality and inevitability of time preference. He deplored Böhm-Bawerk's concessions to the productivity theorists. He rejected Böhm-Bawerk's notion of capital as an aggregate of produced means of production.

Time preference, then, is no single, uniform rate describing human tastes. Not even an individual has just one fixed rate like a definite height measured in centimeters. A person's marginal rate of time preference expresses the relative importance of present and future goods to him at the margin, just as the marginal utility he attributes to shirts depends on how many shirts (and other things) he owns. He can adjust either margin by responding to market opportunities. Not being a single, definite, uniform rate, time preference cannot pull the interest rate into line with itself in a one way manner.[10]

Other things besides preferences between present and future goods enter into the demand for and supply of waiting. These include the productivity of waiting, still to be further explained. We can make only one trivial and far-fetched concession to a preferences-only explanation. It would hold if everyone's marginal rate of time preference were identical and constant, unaffected by how much or how little command they held over present and future goods. If people's time preference were not merely symmetrical but persistently neutral, expressing complete indifference between equal marginal quantities of present and future goods no matter the total quantities, then present and future goods would indeed trade at par with each other. If people were willing and able to exchange still more present goods for future goods at no agio, no matter how extensively they were already doing so, waiting would be free and the market interest rate zero.

[10] Although Mises conveys the view criticized here, an uncharacteristic passage (1963, p. 490; Scholar's Edition, p. 487) does obliquely recognize the distinction between time preferences in some overall sense and at the margin. "The miser, too, in spending some of his means for a scanty livelihood, prefers some amount of satisfaction in the nearer future to that in the remoter future. ... The postponement of consumption and the accumulation of stocks of consumers' goods destined for later consumption would be practiced even in the absence of the stimulus offered by the technological superiority of processes with a longer period of production."

Murray Rothbard explicitly recognizes that no single figure can describe time preference. Individuals bring their marginal rates of time preference into line with each other's rates through market transactions. Yet Rothbard still inadequately recognizes how investment opportunities, including the productivity of roundaboutness, also influence the *level* at which market transactions harmonize people's marginal rates of time preference ("Introduction" to Fetter 1977, esp. p. 4, as well as Rothbard 1962, pp. 323 ff., 329–330).

Most other Austrians also seem to recognize that time preference is a marginal concept not to be expressed in any single figure. See Böhm-Bawerk (1959, I, pp. 393–397, II, pp. 287–288); Hayek (1941, pp. 413ff.); Arnold (1977); and Levatter (1979).

This statement is just as empty as it would be to say that the wage rate would be zero if people could and would perform unlimited amounts of labor for free, remaining indifferent between labor and leisure no matter how much labor they were performing and how little leisure they were enjoying. Similarly, the rent on land would be zero if more than enough of it were available in suitable qualities and locations to meet all demands for its services even at a zero price. It is true but vacuous to say that interest, wages, and rent are greater than zero because waiting, labor, and land use are not as superabundant as the air in a scantily populated and pollution-free region.

4.5 Interest-Rate Equalization by International Capital Movements

As used in "international capital movements," how does the word "capital" reconcile with the concept of waiting? Apart from government controls and use of different currencies, nothing makes *international* capital movements essentially different from interregional or even interpersonal lending and investing and borrowing.

A review of balance-of-payments accounting leads to the reconciliation. Exports of goods and services and imports of financial capital are classified on the same side, the "credit" or "plus" or "receipts" side, of a country's balance-of-payments statement. Export sales ordinarily involve residents of the home country receiving payment from foreigners. So do imports of capital in the financial sense, consisting of foreign loans to and investments in the home country and evidenced by foreign acquisition of home securities, bank accounts, and properties. On the other side, the "debit," "minus," or "payments" side of the statement, imports of goods and services and exports of financial capital appear together, since they all ordinarily involve payments to foreigners.[11]

The same classification puts exports of goods and services on one side and exports of financial capital on the opposite side of a country's balance of payments. Likewise, imports of goods and services go on the opposite side from imports of capital. Apart from details of measurement errors

[11] The hedge word "ordinarily" allows for transactions, like gifts, that are not two-sided in a straightforward sense.

and classification, then, the two sides of a country's balance of payments must add up to the same total.

This equality means that a country making net exports of goods and services must enable foreigners to pay by exporting financial capital (e.g., lending) to them or by seeing them repatriate funds previously placed in the home country.[12] Capital export could include loans to foreigners, purchases of foreign securities and real estate, and repurchase of domestic assets previously held by foreigners; it could even take the form of a buildup of accounts held in foreign banks and of holdings of foreign currency and a rundown of foreign holdings of home country bank accounts and currency. Official acquisitions of gold or foreign exchange could also count in this category. In the opposite direction, a country making net imports of goods and services must be paying for them by importing capital, as by selling securities and real estate, running down deposits in foreign banks and holdings of foreign currency, experiencing increases in foreign holdings of domestic bank accounts and currency, and by the rundown of official reserves.

International transactions in financial capital, then, match trade in goods and services. A country exporting capital is using less worth of goods and services at home than it produces, the difference being its net exports of goods and services. Its savers are lending and investing money abroad that they might otherwise have spent on consumption or on their own investments; they are *waiting* to exercise their command over productive resources. By the same token, a country importing capital is consuming and investing more worth of goods and services than its own resources are producing; it can avoid waiting and have advanced command over resources because foreigners are waiting on its behalf.

But how is this accounting-wise match of trade and capital transactions reflected in reality? An *independently motivated* capital movement is one carried out for ordinary business or personal or government-policy reasons rather than out of concern for a country's overall balance of payments, such as might concern a government or central bank. One aspect of such a transaction, the mere transfer of purchasing power from lenders to borrowers, would be unlikely by itself and from the start to accomplish the full adjustment of trade. According to the logic of an international gold standard or firmly fixed exchange rates, until trade had fully

[12] Not countries as such but individuals and private and government institutions carry out transactions, but the word "country" is convenient.

adjusted, the money supply would shrink in the lending country through its overall deficit in independently motivated transactions and expand in the borrowing country. That is because an overall deficit or surplus is matched and measured, by definition, by an opposite imbalance in official transactions *not* independently motivated.

In the first country, people try to conserve or restore their shrinking cash balances by buying fewer goods and services and by pushing their sales. This behavior shows up partly "at the water's edge" as net exports. Opposite processes operate in the borrowing country, resulting in net imports of goods and services. If flexible exchange rates largely insulate domestic money supplies from outside influences, depreciation of the lending country currency and appreciation of the borrowers' currency then help adjust trade to the financial capital movement.

Although a country's export of financial capital is matched in goods and services, those net exports need not take the form of machinery or other capital goods nor of goods going only to the particular capital-importing country. They might well consist of consumer goods and services. In the other direction, capital imports need not be matched by imports of capital goods; unbalanced trade in consumer goods and services could be the real counterpart of an outward or inward capital movement. Here again, a sharp distinction between capital and consumer goods is pointless and impossible.

4.6 Multilateralism

Much as the real side of a financial transfer need not take the form of just those goods that the borrowers want to buy with the money, so real and financial trade need not match between pairs of countries. A lending country may make net exports of goods, even though these may be bought by others than the actual borrowers or may be demanded even only in third countries. Similarly, borrowers need not buy the goods they want from abroad. If they can buy them more advantageously in some third country or even at home, a net transfer of other real goods and services into their country still means that they obtain more real resources for their own projects without, on the whole, taking resources away from their fellow countrymen. International real transfers can take place in a multilateral pattern. Although arrangements for an international transfer of financial capital may take place between persons in two countries only, this financial bilateralism need not deprive trade of its multilateral character. Countries still can specialize according to their opportunities to gain from trade.

The same principles of comparative advantage count against trying to match capital transactions pairwise between countries. But how can trade adjust to capital movements if borrowers or their fellow countrymen increase their purchases not in the lending country but elsewhere and if lenders or their fellow countrymen reduce their purchases not in the borrowing country but elsewhere? The borrowing country then tends to develop a trade deficit with third countries, while the lending country develops a trade surplus. Balance-of-payments adjustments work toward overall equilibrium in the balance of payments of third countries.

A bilateral example will illuminate multilateralism by contrast. Country A is running a surplus on current account (making net exports of goods and services) and a deficit on capital account (transferring funds abroad). Country B is running a deficit on current account and a surplus on capital account. The real counterpart of the financial capital movement is a net flow of goods and services from A to B. B can consume or invest more than its own resources would otherwise cover, thanks to A's *waiting* to consume or invest.

For multilateral transactions, Country C here stands for the whole rest of the world. It receives net imports of goods and services from A and imports financial capital from A or B or both. At the same time, it makes net exports of goods and services to B and exports financial capital. Overall, C's balance of payments is equilibrated; its bilateral trade and capital imbalances cover one another multilaterally. In effect, C intermediates transactions whereby A exports capital and net goods and services to B *indirectly*, while B finances a current account deficit by importing capital. A net shipment of goods and services from the lending to the borrowing country occurs indirectly, through the intermediary country. C might even host an international financial center that specializes in borrowing on the one hand and lending on the other.

"International capital movements" is an unfortunate but entrenched term. Capital movements are not shipments of capital goods in particular. People in the lending country are giving up current command over goods or resources in general and people in the borrowing country are acquiring it. The lending country performs waiting; the borrowing country buys the result. Through adjustment of exchange rates, price levels, or incomes, imbalance on capital account is matched by opposite imbalance on current account. With a coherent definition of concepts, this overall balance holds even as a matter of sheer arithmetic. The financial side of the capital movement develops its real counterpart as net flows of goods and services out of the lending country and into the borrowing country. This net flow need not consist entirely or even at all of direct shipments from the lending to the borrowing country; trade patterns involving third countries also adjust.

While in general the borrowing country increases its imports, reduces its exports, or both, with opposite changes in the lending country's trade, this is not necessarily so. For example, in an extreme case, the borrowing country might develop a net inflow of goods and services entirely by reducing its exports. The real transfer could take place, furthermore, even if no trade in tangible goods adjusted but only trade in services. In all such cases, nevertheless, lenders are postponing command over real resources and borrowers are obtaining advanced command.

The story is much the same if, instead of by purchase of foreign bonds, capital export occurs through purchase of land abroad. By acquiring and holding land, the investors postpone current command over resources that they might otherwise have exercised. The capital account land transaction has a current account counterpart in a net movement of goods and services into the country where the land is located. Its residents are obtaining advanced availability of command over real resources, thanks to the waiting being performed by the foreign investors.

Multilateralism occurs in domestic credit markets also. Rarely does an individual saver lend money to the ultimate user of borrowed money. Typically, lenders and borrowers deal with one another indirectly, as through financial institutions.

4.7 Trade in Embodied Waiting

Conceiving of capital as waiting meshes smoothly with the theory of how international trade tends, roughly, to equalize the prices in different countries of the factors of production embodied in the goods traded. New wine is produced with relatively little waiting, matured wine with much. If waiting is relatively scarce and the interest rate is high in the home country, matured wine commands a corresponding price premium over new wine before trade. Abroad, where waiting is relatively abundant and cheap, matured wine commands only a small price premium. When trade opens up, the home country imports high-waiting-content matured wine and exports new wine or other low-waiting-content goods. Trade tends to equalize product prices, reducing the price premium of matured over new wine in the home country and shrinking its production of matured wine. Waiting formerly devoted to the maturing of wine is freed for other uses. Trade thus lessens the effective scarcity of waiting and so reduces the interest rate. Incidentally, Paul Samuelson (1965) reaches a similar conclusion, though without the concept of waiting and so less straightforwardly.

The interest-equalization tendency does not depend on whether waiting enters directly or only indirectly into producing goods.[13] Perhaps waiting goes directly into widgets, which, like wine, require time to mature. Or widgets are manufactured with machines that embody much waiting or are made by specialists who undergo years of expensive training. What difference does any direct/indirect distinction make for the interest-equalization tendency? The cost of widgets includes the high cost of the waiting embodied indirectly as well as directly. If international trade brings imports of cheap foreign widgets, the home industry shrinks. Waiting formerly devoted to the machines or to training technicians becomes free for other training or other purposes; and, as in the wine example, the interest rate falls.

4.8 Avoiding Diversionary Formulations

One old idea regards capital as a wages or subsistence fund. The idea goes back to Cantillon, Quesnay, Hume, Turgot, and Adam Smith (Blyth 1987, p. 836). Capital is seen as an accumulation of wealth from which to pay workers their means of subsistence. Later economists, including Böhm-Bawerk, John Stuart Mill, Richard von Strigl, Walter Eucken, and Lester Taylor, have also accepted this idea in some form or other.

Nevertheless, the doctrine is worse than unhelpful. It is an example of conceptual realism or misplaced concreteness—roughly, supposing that if a term exists for "wages fund" or something else not patently fictitious—it stands for something out there in reality. The example illustrates how researchers may face not only empirical and logical problems but even

[13] As already argued, just how to conceive of a production function is a matter not of right or wrong but of convenience in each piece of analysis. Peter B. Kenen (1965) expresses a contrary view, however, making the direct/indirect distinction.

conceptual confusions (cf. Harsanyi 1976, p. 64 and Laudan 1977, p. 50 and Chapter 2).

The doctrine is perhaps barely plausible for a primitive economy in which almost all consumer goods are foodstuffs harvested once a year. Between harvests, workers' real wages must come from stockpiles of enough food to last until the next harvest. Somebody—employers or capitalists—must therefore have *saved* enough to provide workers with these so-called advances. Without these stockpiled savings, time-consuming production would be impossible. Time, waiting, and the subsistence fund are intimately connected.

Robinson Crusoe on his desert island wants a boat, net, or both for more productive fishing. Peter Lewin (1999) imagines Crusoe spending many days accumulating dried fish to live on while later constructing his capital good. During this construction, he forgoes the further consumer goods that he could otherwise have produced and consumed. This productive waiting presupposes the previously accumulated fish.[14]

In a less artificial context, Adam Smith argued that the division of labor presupposes first accumulating materials and tools as well as subsistence goods. Growth of employment and of wages depends on growth of this accumulation (Blyth 1987, p. 836). The wage rate is determined by the ratio of wage fund to labor force. The implication that labor unions and collective bargaining are useless for improving the condition of labor made some economists uncomfortable with the doctrine; John Stuart Mill famously "recanted" his earlier acceptance of it (Blyth pp. 835–836, Blaug 1985, pp. 186–188).

Böhm-Bawerk wrote a few pages about the concept without finding it important. If production does not occur continuously, accumulated wealth must suffice to support the population through the period of production. Actually, current labor and existing investment goods do continuously transform themselves into consumer goods; so, a stock sufficient to support the population through a period of production need not

[14] Trivially different versions of the story postulate different subsistence goods and capital goods, such as wild fruit and a fruit-plucking rod. Lester Taylor (2000) imagines a bread mine where Crusoe works extra hours each day to accumulate a stock of bread to sustain him when he shifts his labor to building a house. The bread stock represents fluid capital, which Taylor calls "myros" and is the book's unifying concept. Myros is some sort of wages fund (although the book's index has no entry for it or "subsistence fund").

have been accumulated in advance (1959, II, pp. 316–319; III, pp. 211–212; the term "subsistence fund" actually occurs on the latter pages of the English translation).

Richard von Strigl (2000, Chapter 2 and throughout) makes much of such a fund. He recognizes, however (pp. 9 ff.), that if production is echeloned—synchronized in the Clark-Knight sense to be explained in Chapter 7, with inputs continually being applied to production and goods in process continually ripening into final goods—then any stock of finished goods can be correspondingly small. But if synchronization rules out any definite relation between size of a fund and length of a period, what is the point of supposing such a relation in the first place? As Henry George insisted (1879/1940), labor is paid not out of some pre-accumulated fund but out of the value of the output to which it contributes continuously. Of course, the ripening of goods in process into finished goods presupposes waiting by someone.

Defining free capital as "the subsistence fund (supply of consumer goods) which is made available for the support of roundabout methods of production," Strigl says that "every capital good must have been preceded by free capital. The capital good is produced as a result of the expenditure of free capital" (pp. 27–28, evidently what Lester Taylor, 2000, called "fluid capital"). But what about a simple tool like a club shaped from a fallen tree branch? Where are the previously accumulated consumer goods? But perhaps Strigl's meaning is trivial—that someone who produces a capital good must have been nourished. Investing labor or other resources for the future means *not* using those same resources for immediate consumption, which implies that persons making that allocation must be *able* to make it. Persons who wait must be *able* to wait.

Even Walter Eucken, whose work on capital theory otherwise deserves admiration, criticizes the concept of waiting as he understands it (1954, pp. 53–54, 91–95). His dismissal of that factor seems to derive partly from preoccupation with a stock of consumer goods and from sympathy, though much qualified, with the classical wages-fund doctrine (1954, pp. 119–121, 124–125, 312). That fund must be available for workers to live on if roundabout methods of production are to be possible. It supposedly enters into determining the length of the production period, the productivity of labor, and wage levels (1954, p. 121; again, on period of production, see Chapter 7).

Eucken repeats the Crusoe story. The important thing, he says, is the stock of fish, not Crusoe's waiting. But of course, Crusoe could not eat his entire initial stock at once anyway; he must consume it gradually while building his equipment. If he could somehow borrow additional fish, he could undertake a more ambitious and time-consuming construction program and afterwards enjoy a perpetually larger daily fish catch than otherwise. This additional yield would be the counterpart of interest in a market economy. Yet, Eucken thinks that the waiting performed, instead of being a distinguishable service and factor of production, arises necessarily from the data of Crusoe's little world.

4.9 Criticism of the Wages-Fund Doctrine

Henry George was an early critic of the idea of a wages or subsistence fund, although without using those terms. He entitles three chapters of his book, *Progress and Poverty,* as "Wages and capital," "Wages not drawn from capital, but produced by the labor," and "The maintenance of laborers not drawn from capital" (1879/1940, Book I). Workers currently earn—*produce*—their wages by producing current output or by contributing to the increase in value of time-consuming projects; yet they get paid only at stated times. Meanwhile, they are "advancing capital" to their employer, that is, supplying a resource and *waiting* for the result or compensation. Never, unless paying wages in advance, does an employer advance capital to his employee (1979/1940, Book I, recapitulated in George 1897/1941, pp. 202, 333–334).

The conclusion that wages are drawn from capital, George continues, "is no more valid than it would be from the acceptance of the proposition that a laborer cannot go to work without his breakfast and some clothes, to infer that no more laborers can go to work than employers first furnish with breakfasts and clothes. Now, the fact is that laborers generally furnish their own breakfasts and the clothes in which they go to work" (1879/1940, pp. 57–59).

Gustav Cassel also criticized the concept of the fund. He thought that far-fetched assumptions were necessary for it: a working population of definite size, a definite sum to be advanced as wages, and the same duration of advances in all branches of production. Reasoning with averages rather than actual facts, he thought, was a vicious habit. Classical supporters of the doctrine maintained that every attempt by workers to get higher wages would reduce accumulation and the wages fund and so make wages fall to their old level or below. They applied the results of their extremely abstract and hypothetical reasoning to questions of actual life and policy. This is an example of what Schumpeter later (1954, p. 473) called the Ricardian Vice. Supporters of the doctrine thereby helped discredit economic theory in the eyes of practical men; they impeded development of a sound theory of interest. In fact, the commodities or services "abstained from" are never produced. Instead, saving and investment permit diverting productive forces from serving current consumption toward future ends (Cassel 1903/1956, pp. 34–37, 134).

Hubert Henderson emphatically insisted that capital is not a stock of consumer goods. The longer the period of production, the larger this stock supposedly must be. Its magnitude "determines how far we can devote our energies to purposes which are remote in time. Now this is pure mysticism. Regarded literally, it is in direct conflict with the facts." Various stages of production are going on at the same time. To argue that the power to produce consumable goods is "*in effect* a store of consumable goods" is to use "the language of symbolism, not of science.... The false conception of capital as essentially a store of consumable goods has led and still leads to many serious fallacies. It was this that gave rise to the notorious ... notion that the sum which can at any time be paid in wages is equal to the quantity of capital, *alias* consumable goods, which happens to exist." It mingles "with an undergrowth of obscurantist controversies" (1921/1958, pp. 99–101, quotations from pp. 100–101).

Of course, waiting for the results of more time-consuming and more productive processes presupposes its possibility; people must be able to afford it. Of course, the more abundant the available resources, including consumer and capital goods and natural resources, the higher will be the marginal productivity of labor and the higher wages can be. But what is gained by postulating some particular fund?

By assumption, the role of Crusoe's stock of fish is to make his productive waiting possible. That stock, besides embodying labor and nature, represents waiting already performed by Crusoe himself or by whoever else accumulated the stock and lent it to him. The waiting already accumulated in the fish is in effect being extended in duration and transformed in its particular embodiment as Crusoe creates his new capital equipment.

More generally, poverty impedes, and wealth facilitates, waiting and its benefits. So does thrift. But waiting must not be confused with these favorable background conditions. For labor also, health and so forth are necessary for supplying it; but we do not confuse those conditions with labor itself or take their necessity as a reason for refusing to count labor as a factor of production.

The notion of the subsistence fund is at best just a dramatic but unnecessary reminder that capital goods construction cannot occur unless the workers are able to survive and work; it is not possible to devote *all* labor and other resources to future consumption and nothing to current consumption.

Especially in an economy with an elaborate division of labor, workers constructing capital goods, instead of subsisting on previously accumulated goods, are consuming mostly the current outputs of other specialized producers and paying from their wages. Their employers had to obtain finance for their projects, and its providers are waiting, but all this has nothing in particular to do with any fund.

Any sharp distinction between capital and other goods is idle. True, Crusoe's accumulation of fish or whatever could count as a capital stock does get effectively transformed into a boat, a tool, or a house. His having something to consume without currently replacing it is what allows him to divert additional labor and resources into constructing those capital goods. In effect, he is performing a *real counterpart of the financial intermediation* occurring in advanced economies. Crusoe's earlier thrifty self is transferring command over labor and resources to his later equipment-building self. As the accumulator of the supposed subsistence fund, he performs waiting for his own subsequent incarnation as investor of labor. His earlier self allows his later self's stinting on consumption to be slighter than otherwise necessary. Waiting and labor are embodied in the accumulation being transformed. In less primitive conditions, people other than an investor himself typically perform the postponement of consumption that permits allocating labor and other resources to constructing capital goods. This is a case of intermediation in waiting: some persons perform it so that others need not perform so much.

A worker need not perform his waiting by accumulating a fund. He might work more hours a day than before to produce both consumer goods and his capital goods. Or, the worker-investor might borrow consumer goods from other workers, not necessarily from previous accumulations of theirs but from their current outputs in excess of their own current consumption. Stocks of consumer goods and partially finished goods are held for the same reasons that any inventories are held.

4.10 Influences on the Interest Rate

Supply and demand determine the interest rate; so do time preferences and investment opportunities. These two classifications reconcile but are not identical. Both subjective and objective influences operate on both the demand side and the supply side of the market. Waiting, like other factors of production, commands a price because it is both useful and scarce. But how is it useful? And why must a positive price ordinarily be paid for enough of it to meet the demand?

Consumer borrowing is one element on the demand side. A consumer may buy a piano or a television set and enjoy it sooner than if the family first had to save its price. By borrowing, a young family expecting an uptrend in income can in effect transform some relatively low-marginal-utility consumption from its affluent future into relatively high-marginal-utility consumption in the present. An expected uptrend in income illustrates the first of Böhm-Bawerk's "three grounds" for preferring present over future goods.

By either renting a house or apartment or borrowing to buy one, a family obtains housing sooner than if it had to save money for a purchase. If it rents, it pays for housing services only as it consumes them. Its landlord ties up wealth in the property while receiving the value of its services only gradually. For the borrower and renter alike, sooner rather than later availability is worth enough to pay someone else to perform waiting required.

Time preference also appears on the supply side of the market. Most obviously, waiting is limited by the income, wealth, and resources that could be withheld from current consumption. On the demand side, opportunities for profitable investment operate.

4.11 Capital Paradoxes and Their Resolution[15]

Some critics of orthodox economic theory take aim, or used to, at the idea that the rate of interest (or profit, as they sometimes said) is related to the marginal productivity of "capital" in any sense of that word. The discussion is one example of misunderstandings wrought by the very word

[15] This section draws on Yeager 1979. For citations, technicalities, and bits of arithmetic omitted there and here, see Yeager 1976.

"capital." Abstract examples supposedly discredited orthodoxy. This literature has mostly gone out of fashion (apart from a 2003 article by Cohen and Harcourt). Still, resolving the supposed paradoxes remains instructive. Despite the paradoxes, "capital," or whatever the interest rate is the price of, must not be understood in purely physical terms.

Paul Samuelson (1966), though not necessarily a paradoxer himself, offered a simple example. Either of two techniques can produce a definite amount of champagne. Technique A employs 7 units of labor two periods before the final product emerges and no further input. Technique B employs 2 units of labor three periods before and 6 more units one period before the output. In each technique, while ripening into the final product, labor is embodied in unfinished champagne and perhaps in machinery also.[16]

In each technique, something like compound interest accrues on the value of invested labor. Straightforward arithmetic shows that technique A is the cheaper at interest rates above 100 percent per period, B is cheaper at rates between 50 and 100 percent, and A is cheaper again at rates below 50 percent. This is the paradox of reswitching.

If a decline of the interest rate through the upper of its two critical levels brings a switch from the less to the more capital-intensive of the two techniques, which might seem normal enough, then the switch to the other technique as the interest rate declines through the other switch point is paradoxical. If we view the latter switch in the other direction, an increased interest rate prompts a more intensive use of capital. This perverse response of capital intensity to the interest rate is capital reversal.

The very word "capital" invites trouble, but examples of reswitching or reversal do not depend on purposive trickery in measuring its stock. A technique is defined by its ratios of inputs to each other and to output, by their timing, and by everything else that physically characterizes it, including whatever stock of capital and intermediate goods may exist at each of its time stages. These physical characteristics stay the same regardless of whether the technique is actually in use and so regardless of the interest rate. If technique A has physically more capital per worker than B at one interest rate, then it still has more at any other rate. This remains true by any physical index of whatever so-called capital may be involved, even for measurement in tons of steel, provided only that measurement

[16] That distinction is inessential: inventories and capital goods alike are intermediate stages in transforming ultimate factors into finished goods.

conventions do not change mid-example. If the capital/labor ratios of A and B are such that the switch between those techniques at one critical interest rate is nonparadoxical, then the switch at the other must be paradoxical: a change of capital intensity in the *same* direction as the interest rate. We cannot, with consistency, deny perversity at both switch points unless—which is decisive—we abandon a purely physical conception of capital in the first place.

We can concoct examples in which capital reversal occurs without reswitching. Suppose that some third technique C happens to be cheaper than both A and B in a range in interest rates including the rate at which the nonparadoxical switch between those two would otherwise occur. In the interest-rate range where the paradoxical switch between A and B occurs, however, technique C happens to be too costly. Since C dominates both A and B at what would be their nonparadoxical switch point in C's absence, no actual reswitching occurs. Yet, with C out of the running at the paradoxical switch point between A and B, capital reversal does occur.

This perversity is a bothersome phenomenon. The chief role of reswitching in the whole discussion is to provide the simplest example of capital reversal. Reswitching cannot occur with production functions having the neoclassical properties of constant returns to scale, diminishing marginal returns, and smooth, continuous substitutability among factors (Burmeister and Dobell 1970, p. 279, Theorem 5). Even so, such production functions can exhibit the capital reversal just described.[17] No real world examples of this paradox have been described, to our knowledge, but it remains an instructive challenge.

With emotions ranging from glee to gloom, some economists viewed reswitching and especially capital reversal as an embarrassment for neoclassical capital and interest theory and even for the whole marginalist theory of production and functional income distribution. Modern orthodoxy sees the prices of factors of production as determined by supply and demand, with demand mainly reflecting how a bit more or less of a factor would change the total value of output in each line of production or firm employing it. In brief, factors of production tend to be paid in line with

[17] On whether the neoclassical properties preclude reswitching (but not capital reversal and a consumption paradox explained in the coming pages), Yeager and Burmeister (1978) so argued in replying to Rosser (1978), who had commented on Yeager (1976). Different views appeared in the literature, but the issue is a subsidiary one.

their marginal contributions to the value of output. The theory aims to explain but not in itself to justify the incomes of factors.

The controversy would be important if the paradoxes referred to the real world. Actually, and whether or not the controversialists realized it, the paradoxes arose from paper and pencil exercises with inappropriate theoretical concepts. Economic theory became its own subject matter. Academic narcissism reigned.

4.12 The Root of the Paradox

Unfortunately, most would-be defenders of orthodoxy did not pinpoint the source of error. It lies in a purely physical conception of capital or whatever it is whose yield or price is the interest rate. The paradoxes dissolve when we recognize that the amount of that factor—waiting—required in a physically specified production process can indeed depend on its own price.[18]

Reswitching turns out to be closely akin to the long-familiar concept of multiple internal rates of return in an investment option.[19] The criterion of maximizing the present value of a project or of one's options implies that a low-interest rate favors projects or techniques whose revenues occur late relative to outlays, while a high rate tilts choices toward projects whose revenues occur relatively early. In examples of reswitching, neither of the options considered has revenues that are unequivocally later in relation to outlays than the other option. In Samuelson's champagne example, technique B employs some of its labor earlier and some later than A. Which technique employs its labor effectively earlier? The answer depends on the weights accorded to labor employed at different times; and that is a matter of time-discounting via an interest rate.

[18] Although F. A. Hayek did not endorse the conception of waiting as a factor, writing before the literature on capital paradoxes appeared, Hayek (1941, esp. pp. 76–77, 140–145, 191–192) did note that one cannot always say, on purely technical grounds, which of two different investment structures involves more waiting or is longer in time. Once one knows what one is looking for, one can find passages in Hayek's book that indeed suggest how to dissolve the paradoxes.

[19] Garrison (2006) finds the concept long familiar in the field of "engineering economy." Fisher (1930/1955, around pp. 170–171) makes the point, although implicitly at best.

We can show this ambiguous relation between the two techniques by subtracting A's outlays and revenues from B's to construct a fictitious project. The champagne emerging at the same date and in the same amount by both techniques subtracts itself out of the picture. The subtractions for the earlier time periods yield a stream, valued in labor units, of -2, $+7$, and -6 in three successive time periods (the negative and positive signs indicate outlay and revenue). We might interpret these figures as referring to a strip-mining project. The coal is ready for sale in the middle period, an outlay to repair the damaged landscape being required afterwards. A familiar formula calculates the present value of this mining option at its start at each interest rate. The option has a positive present value only at interest rates between 50 and 100 percent, has a negative present value at both lower and higher rates, and has two internal rates of return (rates at which the discounted present value of cash flows is zero).

Our project's crucial feature is that its outlays occur neither unequivocally earlier nor unequivocally later than its revenues, each time-discounted. A clear-cut outlay-before-revenue project has a lower present value the higher the interest rate, for its remote revenues are more exposed to discounting than its early outlays. A clear-cut revenue-before-outlay project, conversely, has a higher present value the higher the interest rate; for discounting affects its remote outlays more strongly than its early revenues. Whether, in some overall sense, our strip-mining project is of the outlay-before-revenue or revenue-before-outlay type thus itself depends on the interest rate. At high rates, the project is of the outlay-before-revenue type; and as with any such project, its present value falls as the interest rate rises. Very high interest rates not only have their normal effect of diminishing the present value of an outlay-before-revenue project but themselves intensify that outlay-before-revenue character. At the other extreme of low interest rates, the revenue of the coal-mining project falls short of its total outlay quite straightforwardly. Furthermore, the fact that its revenue comes before most of its outlay (discounting being too slight to upset this comparison) means that the project is of the type whose present value suffers from the lowness of the interest rate. The project's relative timing of outlay and revenue is particularly ambiguous in the intermediate range of interest rates. There, neither discounting at a high interest rate of revenue coming effectively after outlay nor discounting at a low rate of outlay coming effectively after revenue makes the project's present value negative. A single shift between effective outlay-before-revenue and revenue-before-outlay characters occurs in this intermediate range, at 71.429 percent, where the present value is a maximum.

Constructed as it is by subtracting A figures from B figures, the strip-mining example compares the *relative* outlay and revenue times of the two techniques. Technique B has a lower time-remoteness of revenue relative to outlay than A at interest rates below 71.429 percent and the reverse above this rate. Since the effect of the interest rate on the relative present values of the two techniques depends on their relative degrees of remoteness, and since they do change with the interest rate itself, the reswitching of which technique has the greater present value is hardly surprising.

The waiting- or capital-intensities or roundaboutness of alternative techniques or options cannot, then, always be compared or even ranked in purely physical terms (see Chapter 7). In a physically specified process, a reduced interest rate not only cheapens the waiting that must be done but also reduces its required value-amount. It reduces the interest element in the notional prices of semi-finished and capital goods whose ripening into final consumer goods and services requires further waiting. Increased thrift is productive not only because it supplies more of the waiting required for using capital and intermediate goods but also because, by lowering the interest rate, it reduces the amount of waiting required by any physically specified technique. The amounts of waiting required by alternative physically specified techniques will in general decline in different degrees, which gives rise to the possibility of reswitching.

This same line of reasoning also clears up the puzzle of supposed capital reversal even in the absence of reswitching. When a decline in the interest rate brings an apparently perverse switch to a technique that is less capital-intensive by some physical criterion, the explanation is that the decline in the interest rate, although reducing the waiting-intensities of both techniques, reduces them differentially in such a way as to bring a larger reduction in the overall cost of producing by the adopted technique.

When increased thrift lowers the interest rate, the associated decline in the waiting requirements of a physically specified process is not so merely arithmetical as it might seem. Production of various goods by various techniques may ultimately expand not only because of the increased total supply of waiting but also because of a genuine economy in the waiting required per unit of output. A decline in thrift and rise in the interest rate, conversely, intensifies the status of waiting as a scarce factor to be economized on. It becomes scarcer not only because of its reduced supply but also because of increased requirements per unit of output produced in any physically specified way. The double-barreled advantages of thrift appear in reverse.

Preconceived insistence on measuring all factor quantities and factor-intensities in purely physical terms clashes with the fact of arithmetic that the amount of waiting required for a physically specified purpose does partly depend on its own price. Not only the waiting-intensity of a physically specified process but also the relative waiting-intensities of alternative processes really are affected by the interest rate.

The seeming paradoxicality of reswitching and capital reversal depends on overlooking this truth. When a switch of technique occurs, the technique adopted really is the more economical one on the whole, the inputs, waiting included, being valued at their prices. When one technique displaces another upon a rise in the interest rate, the displaced one has become relatively too waiting-intensive to remain economically viable. It is irrelevant as a criticism of standard theory that *by some other criterion* the displaced technique counts as less capital-intensive.

Waiting for value through time is a scarce factor of production whose rationing by the interest rate is quite in accord with the logic of a price system. It cannot be measured in purely physical terms, and the amount required in a physically specified production process does depend partly on its own price. If these truths run counter to familiar prejudices about capital theory, so much the worse for them.

4.13 Afterthoughts About the Paradox

One remnant of the paradox calls for a further word. With the interest rate above 100 percent, technique A produces the champagne with only 7 units of labor. Now, a fall in the interest rate below 100 percent cheapens production by both techniques but more by B, which is adopted. The same output now requires 8 units of labor (2 early plus 6 later); output per worker falls. Increased thrift, if that is what reduced the rate, seems counterproductive.

If the example describes the entire economy rather than only one line of production, furthermore, we wonder how the technique yielding less output per worker could ever be preferable, regardless of the interest rate. It seems inadequate to reply that labor is not the only factor of production and that the higher output per man in technique A does not, at all interest rates, mean higher output in relation to labor and waiting together. It is people, not abstractions, whose welfare concerns us; and more output per worker allows more consumption per worker. Since this consumption paradox is a direct arithmetical implication of paradoxes already cleared up, however, arguably, no paradox remains.

Yet saying so is not wholly satisfying. The lower output per worker of technique B than of technique A must have some physical interpretation: it must trace to labor's having a smaller aggregate physical amount of capital and intermediate goods to work with. The shift of techniques as the interest rate falls below 100 percent involves a transitional rundown in this stock of goods and a corresponding spurt in current consumption. This spurt comes at the cost of reduced future consumption, which, after all, hardly suggests an increase in thrift. If increased thrift is not what caused the fall in the interest rate that prompted the switch of techniques, the example casts no discredit on traditional ideas about the productivity of thrift.

What, then, did make the interest rate fall? Conceivably the supply and demand curves of waiting had been intersecting at an unstable equilibrium, so that *decreased* thrift, represented by a leftward shift of the supply curve of waiting, makes the new and again unstable intersection occur at a lower rate.[20] We may well ask whether interest rates in the real world would ever settle at *unstable* equilibria.

Actually, the literature on the paradoxes was silent or vague on what determines the interest rate and changes in it. Strictly speaking, the literature dealt with alternative steady states ("on separate planets") rather than with processes of change. How these steady states come to be went unexplained. References to changes in the interest rate and switches of techniques served stylistic convenience only.

A further question concerns whether it is legitimate to aggregate, as just plain labor, labor performed at different time stages of the production process, even though the labor is performed at the same calendar dates in the steady state of echeloned production. Labor performed three periods before and labor performed one period before the final product emerges in technique B may count as different sub-factors of production. Can we simply add their amounts together and compare their total to the single amount of labor performed two periods before output emerges

[20] Such a possibility recalls out-of-fashion worries about perverse elasticities in the foreign-exchange market.

in technique A? Not to distinguish between the time stages when labor is performed ignores the role of time in production, even steady state echeloned production. There lies the root of the paradoxes.

A related question suggests that a steady state using technique A is preferable to a steady state with technique B because of the greater output per worker. How, however, could an economy in state B make the transition to state A? Doing so would require accumulating the larger physical stock of capital and intermediate goods characteristic of state A; it would require a transition period of frugality in consumption. Do the long-run gains adequately reward the transitional sacrifice? The answer is not obvious; it depends on time preference.

Theorists who insist on crying paradox over examples of the kind reviewed here should spell out what they supposed to be happening in enough detail to disclose crucial assumptions and permit comparing their story with the real world. Standard theory need not be embarrassed by stories that do not even say how the interest rate is determined and changed, why one economy might be in a steady state employing one technique and an otherwise supposedly similar economy in a steady state employing another, and how an economy might make a transition between such states.

What *does* determine the interest rate and changes in it? After all, it measures the opportunity cost of employing waiting in each particular way. Why might it rise when it does? Perhaps new and especially productive uses for waiting, or perhaps a reduction in thrift, have made waiting scarcer than before and require greater economies in using it. It need not be paradoxical, then, that a rise in the interest rate calls for a different mix of factors of production in some industry, with relatively *more* capital equipment employed in some physical sense.

Despite everything, Cohen and Harcourt provide an example, as late as 2003, of how a few people still welcomed the Cambridge (England) position in the old paradox controversies as an embarrassment for standard economic theory. Cohen and Harcourt rehearse Samuelson's champagne example, reswitching and capital reversal, difficulties with the aggregate production function, questions about the meaning and measurement of capital, metaphors about capital (Meccano sets, putty), and so on. They briefly mention neoclassical replies but completely neglect the line of reply previously summarized.[21]

4.14 Conclusion

This chapter claims several advantages for treating waiting as a factor of production and interest as its price. That approach bypasses brooding over what capital really is and what goods count as capital goods. It can handle negative interest, conceivable though normally rare. It reconciles with alternative conceptions, as of a pervasive agio in value of present over future goods and of a pervasive ratio of services-to-sources values. It rejects a supposed pure time-preference theory of interest. It rejects a wages fund or subsistence fund. This approach can handle international capital movements and explain how even trade in goods can tend, if slightly, to equalize interest rates internationally. It shows how both subjective factors and objective factors operate on both sides of markets determining interest rates, both strictly and broadly conceived. Dissolving the Cambridge capital paradoxes, it shows why whatever it is that the interest rate is the price of must be conceived of in value terms and not just physical terms.

We have paved the way for considering how decision makers respond to the interest rate and how further conditions join in determining it. Later chapters will review roundaboutness and its productivity, as well as how monetary conditions influence or distort interest rates.

[21] They quote (p. 207) the surprising conclusion contained in Christopher J. Bliss, *Capital Theory and the Distribution of Income* (1975, p. 85) that "there is no support from the theory of general equilibrium for the proposition that an input to production will be cheaper in an economy where more of it is available." They conclude: "The Cambridge controversies were *not* a tempest in a teapot. ... Major issues—explaining (and justifying) the return to capital, visions of accumulation, limitations of equilibrium tools—were and are at stake. While many of the Cambridge, England combatants stopped asking questions because they died, the questions have not been resolved, only buried. When economists decide to delve again, we predict controversies over these issues will be revisited, just as they were time and again in the 80 years prior to the Cambridge controversies" (Cohen and Harcourt 2003, pp. 211–212). Garrison (2006) comments insightfully on this article.

CHAPTER 5

Responses to the Interest Rate

5.1 Interest-Rate Determination

Some topics in this chapter may resemble business administration and personal finance more than economics. They appear here not as advice but to show how market signals and incentives coordinate the actions of firms and individuals throughout the economy. Individual experiments concern how the interest rate affects the amounts of waiting supplied and demanded and investors' decisions. They pave the way for market experiments which concern how the interest rate and affected variables respond to postulated changes in "wants, resources, and technology."

Several sections of the chapter illustrate interest-rate determination by tangencies of curves and lines or refer to Böhm-Bawerk's "three grounds" for a normally positive rate of interest. These expositions in no way contradict representing the equilibrium interest rate as the intersection of supply and demand curves for waiting. They explain, rather, why those curves intersect as they do. Chapter 8, which postulates various changes in "wants, resources, and technology," will further reconcile the approaches of this chapter with supply and demand analysis of waiting.

L. B. Yeager and S. H. Hanke, *Capital, Interest, and Waiting*,
https://doi.org/10.1007/978-3-031-63398-0_5

5.2 Individual Experiments and Market Experiments

Whether it is legitimate to ask about the effects of a change in the interest rate or in any price depends on the context and purpose of the question. A price change does not occur in a vacuum; it is one among other results of a change in underlying determinants—"wants, resources, and technology," including policy. Unless the causes of a price change are specified, it is just as meaningless to ask about the complete effects of that change as to ask about how an arbitrarily postulated change in the price of wheat would affect the volumes of wheat produced and consumed.

Don Patinkin made the illuminating distinction between individual experiments and market experiments (*Money, Interest, and Prices*, 1956, pp. 15, 275–281; 1965, pp. 12, 48–50, 265–268, 352, 387–392). An individual experiment discovers, at least conceptually, the actions desired under specified circumstances by one or many individual agents or even all individuals in a particular economic position. Whether these circumstances are compatible with other economic conditions and so could in fact prevail is beside the immediate point. An individual experiment is not meant, by itself, to describe the equilibrium that may emerge.

An ordinary demand curve is an example of an individual experiment. It shows the total amount of a thing that its buyers and potential buyers would want to buy at various alternative prices. It is true that economic realities may rule out many and perhaps all but one of the contemplated prices. Although the price is postulated to be a datum at various alternative levels for the buyers, it is an endogenous variable for the economy as a whole, depending on innumerable facts and preferences, and so it cannot be just "given." This consideration does not make the demand curve illegitimate; for it is not meant, by itself, to identify the one or more prices that can in fact prevail.

Identifying equilibrium prices presupposes taking into account the results of other individual experiments reflecting the circumstances and attitudes of groups beyond the actual and potential buyers of the thing in question, notably its suppliers. Or, if this first experiment is focused on suppliers, the further experiment would involve demanders.

This other type of analysis is what Patinkin calls market experiments. It pulls the results of individual experiments together, examines under what conditions the plans of market participants would and would not mesh, describes what happens when plans fail to mesh, and describes the equilibrium toward which market processes may be driving.

This distinction between two kinds of experiments applies more widely than to analysis of particular markets. Here, examining how an individual firm's investment decisions respond to interest rates is just an example of the individual-experiment *part* of market experiments on the economywide behavior of interest and waiting. That a reduced interest rate would incline business firms to undertake more real investment may be the individual-experiment *part* of the broader market experiment.

5.3 The Supply of Waiting

Waiting is useful, and people will pay to get it done or avoid doing it themselves. Individual experiments show why not enough waiting is ordinarily supplied to meet all demands for it at a zero price. People do not have unlimited incomes and wealth or unlimited productive resources to tie up over time. Much of their limited resources must go for current consumption.

Still, people would do some waiting at a zero interest rate, just as they would do some work of some kinds even at a zero wage rate. Normally, though, people would save or work less at a zero interest or wage rate than at a positive rate; at the margin, a positive reward is necessary to get more waiting done. The opposite, "perverse," response is possible, however, or sometimes even plausible. The most familiar such case is that of a person trying to accumulate a fortune to generate a target flow of retirement income. A reduced interest rate might motivate him to increase his saving.

The more consumption individuals postpone, the more future consumption they can expect.[1] For society as a whole, the productivity of roundaboutness contributes to future consumption potential. The increase of future relative to present consumption lowers its relative marginal utility; and if the marginal waiting is to be motivated anyway, this lower marginal utility per unit of future consumption must be compensated for by interest.

Even if the interest rate did not motivate supply and left waiting unresponsive, it would still perform a rationing function. In this respect it

[1] The possibility that inflation will destroy savings is a big qualification to this statement.

is like land rent. It is irrelevant that the pure gifts of nature are available without anyone's creating them and in amounts unaffected by the level of rents. Using a resource in any particular way has opportunity costs. Similarly, it is irrelevant to the rationing function of the interest rate that some or even all waiting might conceivably be performed without disutility and without reward.

Now let's look more closely at time preference. If investment in well-chosen roundabout processes has positive marginal productivity, a positive rate of interest presupposes time preference only in the broadest sense: people care about the timing of their consumption; they do not remain perfectly indifferent between one unit now and one later regardless of how much consumption they enjoy now and can count on later. But if people were perfectly (and impossibly) indifferent and ready, without payment, even to postpone all consumption, then the interest rate could be zero, and investment would have gone so far as to reduce its marginal productivity to zero also. Wages or rent could be zero, likewise, if enough labor or land were available to meet all demands for free.

The indifference map with 135-degree straight lines in Fig. 5.1 represents the quite unrealistic complete absence of time preference. Present consumption is measured along the horizontal axis and future consumption along the vertical. This two-period-only diagram is a permissible simplification, taking a slice out of a multidimensional hyperspace with an axis for goods available in each distinct future period. One underlying assumption is that the amounts of goods available in the various periods can be known or arranged for with certainty.

Figure 5.2 shows more realistic cases. To avoid clutter, it shows only one of the indifference curves belonging to each of two alternative indifference maps. The dashed curve shows time preference in the broadest sense: symmetrical or unbiased time preference. The 45° line shows equal provision for present and future goods. At its intersection with it, the dashed curve has a slope of (minus) one. A person having command over equal amounts of present and future goods is indifferent between marginal units of each. The line's curvature, contrasting with the straight lines in Fig. 5.1, illustrates the principle of diminishing marginal rate of substitution: the more goods the person has in one time period (present or future), the less is their marginal importance to him relative to goods in the other period. The more future goods and fewer present goods the person has while remaining on a given utility level, the larger must be an increment of future goods to just compensate for a one unit loss

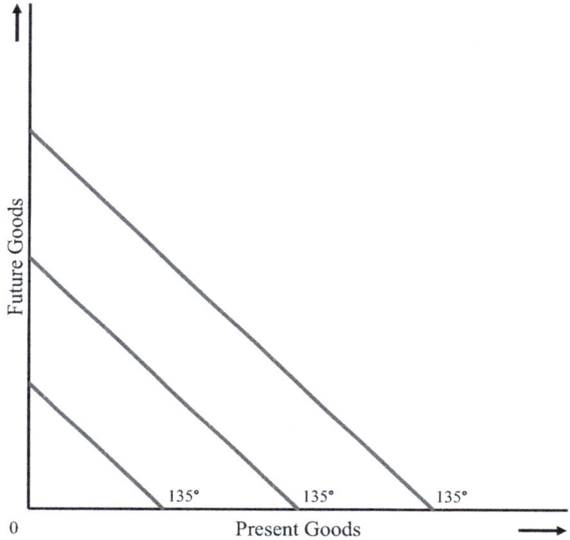

Fig. 5.1 Indifference curves of a person with no time preference

of present goods. The same principle holds for fewer present goods and more future goods.

The symmetry portrayed here holds even in degree: if the person has x present and y future goods and would be no better and no worse off having $x + a$ present goods and $y - b$ future goods, the same proposition holds true with the words "present" and "future" interchanged. If the diagram were folded along its 45-degree ray, the two halves of the dashed indifference curve would make exact contact with each other. For a person with unbiased preferences like these, the only reason for preferring a given marginal quantity of goods in one period over an equal marginal quantity of goods in the other period would be relative scarcity of goods in the one and relative abundance in the other.

Briefly, the person with an indifference map of curves like the dashed one *cares* about the time pattern of his consumption; he does not remain indifferent between equal marginal amounts of present and future goods regardless of the total consumption assured him in each of the two periods. He has no systematic bias, however, toward either present or future consumption. Nothing other than having unequal totals of present

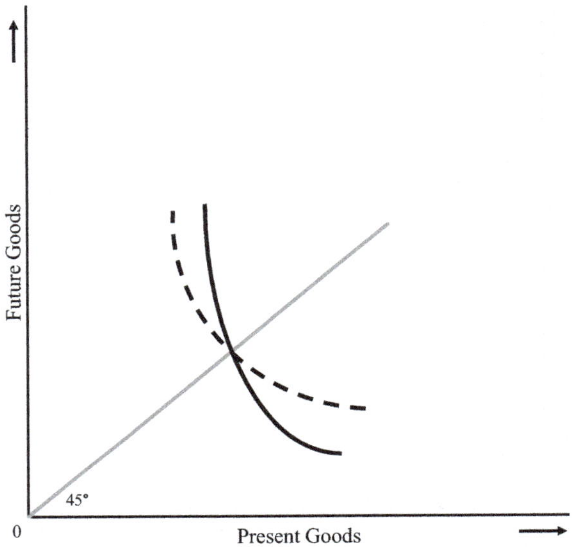

Fig. 5.2 Indifference curves showing symmetrical and present-biased time preference

and future consumption would give him a preference between equal marginal amounts of the two.

In contrast, the solid and steeper indifference curve in the same Fig. 5.2 shows systematically biased preferences. At its intersection with the 45-degree ray showing present and future consumption equal, the person *does* prefer a marginal unit of present goods to a marginal unit of future goods. Compensation for losing 1 unit of present goods would require more than 1 additional unit of future goods; the *waiting* would require a price. The price required would increase as the person moved to positions represented by points further to the northwest on his indifference curve. The curvatures of the indifference curves in both figures represent diminishing marginal rates of substitution. The only thing that, despite systematic bias, could make the person indifferent at the margin between present and future goods, or even make him prefer future goods, would be relative abundance for him of present goods and scarcity of future goods. Such positions are represented by points toward the south-east end of the solid curve, where its slope becomes (minus) 1 and then even flatter.

The last several paragraphs imply that time preference in the specific sense shown by the solid black indifference curve is unnecessary for a positive rate of interest. Even a person with the unbiased time preference shown by the dashed indifference curve would have a *marginal* preference for present over future goods if he could borrow and lend at a positive interest rate.

Figure 5.3 shows the market rate of interest uncluttered with indifference curves. The straight lines represent three alternative budget or opportunity lines. Line a, with a 135-degree slope, represents a zero-interest rate; present and future goods trade flat against each other. Line b represents a positive rate: a definite amount of present goods trades against a larger amount of future goods. Line *c* represents a higher rate. The slope of a budget line (algebraic sign ignored) represents 1 + *i* (*i* being the interest rate expressed as a decimal rather than a percentage). This slope shows how many units of future goods exchange against 1 unit of present goods (see the small triangle to the right of the main figure). The line's distance outward from the origin represents the scale of the person's opportunities, which depends on his "endowments" of present and future incomes or wealth available to be rearranged over time by borrowing or by saving and lending. To represent a definite interest rate without saying anything about the scale of opportunities, we should draw a whole family of parallel lines. For neatness, a single line represents each interest rate. Letting these alternative lines have the same intercept on the horizontal axis is arbitrary. Arguably, the lines should intersect at whatever point represents the position from which the person starts borrowing or lending.

Near flatness of the common tangent to an indifference and transformation curve shows a low interest rate because the interest rate is the gain in future goods per given sacrifice of present goods.

In Fig. 5.4, the slope of opportunity line b represents a market interest rate (strictly, 1 + the interest rate) confronting a person with unbiased time preference as represented by the symmetrical dashed indifference curve. Much as in an ordinary choice between consumer goods, the point of tangency between the opportunity line and the person's highest attainable indifference curve represents his choice between present and future goods. Since 1 unit of present goods trades for more than 1 unit

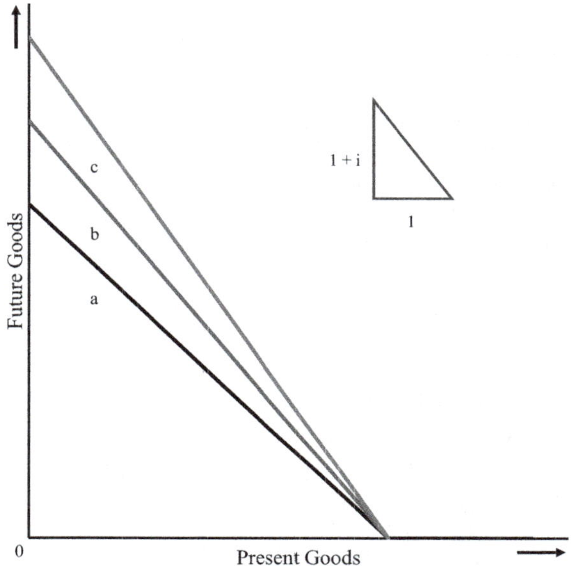

Fig. 5.3 Alternative interest rates

of future goods, the tangency can occur only on the northwest stretch of the symmetrical indifference curve. At that margin, if faced with a choice between 1 unit of present goods and *only* 1 unit of future goods, the person would prefer the present goods, according them a subjective agio. At a higher interest rate, represented by a steeper opportunity line (like line c, not redrawn here), the tangency with a higher indifference curve would occur somewhere northward in the diagram. At that new margin, the subjective agio accorded present over future goods would be larger than in the case drawn. In either case, the agio would develop, despite lack of asymmetrical bias in time preference, because the person would respond to borrowing or lending opportunities so as to become more abundantly supplied with future than with present goods. Even if no one had any asymmetrical time bias, the productivity of roundaboutness could affect the demand for waiting so as to make the equilibrium rate of interest positive, which would cause people to exhibit a *marginal* preference for present goods.

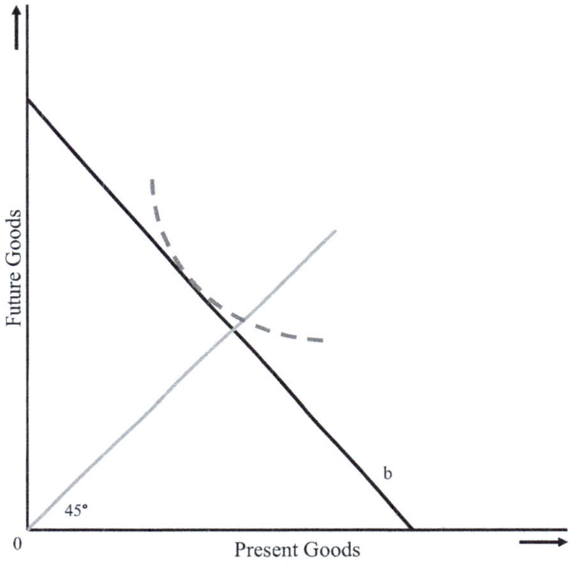

Fig. 5.4 A positive interest rate confronting unbiased time preference

Saying so does not deny that a systematic bias in favor of present goods may well limit the supply of waiting and so help account for the positive interest rate actually observed. But no such bias is the very precondition and essence of the interest rate; again, the pure time-preference theory of interest is wrong. Only in the weakest sense, the one ruling out the preposterous straight lines indifference map of Fig. 5.1, is overall time preference necessary for a positive interest rate.

Confronted with a positive market interest rate, even a person with unbiased time preference exhibits positive time preference at the margin. He takes advantage of the market opportunity to give up some present goods for a larger amount of future goods. If he happened to be "endowed" with more future than present goods, he might borrow rather than lend but would still choose to have more future than present goods. In his chosen position, he has command over fewer present goods than future goods and accords them a marginal agio equal to the interest rate. The person would supply waiting and receive its price; or, if the person was a heavily future-endowed borrower, he might still demand waiting and pay its price.

In an implausible but instructive analogy, a person with no systematic bias between leisure and work finds some work positively satisfying; and when spending equal numbers of waking hours on leisure and on work, he would be indifferent about reallocating a few minutes of his time in either direction. At a positive wage rate, however, and if he can closely adjust his schedule, he works to the point that work does have marginal disutility for him. His marginal preference for leisure over work corresponds to the wage rate. Similarly, a positive market interest rate leads even a person without time bias to allocate his command over present and future goods so as to have a marginal preference for present goods.

So far, we have mostly assumed that it is the interest rate which persuades people to *arrange* for a greater abundance of future than of present goods and to exhibit marginal time preference. A plausible case, not contradicting anything already said, is that real incomes are trending upward over time, thanks to growth in personal and general production. Apart from saving and lending, then, a person's expected future consumption would exceed his present consumption; and he would consider future goods less important at the margin than present goods. People would want to transfer some of their abundant future goods to the present by borrowing. This is Böhm-Bawerk's "first reason" why interest exists: if people generally expect their incomes to rise in relation to their needs, the abundant future goods have less marginal utility for them than the relatively scarce present goods. A traditional example cites a person living lavishly on credit in expectation of an inheritance. A positive interest rate would emerge, holding borrowing in check and perhaps even promoting saving and lending after all.

The interest rate could well be positive even in the absence of present-biased time preferences. Still, such a bias could generally prevail, restricting the supply of waiting and making the interest rate higher than it would otherwise be. Böhm-Bawerk lists this "underestimation of the future" as his "second reason" why positive interest exists. His third reason is the productivity of roundaboutness, a topic for Chapter 6.[2]

[2] Below is a less condensed summary of Böhm-Bawerk's three reasons:

1. Present wants are more intense than future wants relative to the means for satisfying them, chiefly for the following reasons:

   (a) Earning capacity may be greater in the future than at present.
   (b) Some people are in more urgent need now because of illness, loss, and so forth.

A person with this bias would prefer a marginal unit of present goods over a unit of future goods even when holding command over equal total amounts of each. Such an attitude might reflect a deficient capacity for perceiving and assessing future wants and satisfactions in relation to present ones. A. C. Pigou (1932/1950, pp. 24–26) spoke of a "defective telescopic faculty." Maurice Allais (1947, I, pp. 220n., 223, 592–593) noted that the allocation of consumption between a person today and the same person 10 or 20 years later was decided without any input from the future self.

But must a bias toward present satisfactions be irrational? Goods to be consumed only in the future may be genuinely different in view of a person's own changing purposes and personal characteristics, and different even from physically identical goods available now. Future satisfactions are more uncertain, furthermore, than present ones. More conditions are uncertain than whether debtors will pay, whether money will retain its purchasing power, and thus whether the expected future goods will in fact be available. One's future self may have a lesser capacity for enjoyment than one's present self. It is plausible advice to travel while young enough for the exertions to be a joy rather than burden.

As Cassel reminds us, no one can even count on being alive to enjoy future goods.[3] If life expectancies were much longer than they are in

(c) The holder of a durable asset is at liberty to use or sell it either now or in the future. Money, in particular, is durable and cheap to store (abstracting from price inflation); hence, someone intending to spend it only in the future nevertheless values it more highly now as a way of keeping his options open.

2. Many people underestimate future wants relative to present wants because they lack imagination, will power, or are uncertain about their life spans.
3. Present goods have a technological superiority over future goods; roundaboutness is productive.

Other summaries appear in Conard (1959), pp. 36–37; Blaug (1962), pp. 451ff; and Kuenne (1971), pp. 25–34. In Böhm-Bawerk's *Capital and Interest* itself, see II, pp. 259–289.

[3] Under unrealistic conditions, an uncertain life span would not recommend present-biased choice. The key assumption is "perfect" life insurance, which would give the individual broader opportunities than merely to insure against an unexpectedly short life in the usual way. He could obtain loans secured by life insurance and could also insure against unusually long life by buying an annuity. These kinds of insurance would be available on actuarially fair terms. Then, although an uncertain life span would still introduce a discount on future satisfactions, it would also discount just as much the costs of providing for them. Furthermore, having an uncertain life span of definite average expectation yields

fact, a stronger concern for the future would guide choices, and the interest rate would fluctuate in a lower range than nowadays (1903/1956, pp. 12–13, 151–152). Böhm-Bawerk makes a similar observation about "the brevity and uncertainty of human life" (1959, II, p. 270). Rothbard notes that if the world were sure to end soon, the interest rate would rise very high; but if some new drug made people immortal, time preferences would weaken, the pure rate of interest would fall sharply, and investment would increase (1962, p. 381).

A diagram similar to Irving Fisher's helps represent Böhm-Bawerk's "three reasons" for a positive rate of interest. The indifference curves in Fig. 5.5 form a social indifference map, somehow derived from the indifference maps of individuals. The lines are curved, not straight, showing that people care about the timing of their consumption. This fact is loosely akin to Böhm-Bawerk's first reason. The curves do not represent his reason exactly since he referred to a difference between present and future needs *relative* to the means of satisfying them. The asymmetry of the curves, obvious in their crossing the 45-degree line with slopes steeper than (minus) 1, represents Böhm-Bawerk's second reason—a systematic bias in favor of present goods, a tendency to attribute lower satisfactions to future goods than to present goods. The third reason, the productivity of roundaboutness, is represented by the transformation curve. It represents opportunities to invest resources productively and so obtain more future consumption than the present consumption sacrificed. Such opportunities are represented by the steep slope of the curve and by its greater intercept on the future goods than present goods axis. Its curvature, with its slope becoming less steep toward the northwest, represents the plausible but nonessential assumption that the more present consumption has already been sacrificed in favor of future consumption, the smaller is the payoff to further such postponement. The curve's shape thus represents both the productivity and diminishing marginal productivity of waiting; present goods can be transformed into larger quantities of future goods, but at a diminishing marginal rate. The diagram represents possibilities of

the person a higher value of expected lifetime utility, evaluated at the start of life, than having a definitely known span of the same length. The insurance companies would also presumably know his predetermined life span, making mutually advantageous insurance transactions impossible; yet he could not have escaped the initial determination of his life span. On the other hand, a known life span might afford better opportunities than an uncertain one for planning one's education and the like. See Barro and Friedman (1977).

transformation over a definite time span. In reality, both the amounts of resources invested and the expected times of waiting for their outputs are subject to decision. The diagram can represent variations in the quantity dimension but not also in the time dimension of waiting.

Equilibrium is represented by the point of tangency between the intertemporal transformation curve and the highest attainable indifference curve. There, the marginal rate of transformation between present and future goods, represented by the slope of the transformation curve, equals the subjective marginal rate of substitution between present and future goods, represented by the slope of the indifference curve. The straight line drawn tangent to both curves emphasizes their common slope at equilibrium. This slope (sign ignored) represents the market rate of exchange between present and future goods, the interest rate (strictly, 1 + the interest rate).

Modifications in Fig. 5.5 will show that if the transformation curve were symmetrical about the 45-degree line, and especially if it were a straight line perpendicular to it, while the indifference curves remained as

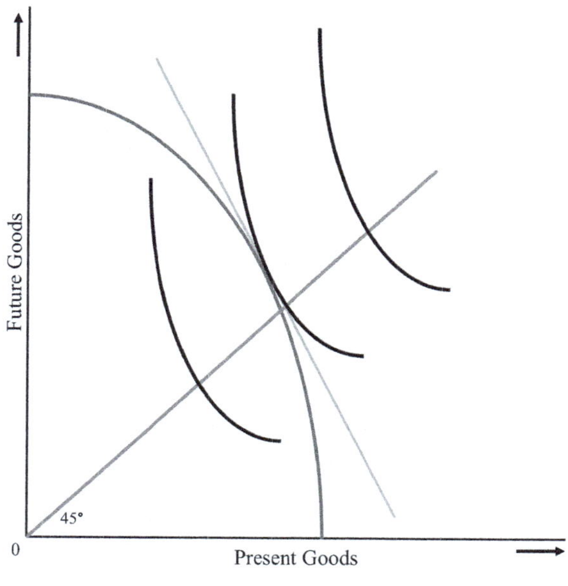

Fig. 5.5 Interaction of tastes and opportunities of the community

drawn, the point of tangency would be further southeastward. In words, if production possibilities were no longer skewed in favor of future output and if tastes remained unchanged, future output would decline relative to present output, and the interest rate would be lower. In the original situation of Fig. 5.5, the productivity of roundaboutness makes the interest rate higher and production more future-oriented than they would otherwise be.

Alternatively, the transformation curve remains as drawn while the indifference curves become symmetrical around the 45-degree line. The point of tangency moves northwestward, and the straight line through it becomes less steep. In words, eliminating the present bias of time preferences increases future output relative to present output and reduces the equilibrium rate of interest. In the original situation as diagramed, present-biased time preferences make the interest rate higher and production more present-oriented than they would otherwise be. The function of the interest rate in that situation is to restrain future-oriented investment in line with people's impatience to consume; only relatively high-yielding investment projects can meet the test posed by the high price of waiting.

Let us pull together the conclusions of the last two paragraphs. Both the productivity of roundaboutness and any present bias of time preferences tend to make the interest rate higher than otherwise, while these productive and subjective conditions pull in opposite directions on the allocation of consumable output over time. The productivity of waiting and the consequent demand for it, on the one hand, and people's reluctance to wait, on the other hand, raise the price of waiting while keeping its volume performed below what its productivity alone would suggest.

5.4 Present Consumption Versus Future Flows

So far, our diagrams measured consumption available in the "present" (or near future) on the horizontal axis and consumption in the "future" (or remoter future) on the vertical axis. Figure 5.6, a variant of Fig. 5.6, takes account of many time periods. As before, consumption available in the present year is measured along the horizontal axis. The vertical axis, however, measures goods available not in one particular year but in each future year in a perpetual steady flow. The diagram represents possibilities of a one-time sacrifice of present consumption in return for an increase in continuing future flow (a similar construction appears in Hayek 1941, pp. 222ff.) A close analogy is the case of an investor considering a cut in consumption this year to buy a perpetual bond yielding annual interest and thus a flow of consumption through all future years.

As before, a transformation curve concave to the origin represents investment opportunities. In contrast with Fig. 5.5, however, the consumption represented by the vertical axis intercept is much smaller than what the horizontal intercept represents. This difference represents the fact that the consumption obtainable in *each* of indefinitely many future years by devoting all current resources to providing for that future flow is normally only a small fraction of the amount of consumption that could have been enjoyed in the single present year by devoting all available resources to it. Cumulated over the fullness of time, of course, the volume of consumption obtainable by shifting resources toward that future flow is larger, perhaps much larger, than the necessary one-time sacrifice of present consumption. Roundaboutness is productive.

Indifference curves, as in the earlier diagram, are convex to the origin. Here, however, they represent consumers' indifference between amounts

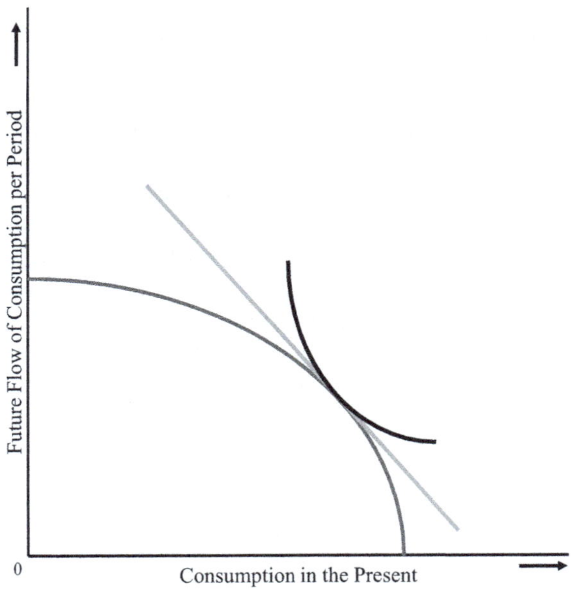

Fig. 5.6 Present consumption and future consumption flow

of consumption in the present year and in *each* of all future years. Zero marginal time preference can no longer be represented by indifference curves cutting a 45-degree line at right angles. To avoid clutter, the diagram shows only the highest indifference curve attainable with each available investment opportunity. The straight line emphasizes the slope that this indifference curve and the transformation curve have in common at their point of tangency. This slope (ignoring algebraic sign) represents the equilibrium interest rate (and not 1 + the interest rate, as in Fig. 5.5). Consider the change in vertical distance associated with the change in horizontal distance in a move along the line. Their ratio, which is the line's slope, is the change in goods per future year divided by the change in the single amount of goods given up in the present year; and this ratio has the dimensions of a percentage per year. At the margin, a definite cutback in present consumption devoted to buying a perpetual bond, for example, provides interest earnings that pay for a definite annual increment to future consumption. In the other direction, a definite one-time increment in present consumption can be obtained by borrowing and making interest payments costing a definite annual cutback in future consumption.

The common slope of the straight line, the transformation curve, and the highest indifference curve at their point of tangency represent the equilibrium equality among the interest rate, the marginal rate of transformation between present consumption and annual future consumption offered by real investment opportunities, and the subjective marginal rate of substitution between present and annual future consumption. It is worth noting that this entire discussion realistically assumes that people do not opt entirely for present or entirely for future consumption. If the terms on which people were objectively able and subjectively willing to shift between present and future consumption were not equal, they could gain by adjusting the amount of resources devoted to investment and so altering the time pattern of their consumption. In so doing, they would move in the direction of equality between the objective and subjective marginal rates and the interest rate.

5.5 Opportunities and Decision Criteria of the Firm

A different modification of our two-period diagram, following Irving Fisher, shows a person or a firm facing both investment opportunities and credit-market opportunities. In Fig. 5.7, the quantities no longer represent consumption specifically but goods or incomes available for use as the owner sees fit in the single present or future year. As before, the transformation curve shows the productivity of waiting: more goods or income can be obtained in the future year than the amount forgone in the present. The interest rate (strictly, 1 + the interest rate) at which the person or firm can borrow or lend is represented by the slope of the straight line (ignoring algebraic sign). Since the slope and not the position of the line is what represents the interest rate, a whole family of parallel lines belongs in the diagram. To avoid clutter, however, only the one that proves relevant is drawn, the one furthest from the origin touched by the transformation curve. Reaching this outermost interest-rate line represents reaching the largest or best set of market opportunities attainable, given the opportunities described by the transformation curve. The tangency at point b between the transformation curve and the highest attainable market-opportunity line represents the intertemporal production pattern that *maximizes the present value* of the firm. The diagram illustrates the *maximum-present-value rule* for investment decisions.

The diagram also illustrates the *separation theorem* (so-called by Hirshleifer 1970, p. 63 and *passim*): making the best of both the investment and borrowing or lending opportunities requires separate investment and consumption decisions. Regardless of tastes, a firm chooses production point b in the diagram. The present value thus maximized can then be allocated by borrowing or lending to achieve the time pattern of consumption preferred by the firm's decision makers. Their choice is represented by the point of tangency between the market-opportunity or interest-rate line and the highest attainable indifference curve. In the case shown, the firm borrows, producing as represented by point b and its owners consuming as represented by point c.

The separation theorem presupposes that the firm can borrow and lend as much money as it wants at a single, definite market rate of interest, represented in the diagram by the unkinked straight line. If the borrowing or lending rates diverge or if the firm must pay a different rate of interest on large than on small borrowings, the analysis and diagram must be

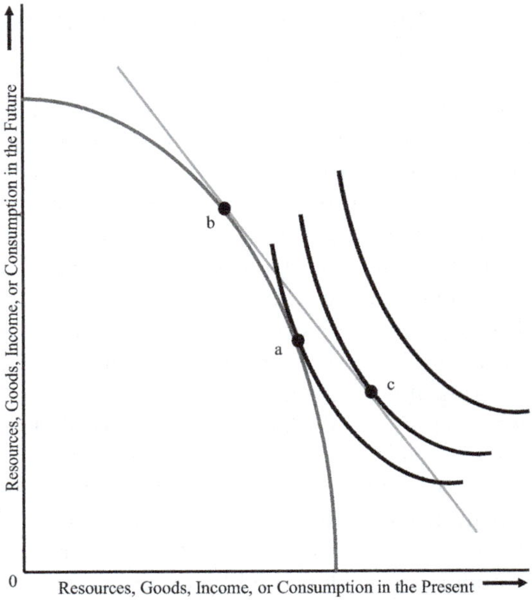

Fig. 5.7 Production, borrowing or lending, and consumption decisions of an individual person or firm

modified. If the firm cannot borrow or lend at all, the investment and consumption decisions are thoroughly intertwined. The firm can then attain no position preferable to the one represented by point a, the point of tangency between the transformation curve and the highest attainable indifference curve.

5.6 Analogues of Intertemporal Choice

The theory of intertemporal choice resembles the theory of gains from international trade. Being able to trade on the world market at definite terms enables the home country to separate production and consumption decisions, to rearrange both activities, and so to achieve the most preferred position attainable by the technological and trading opportunities. Admittedly, this metaphor is to speak of the tastes and decisions of a "country" just as one speaks of a "firm."

The theory of interest centering on the demand and supply of waiting is eclectic, but no more so than the theory of any other price. This eclecticism is another parallel between the theories of the interest rate and of other factor prices. The "productivity" and "time preference" concepts of interest theory have analogues in the "productivity" and "disutility" concepts of wage theory. In equilibrium, under appropriate simplifying assumptions, the marginal value productivity of labor equals the wage rate which equals the monetary compensation for the marginal disutility of labor.

The traditional term "disutility" need not be taken literally. It just as well means the subjectively appraised marginal opportunity cost of labor. Perhaps the worker actually enjoys working, even at the margin, but would enjoy some other activity even more, so that his wage is necessary to persuade him to do the marginal work. Neither the quasi-objective marginal productivity nor the subjective marginal disutility or opportunity cost of labor determines the wage rate. All three equilibrium magnitudes emerge from a system of general interdependence in which the *schedules* of marginal productivity and marginal disutility or opportunity cost largely account for the demand for and supply of labor.

The market for waiting operates similarly: the marginal rate of transformation of present into future goods equals the interest rate which equals the marginal rate of time preference. Neither the quasi-objective productivity element nor subjective time preference determines the interest rate. All three equilibrium magnitudes emerge from a system of general interdependence in which *schedules* of marginal returns and marginal time preference largely account for the demand for and supply of waiting.

Further parallels occur in labor-market analogues of Böhm-Bawerk's "three reasons" for interest. (1) Just as the relative marginal utilities of present and future consumption depend on the actual or prospective amounts of each, so the relative marginal utilities[4] of leisure and of labor income depend on the times devoted to each. A person enjoying little leisure and doing much labor would require a high wage rate for the marginal labor. (2) Just as people might systematically underestimate

[4] Someone might object to the term "relative marginal utilities" on the grounds that it takes utilities as cardinally measurable and interpersonally comparable. Yet, that phrasing appeals to intuition, especially considering the general principle of diminishing marginal returns. The reader who objects is free to substitute the term "marginal rate of substitution."

satisfactions of future wants relative to the present sacrifices necessary to obtain them, so they might underestimate the utility of earned income relative to the disutility of labor. Or, conceivably, the underestimates might run in the opposite direction. (3) The productivity of waiting is analogous to the productivity of labor.

One final analogy ends this section on supply and demand. Just as many more wage rates exist than a single one for a single type of labor, likewise, many interest rates remunerate waiting performed over different spans of calendar time and by holding various assets and financial instruments.

5.7 Investment Criteria of the Firm

In an individual experiment, a reduced interest rate would make a firm want to invest more resources now for the future payoff. But in the broader market experiment, could it find the financing? Does something cause more saving, allowing more resources to shift from current consumption into investment? Answering these questions requires considering what underlying change has disturbed the original situation and how market participants react to it.

Writers in the tradition of Böhm-Bawerk and Fisher are fond of examples showing how the best time to cut a tree, the best durability for an apartment building, and similar optima depend on the rate of interest—"best" meaning most advantageous for the project's owner. The best volume of waiting used in producing a good or service depends, among other things, on the prices of waiting and other factors. Waiting a long time before cutting the tree ultimately yields more timber than an early cut (and more revenue, barring a price drop). Whether this high-waiting-intensive production is advantageous depends on the interest rate and other factor prices.[5]

[5] Although the following quotation alludes to capital and interest by mentioning "initial investment," it illustrates the role of prices more broadly:

What factors go into the decision to build a pipeline versus hauling the oil by truck or barge? Key considerations include the volume to be moved, the distance from origin to destination and the type of terrain to be traversed. In general, the initial investment required to build a pipeline is large; but the cost to transport each barrel is small when compared to the truck or barge alternative. Therefore, smaller volumes tend to be transported by trucks and larger volumes are more likely to be transported by pipeline (Koch Oil 1996).

A decline in the rate tends to increase timber production in either or both of two ways, especially if timber is a more waiting-intensive good than most others in the economy. First, forest owners would probably let the typical tree grow more years before cutting it, so combining waiting more intensively with other factors. Second, even if some biological inflexibility in growth periods barred this option, owners would raise more trees than before. The amount of waiting demanded could thus expand either intensively or extensively; in equivalent language, the use of waiting could be either deepened or broadened.

In deciding when to cut a tree, the owner considers both the productivity and price of waiting. The most profitable growing period is just long enough for the percentage increment in the amount (strictly, value) of timber attributable to the "last" increment in the period's length to equal the rate of interest over that incremental period.[6] As with other factors, the owner employs waiting to the extent that its marginal revenue product equals its price.

Constructing apartment buildings that will last many years with little maintenance is a more waiting-intensive way to provide housing services than constructing buildings with shorter lives or requiring more maintenance. Even though the more durable buildings require more labor and other inputs at first, their total services over their entire lives will be larger in relation to total inputs of factors other than waiting. This does not mean that constructing the more durable buildings is unequivocally advantageous; for the longer average interval between inputs of resources and outputs of services, as well as the fact that the economies in maintenance accrue not all at once but only over time, implies an opportunity cost. That cost is other projects forgone because the scarce capacity to wait for results has been devoted to the durable apartments. The market brings this cost to the attention of investors in the form of interest.

Which one of the many actual interest rates best expresses the opportunity cost of using waiting in a particular project? For an individual firm's decision, the answer is obvious: the best rate it can obtain. In a more "social" context, as in deciding on a government project, the answer

[6] We also assume that the second-order conditions for a maximum are satisfied, that any additional costs other than of waiting are netted out of the incremental value of timber, that the relevant markets are competitive, and so forth. These simplifications do not undercut the principle illustrated.

is more complicated. Against which target rate should such a project's prospective yield be compared?

A high cost of waiting discourages supply of housing services in a way that ties up resources for a relatively long time. A fall in the interest rate makes constructing durable apartment buildings more attractive. In another standard example, a fall in the rate cheapens mature wine relative to new wine and favors its production and consumption. All of this presupposes that the interest-rate change resulted from increased availability of waiting, i.e., that it was a market-experiment result.

A more general formulation covers what the forestry, housing, and wine examples illustrate. N and R label two projects with streams of net receipts (revenues minus expenses) relatively Near and relatively Remote in time.[7] Since investment expenditures typically occur before revenues begin, Fig. 5.8 shows net receipts as negative during each project's early stages. Counting net receipts even in the far future on a dollar-for-dollar par with net receipts in the near future, project R yields a greater total than project N, as shown. Suppose that the two projects are mutually exclusive, like building one structure or another on a definite site, cutting a tree after 10 years or after eleven, or equipping a winery to produce sparkling wine by one method or another. Which of the two is the more advantageous depends on how sharply future net receipts are discounted in calculating present value.[8] Project R is worth more at discount rates below a certain level and project N at higher rates.

An individual investor's cost of waiting depends on his specific circumstances. It may be his subjective estimate of the disadvantage of delay in receiving benefits, or the interest paid for shifting the delay to some lender, or the opportunity cost of forgone earnings on some other investment of his own money. For Crusoe, the cost is his subjective aversion to delay. In a competitive market economy, where arbitrage and substitution tend to equate net returns on all claims and assets (apart from standard qualifications about risk and so forth), the interest rate measures the cost of waiting. As already explained, furthermore, individuals tend to pull their marginal rates of time preference into line with the market interest

[7] Here we consider projects for which such a comparison is unambiguous. Examples can be devised to exhibit ambiguity in the ranking of projects or production methods by the remoteness of revenues or outputs relative to costs or inputs. Such examples give rise to paradoxes that the concept of waiting can clear up, as Chapter 4 showed.

[8] For a further explanation of present-value calculations, see the Mathematical Appendix.

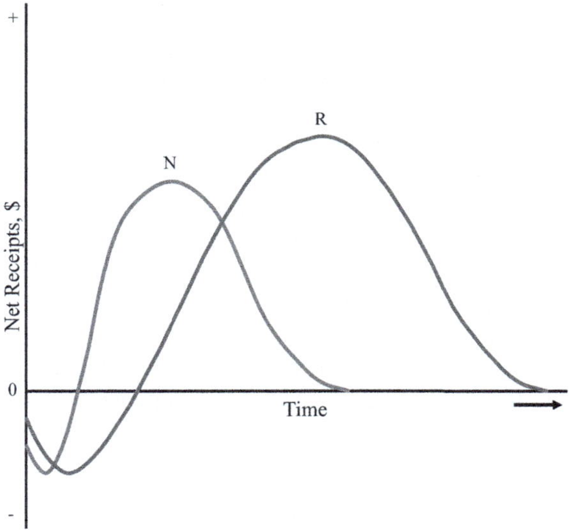

Fig. 5.8 Relatively near and remote investment projects with streams of net receipts

rate. At a high interest rate, the investor chooses project N over project R, since R's cumulative undiscounted net receipts are not large enough in view of the high cost of waiting. At a low enough rate, the investor will choose R, since the cost of waiting for its larger but more remote net receipts is not too high.

The borderline rate at which two investment options would have the same present value is what Irving Fisher called "the rate of return over cost" (Fisher, 1930, p. 150). Fisher emphasized that an investment decision involves comparing alternative actions (or inaction) and that the ranking of alternatives by their present values depends on the level of the interest rate applied.[9]

[9] Despite J. M. Keynes's assertion, his own "marginal efficiency of capital" is not the same as Fisher's rate of return over cost; it is more closely related to the internal rate of return on the most attractive of the not-yet-undertaken investment projects in the economy. Since presumably many not-yet-undertaken projects offer internal rates appearing about the same, Keynes's marginal efficiency refers to the economy in general rather than to any specific project. On these distinctions, see Armen Alchian in Ezra Solomon (1959, ca. p. 67).

Fisher's rate of return over cost is not the same as a project's "internal rate of return." The latter is the rate that discounts the project's present value to zero: expected gross receipts and expected gross outlays, discounted at that rate, are equal. For example, a project requires an immediate outlay of $1000, yields revenue of $500 1 year from now and $609.90 2 years from now, then ends. Its present value is zero at an interest rate of 7%, which is its internal rate of return.

A rate of return over cost compares projects, while an internal rate describes a single project. The two rates are, however, related. The rate of return over cost that compares our projects R and N is the same as the internal rate of the imaginary single project whose stream of net receipts we obtain by subtracting, at each time, N's net receipts from R's. This is obvious: the interest rate that gives the two projects the same present value is also the rate giving a zero-present value to the imaginary project consisting of the difference between the two.

In one sense, after all, the concept of rate of return over cost *can* apply to a single project. The obvious rival "project" is then simply doing nothing and receiving no return. The rate of return over cost that makes the investor indifferent between the contemplated project and doing nothing is trivially the same as the internal rate of return of the imaginary project obtained by subtracting a stream of zeros from the stream of net receipts of the contemplated project. It is excusable to describe this rate as the rate of return over cost of the contemplated project, *provided that* "cost" is then interpreted as an initial and entire investment outlay with which the project's stream of *subsequent* net receipts is compared. This peculiar formulation supposes that all cost, or all cost ahead of what is netted out of subsequent revenues, occurs at the beginning or can be treated as equivalent to one initial lump sum and not subject to time-discounting. Buying an asset for a one-time-only payment is the obvious example. On this strained interpretation, the interest rate making the present value of subsequent net receipts equal to initial investment outlay may be thought of as the project's rate of return over cost or, equivalently here, as its internal rate of return.

Despite this way of forcing the concept of rate of return over cost onto even a single project, the concept remains basically comparative. This aspect is clearest when an investor compares a contemplated project with another of the same type but *marginally* different in scale or duration and so, either way, employing a marginally different amount of waiting. For example, the investor compares a forest of x trees with one of $x - 1$

trees or cutting a tree after y months with cutting it after $y - 1$ months. The rate that gives the two projects the same calculated present value, equivalent to the internal rate of return on the imaginary project of tiny scale or duration obtained as the arithmetical difference between the two, is the *marginal rate of return over cost* that summarizes the comparison.[10] When the projects to be chosen from can differ by fine gradations, the investor does best to choose the one whose marginal rate of return over cost equals the relevant rate of interest. That project has maximum present value.

In ordinary timeless theory, analogously, a firm employs a competitively hired factor most profitably in whatever amount makes its marginal revenue product equal its price. In our present context and terminology, the investor does best to employ waiting in just the amount, in both scale and duration, at which its marginal revenue product equals its marginal cost.

We have been supposing that the investor chooses according to the maximum-present-value criterion, assuming all along that he can borrow and lend at a definite rate of interest. However, maximum *present* value—maximum value at the present moment—has no special significance beyond analytical convenience.[11] That criterion in no way supposes that the investor will spend the maximized value on consumption right now or at any other particular time. Instead, the logic of the criterion is that the larger the present value of his investments, the more wealth the investor can reallocate over time, by borrowing and lending, to pay for consumption when he prefers it. The investor does best to undertake the

[10] Schneider (1966, pp. 43–57), lucidly explains marginal rate of return over cost as equivalent to the internal rate of the marginal investment.

[11] As Mishan says (1975, p. 232–238), to what time to discount (or compound) outlays and revenues is an issue not of right or wrong but of naturalness and convenience. He prefers compounding *forward* to a terminal period.

Maximizing total present value discounted at a definite interest rate implies, incidentally, also maximizing the value expected at each future date at that same interest rate. "Maximizing present value" is a shorthand expression for achieving what promises to be the most extensive set of consumption opportunities stretching out over time that can be achieved by present choices, given technological and market opportunities and present knowledge. In the previous diagrams, it means achieving the opportunity set represented by the farthest-from-the-origin attainable straight intertemporal budget line. Maximizing value discounted to the present amounts to the same thing as maximizing value discounted to any subsequent date. Phrasing the criterion in terms of *present* value serves definiteness and avoids arbitrarily specifying some other date.

investment program yielding the highest present value and reconcile it with a preferred consumption schedule by borrowing or lending. As the "separation theorem" says, he advantageously *separates* decisions about the time patterns of production and consumption. His overall optimum combines a production optimum and a consumption-timing optimum (Hirshleifer in Solomon 1959, esp. pp. 226–228, and Hirshleifer 1970, pp. 13–14, 63, 204, 273, 312).

The maximum-present-value criterion appears in individual experiments concerning how the interest rate affects choices of products to be produced and of the waiting-intensities of methods employed. That criterion presupposes a definite market rate of interest at which waiting can be both bought and sold, just as the ordinary analysis of the competitive firm presupposes market prices at which the firm can buy and sell factors and products. Recognizing "imperfections" in the loan market requires qualifications to the present-value criterion.

That criterion bears an analogy with the maximum-profit criterion of timeless theorizing. Maximizing present value is the time-conscious analogue of choosing the factor combination and output scale that maximizes a firm's profit in a timeless context; the timeless analogue blurs the distinction between income and wealth. The firm selling its output and buying its factors in pure competition seeks an optimum position in which, for each of its products, price and marginal cost are equal and, for each factor employed, price and marginal revenue product are equal. The maximum-present-value criterion of time-conscious theorizing is a more general or inclusive formulation embracing, as a special case, the timeless criterion of maximum excess of revenue over costs of inputs (Alchian in Abramovitz and others 1959). Often, it has heuristic value, as this book argues throughout, to think of waiting and the interest rate as we would think of any other factor and its price in a timeless context.

5.8 A Supposed Rival Criterion

In rivalry with maximum-present-value criterion of investment choice, the internal rate of return is—or was—sometimes suggested. The internal rate, we remember, is the rate of discount that would make a project's present value zero, giving equal present values to its receipt and outlay streams. That single rate supposedly describes a project's attractiveness, apart from its size. It takes account of differences in the time patterns of expected outlays and revenues. As its name implies, the internal rate characterizes the project itself, unaffected by outside changes, including changes in the market interest rate. It supposedly can rank all types of projects against each other and against the cost of finance to the investor (Solomon in Solomon 1959, p. 79).

This mistaken criterion recommends adopting all investment projects and increments to projects whose internal rate exceeds the firm's cost of capital at the market rate of interest. It means adopting all projects and increments having any positive present values when revenues and outlays alike are discounted at the cost-of-capital rate. Failure to undertake all projects satisfying this criterion means passing up opportunities to increase the present value of the firm's net worth. Or so it might seem.

The present-value and internal-rate criteria apparently agree on whether to undertake or reject a particular project. So, we might wonder: who cares? The question is whether they can disagree on the *ranking* of projects.[12] If they agree on adoption and rejection, who cares if they disagree on how enthusiastically to adopt some projects and how scornfully to reject others?

A difficulty arises when two or more proposals, each endorsed by both criteria, differ in scale or duration and are mutually exclusive—if undertaking one would rule out the other. Examples might be establishing a brewery and a pig farm both on the same site or erecting both of two factories, each of which alone could fully serve the market contemplated. Their own characteristics make the rival projects mutually exclusive. Being unable to undertake both or all of them because of scarcity of finance is a different matter.

Suppose you can invest \$1 at 100% or \$1000 at 10%, but not both. Is it obvious that you prefer the higher internal rate? Suppose that of two rival projects, the first yields a much higher internal rate but only for 3 years, after which it is finished and unrepeatable. The second project yields a lower internal rate (but still above the cost-of-capital rate) but will continue affording that rate for 10 years. Is the choice so clear? What warrant is there for assuming that the proceeds of the first project can be reinvested upon its completion at its more attractive internal rate? Somehow the investor must balance attractiveness of rate of return against attractiveness of duration. The present-value criterion accomplishes that balancing.

[12] One possible difficulty with ranking is that one or more of the projects compared may have more than one internal rate of return.

The conventional internal-rate criterion implicitly assumes that early revenues can be reinvested at the internal rate itself. In general, this is not true. Consider two investment opportunities of different sizes. A benefit-to-cost-ratio criterion tacitly assumes that the stream with the smaller outlay can be multiplied to employ all available funds. If this is not so, the larger project should be compared with the smaller one *plus* what can be done with the difference in funds, like investing them at the general rate of return. If one stream ends earlier than the other, the present-value criterion may conflict with the supposed internal-rate criterion. Then, we should consider how best to invest the funds accruing from the shorter stream for the time remaining until the end of the longer stream. Mishan (1975, Chapter 28) suggests "normalization" rules: (1) establish a capital outlay common to all the projects; (2) calculate and utilize the maximum reinvestment potential for the revenues from each stream; (3) extend all investment streams compared to run for the same length of time.

When the two criteria disagree on the choice between projects of different durations, the explanation may well hinge on different implicit assumptions about use of revenues yielded by the short-lived project between the time they accrue and the end of the long-lived project. In general, recommending the project with higher rate of return but shorter duration would implicitly assume that the funds it yields can be reinvested somewhere *at that same rate*. It simply assumes away having to choose between a high return for a short period and a lower return for a longer period. The alternative recommendation of the project with the higher present value (still assuming that the projects are mutually exclusive) implicitly assumes that the funds yielded by either can be reinvested when the time comes at the interest rate used in calculating present values (Solomon 1959, p. 76). One must beware of tacit assumptions.

A correct choice between mutually exclusive investment opportunities lies not between projects, narrowly described, but between entire courses of action, including reinvestment of funds. If some rate of return measures relative profitability, then the relevant rate is the yield per year promised by each alternative course from its beginning to a common end date, probably the end of the longer-lived project. This thought would support Mishan's preference, noted in Footnote 54, for the criterion of maximum *terminal* value. This formulation presupposes an explicit assumption about the rate at which cash flows generated in either course of action can be reinvested until that date (Solomon 1959, pp. 77–79). Even if the rate-of-return criterion can be salvaged in this way despite the problem of different durations of rival projects, the problem of differences in scale remains.

The supposed rule of maximizing the internal rate of return without regard to the market interest rate appeals to intuition, but deceptively. The investor wants his wealth to be as large as possible, thus growing as fast as possible. But maximizing the growth of wealth (in the broad sense)[13] does not call for choosing among alternative *parts* or *strands* of a comprehensive program, such as specific investment projects and increments to projects, by their own internal rates of return alone. The best program fits individual projects together in view of all opportunities to construct, produce, buy, sell, borrow, lend, and invest, as well as the related prices and interest rates. The most advantageous choices can no more be made without reference to market interest rates than without reference to other prices. The interest rate is relevant both to investment choices and to the allocation of consumption over time.

The program of present choices and actions that maximizes the discounted present value of the investor's wealth (in the extended sense of Footnote 56) is made up of components. The present value of each one is also to be maximized individually—so far as doing so is not outweighed by impairment to the present value of other components.

There is thus no contradiction between maximizing present value and aiming at maximum wealth at each date in the future. Although the latter formulation may *sound* like a rule of maximum internal rate of return, it is not. In particular, it in no way justifies putting together a comprehensive investment program out of components chosen by their separate internal rates of return without regard to the market interest rate.

Some writers, goaded by fallacies of the internal-rate rule, call the present-value rule the "universally correct criterion" (Solomon 1959, p. 15; Alchian in Solomon 1959, p. 67). While supposed rival rules are actually fallacious, the present-value rule does require some qualification, just as do generalizations in many fields of knowledge. It applies strictly only under idealized conditions. It sharpens or epitomizes Irving Fisher's

[13] Strictly speaking, the investor wants to maximize all consumption ever enjoyed or available, somehow properly discounted and cumulated over time. The text tacitly invokes the separation theorem: the "wealth" to be maximized is the investor's affordable consumption, allocated over time in a pattern considered best in view of the interest rate and all other circumstances confronting him. It may help to think of the investor not as a consumer but as a business firm maximizing its profits and distributing them as its owners prefer.

analysis of investment decisions as a way to an optimum time pattern of consumption, which distinguishes between productive and market opportunities. For all proposed investment rules, Fisher's approach helps show where they apply and how they may fall short. It stands as the general guideline to investment decisions under certainty (Hirshleifer in Solomon 1959, p. 228).

The maximum-present-value rule, to repeat, presupposes some single, definite market rate of interest used for discounting expected future revenues and outlays. Ideally, in full competitive equilibrium, it is also the firm's "cost of capital": it is the rate on money borrowed or raised as equity capital and also the opportunity-cost rate at which owned money could most advantageously be used for projects other than the ones under consideration. In competitive equilibrium under conditions of certainty, all these rates would be equal.

In the uncertain, imperfectly competitive, and disequilibrated world of reality, no such single and unambiguous rate prevails. Like the various rates at which a firm could invest, the rates at which it could borrow and could lend are different. Its borrowing rate, in particular, is likely to rise with the amount borrowed. Its situation is then represented by a market-opportunity line which, instead of being straight, is either kinked at the point representing the firm's present situation, or curved, as in Fig. 5.9.

In reality, furthermore, the firm cannot borrow unlimited amounts of money; it faces credit rationing.[14] Obviously, also, investors cannot expect future revenues and outlays with great definiteness and confidence. Such conditions narrow the opportunities open to the firm to choose the time pattern of its production and to separate its production decision from its owners' consumption decisions. For these and other reasons, there is no such thing as a single, unambiguous present value for each of the investment opportunities being compared; and the choice among them is not straightforward after all.

As Tibor Scitovsky said (1971, pp. 206–208), a firm does not demand money capital to the point where its marginal value productivity equals its

[14] Mention of credit rationing reminds us that the projects called mutually exclusive were so not because of any limitation of funds but because of their own characteristics. The financial limitation considered here may be described as a rising average and marginal "cost of capital," and any absolute ceiling to the funds available makes the marginal cost of capital infinite at that ceiling. The term "cost of capital" is still another example of using the word "capital" for the factor whose price is the interest rate.

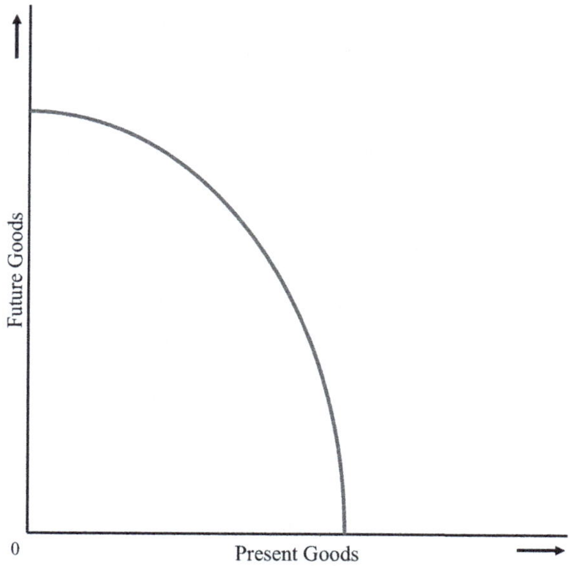

Fig. 5.9 Market opportunity for which the interest rate becomes increasingly unfavorable

price if it is rationed otherwise than by price alone. If capital were rationed only by an interest rate rising with the size of the loan, the borrowing firm would maximize profit by operating so that the rate of return on invested capital and the interest rate payable on borrowings were equal *at the margin*. This case resembles that of a monopsony employing a factor to the degree that its marginal value product equals marginal expenditure on it. Faced by nonprice rationing, the firm maximizes its profit by obtaining all the capital it prudently can and investing it advantageously. Labor, too, is nonprice rationed to some extent, as by legal and ethical considerations. Zoning is an example of the nonprice rationing of land.

Because of nonprice rationing, the individual firm cannot make the rate of return on its investment equal to a uniform market rate of interest. Still, unrestricted entry would create a long-run tendency for rates of return in different firms to become equal to the market rate of interest and to each other. The size or growth of each individual firm is limited by its ability or willingness to borrow, but nothing comparable limits the *number* of firms that can expand or be founded (Scitovsky 1971 pp. 210–211).

These major qualifications should not be disconcerting. In the imaginary world of complete knowledge, perfect competition, and continuous equilibrium, marginal rates of return on all chosen opportunities would be equal to each other and to a single, unambiguous market interest rate. People could be indifferent about marginal choices among many investment opportunities. No particular person or firm would have to exercise entrepreneurial judgment (although some people would have to exercise it to maintain the characteristics of such a world). Reality demands *more* entrepreneurial judgment.

A firm's "cost of capital" and its cost of labor are both ambiguous. Firms pay different wage rates for otherwise much the same labor because of overtime, choices between salaries and piece-rate wages, not fully foreseen costs of fringe benefits, circumstances motivating the hoarding of labor, and so forth. Ambiguities appear in choices among more or less waiting-intensive and more or less labor-intensive opportunities alike.

Although complexities of reality restrict its scope, the maximum-present-value criterion is broadly correct. Being worth more now rather than less carries a wider range of opportunities, including choices for the firm's owners of when and how much to consume. The present-value criterion fits in nicely with our intuition that the choice among projects of different degrees of waiting-intensiveness, among long-lived and short-lived projects, does depend on the price of waiting. It is a market-oriented criterion, fitting nicely under the more general principle that a firm's most advantageous line of action depends on factor prices and other prices and circumstances.

5.9 Conclusion

We have been considering the best choices not to advise investors but to examine how the interest rate, like other prices, links sectors of the economic system together. Examining how the individual investor or firm would respond to changed price signals helps us understand how the system as a whole responds to changes in "wants, resources, and technology." Individual experiments prepare for market experiments.

As Armen Alchian has said, Irving Fisher's model shows how the economic system reacts to changed circumstances. Different kinds of investment appear in a low-interest economy than in a high-interest economy. His model explains how cultural attitudes and technology affect the rate. Its theorems are broadly valid for the whole economy even when uncertainty degrades them for describing and advising the behavior of individuals and firms (Alchian in Solomon 1959, p. 70).

CHAPTER 6

Time Preference and the Productivity of Roundaboutness

6.1 Interaction of Time Preference and Productivity

Except in implausible extreme cases, neither time preference nor the productivity of roundaboutness alone determines the interest rate, just as neither subjective factors nor objective factors alone determine the wage rate or any ordinary price. The pure time-preference theory is just wrong.

Suppose that the marginal rates of time preference and intertemporal transformability diverged from each other and from the market interest rate. People are indifferent at the margin between 100 goods now and 105 a year from now. Lengthening production by a year would convert 100 goods sacrificed now into 120 a year from now. The market rate of interest is 10 percent, here a disequilibrium rate. By lending at interest, savers could obtain 110 future goods, more than they would have been satisfied with, in exchange for 100 given up now. Seizing this opportunity, they would make their present goods less abundant and so of increased relative marginal utility and make their future goods more abundant and of reduced marginal utility. They would carry these transactions to the point where an increased number of future goods, say 108 initially, were required to compensate at the margin for the loss of 100 present goods.

L. B. Yeager and S. H. Hanke, *Capital, Interest, and Waiting*, https://doi.org/10.1007/978-3-031-63398-0_6

Meanwhile, if producers could borrow at the supposed 10 percent interest rate, they would produce the supposed 120 of future goods for each 100 of current consumption postponed at the margin by savers. This extension of roundaboutness would reduce its marginal productivity, say to 107 future goods for 100 currently sacrificed. Also, the borrowing by producers and the increased marginal reward required for postponement by savers would raise the interest rate above the initially supposed 10%, say to 15%.

Qualified by standard simplifying assumptions, this process would tend toward an equilibrium with the marginal rates of time preference and productivity of roundaboutness and the market interest rate all equal, say at the just-supposed 15%. Different consumers would have the same *marginal* rate of time preference and different producers the same *marginal* productivity of roundaboutness because all were adjusting to the same (increased) market rate of interest. Although market forces make the three rates equal in equilibrium (again subject to standard assumptions), they are not conceptually identical.

This example illustrates the *interdependence* of the three rates: neither time preference alone nor the productivity of roundaboutness alone determines the interest rate (except only in the empirically preposterous case of a rate of time preference or of productivity fixed regardless of the quantities involved; Brown (1913) already gave a good exposition of this interaction).

The production-possibility and social-indifference curves in Fig. 6, Chapter 5, show three magnitudes all equal in equilibrium: the marginal rate of transformation between present and future goods, consumers' marginal rate of substitution between them, and their intertemporal price ratio. Analogously, labor's wage rate is determined not by any fixed marginal productivity nor by any fixed subjective tradeoff between labor and leisure but by interaction that equalizes those three conceptually distinct rates.

6.2 Time Preference and Influences on Its Marginal Rate

Before continuing with the standard theory of intertemporal choice, we should recognize some psychological anomalies.[1] People do not dependably discount future pleasures and pains to the present as if they applied a single uniform discount rate or discount function that would take account of their prospective present and future quantities of goods. Anomalies turn up in questionnaires and in laboratory experiments, typically on students but even on pigeons and other animals. Given a choice between $700 delayed for 12 months and $800 delayed for 13 months, an experimental subject would typically prefer the larger amount delayed one further month. But if 12 months had already elapsed, leaving the choice between $700 immediately and $800 1 month later, the subject might well prefer the immediate but smaller amount. This so-called reversal could not result from discounting at a uniform percentage rate per period ("exponential discounting"); but it has been observed with "hyperbolic discounting" such that the discount rate is higher for choice over short than over long periods. Taking "payday loans" may be an example.

This reversal is intuitively understandable. If alternative benefits are available rather far in the future, just *how* far may seem less important than their difference in size; but a difference between *now* and later, even if not much later, may loom large enough to prompt choosing the smaller gain. People are more sensitive to an early than to a late delay. Böhm-Bawerk and, much earlier, Baruch Spinoza understood this phenomenon (both quoted in Loewenstein and Elster 1992 Preface, p. xiv).

Hyperbolic discounting shows up in intending to do the farsighted thing (save) and then doing the shortsighted thing (splurge). Rather the opposite is postponing a pleasure, meanwhile enjoying the anticipation, and then for the same reason further postponing the planned moment of consumption (Frederick, et al. 2002, p. 371).

"Mental accounting" appears in classifying small gains as money to spend and large gains as money to save (Richard Thaler, summarized in Frederick, et al. 2002,373–374 pp.). Experimental subjects often depart from marginalist thinking. They tend to equalize average rather than marginal returns in allocating time or resources among activities. People

[1] See papers gathered in Loewenstein and Elster (1992) and a review article by Frederick, et al. (2002).

often let small decisions have cumulative effects that they would not desire if they faced the choices directly; this is a notorious result in politics.

The very concept of uniform time preference comes into question, as if choosers had compartmentalized utility functions and applied different discount rates to different *kinds* of experiences and goods and services and their utilities or disutilities. Discount rates are affected by whether expected streams of income or utility are rising or falling, by effects of past consumption (even addiction), by comparing oneself with other persons, by whether gains or losses are at stake, and by culture and fashion. People procrastinate. Uncertainty operates: one reason for preferring earlier to later pleasures is the uncertainty of still being alive and healthy enough to enjoy the postponed pleasures. Inflation risk has an understandable influence. People sometimes strategically narrow their options to compensate for weakness of will. Opposing forces affect intertemporal choice: "diminishing marginal utility motivates a person to spread consumption over time, while positive time preference motivates a person to concentrate on consumption in the present" (Frederick, et al. 2002, p. 359). On the other hand, a desire to enjoy income or consumption rising over time might work against a preference for early consumption.

Some experiments suggest split personalities, as if a chooser distinguished between a present self and a future self. Sometimes people adopt commitment devices to block or punish departures from their good resolutions (as to stop smoking, lose weight, or waste less time on television); the farsighted self tries to constrain the shortsighted self. People forgo short-run advantages to conserve good reputations. Past and future affect current well-being: people get utility from memory and anticipation, disutility from regret and dread.

Loewenstein and Elster (1992, Preface, p. xxiii) name many problems apparently due to suboptimal time discounting and requiring explanation and perhaps remedy. These include low rates of saving and corporate investment, growing private and public debt, teenage pregnancy, high infant mortality, crime, environmental degradation, and AIDS. Many American consumers, managers, voters, parents, students, and criminals evidently weight the present heavily relative to the future. Economics that simplistically ignores psychology "provides few useful insights into these problems."

Employees and entrepreneurs often act on whim, impulse, and hunch. Such behavior invites self-examination, conversation, and even a little preaching. Psychological research into extreme time discounting can be relevant to shaping personnel policies within firms, public welfare programs, pension plans, and other private and public arrangements for saving. Such research may especially be relevant if foresight and concern for the future are judged somehow deficient under laissez faire.

People are more complicated than economic theory can conveniently recognize. Their utility functions are poorly defined and hardly even exist in advance of trial and error in actual markets.

Despite such psychological realities and quirks, economic theory ordinarily serves well enough by putting forward more or less average or typical people whose idiosyncrasies somehow average out and who do respond to prices and other incentives.

Much the same is true in the markets for "capital" or waiting. Nothing obviously requires reformulating capital and interest theory so greatly as to discredit the concept of waiting as a productive factor and interest as its price. Here we find another parallelism, not contrast, between waiting and labor and other factors of production.

6.3 The Naive Productivity Fallacy

The "naive productivity theory," duly criticized by Böhm-Bawerk (1959, I, pp. 79–95), fails to distinguish between the productivities of capital goods and of waiting. Crusoe can catch more fish per hour of current labor with a net than without; the net itself is productive. His investment of labor in making the net may well have been worthwhile, but to take as proof the mere fact of the larger catch with the net is the fallacy. Conceivably, on the contrary, the net, over its entire usable life, might add fewer fish to what Crusoe would have caught without it than his labor invested in it would have caught if applied directly to fishing. Crusoe would then have invested his labor mistakenly; his waiting would have had negative productivity.

The principle of the greater productivity of roundabout productive processes holds, as Böhm-Bawerk insisted, only for *well-chosen* roundabout processes. A forthcoming section on "Misconceived Counterexamples" emphasizes this point.

By the time Crusoe realizes his mistake, it is ancient history; and he may as well continue using the net as long as it adds anything to the output of his current labor. Of course, he would not have invested labor in the net unless he had expected this roundabout process to yield more fish than his direct labor alone—and *enough* more to compensate him for having to wait for the results of the labor channeled through the net. It is fallacious to confuse the productivities of the net itself and of the waiting or roundaboutness applied to it.[2]

6.4 The Productivity of Roundaboutness[3]

The most challenging element on the demand side of the market for waiting is its productivity. The following discussion aims at anyone who denies any importance of roundaboutness to the interest rate (recall the section on pure time-preference theory in Chapter 4). Readers already persuaded may hurry over this section.

The word "roundaboutness" is loose but convenient. It does not imply the actual measurability of any period of production. Just as it can make sense to judge one vacation more enjoyable than another, so it can make sense to speak of one process being more roundabout than another.

Even one champion of the pure time-preference theory indirectly recognizes the greater productivity of well-chosen roundabout processes:

> [C]ivilization advances by virtue of additional capital [goods], which lengthens production processes. Greater quantities of goods are made possible only through the employment of more capital in longer processes. Should capitalists shift from saving-investment to consumption, all these processes would be necessarily abandoned, and the economy would revert to barbarism, with the employment of only the shortest and most primitive production processes (Rothbard 1962, 341; cf. Mises 1966, chapter XVIII).

[2] Böhm-Bawerk (I, pp. 86–87) describes the naïve productivity fallacy pretty much as done here, if perhaps less precisely. He pins it on J.-B. Say, among others. Böhm attributes something like its Crusoe-and-net version to Wilhelm Roscher.

[3] Such language is often convenient, even though "waiting" and "roundaboutness" are not exact synonyms. Loosely speaking, roundaboutness characterizes processes employing much waiting relative to other factor inputs.

6.5 Böhm-Bawerk on the Technological Superiority of Present Goods

The productivity of roundaboutness or waiting is related to what Böhm-Bawerk called the technological superiority of present goods over future goods (1959, II, pp. 273–289, and *passim*). In an example offered by Robert Dorfman (1959, pp. 359–360), goods available now rather than a year from now facilitate investment and permit having more goods available at any subsequent date. Suppose that the United States offers an underdeveloped country 100 units of goods in either this year or next year. The country would do well to choose the earlier delivery. It brings the opportunity to invest goods in roundabout processes. What is invested, more precisely, is not the donated goods themselves but the productive factors released from producing for current consumption because the donated goods can be consumed instead. The sooner the released factors are invested in time-consuming production, the greater the cumulative results over time.

Another Crusoe story illustrates how borrowing abroad can facilitate a country's capital goods formation even if the "real" counterpart of the loan takes the form of imports of consumer rather than capital goods or even of a cut in exports. When Crusoe lands on his island with no food, he can keep from starving only by applying his labor in ways that yield quick results. But, if he starts well supplied with food, he can devote more of his time to making a fishing net and other instruments of roundabout production.

Examples of the productivity of being able to wait for results point to the reasons for this productivity. The reasons appeal not to abstract logic alone but to facts of experience. All production, in the last analysis, consists of moving and rearranging matter. Most rearrangements require capital equipment or human training. Man's soft, weak hand, as Böhm-Bawerk said, cannot overcome the cohesiveness of the granite cliff; but the hard, sharp steel of the crowbar can; and man can control the crowbar and the sledge that drives it. Man cannot directly combine atoms of phosphorus, potassium, carbon, and oxygen into a grain of wheat; but he can learn and apply the principles of organic chemistry. Some rearrangements involve masses of matter that are enormous in relation to man's physical strength. At the other extreme, man's purposes require delicate manipulations; his unaided hand would be a fistful of thumbs. But, by adopting elaborate processes, man can bring the forces of nature and the properties of matter to bear at times and places of his own choosing (Böhm-Bawerk 1959, II, pp. 7–9, 12–13).

> Every "detour" denotes the conscription of an auxiliary power that is more potent or more clever than the human hand; everything that lengthens the roundabout road signifies an increase in the number of the auxiliary forces that enter man's service, and means the shifting of the burden of production from the shoulders of human labor, which is scarce and costly, to those of the natural forces, which are available in prodigal profusion (Böhm-Bawerk 1959, II, p. 14).

"[S]ome consumers' goods cannot be produced at all, except by indirect methods. Here we might say the indirect method is so much the better way that it is often the only way!" (Böhm-Bawerk 1959, II, p. 12, with picturesque examples on pp. 10–11). Additional waiting or roundaboutness can thus increase the value of output relative to other inputs by yielding not only increased outputs of specific goods but also improved and even entirely new types of goods. On the one hand, this fact brings further insight into the productivity of roundaboutness. On the other hand, it becomes harder to compare quantities of output per unit of input yielded by direct and indirect methods.[4]

We may dodge this complication by recognizing that consumer goods themselves are just intermediate stages on the way to value or utility for consumers. Just as two production methods yielding physically identical final products can involve qualitatively different capital and semi-finished goods along the way, so two different methods yielding similar value or utility for consumers may well involve qualitatively different physical products. Several distinct systems, for example, all have the end result of the pleasure of music in the home.

An analogy holds here with the twofold nature of gains from international trade. The people of a country can produce widgets directly or "produce" them indirectly by producing exports to trade away for them; likewise, people can produce satisfactions for themselves by consuming either widgets or other goods. Imported bananas and domestic apples, or imported wine and domestic beer, are alternative intermediate stages

[4] Not only outputs but also inputs differ between methods in *kind* as well as in amount.

in producing consumer satisfactions. The opportunity for greater roundaboutness resembles trade in broadening the range of choice of product-routes to satisfactions as well as of production-routes to products.

A farmer who borrows money to buy a tractor gets its services sooner than if he first had to save for it. Without it, he might not have been able to earn and save the money. If all goes as expected, the tractor's earlier availability adds more than enough to the farm's revenue to cover the interest paid. Resources that might have been applied directly to farming are channeled through the tractor instead and emerge as increased output. Saying so does not commit the naive productivity fallacy. The tractor has more than merely *some* usefulness to justify paying the interest.

A farmer, manufacturer, or builder may be able to wait for the results of his process because someone else performs waiting for him by lending him money or renting him equipment. If so, he becomes not an ultimate supplier of waiting but an intermediary between ultimate savers on the one hand and his suppliers of inputs and his customers on the other hand. The more time his process can take (within some limits, anyway), the smaller is the amount or value of inputs other than waiting necessary for a specified final output.

This substitutability at the margin for other inputs is a further parallel between waiting and other factors. Consider a house of definite specifications to be built by a definite date. The sooner (within limits) construction can begin and so the more time it can take, the smaller are the required quantities of some of the inputs other than waiting. The house could perhaps be built in only 5 days as a stunt but imagine the inefficiencies and expense![5]

Henry George expressed the idea well:

> [I]f I go to a builder and say to him, "In what time and at what price will you build me such and such a house?" He would, after thinking, name a time, and a price based on it. This specification of time would

[5] Armen Alchian expounds the costliness of hurried processes and the economies of taking more time (1959, esp. pp. 31–35, 39):

A longer construction process not only uses less of the nonwaiting factors but also uses them in different proportions. Hence an index-number problem arises in measuring their total amounts. Here it seems legitimate to use their total money value, especially since competitive prices indicate economywide substitutabilities among factors, apart from problems of time-discounting. The point being made does not depend on resolving such fringe complications.

> be essential.... This I would soon find if, not quarreling with the price, I ask him largely to lessen the time.... I might get the builder somewhat to reduce the time...; but only by greatly increasing the price, until finally a point would be reached where he would not consent to build the house in less time no matter at what price. He would say [that the house just could not be built any faster]....
>
> The importance ... of this principle that all production of wealth requires time as well as labor we shall see later on; but the principle that time is a necessary element in all production we must take into account from the very first (1897/1941, pp. 369–370).

Examples come to mind of inefficiencies of rush jobs in putting on a play, preparing a banquet, repairing a car, delivering a parcel, fashioning a dress, or building an electric power station. Doing such things at a more deliberate pace substitutes waiting for other resources that might otherwise be inefficiently employed. Morris Adelman (although questionably calling interest "the value of money") gives an example of factor substitutability in the oil industry:

> The productivity of a pool is less than proportional to the number of wells because past a certain point there is well "interference." The area over which oil migrates through permeable sands is very wide, so that one well could ultimately drain a very large reservoir. If time—meaning the value of money—were no object, that would indeed be the best because it would be the cheapest way. ... If time were no object, with zero rate of return or cost of capital, one well would drain a whole reservoir at lowest cost (Adelman 1972, pp. 19–63).
>
> "When land is so dear that railway companies prefer underground lines," says Cassel (1903/1956, pp. 110–111), "a substitution of waiting for the use of land takes place." The new LED (light emitting diode) bulbs offer another example. They cost much more than incandescent bulbs but last ten times as long; they tie up wealth longer while economizing on energy and labor. Fewer ladders block frozen-food aisles, moreover, and fewer scaffolds tower in hotel lobbies while workers replace blown-out bulbs (Linebaugh 2011). Such examples show how waiting can indeed "enter into the production function."

6.6 Eucken on the Productivity of Roundaboutness

Walter Eucken further clarified the greater productivity of roundabout methods.[6] He cited numerous misunderstandings in the literature. A more subtle fallacy, identified by Eucken yet subsequently committed by Donald Dewey (1965), links the productivity of roundaboutness to the advance of technical knowledge. Actually, roundaboutness is productive even when technical knowledge is constant, as the clearest exposition does assume. That principle does not deny that some technical inventions shorten and others lengthen the ripening times of productive factors, for it says nothing about inventions (Eucken 1954, p. 69).

The principle is an empirical generalization; it rests on pervasive facts and cannot be proved by abstract logic alone (Eucken 1954, p. 214; Böhm-Bawerk 1959, II, p. 12, III, pp. 45–56). The same is true of the productivity of labor or fertilizer. Eucken's discussion offers no proof but points instead to decisive experience.

The opportunity to *wait* for results makes other factors more productive by widening the usable ranges of both natural resources and human skills and so making a finer division of labor advantageous. Without a stock of consumer goods, Crusoe must produce quickly. An abundance of game does him no good if he cannot take time to make hunting weapons. Fertile ground is worthless if he cannot spend time to make farming tools and wait until the crop is ready. Skills he might have as a toolmaker, hunter, or farmer are likewise irrelevant. But if he starts with or can somehow borrow a stock of consumer goods, he can take time to make a fishing boat and other tools, hunt game, and cultivate land. Otherwise, useless wildlife, arable land, offshore fishing banks, trees, and fibers become valuable. He may develop skills as a butcher, tanner, and shoemaker. With no other change in the objective situation than a stock of consumer goods that permits a longer wait for the results of his current

[6] Eucken 1954, pp. 89–90 and throughout, interpreted and supplemented here. Most of Eucken's points already appear, it seems, somewhere or other in Böhm-Bawerk's three volumes on *Capital and Interest*. Eucken pulls them together and frames them persuasively, free of Böhm's distracting polemics.

efforts, the range of resources and skills that Crusoe can use has greatly broadened.[7]

These points obviously apply better to a *group* of Crusoes practicing the division of labor. In a complex modern economy, comparable examples of resources that would be worth little if anything without opportunities to wait for results include deep-lying coal and ores and other minerals, offshore oil and natural-gas deposits remote from centers of consumption, minerals in sea water, river gorges suitable for hydroelectric plants, waterways, dredgeable rivers and harbors, and suitable places for canals and bridges. Skills that are relevant only thanks to time-consuming production methods include those of rolling-mill workers, tool-and-die makers, construction workers, agronomists, and scientists and research workers of all kinds. Specialized skills take time to acquire. Specialization occurs not only among workers but also among firms; horizontal and vertical disintegration of industries likewise contributes to productivity. The productivity of an economy is more than a simple composite of the productivities of its component firms (Eucken 1954, pp. 75–76, 89–90).

More roundabout production methods typically employ qualitatively different factor combinations. In this respect, too, a parallel holds between waiting and other factors: use of more or less waiting, as of labor, probably requires different combinations and even qualitatively different types of other inputs. But given these differences, can we still compare the amounts of factors of production required per unit of output in more and less roundabout processes?

Eucken sees no genuine difficulty. Qualitatively different specific inputs still derive from the basic potentialities of nature and human beings, which are the ultimate data (Eucken 1954, pp. 75–76). Physical input quantities required per unit of output in short and long processes cannot be rigorously compared for an individual firm or industry or economy, depriving the notion of its production function of definiteness; but just how to conceive of the production function is a question not about reality but of analytical convenience in each particular context. Problems of conceptualizing and precisely measuring the demand, supply, and productivity of waiting may bedevil describing a whole economic system but pose no difficulty for individual households and firms.

[7] In emphasizing a stock of consumer goods, however, Eucken unfortunately flirts with the wages-fund idea.

A distinction between linear and circular aspects of roundaboutness, though of slight importance, serves clarity. Böhm-Bawerk, as interpreted by Eucken and others, usually envisioned a one way ripening of original factors through intermediate stages into final consumer goods. So did Menger's stages of production. An opposite extreme view, preoccupied with plow-backs of intermediate goods and the services of capital goods into creating further means of production, would seem to neglect the ultimate purpose of satisfying consumers' wants. Actually, the economy-wide process shares both aspects. Original factors ripen into final goods not steadily but with many zig-zags and backward loops. Capital or intermediate goods are always being shifted farther from final consumption on a vast scale; examples are feeding wheat to cattle or using it as seed instead of baking it into bread and using tools to make tools or to dig ore (Eucken 1954, pp. 210–212, 226–236, 267).

6.7 Eucken's Rules of Roundaboutness

Eucken states four rules of roundabout methods (1954, pp. 68–85). The latter three, he says, complete and extend the first one; and together they express a single truth.

First rule: Productive factors generally produce more consumer goods the more time elapses on average between the inputs and their ripening into final product—*provided* that the method of lengthening the time is wisely selected. Böhm-Bawerk had already stated the proviso about wise choice, and Eucken thought further emphasis was unnecessary, since economic theory presupposes rationality (1954, p. 69).

Experience repeatedly testifies to this rule. Bread output would be skimpy if people picked wild grain by hand, threshed it with wooden flails, ground it with stones, and baked the dough on open fires. The rule is illustrated in the growth of trees for timber (and so is the *diminishing* marginal productivity of lengthening, as the fourth rule states). The denials of the rule that still turn up in scholarly works remind Eucken of Hegel's remark that familiarity renders invisible things that our existence depends on (1954, pp. 69–70).

Second rule: Making the average ripening time longer or shorter typically involves changes in the productive services applied. Fishing with nets enlists different labor skills and natural resources than fishing with hooks or with bare hands. Mines, blast furnaces, and farm-machinery factories newly established in a formerly agricultural country bring different resources and labor services into use. Longer production periods bring fuller development and use of the country's natural fruitfulness and human capacities (1954, pp. 75–77).

Third rule: Lengthened ripening times bring forth both quickly used-up *(verbrauchliche)* means of production and durable ones—fuels, ores, wool, rubber, and other raw materials and semi-processed goods, as well as the proverbial fishnet.

No such things as durable consumer goods exist, says Eucken (1954, pp. 77–79), only durable means of production. So-called consumer durables—furniture, pianos, appliances, clothing, and so forth—are tools in the time-consuming production of consumer services. They not merely resemble durable means of production but belong to that category. Eucken may be faulted for this quibble, and convenience often suggests the term capital goods for undoubted means of production like buildings and machinery; but it is indeed pointless to brood over just how to draw a line between capital goods and durable consumer goods. All ownership of durable goods involves tying up wealth while *waiting* for their services to emerge.

Eucken supposes that some catastrophe destroys most of a country's durable means of production and the partially ripened consumer goods embodied in them. The productive powers of nature and labor remain fundamentally the same. Still, without stocks of consumer goods to live on, people must shift to quicker but lower-yielding methods of production. Some previously exploited mineral deposits now remain temporarily unexploited, and specialized workers like miners and metal workers turn to primitive agriculture (1954, p. 76).[8]

Durable production goods contribute vastly to human welfare, but they can also make the productive apparatus inflexible. Expanding the quantity of money has different effects according to whether the economy employs a large or a small apparatus of durable means of production (1954, p. 80). On the other hand, a large and varied stock of durable goods gives an economy a certain elasticity. The ripening times of labor and means of production can be adjusted. Repair and replacement of

[8] In some strands of capital theory, as in considering what determines the level of interest rates, it is instructive to trace out the consequences of the destruction (or the magic appearance) of resources and capital goods. Often it is important to be specific about the nature—especially about the capital-intensity or "waiting" content—of the items supposed to be destroyed or created. Chapter 8 considers such cases.

equipment might be postponed to maintain consumption in some emergency.[9] This is a cheerier side of having wealth trapped in the form of specialized durable producer goods that might be unsuitable for changed circumstances. Without explicitly developing this point, Eucken clearly hints at it (p. 255).

Eucken's whole discussion, like Menger's stages of ripening of ultimate factors into final consumer goods and services, takes for granted the great variety and changeability of an economy's stock of capital and intermediate goods. Yet some economists (Lachmann 1956/1978, pp. 2–7) have made a point of insisting that an economy's real capital is not a homogeneous mass. Whoever thought it was? Furthermore, this assortment of objects, while embodying the labor and other factors that went into producing it, is not the same thing as the "waiting" described as a factor of production. Again, the word "capital" is slippery.

Fourth rule: Beyond some point, the incremental yield of productive factors declines as the average ripening time lengthens further: the general principle of diminishing marginal returns applies even here.

In some historical epochs the stage of diminishing marginal returns sets in sooner, in others later. In modern times, vast technological knowledge avoids narrow technical limits to the advantageous lengthening of production processes; marginal returns diminish more slowly than in times of more primitive technology. In the Middle Ages, a relatively limited variety of ways of advantageously lengthening production times helped account for the frequent absence of interest (1954, pp. 81–83).

In housing, Eucken sees no limit to the gain in productivity from lengthening the period. How long a building remains useful seems always to increase more than in proportion to the inputs employed in constructing it. Valid or not, Eucken (p. 84) attributes this point to John Rae.

[9] A central administration could increase the current output of consumer goods at the cost of future output by slaughtering cattle and using less rye for fodder and more for milling and baking. It might cut back maintenance of steel mills and railroads and devote more iron to armaments. It might operate textile mills twenty-four hours a day. Thus consumption (or military capacity) could be temporarily increased or maintained by a shortening of ripening times (Eucken 1954, pp. 252–253).

6.8 Misconceived Counterexamples

Supposed refutations occasionally cite a roundabout method less productive than a quicker one. A Rube Goldberg machine (called a Heath Robinson in England) is an extreme example. Crusoe might adopt an overly elaborate method of fishing with a boat, tackle, nets, weirs, and dams; or he might construct an elaborate pipeline to bring water from the spring to his cabin. The ultimate amounts of fish caught or water delivered could be smaller per hour of Crusoe's direct plus invested labor, despite the waiting also performed, than the output of a more direct method.

The proposition about the productivity of roundaboutness postulates intelligent choice of more time-consuming methods. Böhm-Bawerk spoke of "well-chosen roundabout capitalist methods," of "skillfully chosen circuitous methods," and of "a wisely selected extension of the roundabout way of production" (1959, II, pp. 82, 84; compare III, pp. 45–56). Of course, one can conceive of excessively time-consuming, complicated, and wasteful ways of doing almost anything. For example, an arbitrarily imposed roundabout method might be less efficient than a more direct method freely chosen. A producer will not freely choose a more over a less roundabout method unless he expects it to be more advantageous. The opportunity to wait for results is productive because it broadens the range of production processes among which intelligent choice can be made.

Keynes, implicitly referring to Böhm-Bawerk,[10] offered an analogy. Processes are not physically efficient just for consuming time. We can easily imagine wasteful roundabout ones. Similarly, processes are not efficient for being smelly or risky; producers choose them from an expanded set of possibilities because they are more efficient enough to justify putting up with the smell or risk and paying people to do so. "But we do not devise a productivity theory of smelly or risky processes as such" (Keynes 1936, pp. 214–215).

According to a news broadcast in Auburn, Alabama, on 22 September 1989, University of Tennessee football coach Johnnie Majors accused Auburn University coach Pat Dye of seizing an unfair advantage by recruiting academically substandard players. Whether Dye had violated

[10] Böhm-Bawerk's analogy (1959, III, pp. 49–51) involved short and long railway routes between Hamburg and Frankfurt and Hamburg and Munich. He began with an apology: "I must endeavor to create clarity at any price, even at that of utmost tediousness."

any rules and whether the rules were wise is not the issue here. A side issue is whether academic deficiency actually promotes athletic prowess. Probably not, and Majors was hardly supposing so. He was complaining about Dye's drawing from an illegitimately widened set of potential recruits, including even academically deficient ones. Although dumbness as such does not make good players, more good players are to be found in the wider set of both dumb *and* smart players than in the set of smart players alone.

Similarly, a set of production methods widened to include relatively time-consuming ones is likely to contain ones more productive than a set of quick methods only. Being able to select from a thus widened set hinges on capacity and willingness to wait for results, which ordinarily commands a price.

Again, we see that waiting parallels other inputs, say labor or fertilizer. Conceivably, use of more of either, arbitrarily imposed, would reduce output. Too many cooks spoil the broth. But this does not happen if the use of waiting, labor, or fertilizer is wisely chosen. An opportunity that a producer can either use or reject will not harm output, mistakes aside; so, if it makes any difference at all, it makes a beneficial difference.

Business firms will pay for such opportunities. They will pay for loans enabling them to adopt more time-consuming production methods or to install plant and equipment already embodying waiting along with other factors. Business demands for waiting (i.e., for shifting the burden of waiting onto lenders or other parties) derive, then, from its productivity and from consumers' demands for goods embodying it.

This view fits in nicely with the Austrian theory of imputation, which traces the values of capital and intermediate goods and factors of production to the subjectively appraised values of the final consumer goods and services into whose production they directly or indirectly enter. Counting interest among the factor prices does not challenge the Austrian position but extends it. But we must not forget assessment *at the margin* or deny general interdependence and *multidirectional* causation; we must not share the extreme and erroneous or carelessly expressed view that causation runs in one direction only, from consumer utility to everything else.

Böhm-Bawerk recognized both the subjective and productive elements in interest-rate determination. Hayek did so throughout his 1941 book, and in one passage (pp. 420–421) he even criticized Irving Fisher for underplaying productivity relative to time preference. Only an extreme subjectivist wing of contemporary Austrianism denies the role of productivity in favor of a pure time-preference theory, a position we have criticized in Chapter 4.

Even Frank A. Fetter, whose reprinted writings have been in vogue with extreme subjectivists, does recognize, if in a backhanded way, that objective reality, including "productivity," influences the interest rate (Fetter 1977, pp. 242–247, 312). On the whole, his analyses are excellent. He understands the logic of the price system, the interrelation of prices, and the status of interest as one class of prices interlocking with all others. He distinguishes between the prices of a durable good and of its services, the ratio of those prices being one manifestation of the interest rate broadly conceived. He emphasizes that the values of future services are not just arithmetically capitalized at a predetermined interest rate into the price of the durable good itself. On the contrary, determining the relation between the values of future services and of the good is part and parcel of how the interest rate is determined. Fetter has a good grasp of how arbitrage links together the nooks and crannies of the market for waiting (although he does not use that term) into one substantially unified market. He refutes the old doctrine that rent is not a cost. He seems to recognize prices as determined by the interaction between cost schedules and demands, with factor prices *not* being unidirectionally imputed back from predetermined marginal utilities of ultimate consumer goods alone. Objective circumstances and market transactions enter into determining the margins at which people's marginal rates of time preference tend to be roughly equated. Why, then, isn't Fetter willing to recognize this mutual interdependence more explicitly than he does throughout his theory of interest?

The mere fact that labor or fertilizer or waiting has a positive marginal product does not prove that using more of it is profitable. Price also counts. Similarly, a more waiting-intensive method might yield a bigger output in relation to the quantity of inputs *other than* waiting, yet not necessarily pay.

6.9 Opportunities to Employ Waiting

An advanced economy affords innumerable opportunities to use more waiting to good advantage—if only it were abundant, cheap, and dependable enough. A railway tunnel through a mountain lets trains run on straight and level track, saving transport time and fuel and reducing wear and tear on equipment. Quicker trips save labor and reduce how many locomotives and cars are needed to carry a given volume of freight and passengers. But these savings come mostly in the future; meanwhile, labor and resources digging the tunnel must be withheld from other uses. Eventually, the resources saved in operation will equal in value the resources used in digging the tunnel; further savings from then on will be pure gain in a physical or engineering sense.[11]

Since these gains require investing resources in the tunnel and then *waiting*, and since waiting is scarce and might well yield a bigger payoff elsewhere in the economy, the tunnel is not necessarily worth constructing at the prevailing interest rate. But it would be so if waiting had a low enough opportunity cost—if it were dependably abundant and cheap enough.

Martin Bailey mentions other projects that would yield *some* return to waiting. Flattening mountains and filling marshes and lakes could create arable land. "In some instances, such as filling along the coast of the Gulf of Mexico and topping the fill with dredgings from the Mississippi River silt deposits, land of productivity comparable to the highest now existing could be created" (Bailey 1962, p. 111). Cassel (1903/1956, pp. 107–110) gave many examples of how the use of waiting would be profitable at very low interest rates, as in erecting extremely durable buildings. Such projects seem far-fetched precisely because we can think of many others that better exhibit the productivity of waiting and come closer to covering their opportunity costs as reflected in the interest rate and other prices.

Far-fetched examples of investment opportunities bring to mind Frank Knight's contention that decline of the marginal productivity of investment or waiting to actual zero is almost inconceivable.[12] Until all

[11] Examples of the productivity of waiting legitimately abstract from disasters and changes in technology or tastes that might disappoint expectations. Unexpected events could just as well make the labor applied to some projects go to waste, yet that possibility does not deny the general productivity of labor.

[12] Although Knight's theory is avowedly eclectic in recognizing some interaction between time preference and the transformability of present into future consumption

possibilities have been exhausted of leveling and straightening railroad tracks and converting mountains, swamps, and coastal waters into arable land, opportunities remain to obtain benefits that accrue indefinitely at finite initial costs. Waiting will never become superabundant in relation to opportunities for its productive use. Reasons more fundamental than risks of default and the like explain why the interest rate will never sink to zero. This, anyway, is the view of theorists like Eucken, Bailey, and Knight.

6.10 Deepening and Broadening

If people become thriftier, making waiting more abundant and cheaper, production can become more roundabout in two ways, often called "capital deepening" and "capital broadening" (or "widening"). Eucken's German terms convey this distinction (1954, pp. 146–147, 307): *Umbau*, deepening, refers to the *reconstruction* and *Anbau* to the *extension* of the productive apparatus. *Umbau* means adopting technically more sophisticated, equipment-intensive, or time-consuming methods of production—hunting rather than mere gathering, fishing with more elaborate tools, electrification of railroads, construction of stone rather than wooden houses and steam mills rather than primitive windmills. *Anbau*, broadening or widening, means merely expanding existing waiting-intensive types of production without a shift toward more individually roundabout ones. Examples are constructing additional railroads, houses, mills, and factories of the same old kinds. Another example is the introduction of some new good whose production is waiting-intensive, even though no more so than existing lines of production. If the economy's more roundabout sectors thereby expand relative to the less roundabout, both *Anbau*

potential, dominance of the latter element in effect makes his a productivity theory. The total stock of capital goods existing at any one time is so large that any short-period change in it, given the state of technology, must be too small to affect its yield appreciably. For Knight, the marginal productivity of investment is practically a fixed magnitude, and it one-sidedly determines the interest rate. Conard (1959, pp. 79–89, 115) so interprets Knight's position, giving citations. Emphasis on productivity also appears in Knight's metaphor of the Crusonia plant, a "perennial which grows indefinitely at a constant (geometric) rate, except as new tissue is cut away for consumption," which "requires no cultivation or other care," and which is the sole productive agent gratifying the sole "want" of the hypothetical Crusonia economy (Knight 1944, p. 30).

On the possible zero marginal productivity of capital, compare Scitovsky (1971, Chapter 9).

and *Umbau* make the whole economic process more waiting-intensive, time-consuming, or roundabout; the economywide ripening time of primary productive factors grows longer on average.[13] Increased thrift permits both types of investment in capital goods—qualitative changes and mere additions to quantity.

As Hayek writes of widening,

> It is not only conceivable, but it is probably a very frequent occurrence that an increase in the supply of capital may lead not to a change in the technique of production in any particular line of industry, but merely to a transfer of factors from industries where they have been invested for shorter periods to industries where they are invested for longer periods. In this case the periods for which one has to wait for any particular type of produce have all remained unaltered, but the periods of investment of the factors that have been transferred from one industry to another have been lengthened.[14]

Hayek's point may be pressed further. It is even arithmetically conceivable that the average period of investment of primary factors in producing ultimate consumer services might lengthen for the economy as a whole while growing shorter in each individual line of production. The most roundabout or waiting-intensive lines of production, while becoming slightly less so, might expand at the expense of the less waiting-intensive lines. It is hard to think of a realistic example, but expanding production in a relatively waiting-intensive industry in response to a reduced interest rate might for some reason involve installing machines less durable than the ones used before. Their lesser durability could indicate a shorter average period of investment in producing the specific final product.

[13] The distinction may be expressed in terms of roundaboutness. *Anbau,* widening, involves an increased number of projects using roundabout methods without any project itself necessarily being more roundabout than before. *Umbau,* deepening, involves methods of production that are individually more roundabout; they are not necessarily more numerous but more capital-intensive than before.

[14] Hayek (1936/1946, p. 361). Hayek objects to the term "period of production" because it tends to direct attention to the methods of producing particular products; yet when additional waiting is applied more broadly but not more deeply, the production periods of particular products do not lengthen. Hayek prefers to focus on factors of production and their periods of investment. We, in turn, may quibble about Hayek's possibly ambiguous use of the term "supply of capital" in the passage quoted.

The durability of capital equipment does not infallibly measure how intensively an industry employs waiting relative to other factors. Two opposite extreme cases provide a counterexample. Very durable capital goods represent much waiting done by owning them, but precisely because of their durability, they transform only small fractions of themselves per period into final goods and services. Although every unit of factor services flowing out of the durable equipment and into final consumer goods has been locked up a relatively long time, that outflow could be small relative to the amounts of labor and other nonwaiting factors also employed in constructing and using it. At the other extreme, *non*durable capital goods or goods in process are transformed quickly into final consumer services. Given a large amount of such intermediate goods used, however, their release into final consumer goods of factors that had been locked up for at least a short time could be large relative to the employment of nonwaiting factors.

To recapitulate: Given the flow of final output and the stock of capital goods, high durability implies a mere trickling outflow per period of factor services that had long been locked up in them. At the other extreme, capital goods of slight durability release a heavy flow of embodied factor services per period; but little waiting is associated with each unit of the services passing through them.

Thus, the durability of the capital goods is not in itself an infallible clue to the waiting-intensity of processes yielding a given outflow of final consumer goods. A probably better indicator, examined more closely in Chapter 7, is the ratio of the value of capital and intermediate goods, reflecting both their durability and quantity, to the value of final output per period. Meanwhile, until Chapter 7, a merely rough-and-ready understanding of these and related concepts like periods of production and investment will suffice.

The stock of capital goods is no measure itself of the waiting-intensity of the production process served, for its size is not the capital-output *ratio*. The ratio's denominator, the outflow value, could vary widely between stocks of capital goods of equal total values, as could the inflow per period of original factor services.

Is it even true that for a given capital-output ratio, the more durable the capital goods are, the more waiting or capital-intensive the production process is? Probably not. For a given flow of housing services but with the capital goods more durable in one case than in another, it is hard to conceive of the capital-output ratio being the same in both cases.

Especially for a whole economy, the distinction between broadened and deepened uses of waiting helps show why durability, average investment period, and waiting-intensiveness are not unambiguously associated.

Here too we find a parallel between waiting and other factors. Their use, likewise, may become either broader or deeper. An increased supply and reduced price of a particular kind of labor could conceivably spur production of a wider range of goods embodying it even while technological requirements in each particular employment kept the various factor quantities relative to each other and to output nearly rigid and insensitive to price. Substitution of the cheapened labor for other inputs would occur in the economywide pattern of production and consumption but scarcely in the individual firm. Labor's use would be broadened but scarcely deepened. In reverse cases, a reduced supply and higher price of waiting or of labor might shrink the factor's employment economywide but scarcely in the individual firm.

Anyway, possibilities of broadened as well as deepened use of a productive factor further support the idea of wide opportunities for productively employing any increase in the supply of waiting.

6.11 Technological Progress

Opportunities to use waiting productively do not depend on ongoing technological progress and growth of knowledge, even though such developments do expand those opportunities. Even in a static economy with unchanging technology, production requires time; a decrease in waiting employed would reduce production. Refuting the contrary view can strengthen our grasp of the correct one. Donald Dewey (1965) argues, wrongly, that

> to explain capital productivity, one would have to explain the growth of knowledge itself. For capital accumulation in the real world always involves the use of an existing set of machines and men to create a "better," i.e., more efficient set of men and machines. This achievement presupposes in turn that the economy knows how to create the better man or machine before the task is undertaken (pp. 8–9).
>
> Capital productivity does seem to be inextricably bound up with the creation and utilization of knowledge that is technical progress. Unhappily, the relationship is still extremely obscure and, given the philosophical difficulties in explaining change, is probably destined to remain so (p. 50).

Dewey blames "the major obscurities and errors" in Böhm-Bawerk's capital theory on his seeking "to analyze capital accumulation within the context of a steady state—one where technology is 'given.'" (p. 43)

> The effort to establish the possibility of capital accumulation, in an economic model where technology is given, and the most efficient productive techniques have already been adopted, is best avoided. It can only lead back to Turgot's natural fecundity of nature, the unfathomable mysteries of Marx's "labor process," Böhm-Bawerk's superiority of more roundabout methods of production, or some equally unconvincing explanation (p. 45).
>
> We dimly perceive that the rate of return on most investments is positive because knowledge is increasing or has recently increased" (p. 48; further such passages occur on pp. 44–45 and 47).

Actually, Böhm-Bawerk was correct in explaining that roundaboutness is productive even in a steady state. Dewey fails to distinguish adequately between new knowledge and old knowledge not yet fully exploited. The productivity of waiting no more depends on the growth of knowledge than does the productivity of labor. The points made by examples of Crusoe's fishing net, the railroad tunnel, land improvements, and various ways of broadening as well as deepening investment all remain valid even on the assumption that technological knowledge is unchanged. People already know how to reap an eventual gain by investing resources in such projects and waiting for the results. What keeps them from embarking on the less attractive of such projects is that they have better uses for their scarce resources, which include waiting.

6.12 Investment in Training

Creating specialized labor—human capital—can be a rewarding investment. Employers who offer their workers experience, new workers who accept temporarily low wages, and students who postpone paid employment while paying tuition all presumably consider their short-run sacrifices justified by their longer-run prospects. Many borrow to finance such investments. What is it that the borrowers are paying interest for, and why do they consider the transactions advantageous? What are lenders supplying? What are the market values and yield of human capital? Such questions are awkward to handle with the services-to-sources ratio and agio conceptions of interest noted earlier, but they are easy with the concepts urged here. The training of human beings requires that somebody perform waiting, and people perform it (or buy its performance by others) because they expect it to be productive.

An earlier section of this chapter warned against the "naive productivity theory" of interest. Just as we had to avoid confusing the productivity of a capital good with the productivity (if any) of the waiting associated with it, so we must avoid confusing the greater productivity of a trained than untrained worker with the productivity (if any) of the waiting associated with his training. Just as investment in a capital good might prove with hindsight to have been mistaken—obviously so if the resources embodied in it would have yielded more output if employed more directly—so something similar could prove true of a worker's training. He can indeed produce more than an untrained worker, and he would be silly to take a pill erasing what he had learned. Yet hindsight might show that he could have produced more output over his entire working life if he had begun actual work sooner and had not sidetracked time and effort into training. More generally, the fact that well-educated people produce more income over their lives than less well-educated people with similar innate capabilities suggests but does not by itself prove that the incremental expenses and sacrifices of obtaining more education have had a positive payoff. The question remains whether the higher incomes more than fully recoup the expenses and sacrifices. An obvious qualification applies to people who enjoy the education experience or its nonmonetary payoffs as a kind of consumption.

Even if increased earning capacity does more than recoup its obvious costs, the investment may still not be worthwhile. The further question remains whether the over-recoupment is large enough to warrant the costs. As educators, we like to think that it is. Our purpose here is not to disparage education but to clinch some theoretical points. So, is the return to waiting large enough to cover all of its further costs? These costs include the loss of utility through delay of income and also the payoff that income from earlier employment could have yielded if invested in projects other than education. The waiting involved in education is worthwhile only if it yields a net gain at least as large as alternative uses of waiting would have yielded. A just-mentioned qualification requires emphasis. Calculating net gain should go beyond considering enhanced productivity in a narrow business sense; it should also recognize that education also may be a consumer good and a way to make life more enjoyable.

The interest rate measures this opportunity cost of waiting, brings it to the attention of potential investors in and borrowers for particular projects, including education, and so guides choices in view of the forgone prospective benefits of alternative uses. The prices of waiting, labor, and land use all are similar in this respect. Waiting, like labor or land, might well be productive in a particular use, yet not productive enough to cover its money cost, which measures its opportunity cost, its potential contribution to the value of output in other lines of production. Opportunity cost does not pertain just to some specific next best financed alternative; it is the value in general of attractive opportunities forgone.

6.13 The Productivity of Waiting Summarized

Waiting widens the range of production methods to choose from by including more time-consuming ones, it widens the range of opportunities for using other factors, and it makes a wider variety of them, including natural resources and human capabilities, economically relevant. It permits a finer division of labor. It permits producing goods and services in greater quantity, better quality, and wider variety. While not every more roundabout process is more productive than a less roundabout one, some are; and waiting makes choosing them possible. Much the same is true of any factor of production: employing more (but not too much) of it makes complementary factors more useful and broadens the range of choice among production processes and qualities and varieties of output. Waiting appears to be a particularly versatile factor and highly complementary with others; so, it offers these benefits to a high degree.

6.14 Waiting and Saving Even in a Static Context

Waiting is productive even when net saving and investment are zero and the amount of waiting performed remains unchanged, just as labor is productive even when the labor force is not growing. Even in a stationary economy, waiting would be necessary merely to keep the economy stationary—merely to maintain output by maintaining the stock of capital equipment and human skills and knowledge and forestalling deterioration. That stock could, after all, be gradually consumed. People could employ resources for current consumption—at the cost of future consumption—by diverting them from repair and replacement of equipment and from education. To prevent this decline, some members of society must continue holding capital goods, land, and financial assets; they must refrain from neglecting their maintenance or selling them to spend the proceeds on consumption. The waiting performed by assetholders permits maintaining equipment and skills and knowledge and so it is productive. Even in a stationary economy, there is scant reason to suppose that all the necessary waiting would be forthcoming at a zero-interest rate.

Waiting is a broader concept than saving. Saving is nonconsumption of current income; waiting is nonconsumption of current income or of accumulated wealth or both. Waiting can continue even without growing in volume, without the accumulation of additional wealth through saving out of current net income.

Waiting can either maintain or increase the stock of capital goods, including human capital. If the distinction between maintenance and increase is fuzzy (notably because capital goods are usually not replaced identically), the waiting concept lets us de-emphasize that distinction. An analogy with labor holds. Labor can work not only in producing consumer goods but in maintaining or replacing or further accumulating capital goods, but often that distinction is unnecessary. We can explain the price of labor by its productivity and scarcity, and a parallel holds for waiting.

How, if at all, is the distinction between waiting and saving related to the distinction between the marginal productivity of capital and the marginal productivity of investment (a distinction made by Abba Lerner 1944/1947, Scitovsky 1971, and others)? Those two productivities are supposedly equal only in long-run equilibrium.

In an economy where current saving adds to the stock of capital goods, the market interest rate is higher than the prevailing marginal rate of time preference; otherwise, positive net saving would not occur. The interest rate is lower, however, than the marginal productivity of capital goods; otherwise, their stock would not be growing. Its growth depends on a marginal productivity of investment exceeding that of capital goods. Eventually, however, in complete long-run equilibrium, no more capital goods would be accumulated. In this hypothetical state, the parallelism between waiting and labor would be complete: each would be remunerated at a rate expressing both its marginal productivity and the marginal sacrifice involved. The marginal productivities of capital and investment, as well as the interest rate, would be zero, even though the marginal productivity and wage of labor could still be positive (Scitovsky 1971, pp. 218–219, paraphrased and interpreted). A situation is equally imaginable with a zero marginal productivity of labor, as in the old economic-development literature on disguised unemployment.

In full equilibrium, the marginal rates of return on capital goods and on investment and the interest rate are all equal. In disequilibrium, they can be unequal. A rate of return on capital goods in excess of the rate of interest motivates investment, but investment could conceivably be proceeding either at an inefficiently rapid rate (reducing its marginal rate of return) or at an inefficiently slow rate (leaving its marginal rate of return too high in some sense). The concept of waiting may bypass the necessity for some of these distinctions. Waiting is qualitatively the same whether devoted to maintaining or accumulating capital equipment.

6.15 Diminishing Marginal Returns to Waiting

The principle of diminishing marginal productivity applies to waiting as to other factors of production, as Eucken's fourth rule states.[15] This principle of diminishing returns, as of the productivity of roundaboutness itself, is an empirical generalization and not a purely logical truth. Consider a firm operating with borrowed money. Beyond some point, each additional $1000 borrowed would add less and less to its expected profits before interest; and a lower interest rate would be necessary to persuade it to borrow still more. For the economy as a whole, at some range of already feasible choice among inputs, methods, and outputs, the still wider range made possible by each further extension of the scale or duration of waiting becomes less and less significant. Contrary examples might be found, just as additional amounts of an ordinary factor of production in a particular use might yield increasing marginal returns "for a while." It is not realistically conceivable, however, that each successive dose of waiting, without more of other factors, should go on "forever" yielding equal (let alone larger) increments to output.

Take the example of wine. Beyond some period, each additional month of storage adds less and less to its quality and value, and eventually

[15] Böhm-Bawerk had already recognized this point (1959, II, p. 85 and *passim*). However, he does not treat waiting as a factor; he refers to the diminishing incremental advantages of extending the roundaboutness of production.

further waiting would degrade it. In building a house, waiting and other factors are substitutable at the margin. The inefficiencies of a rush job are obvious. Smaller amounts of the nonwaiting factors are probably required if they are available 4 months instead of only 3 months before the agreed date of completion. But if they are already available 22 months in advance, having them available still one more month earlier would bring only slight additional economies. The more durably built an apartment building is, beyond some degree, the smaller are the benefits in lower maintenance costs and a longer-lasting flow of services to be expected from making it still more durable.

The diminishing marginal value productivity of further-lengthened production periods bears an analogy to diminishing marginal utility of goods. Carl Menger (1871/1950, pp. 129–130) explains diminishing marginal utility, without invoking psychology. When an isolated farmer has very little grain, he devotes it to what he considers the most urgent uses; he selects. With more grain available, the farmer would devote units of it to successively lower-valued uses. Similarly, if business firms or the central planners of a socialized economy were to consider using a definite increment of waiting—a lengthened production period—they would use it in the ways they thought most productive; and they would use successive increments in ways that increased valued output less and less. They would have used the better opportunities first.

Recall the analogy of recruiting football players. Each further increase in the size of the pool chosen from (permitted, perhaps, by reductions of the cutoff grade-point average) would add less and less to the quality of the squad recruited. The best results of expanding the pool would be chosen first.

6.16 Zero Interest?

Might waiting become so abundant that its marginal productivity falls to zero? Might no opportunities remain for productively extending the degree of roundaboutness? If an actually negative interest rate is conceivable under peculiar circumstances, why couldn't a merely zero rate occur even under less peculiar ones? If labor were so abundant relative to other factors as to have zero marginal productivity—and some cases of "disguised unemployment" have indeed been reported in underdeveloped countries—why isn't the same possible with waiting? That result might well presuppose an end to technological progress that keeps creating investment opportunities afresh. As cautioned, continuing technological progress is not necessary for a positive interest rate. A zero rate might also presuppose a greatly increased supply of waiting, perhaps by measures like forced saving through the government budget.

Some economists apparently would like to see investment carried far enough to reduce its marginal productivity essentially to zero. Their argument could involve the ethical premise that each marginal real dollar's worth of consumption by members of different generations should count equally; future consumption should not be discounted relative to present consumption, no matter how much better off than the present generation future generations will be.[16]

Schumpeter (1911/1934/1983, Chapter V) maintained that interest—on what he called "productive loans," anyway—would be zero in a stationary economy. Businessmen are willing to pay interest to finance innovations because they expect the profits of temporary monopoly from them. The functions of innovator and owner cannot be completely separate; innovation requires some investment of capital. Interest derives from and is practically a part of the profits of innovation, which derive from change and disequilibrium. In the static economy, in Schumpeter's view, no entrepreneurial profit would arise distinct from the "normal profit" that is really a wage of management. With no entrepreneurial profit in prospect and no attendant demand for borrowed money, there would be no interest either.

In Schumpeter's imagined stationary state, would the interest rate be zero or, more exactly, would no business loans and so no interest on them exist at all? More fundamentally, a circumstance that helps explain a positive interest rate in the real world is not necessarily one whose absence would make the interest rate zero.[17]

Implausible as they may be, zero marginal productivity of waiting and zero interest would not embarrass economic theory. They would not necessarily imply the end of all scarcity and all need for economizing: that something is not scarce does not mean that nothing is scarce. Air might be considered a factor of production, but it (usually) commands no price.

[16] See Allais (1947, II, pp. 542ff.), Ramsay (1928), and Keynes (1936, pp. 374–377). Hayek explains the concept of zero marginal productivity of investment, though without the policy recommendation (1936/1946, p. 379).

[17] Rothbard (1962, pp. 385–386), offers further objections to Schumpeter's theory.

Still, persistently zero interest in a world like ours is empirically implausible. And how plausible is it that consumers, with no reward, might reach and remain at a margin of complete indifference between a unit of goods in general now and a unit only later?

Why is a piece of land priced at less than the sum of the values of its future services? The answer reinforces skepticism about persistently zero or negative interest. The sum of the undiscounted values of land's future services is practically infinite. An infinite price of land would imply a zero rate of return. No one would willingly choose such a position. Current landowners would hasten to sell, reinvesting the proceeds more lucratively or buying consumer goods. Arbitrage would bring land's price and rate of return into line with the general rate of return on assets.

Holders of land, as of bonds and other financial and physical assets, are waiting and refraining from bidding resources into consumption. If people become thriftier and apply their thrift to buying land, their bidding raises land prices and, through arbitrage, raises asset prices and reduces percentage yields generally, including the interest rate. Reduced target yields tend to promote real investment.[18] Symmetrically, a decline in thrift expressed in land sales restrains investment.

Further reason for skepticism about a zero rate is that some assets, like consumer durables, would always afford some positive yield, if only of subjective satisfaction. If assets were so abundant as to yield nothing at all at the margin, not even satisfactions, and if nobody were willing to spend the proceeds of selling some of them on additional consumption because everybody already was consuming all they wanted to, then scarcity would have been abolished; the Land of Cockaigne would have arrived, and economizing would have ceased.

But if waiting is a factor of production on a par with all the others, could such a situation be imagined for it alone? We can imagine a zero marginal productivity of particular kinds of labor—think again of "disguised unemployment" in backward countries or of a highly robotized productive system—but hardly of labor of all kinds; for that, too, would mean a Land of Cockaigne. Waiting is a comprehensive and pervasive factor, performed by the holding of all sorts of wealth. Only if wealth were superabundant—a case we have been considering—would waiting have no marginal yield, not even of subjective satisfaction.

[18] Compare, however, Allais's argument, presented in Chapter 3, about how thrift expressed in landownership might be partially diverted from real investment.

6.17 Derived Demand, Durability, and Arbitrage

Demands for factors of production, and so their prices, derive from their contributing to output demanded ultimately by consumers. In having a demand derived from embodiment in consumer goods and services, waiting is on a par with other factors. The relative strengths of consumer demands for goods embodying various factor services in different proportions affect producers' demands for factors and so affect their prices. A decline of consumer demand for a highly waiting-intensive good tends to lower the rate of interest. This point was illustrated in the example of matured wine, whose import from abroad reduces demand for its domestic counterpart, frees waiting for other uses, and tends to lower the interest rate. These effects can hardly be demonstrated by clear empirical observation, for the postulated changes in the supply and demand of waiting are trivial relative to the vast amounts of waiting always going on anyway. Here we stress the nature, not the strength, of those effects, along with their parallelism with effects on factor prices discussed in standard microeconomic theory.

Consumers perform waiting by buying durable goods and then waiting for their services. If consumers become less willing to wait and arrange either to borrow their purchase prices or to rent them instead and so pay only as they consume their services, and if they do not offset this decline in their willingness to wait by increased willingness to buy and hold other assets and claims, then the rate of interest tends to rise.

What if demand shifts toward low-durability models of goods, but goods still bought, not rented? The effect on the interest rate depends, in part, on whether the high-durability or low-durability goods themselves embody more waiting. This is not the whole story, however, for consumers will wait less for the future services of the low-durability goods bought now.

One methodological point is worth repeating. Explaining how any change in "wants, resources, or technology" affects the rate of interest, broadly conceived, should reconcile with explaining what happens to the interest rate even defined narrowly as the price of money loans. Consumers' choices about how to perform or avoid waiting intertwine with the substitution and arbitrage that tend (subject to standard qualifications) to equalize the interest rate and the yields on various goods and securities.

Consumer durables do have yields—in the form of services that could be appraised in money and compared to the values of their sources, even though this calculation is seldom explicit. A durable refrigerator or building or pair of shoes presumably yields more service cumulated over the fullness of time, not merely in total amount but even in relation to initial cost, than does a flimsy version of the same item. On the supposed false economy of buying cheap consumer goods, Böhm-Bawerk expatiated (1959, II, pp. 89–94). Yet such a purchase may be sensible for a person who is short-run-oriented because of current low income or for other reasons.

Services that a highly durable good will still be yielding, after a less durable version would have been junked, gain in relative significance from a low rate of interest and lose from a high rate. A high rate makes it expensive for consumers to borrow (or to forgo attractive loans and investments of their own funds) to finance purchases of cars, refrigerators, and furniture. Consumers are more likely at a high interest rate than at a low rate to buy low-priced, nondurable models, if any. How interest-sensitive such decisions are is beside the present point. The tendency toward equalization of explicit and implicit rates of return on all assets is central to capital theory and monetary theory, regardless of how sharply or how gradually the subjectively appraised yield on an asset varies inversely with the amount held. The subjective percentage yield on a nondurable model bought at a high interest rate exceeds the yield on a durable model bought at a low interest rate because, during its short life, the nondurable model yields a larger rate of flow of services relative to its capital value.

6.18 Conclusion

Like other prices, the interest rate is determined by "supply and demand," which reflect concern for the timing of consumption and by opportunities to increase the productivity of land and labor by well-chosen time-consuming processes. Psychological quirks counting as departures from strict rationality may affect people's willingness to delay consumption, but marginal time preference—to be distinguished from overall concern about timing—is influenced by how much consumption people expect to have at their disposal in the present and the future.

The principle of derived demand applies to waiting just as much as to other factors: the demand for them reflects consumer demands for the final goods and services into whose production they enter.

To understand the productivity of more rather than less roundabout and time-consuming processes, we must discard the naive productivity fallacy, which identifies the productivity of roundaboutness with the productivity of capital goods. Capital goods, once constructed, may be useful; but that fact does not justify investing resources in them that might better have been used otherwise. The correct view recognizes the benefit of a range of choice among production processes that has been widened by including more time-consuming ones. Examples of the wastefulness of a rush job of building a house or preparing a banquet help make the point. More time-consuming processes are assumed to be well-chosen, of course; supposed counterexamples of wastefully elaborate Rube Goldberg processes are irrelevant.

The principle of diminishing marginal productivity applies to roundaboutness and to the waiting that makes it possible just as much as to other factors of production. Beyond some point, choosing still more time-consuming processes contributes less and less to productivity. An analogy with the diminishing marginal utility of a consumer good is obvious. Potential productive uses of waiting include investment not only in physical capital goods but also in human training and experience. Walter Eucken contributes many examples of the productivity and diminishing marginal productivity of roundaboutness.

Examples of opportunities to reap at least some additional productivity from roundaboutness if enough waiting is available enter into discussions of whether the long-run rate of interest could be durably reduced to zero. Schumpeter thought that a zero rate of interest would depend on an end to innovation and the temporary monopoly profits from it. Committing an instructive error, Donald Dewey thought that a rate of interest depended on continuing technical progress.

CHAPTER 7

Measures of Roundaboutness

7.1 Fuzzy, Controversial, yet Meaningful Concepts

This chapter further examines the related concepts of period of investment of productive factors and period of production of goods and services. An investment period is the time or average time elapsing between application of whatever count as original inputs and their emergence as final goods and services; a good's production period is the time (or average time) taken to make it from its inputs.[1] The two concepts differ in focus, one on inputs, one on outputs. The period of completing production of a good made with some already processed inputs is in general shorter than the periods of investment of the more nearly ultimate factors directly or indirectly employed in making the good. The story of Robinson Crusoe's fishing net is what the two concepts are meant to illustrate even for complex money-using economies.

Those concepts of investment and production periods are attempts to supplement the time-and-money-value dimension of waiting with the natural dimension of time alone. However, one can use both, as Böhm-Bawerk did, without recognizing waiting as a factor.

[1] This chapter uses "average period," "roundaboutness," and "duration" in their everyday senses, looser than the technical financial sense of "duration" in Chapter 9.

L. B. Yeager and S. H. Hanke, *Capital, Interest, and Waiting*,
https://doi.org/10.1007/978-3-031-63398-0_7

The very use of capital goods shows that production is roundabout. How abundant and durable capital goods are may even roughly compare degrees of roundaboutness between countries and industries. However, the connection is not tight. Heavy use of elaborate capital equipment in some industry does not necessarily imply a relatively great waiting content in the industry's own product. Perhaps the equipment is very durable, and its periodic services contribute only a small fraction to the value of output. Or, the equipment itself may be quick to produce and have relatively little waiting content.

The notions of period of production or investment is arguably just a distraction; but their prominence in the literature requires attention. "The average period of production is only intended to provide an ordinal index of capital intensity for purposes of comparing different equilibrium situations characterized by differences in the amount and structure of capital" (Blaug 1985, p. 514). William Vickrey (1964), like Blaug, finds the period of production legitimate "as a measure of the degree of roundaboutness or the degree of 'capital intensity' of a production process." In a very simple process, the period is the time elapsed between an average date of original factor inputs and a single date of output. Complications arise when one firm uses another's outputs as inputs and when some outputs are recycled as inputs. Trying to trace each production process back to ultimately original factors involves contemplating the remote past and the indefinite future. Relating outputs as a whole to inputs as a whole presupposes some weighting scheme, which will involve the interest rate—a point that deserves emphasis. A measure of time dimension may be obtained, Vickrey continues, as the ratio of the values of capital and intermediate goods tied up in a one-shot process to the rate of input of original factors. If the process being considered can be constructed by combining a sequence of one-shot processes at a uniform output level, the period and ratio are approximately the same, both having the dimension of years. Where production is not in a steady state, it is not clear in detail how the necessary averaging of the measure over time should be done. Nor is it clear how to deal with use of intermediate factors of varying degrees of prefabrication. "The whole problem of measuring the capital intensity of production seems to be in a somewhat loose and unsatisfactory state" (Vickrey 1964, pp. 26–27, freely paraphrased).

7.2 The Dimensions and Measurement of Waiting

Waiting and roundaboutness are related but not identical concepts. Discussing productivity and diminishing marginal productivity of either or both seems to presuppose measuring their amounts. A measure in physical, natural, nonmonetary units might improve the parallelism between waiting and ordinary factors of production. However, we wouldn't speak of the price of roundaboutness.

For some fuzzy concepts, trying to quantify them can be plausible. One is the "readability" of a text. At one extreme lies pretentious polysyllabic literary criticism, at the other, a straightforward exposition of a genuine topic in simple language. Another example is a country's degree of economic freedom. Indexes of it and country rankings are published. It can be meaningful to investigate how the rankings correlate with indexes of living standards, economic growth, political arrangements, and personal freedom.

It is easy to mock the idea of a period of production by asserting that if it is conceivable at all, it is either almost infinite or zero. "[T]he schoolboy's pen knife may contain iron from a mine opened in the time of Caesar" (Stigler 1941, p. 205); and the mining, like making the knife, required tools themselves embodying still earlier labor and other resources. Is the production period of the knife or of its continuing services then practically infinite? At the other extreme, one might maintain that periods of production and investment in an established and steady process are zero on the grounds that flows of inputs into and outputs from it are simultaneous.

Estimating a period of production or investment can be a challenge for the observing economist, but ordinary people can get along well without the concept. Also, the individual household or firm need not distinguish between the monetary and real amounts of its command over resources since its own behavior alone does not alter the proportionality between the two. It needs only the facts of technology and tastes and the prices at which it can buy and sell, borrow and lend.

Understanding the economic system, however, requires recognizing that some activities and objects are relatively close to and others relatively remote from yielding ultimate consumer satisfactions. We want a way to compare the time-structures or waiting-intensities of different productive processes, of different sectors of an economy, and of economic systems in different countries and at different times. We want to understand the productivity of roundaboutness as distinct from the productivity of capital goods.

Even only rough comparisons of production or investment periods may be useful, like observing that the average investment period is longer in one process or in one country's economy than in another or that it has become longer or shorter. Indicators of roundaboutness are available. The use of tools, machines, buildings, vehicles, paved roads, graded land, dredged harbors, and the like illustrates the opposite of a hand-to-mouth process like fishing with bare hands. Original factors of production go into capital and intermediate goods that gradually transform themselves into consumer goods and services.

The mere quantity or total value of capital goods does not straightforwardly indicate the degree of roundaboutness. Nor does their durability, although it also counts. The longer the original factors of production remain embodied in them before emerging as consumer goods and services, the more waiting-intensive that final output is. Do original factor services pass through the capital goods only in a trickle per period, with a relatively large amount of current factor services productively combining with them? Office cleaners may use durable floor-polishing machines without making their work a highly waiting-intensive operation. Furthermore, being routed through capital goods in the narrow sense of machinery and the like is not the only way original factors serve in roundabout processes. They can go into accumulating and maintaining inventories of materials and semi-finished goods and into human capital.

7.3 Quibbles About Measurement

Even for the theorist, rough-and-ready notions of more or less waiting will often suffice. It can be a diversionary tactic to demand greater precision than the subject matter requires and permits.[2]

[2] Compare Aristotle: "Our discussion will be adequate if it has as much clearness as the subject-matter admits of, for precision is not to be sought for alike in all discussions.... [W]e must ... not look for precision in all things alike, but in each class of things such precision as accords with the subject-matter, and so much as is appropriate to the inquiry" (*Nicomachean Ethics*, Book 1, Chapters 3 And 7, pp. 309 and 319 of 1947 edition). In a similar spirit, Sowell (1980, pp. 291–292, 324) diagnoses the "precisional fallacy."

However, Cassel, hardly an obstructionist, dismissed the concept of period of production as vague and unnecessary (1903/1956, pp. 64–65).

One purpose of seeking some quantitative measure of roundaboutness is to show how its amount, or amount relative to other factors, might at least in principle be described, unlike waiting, in non-value terms. Economic theory is not ordinarily concerned with cases so similar that ranking them depends sensitively on details of measurement. Ordinarily we imagine processes or products that differ *clearly* in their degrees of roundaboutness or waiting-intensity.

Goods cannot always be ranked by their factor-intensities. The proportions of factors employed in some line of production can respond to prices of land use, labor, waiting, and final products; and a change in the interest rate can conceivably change a good's waiting-intensity even as a matter of sheer arithmetic. Does the imprecision of comparing factor-contents somehow undermine the proposition that a shift of tastes from less to more waiting-intensive goods will tend to raise the rate of interest? Chapter 8 considers such shifts.

A period of production cannot straightforwardly correspond to a good's waiting content because the dimensions are different. The period has the single dimension of years, days, or whatever only, while waiting has the double dimension of value and time. Nevertheless, for activities or economies of roughly the same size in real income and wealth, some rough correspondence is likely between the time period and the amount of waiting. The value dimension of waiting may in some cases be roughly proxied by accumulated wealth, roughly correlated with real income.

For Abba Lerner, also,

> The average period of production is a useful concept because it emphasizes the connection between capital equipment and the *time* aspect of production. It shows how capital is needed only because production takes time, and that more capital is needed when production takes place by methods that take a longer time (1944/1947, p. 328).

Equipment can be viewed as "imprisoned" factor services. Its value tends to equal the present value of those services, taking into account the time that will elapse until they emerge. "[T]he marginal yield from the postponement of consumption equals the marginal yield from resources applied to the lengthening of the period of production" (Lerner 1944/1947, pp. 324–325, interpreted here, quotation from p. 328).

Concepts like period of production, period of investment, and waiting-intensiveness are vague, and not identical. Still, the general notion of greater or lesser roundaboutness is meaningful, and putting numbers on it is a subsidiary issue. The general price level and price-level change are vague concepts also, but they can usefully be estimated. Just as the calculated period of production depends on the interest rate itself (as we shall see), so the measured price level and even its change may depend on the change itself: price inflation may be allowed in interest rates, boosting costs and prices of waiting-intensive goods and perhaps other prices and wages, so affecting the measured level or change of prices.

7.4 An Average Period

Artificially simple cases will sharpen the concepts of average periods of investment and production. Not until later do we again take explicit account of waiting and interest. Inputs are primary factor services like labor and land use. Inputs of intermediate goods like materials are either assumed to be zero or resolved into the primary factor services that they embody. Outputs are final consumer goods or services, not materials requiring further processing and not durable goods whose services emerge only over time. Housing services, for example, not houses, count as output here. In the upcoming diagrams, time runs from left to right.

In Case 1, inputs are invested all at once, when labor plants a crop. The consumer good appears at once at the end of the growing season, with no further effort required for harvesting. The average period over which labor is tied up in the growing crop is simply the calendar period (Fig. 7.1).

In Case 2, inputs are invested in a capital good all at once. A flow of consumer services begins immediately and continues until the good wears

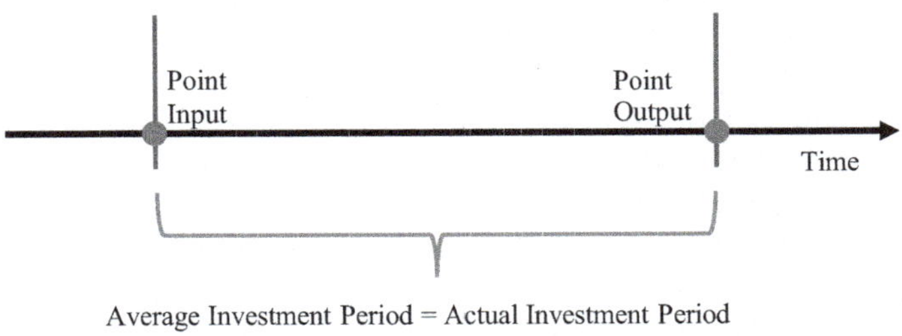

Fig. 7.1 Case 1: Point input, point output

out. Here and in the cases to follow, flows, whether of input or output, are distinguished from one-time events; they continue at a steady rate until ceasing entirely. Here the output flow begins immediately after the one-time inputs and continues until the end of the period. On average, as the diagram shows, the inputs are tied up as unripened output for half of the entire period (neglecting waiting and interest)(Fig. 7.2).

In Case 3, factor services are employed at a steady rate in building a capital good, which then yields all its consumer services in one big bang, as in a fireworks display. The earliest input is tied up for the entire period and the latest input for essentially no time at all; so, on average inputs are tied up for one-half of the entire period(Fig. 7.3).

In Case 4, factors are employed at a steady rate in constructing, say, an apartment building. The earliest input occurs at the beginning and the latest at the end of the construction period. No further inputs are required for maintenance or otherwise. The flow of housing services begins when construction is complete, continues steadily through the life of the building, and ends when it suddenly becomes useless. On average,

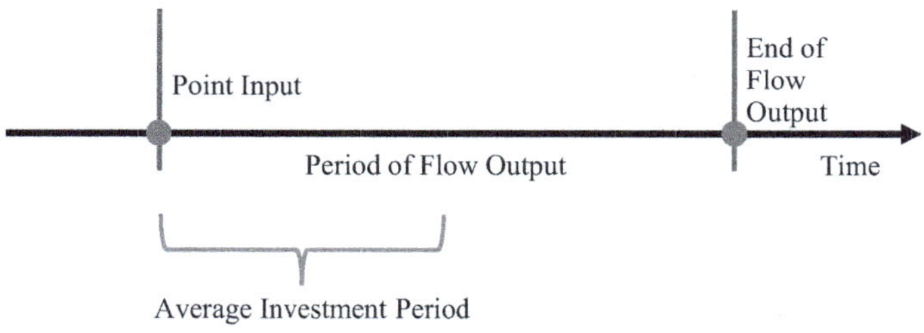

Fig. 7.2 Case 2: Point input, flow output

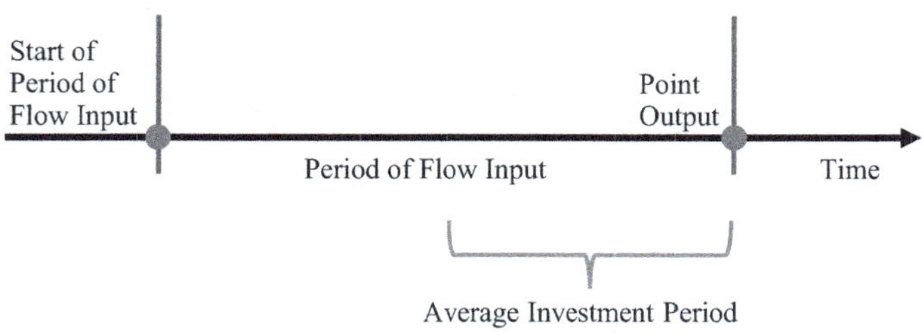

Fig. 7.3 Case 3: Flow input, point output

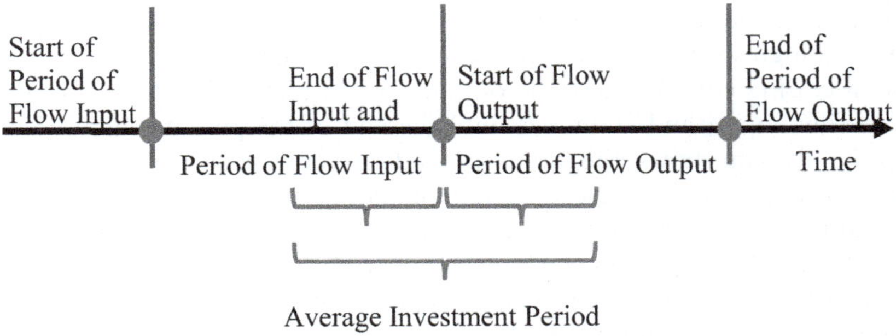

Fig. 7.4 Case 4: Flow input, flow output

inputs are tied up for half the construction period plus half the service period, or, in total, for one-half the entire period elapsing between earliest input and final output(Fig. 7.4).

The cases shown here owe any expository and heuristic value to their simplicity. They assume that all inputs are primary or original factors rather than materials resulting from earlier and unanalyzed productive processes. They assume away any further use of primary factors to operate and maintain the capital good during its period of service. They abstract from waiting itself and postpone questions of how it counts as a primary factor and how its price, the interest rate, might enter into calculating an average period.

In a flow-input/flow-output example, many Case 4 projects are going on at once: buildings are being constructed, yield their services, and are abandoned. In this steady state, new buildings just replace ones wearing out. The stock of buildings holds steady, and the flow of inputs into construction just matches the outflow of housing services. For definiteness, we suppose that each building is constructed over a 2-year period with three units of input each year; then, it yields two units transformed into housing services for each of 3 years. For simplicity, we assume that maintenance costs are zero or that the housing services are measured net of such costs. Over the entire 5 years from start of construction to abandonment of the building, each project transforms six units of factor-service (apart from waiting) into housing services. Output, as just implied, is measured in number of units of its input.

Table 7.1 shows several such projects echeloned in time. The end of year 5 brings the aforementioned steady state. Input and output flows

Table 7.1 Projects echeloned in time

Year	*Project A*			*Project B*			*Project C*			*Project D*			*Project E*			*Project F*			*Projects A-F*		
	I	*O*	*S*	*I*	*O*	*S*	*I*	*O*	*S*	*I*	*O*	*S*	*I*	*O*	*S*	*I*	*O*	*S*	*I*	*O*	*S*
1	3		3																3		3
2	3		6	3		3													6		9
3		2	4	3		6	3		3										6	2	13
4		2	2		2	4	3		6	3		3							6	4	15
5		2	0		2	2		2	4	3		6	3		3				6	6	15
6					2	0		2	2		2	4	3		6	3		3	6	6	15
7								2	0		2	2		2	4	3		6	...	6	...
8											2	0		2	2		2	4	...	6	...
9														2	0		2	2	...	...	...
10																	2	0	...	...	...
11																			...	...	...

I = Flow of Input during the year, O = flow of output during the year, S = end of year stock of inputs that have been embodied in capital equipment and not yet disembodied as output. For assumptions, see the text.

correspond at six units per year, and the stock of inputs embodied in buildings and not yet disembodied as housing services is steady at 15 units. An infinitely wide page would show figures for projects G, H, I, J, and so on and show this steady state continuing indefinitely. The dots in the cells of the totals columns represent figures that would be the same as the figures just above them if only the table could include the figures for the additional projects, each project beginning and eventually terminating 1 year later than the one named with the preceding letter of the alphabet.

7.5 Simultaneity and the Bathtub Theorem

In our steady state, six units of input are employed and six units emerge as housing services each year. It would be misleading, though, to say that input and output are simultaneous. Production has not become timeless (despite a formulation sometimes imputed to J. B. Clark and Frank Knight, reviewed later in this section). Each year's housing services result from inputs applied earlier, not currently; and current inputs emerge as housing services only later, not immediately. As in our Case 4, the average investment period of inputs or the production period of housing services is half of the input period plus half the output period, that is, half of the combined 5-year period, 2.5 years. This average period is equal to the stock of embodied inputs divided by the flow of inputs or outputs: 15 units divided by six units per year is equal to 2.5 years. The dimensions are correct: dividing units by units per year yields a quotient in years. Note that we still postpone the recognition of waiting itself and interest on it.

Merely keeping the steady state steady requires continually investing resources corresponding to resources being disinvested as housing services. Steadiness requires that some people, instead of consuming the equivalent of disinvested resources, continue waiting for the ripening into services of the resources invested in the time-consuming process. Without this reinvestment, the housing stock would shrink; negative net investment is perfectly conceivable and historically experienced.

The stock-to-flow ratio is intuitively appealing = as a measure of average elapsed time. If 20 customers enter and 20 leave a post office each hour and if five are inside at each instant, a customer remains in the post office 1/4 hour on average (five persons divided by 20 persons per hourl/4 hour; cf. Shackle 1962, p. 203). If one pound of meat goes into a grinder and one pound of ground meat comes out every minute and if two pounds are always in the grinder, meat remains in it two minutes on average (Lerner 1944/1947, pp. 325–327, gives further examples). With reference to an obvious example and "in honor of the hydraulic engineers, who use it all the time," Robert Dorfman (August 1959, p. 353) named this stock-flow-time relation, which was originally formulated by Kenneth E. Boulding (1946, p. 127) the "bathtub theorem."

The solera method of producing fine sherry offers a real world example. The wine master periodically pours new sherry into the top cask of an interconnecting series and draws an equal but matured amount from the bottom cask. For our purposes, we ignore evaporation. The contents of the solera are analogous to a stock of capital goods being continuously just maintained, with inflows of resources and outflows of products overlapping. The analogy also reminds us that capital theory need not distinguish between capital goods and goods in process.

A drop of sherry remains within the solera for an average time calculated by dividing the solera's total contents by the rate of flow through it. This "bathtub" relation remains unimpaired by the facts that each liter withdrawn from the solera probably contains at least a fraction of a drop of the sherry put in at the very beginning, that some fraction of a drop of new sherry flows directly through and emerges very soon, and that some sherry whirls around indefinitely without ever emerging during the life of the solera.

That last fact does not imply an indefinitely long period of investment or production, although some paradoxers allegedly so argue, particularly for a complex modern economy as a whole. Nor, as also in the example of apartment buildings, does the steady state mean that the process is instantaneous or timeless. Waiting for results, on the contrary, remains an essential element in producing fine sherry. The amount of waiting involved, whose dimension is quantity or value held through time, is measured by the amount of sherry in the solera multiplied by the average time it remains there.[3] If a solera of the same size had twice as rapid a rate of inflow and outflow, its output would be sherry averaging only half as old.

When we recognize that matured sherry is not the same thing as new sherry, we are on the way to facing the real world's great physical diversity of inputs, outputs, inventories, and capital goods. Calculation of an average investment period requires measuring stocks and flows in a common unit, as in the apartment example; and in practice that unit can only be money. Their ratio, though, still is units of time alone.

One complication of taking into account waiting itself as a factor in a stock-flow ratio is the necessity of supposing that all of it is performed by channeling resources through stocks of capital and intermediate goods rather than partly through such intangibles as training and research. Alternatively, all human capital and research would somehow have to be measured as a stock and included in the numerator of the ratio.

This fact that recent inputs embody earlier inputs suggests why a stock-flow calculation of the average investment period of primary resources may apply better to an entire economy than to an individual line of production.[4] A particular industry might hold relatively small stocks of capital goods and inventories. Yet, if it bought materials in whose production capital goods and inventories had been highly important and if we

[3] The measure is only approximate because we have not yet faced the waiting-for-waiting or compound-interest problem.

[4] Even the concept of "an entire economy" is problematic. Perhaps in estimating the average period of production of one country's economy we should consider not the foreign waiting embodied in its imports but rather the domestic waiting embodied in the exports traded for imports. Still, these questions do not make comparing the degrees of roundaboutness of different national economies meaningless.

could probe beyond those intermediate goods to the embodied primary factors, we might find that the industry's final output (as distinguished from its own processes) was waiting-intensive after all. The average period for which primary resources were tied up in producing its output might even be longer than the comparable period for most other consumer goods and services. In a modern economy, as Eucken observes (1954, p. 218), only a small part of the time taken for the "ripening" of factors into final consumer products elapses within individual enterprises. But this fact does not invalidate the concept of ripening time.

Our solera calculation, for example, considers only the average time for transforming new into matured sherry. It does not probe deeper into the primary resources that went into tending vines, making tools, and training workers, nor into the further resources required in shipping and marketing before the sherry reaches its ultimate consumers. The simplified calculation does not yield the average period for which primary factors, in the fullest sense of "primary," are tied up until they yield ultimate pleasure for consumers.

For such reasons, assessment of waiting in an individual industry might better focus on its value added than on its gross production. Although its stock/flow ratio does not adequately measure the waiting directly and indirectly embodied in its output, we can at least in principle compare industries by how much further waiting they embody in their products—how much they add to the waiting already embodied in the materials bought, trained employees hired, technical knowledge employed, and the like. The concepts of roundaboutness and period of production serve to compare alternative production methods in a firm or industry, degrees of capitalist development, waiting-intensities of different national economies, and so forth.

Whether land is included in the numerator of the capital/output ratio affects the length of the calculated period of production, of course, but possibly not comparative rankings. If we count land services among the original factors, like labor, then it seems straightforward to leave land itself out of the calculation, just as we do not ordinarily count a stock of labor as a capital good.

A simplifying assumption particularly awkward to give up is the steady state process. With production growing or shrinking and inflow greater or less than outflow, the stock-flow ratio becomes ambiguous. The bathtub theorem applies most straightforwardly when the inflows of original services and outflows of final goods and services are equal in value, the flow of waiting itself being counted in a way not yet fully explained. Given that equality, the calculated average period of production is the same whether the inflow rate or outflow rate appears in the denominator. But when inflow rate exceeds outflow rate, the stock of capital and intermediate goods is growing and the average period is rising; when outflow rate exceeds inflow rate, the stock is shrinking and the average period falling. In both cases, the periods calculated with inflow rate and with outflow rate could be regarded as limits to the period at an instant of time.

When inflow and outflows are not equal, one might consider a period calculated with an average of the two rates. A period so calculated, however, is not identical with an average of two periods calculated separately with the inflow and outflow rates–but that is a detail of mere arithmetic. Furthermore, when the inflow rate exceeds the outflow rate, the inflow-calculated period is shorter than the outflow-calculated period, and conversely for the opposite inequality of flows. But how could we know whether inflow units in excess of those in the steady state of equal inflows and outflows remain embodied in the stock more or less briefly than the steady state units? Anyway, the issue here is which–if either–of two conventions for calculation is the more useful.

Less troublesome is the picture of outflow exceeding inflow and the outflow-calculated period being shorter than the inflow-calculated period. Then the capital stock is being run down, and embodied resources are being disembodied. In the previous inflow-exceeding-outflow case, the additional productive units are being embodied for a long time compared with the time of their being embodied in the steady state. Think also of people entering the post office in excess of those leaving.

In the post office example of the bathtub theorem, if more or fewer people enter than leave, the number inside keeps changing. Not only the flow denominator but also the stock numerator seems troublesome. We are in trouble not only with the denominator but also with the numerator in the bathtub theorem. Could the very concept of period of production fail except in the steady state?

No. The stock is rising when inflow is greater than outflow and falling when outflow is greater than inflow, although not without limit. More importantly, at any instant the stock has some definite value free of a time dimension. The flow in the denominator, or some sort of average of flows, does have a time dimension, however; so that the bathtub ratio itself has the correct dimension of a length of time.

If national income per year is the denominator of the bathtub-theorem ratio, what capital and intermediate goods should be included in and what ones excluded from the numerator? Should consumer durables like refrigerators be included and their services count in the flow of final output? Net investment in capital goods conventionally counts as part, but only part, of national income, while disinvestment counts negatively. Nevertheless, stock numerator and flow denominator both still have a positive sign; and the bathtub calculation still gives a time period.

We shouldn't overemphasize the many such fringe complications. Although the period of production is admittedly a fuzzy notion, it and the bathtub way of estimating it can have heuristic value. International comparisons can mean *something* if the national figures are similarly compiled. Even without actual measurements and calculations, qualitative observation may permit rough-and-ready comparisons.

The concept of period of production shows how time is intimately involved even in steady processes, ones loosely called "timeless" because inputs and outputs occur at the same time. This view, as we indicated earlier, has sometimes been imputed to J. B. Clark and Frank Knight,[5] perhaps unfairly; Knight (1936, p. 456) merely recognized that in a stationary highly developed economy, inputs and outputs are simultaneous—in a sense. In the bathtub example, we wouldn't say that each person enters and leaves the post office at the same instant, transacting business in zero time.

[5] Rothbard (1962 p. 402); Rothbard, Introduction to Fetter (1977, p. 6). Kirzner (1966, pp. 76–82), summarizes and criticizes Knight's supposed view of the simultaneity of input and output in equilibrium. Knight defines production so that "actions taken currently exclusively in order to ensure the continued flow during the *future* of the product service, are to be viewed as producing the flow of product service during the *current* period" (Kirzner 1966, p. 77). According to Fetter (1977, p. 271), J. B. Clark "arrived at an explicit denial of any significance for time in the explanation of interest. It is the function of (pure) capital, he declared, to synchronize the outlay of labor and its fruits, and he attempted to prove this by an argument palpably fallacious." Clark's example of simultaneously planting and harvesting trees diverts attention toward an apparent technological datum and away from people's assessments of and choices about future wants and needs. We can indeed say that people "are producing and consuming simultaneously, but there is simply no point in saying it!" (Garrison in Caldwell 1990, p. 143). They are consuming the output of previous inputs while supplying inputs for later outputs.

7.6 Still More Doubts About the Period of Production

Menger and Böhm-Bawerk thought that the prehistory of production is irrelevant—for example, how long the wood for a fence had been growing or whether some of the iron in a knife might have been mined in Roman times. Menger thought so on the grounds that choosing among production processes is necessarily oriented toward the future.[6] Böhm-Bawerk judged prehistory irrelevant on the grounds that inputs from the remote past are minuscule. If decision-makers cannot have some purpose in consulting history, it is irrelevant to choice and to theorizing about it (Garrison in Caldwell 1990, p. 137).

Böhm-Bawerk was less concerned with calculating a period of production than with the time dimension of the structure of stages of production (Garrison in Caldwell 1990, p. 140). Yet he did try to capture his insight into the relation between maturity classes of capital goods with the single number of an average period. Worrying about how to calculate it led him "away from Menger's forward-looking vision in which (subjective) values are to be gauged by entrepreneurs. ... Examples of production processes which allowed for the calculation of the period of production required the assumption of a steady state, which virtually robbed the production period of its economic relevance." Böhm-Bawerk opened the door to the mistaken Clark-Knight-type criticisms (Garrison in Caldwell 1990, p. 141).

Should we dismiss the question of periods of investment or production because "bygones are bygones" in economics? Should we reject asking how existing capital goods came to exist and simply take them as a historical datum, supposedly like land?[7] In one sense, the slogan is good advice. Once a capital good exists, its history and cost are irrelevant to its best use now. It is what it is, regardless of whether it was deliberately created or descended magically from Heaven. Constructing it may have proved

[6] Israel Kirzner has echoed this emphasis on planning for the future. "[C]apital goods ... fall neatly into place in a *teleological* framework. They are the interim goals aimed at in earlier plans; they are the means toward the attainment of still further ends envisaged by the earlier plans" (1966, p. 38). Much confusion can be avoided by resolutely referring to the *plans* behind economic events. Waiting, capital, and capitalistic production must be understood as aspects of exchange across time (pp. 73–74).

[7] Knight likes to deny any fundamental difference between capital goods and land (e.g., 1944, pp. 33–34; 1936, pp. 453–455; 1938, pp. 74, 77).

an expensive mistake, but regrets should not bar using it now to salvage as much value as possible beyond the costs of operating it.

Economic and business history is a tool for the economist's understanding and for business decisions. Contemplating past investments and their outcomes provides information for economic understanding and future decisions. The background and origins of existing capital goods enter into judgments about their continuing maintenance, replacement, and construction. This is one way capital goods remain distinct from land in the sense of sheer space and other irreproducible gifts of nature.

Several critics apparently think that their quibbles about the period of investment or production discredit the entire part of capital and interest theory that the concept is meant to illuminate. Frank Knight dwells on the impossibility of measuring the time elapsed since primary factors were first used in the indirect production of a consumer good or service.[8]

An hour of labor performed today may go toward building machines that will be used for making tools for constructing factories in which other machines will be built for making builders' tools that will be used in constructing apartment buildings many years in the future; and people may still be living in those buildings decades or centuries from now. How much time will elapse, then, before an hour of labor invested today has fully "ripened" into the last bit of housing services to which it will ever contribute? Productive factors, capital goods, and modern industrial processes defy unambiguous classification by stages of remoteness from the ultimate consumer. For example, consider a floor-polishing machine that might be employed either in a research laboratory or by a house-cleaning service.

In even a simpler example of time-measurement difficulties, Crusoe, instead of chasing fish with his bare hands, uses a stone for many years. Isn't the labor spent on picking it up invested for a ridiculously long period, discrediting the concept? Well, so insignificant a fraction of total labor directly and indirectly applied to fishing carries negligible weight in calculating an average period. If picking up the stone, though lengthening the average period only extremely slightly, nevertheless greatly increases

[8] Conard (1959, p. 38n.) gives citations to the long controversy over these matters between Knight and Nicholas Kaldor, including Kaldor (1937); see also Lutz (1967, pp. 97–99, 106–107). Conard comments on Knight's quip that a production or investment period must be either zero or infinite.

the fish catch over the bare-hands method, that fact would simply illustrate the point that when little or none of a factor is used in some process, "first" units of it added may have a much higher marginal productivity than additional units added to already ample amounts. The law of diminishing returns applies even to waiting.

These considerations answer what Walter Eucken called the supposed problem of "endless regress and progress." The relevant concept is some sort of average period of investment of resources or production of goods, not some fantastically long absolute period.[9] Even if some of the factor services now being disembodied into final consumer goods or services were originally embodied in capital or intermediate goods thousands of years ago, and even if some of the primary factors being applied today will yield their last bit of consumer service many thousands of years hence, the average investment period of resources and production period of goods is finite. Similarly, the sum to infinity of a diminishing geometric progression is finite.

Wassily Leontief's input-output system offers another analogy. Steel goes into building ships, while ships transport iron ore for making steel.

[9] Even if Böhm-Bawerk did not satisfactorily handle the problem of endless regress and progress, he did at least explicitly face it (1959, II, pp. 86ff.).

Blaug maintains that the type of average contemplated—arithmetic mean, geometric mean, or whatever—is not important. The purpose of the concept of average period "is served just as well by one mean as by another so long as we do not switch means in the middle of the comparison" (1962, p. 468, 1985, p. 514). Hayek (1936/1946, pp. 362–363) makes a more general comment. Referring to the periods over which different factors are invested, he maintains that it is possible to conceive of a society's capital goods in terms of waiting periods, even though describing their diversities cannot be collapsed into a measurable single average period. This impossibility does not banish time from capital theory. Such an overall measurement would be irrelevant to real world economic decisions, anyway. It is at the margin of growth of each individual industry and firm that the question arises whether extending investment would be productive enough to justify tying up resources until their returns accrue.

Despite this whirlpool character of production[10] and despite the infinite series involved in the iterative computation of, say, the labor directly and indirectly used in making an automobile, the total amount of labor used per automobile is finite. Recall, also, the sherry solera. The average time a molecule of liquid remains in a reservoir is meaningful, even though we cannot date the entry and exit of specific molecules (Dorfman 1959, pp. 367–368); Paul Samuelson's "perpetual stew" can have a finite average age (Blaug 1962, p. 470, 1985 pp. 515–516.).

Quibbles about the supposed "infinite" length of investment or production periods exaggerate the importance of infinitesimal bits of past primary factor services and of future consumer goods and services (Eucken 1954, p. 250). As already mentioned, paradoxers sometimes argued that if the production period is not infinite, then it is zero. In a continuous process, with all inflows of resources, stocks of capital and intermediate goods, and outflows of goods and services remaining steady, no time elapses between production and consumption.[11] But how strained such a notion of simultaneity is! Decisions about the timing of consumption are involved even in keeping the stationary state stationary. People could consume more lavishly in the present and near future if they diverted resources away from maintaining and replacing capital goods, all at the cost of losing more consumption in the more distant future.

[10] The whirlpool character bars strictly classifying goods into Menger's "orders." Lowest-order goods are closest to final consumption, like food on the table; highest-order goods are remote from consumption, like iron ore or machine-tool factories. An extreme example of a high-order good is one of the huge machines that bore tunnels through mountains and under water. The tunnels themselves have long useful lives; and although they may be partly employed for pleasure travel, they are also used to transport equipment and materials for productive purposes.

Furthermore, as Alfred Marshall observed, a good may belong to several orders at once. A train carrying people on a pleasure trip is in that respect a first-order good. If at the same time the train is carrying consumer goods and machinery of different kinds, it is also a good of second and higher orders (Marshall 1920/1947, pp. 64–65n.). Although the concept of "orders" may have some slight heuristic and pedagogic usefulness, it is irrelevant to the supply of and demand for waiting.

Because of the greater time element, decisions about producing high-order goods are presumably more interest-rate-sensitive, by and large, than decisions about consumer goods.

[11] J. B. Clark, Leon Walras, and Frank Knight have been interpreted as saying something like this (e.g. Knight 1936, pp. 455–456). On Clark, see Blaug (1985, pp. 519–520); on Clark and Knight, Dorfman (1959, pp. 354–355, 363); on all three, Kuenne (1971, p. 66).

On a familiar if exaggerated interpretation, J. B. Clark and Knight conceived of capital as a kind of aggregate mass continually being reincarnated piecemeal into new specific capital goods and carrying with it a presumption of being forever maintained or replaced.[12] Such a view shoves aside questions about what guides decisions about accumulating, maintaining, or consuming the capital stock.

This seems to be Eucken's chief complaint against adherents of such a view. From the facts of "infinite" regress and progress and the whirlpool character of modern production, with outputs of some processes being inputs to themselves or to other processes, they conclude that the time element is incomprehensible ("das Zeitmoment sei unfassbar") and consider the matter either hopeless or settled.[13] In quibbling about the period of production, in asserting the simultaneity of production and consumption, and in describing capital as inherently self-perpetuating, such critics do worse than merely spread confusion. Unintentionally, they disparage attention to questions like the following: How, in principle and although only roughly, might the waiting-intensity or degree of roundaboutness of an economy's production processes be estimated? What determines that intensity and any increase or decrease in it? Why are some of the outputs of resources that had been invested earlier plowed back as inputs into production? How is waiting productive, and why is it scarce and costly? What determines the interest rate? However, Eucken does not use the concept of waiting (1954, pp. 250–251; cf. pp. 208–210).

[12] E.g., Knight (1936, pp. 456–460). Stigler (1941, pp. 308–315), and Blaug (1985, pp. 519–520) review these ideas of Clark; Kaldor (1937, pp. 211–212), reviews those of Knight. But of course, Knight did not believe that the capital stock does automatically maintain itself; it can be built up or allowed to deteriorate.

[13] Eucken (1954, pp. 250–251). "If one thinks of an economy in which the problem of temporal structure is solved and if one accordingly assumes that 'real capital' always renews itself in the same material form *[Sachgestalt]*, one then arrives at the result that this problem of temporal structure is solved. One finds the same as one has previously hidden in the assumption" (referring to Albert Hahn's methodological remark about children overjoyed to discover objects that they themselves have hidden). Such playing with concepts *[Gedankenspiel]* leaves economic reality unanalyzed (1954, p. 208).

7.7 Waiting Itself as an Element in the Average Period

No longer can we postpone a thorny problem. If waiting itself counts as a factor of production, then it too should enter into calculating average investment or production periods. Otherwise, the flow of output value would exceed the flow of input value. Even for a process neither growing nor shrinking, the bathtub-theorem calculation of the average period as the stock-flow ratio would become ambiguous. The stock-inflow ratio would overestimate, and the stock-outflow ratio would underestimate that period (Lerner 1968, pp. 273–274). Waiting itself, therefore, must be counted among the factor inflows.

Shackle, who supplied bathtub-theorem examples, recognizes the problem:

> the "quantity of capital" corresponding to a given "length of the average period of production" will vary when the interest-rate itself varies: for a "packet of input" must be conceived of as growing in value at compound interest all the time it is "embodied" in the capital structure. Thus we lose the simple and direct link between quantity of capital and interest-rate, and are reduced to extremely complicated mathematical analysis for the sake of a result which has little realistic relevance even when it is established (1962, p. 205).

Suppose that labor is embodied in capital and intermediate goods only in year 1 and that the final product emerges in year 5. If plans are successful, waiting adds something to the value of the goods in process by year 2. Between year 2 and year 3 their owner ties up value in the further ripening not only of the original labor but also of the value already added by waiting. In each successive year until the end of the process, the owner waits for the further ripening of waiting already performed. At each instant, the value of the stock whose ultimate transformation into consumer goods and services is being waited for depends, other things being equal, on the productivity of the waiting already performed. The greater the rate of growth in the value of this stock, the larger is the element of waiting and of waiting for waiting. Something like compound interest is at work. The rate of compounding itself affects the calculation of the period of investment or production.

Nevertheless, Robert Dorfman shows how, in principle, to calculate the investment period of waiting and other factors averaged together. Before continuing, however, and to focus attention on waiting, we lump all other factor services together as "labor." The use of human capital, including the results of training and experience, fits into this stretched category; so do the benefits of research. As for land, what counts in the calculation is the flow and the embodied stock of its services, just as labor means labor services. Here, however, labor and land services are lumped together; and we need not face the question whether land itself, as the pure gift of nature, and perhaps also as manmade improvements, should be counted as a capital good.

Continuing with Dorfman, we suppose, provisionally, that the average investment periods of labor and waiting services have been calculated separately with the bathtub theorem. For the overall average period, we want a weighted average of these two separate periods. It's worth noting that readers should remain alert to the scarcely avoidable homophones "wait" and "weight." The weights are flows of value per year—prices times quantities—of labor and of waiting. With labor (in the stretched sense mentioned) and waiting counted as the only factors, the sum of their flows of value is national income. National income per year is the denominator in an expression for the weighted average period. Partly for the sake of parallelism, we avoid here the near-standard symbols for wage and interest rates.

The symbols used are:

F_{L} = the flow of labor per year; dimension: worker-hours per year.
S_{L} = the stock of labor embodied in capital and intermediate goods; dimension: hours of labor.
F_{W} = the flow of waiting per year; dimension: dollar-years per year.
S_{W} = the stock of embodied waiting; dimension: dollar-years.
P_{L} = the price of labor; dimension: dollars per hour.
P_{W} = the price of waiting; dimension: dollars per dollar-year, which reduces to the pure number of percentages per year.

In the numerator of the expression for the weighted average period, the labor term is the labor investment period (calculated by the bathtub theorem) times the value of the labor flow per year, which is:

$$\left(\frac{S_L}{F_L}\right) \times P_L F_L = S_L P_L = \text{the value of embodied labor stock}$$

The waiting term in the numerator is the waiting investment period (also calculated by the bathtub theorem) times the value of the waiting flow per year, which is:

$$\left(\frac{S_W}{F_W}\right) \times P_W F_W = S_W P_W = \text{the value of embodied waiting stock}$$

Therefore, the complete expression for the weighted average of the separate labor and waiting periods is:

$$\frac{S_L P_L + S_W P_W}{F_L P_L + F_W P_W} = \text{the total value of the stock of factor services}$$

embodied in capital goods and other goods in process

dividied by national income

The dimension is dollars divided by dollars per year, simplifying to years.

Equivalently, the weights may be interpreted as shares of national income, Y, earned by labor and by waiting. The overall average period of production is the average period of embodiment of labor times labor's share of Y plus the average period of embodiment of waiting times waiting's share of Y:

$$\left(\frac{S_L}{F_L}\right) \times \frac{F_L P_L}{Y} + \left(\frac{S_W}{F_W}\right) \times \frac{F_W P_W}{Y} = \frac{S_L P_L + S_W P_W}{Y}$$

= the total value of embodied stocks of labor and waiting

= the total value of capital and other goods in process,

all divided by national income

(the total value of the annual labor and waiting flows)

We did not need to know just what we might mean by separate embodied stocks of labor and waiting; we did not need to calculate separate investment periods of labor and waiting after all. The bathtub theorem works for the economy as a whole. Dorfman justifiably claims to have carried out an "Alexandrian stroke."[14] We also did not need to, and could not, distinguish between investment and production periods for the whole economy. In the calculation, income earned by waiting should be evaluated by the interest rate understood not just in the narrow sense but also in the most stretched sense of an economywide discount of the future.

Although the estimated ratio has the denomination of units of time, its stock numerator and flow denominator simply cannot be expressed in physical terms; the whole calculation is shot through with money prices. The amount of value tied up in waiting for the further fruition of waiting already embodied in a physically specified productive process depends on the growth rate of the process. Writers at least as early as Wicksell explicitly noted that the rate of interest affects the calculated length of a physically specified process.[15]

Perhaps the most plausible rationale of the exercise just reviewed is that it justifies roughly estimating an economy's degree of roundaboutness or its rank among countries by how abundant its capital goods, broadly conceived, are in relation to income. A developed economy is unmistakably more roundabout than a primitive one whose members scratch out a living with the simplest tools.

Which way does the interest rate affect the calculated length of an average period of production?[16] Whether it is legitimate to just postulate a change in the interest rate without specifying its cause is a question faced

[14] Dorfman (1959, esp. pp. 360–363), with notation changed and some interpretation supplied here. For the unconvinced reader, Dorfman provides a direct computation in a Mathematical Appendix (pp. 367–372). "It is nice," he concludes, "that this elaborate calculation is really unnecessary."

[15] Wicksell (1934, vol. I, p. 184), Blaug (1962, Chapter 12, esp. pp. 468–469; 1985, Chapter 12, esp. pp. 514–515). Dorfman (1959) makes this dependence on the interest rate explicit in his mathematical appendix but does not comment on it.

[16] According to Blaug (1985, p. 515), "[a] lower rate of interest immediately shortens the measured average period of production, even if production processes have not changed, because it lowers the weights attached to earlier inputs." Actually, the matter is not that simple. A case is conceivable for which the calculated total period declines as the interest rate rises. Waiting for the ripening of the interest-increments to the value of labor invested at a definite time occurs after that time, and those increments are waited for over shorter periods than the labor itself. The larger they are because of a high interest rate, therefore, the more weight they carry in shortening the average investment period. One

in Chapters 5 and 8, which adopt Don Patinkin's distinction between individual experiments and market experiments. Possibly the public's time preference has changed. Meanwhile, we return to the expression for the weighted average period:

$$\frac{S_L P_L + S_W P_W}{F_L P_L + F_W P_W}$$

Its partial derivative with respect to the interest rate P_W, for whatever that may be worth, is an expression whose denominator is an inherently positive squared term and whose numerator is.

$P_L \times (F_L S_W - F_W S_L)$. Since the individual terms are nonnegative, the sign of $F_L S_W - F_W S_L$, and, equivalently, whether $\frac{S_W}{F_W} > \frac{S_L}{F_L}$, is decisive for the sign of the derivative. The two ratios are the average investment periods of waiting and labor.

In words, the overall average period of production changes in the same or the opposite direction as the interest rate according to whether the period of investment of waiting exceeds or falls short of the labor investment period. An increased interest rate raises the weight of the waiting period in the overall average period and so pulls the overall average up or down according to whether the waiting period was longer or shorter than the labor period.

As symmetry of the symbols suggests, much the same applies to labor. An increased wage rate raises the weight of the labor period in the overall average period and so pulls the overall average up or down according to whether the labor period was longer or shorter than the waiting period. The economywide period changes in the same direction as the wage rate if the labor period exceeds the waiting period.

These results depend on assuming, questionably, that the individual periods of production of labor and waiting are given and that what is at stake is only the weights accorded to each in calculation of the economywide average. The arithmetic does not take into account what might have made the interest rate change—perhaps a change in thrift—or of price-influenced changes in production methods.

If the economy employed only a single factor measured in purely physical terms, its average investment period would be mathematically

might even imagine a case in which the calculated period first rises and then declines as the interest rate rises.

unaffected by its price. In the real world, the amount of waiting in a physically specified process depends on its own price in a way that is not true of labor. The flow and stock of waiting simply cannot be measured in physical terms; its amounts are expressible only in value terms and are affected, even arithmetically, by the interest rate.

In the real world, the interest rate, decisions about production processes, and whatever else affects the average investment or production period are all determined endogenously in a system of general interdependence. Their interdependence poses no problem for the individual saver, investor, or entrepreneur, who can regard the market interest rate as a datum and need not worry about any average period.

Whether an economist gains any insight from the concept of an interest-rate-dependent average period may be a matter of personal disposition. It is all too easy, however, to reject the concept of period of production and remain unaware of how much poorer one's insight would have been if one had never heard of it. Even this inherently fuzzy concept does foster insights, particularly into how waiting serves as a productive factor. To judge from how durable the concept is in the literature, many economists have thought so too.

7.8 The Crusonia Plant

Next, we consider a model seemingly designed to ridicule the concept of period of production. Frank Knight imagines a society, "Crusonia," where people have only one want, which is gratified by a single resource: a perennial plant growing naturally and "indefinitely at a constant (geometric) rate, except as new tissue is cut away for consumption." The plant "requires no cultivation or other care," and even any labor involved in gathering or eating it may be ignored. If consumption just keeps pace with the plant's growth, income and capital are constant, illustrating a stationary economy in its simplest form. If consumption falls short of the plant's growth for a while—if people save—the difference automatically increases the capital stock (Knight 1944, pp. 29–31, quotations from p. 30; cf. Dewey 1965, *passim*). "Investment consists solely of *not* eating all the cabbage" (Wright 1944, p. 335n.). Such an episode of positive saving and investment increases the plant's size, permitting consumption later to resume fully absorbing its growth, and at a higher level than before and without trenching on capital. Dissaving and disinvestment mean a splurge of consumption, reducing the plant's size and the level of consumption sustainable thereafter.

Knight emphasizes that "nothing in the nature of a 'production period' is present in the situation." Donald Dewey claims two merits for the Crusonia model (1965, pp. 199–215): besides making "precise delineation of the marginal productivity of investment" possible, it largely eliminates the period of production because "every act of investment yields a consumable product 'immediately'" (p. 199).

Yet even in this extreme case of supposedly simultaneous production and consumption, a period of production can indeed be meaningful. Except perhaps for some single act that initially brings a tiny Crusonia plant into existence, waiting is the *only* productive input. Its output is plant growth available for either consumption or investment.

Suppose that a minuscule amount of labor is invested to make a one unit plant only at the beginning of a first year. The plant grows at the rate (expressed as a decimal) of r per year with no further attention until after the end of n years, when it has grown to $(1 + r)^n$ units. From then on, the new growth is consumed at a portion r (also) per year of this now stabilized size, thus $r(1 + r)^n$ units. By the bathtub theorem, dividing this consumption flow per year into the plant's stabilized stock size yields $\frac{1}{r}$ years.

This result makes intuitive sense. The higher the growth-and-interest rate, the larger are the recent and relatively short-period increments of waiting. The higher the rate, the greater the weight accorded to the waiting; and the waiting comes after whatever initially launched the plant. A greater rate would give recent waiting more weight in determining the average period. At the other extreme, an r of zero, meaning that waiting is totally unproductive, yielding no growth and no consumption, would imply an infinite period: the tiny labor input that created the tiny plant in the first place and the subsequent huge inputs of waiting would never pay off in consumption.

But what about that tiny initial labor input? Isn't its investment period, entering into the overall average period of investment or production, extremely long? A partial answer, when waiting is productive, is that the initial labor input is infinitesimal relative to all the ongoing inputs of waiting. One still might object that the long investment period of the tiny initial input carries heavy weight in calculating the average period because that input acquires increasingly great value as time rolls on. That growing value pertains not to the initial labor input itself, however, but to the waiting, which is already recognized in calculating the plant's average period. Furthermore, the initial input does not all remain locked up in the plant. Along with the results of waiting, fragments of that tiny initial input in effect pass through the plant if any growth is cut off for consumption, like sherry through a solera.

Knight may have introduced his Crusonia plant to ridicule the period of production, but a closer look seems to support it.

7.9 Conclusion

Although roundaboutness and its measurement are vague ideas, they reinforce an intuitive grasp of capital and interest theory. As Lerner writes (1944/1947, p. 328): "The average period of production is a useful concept because it emphasizes the connection between capital equipment and the time aspect of production. It shows how capital is needed only because production takes time, and that more capital is needed when production takes place by methods that take a longer time"—"capital" here meaning "capital goods."

Even in the imaginary world of a static equilibrated economy with everything happening over and over again in the same old ruts—an "evenly rotating economy," as Mises called it, a world in which inputs were being applied and outputs being reaped simultaneously in the same old quantities—production is not timeless. A specific dated input does not emerge until later as a component of a specific dated output. Ongoing innovation is not—repeat not—necessary to maintain a demand for waiting as a factor of production.

The concept of period of production, even along with satisfactory and unsatisfactory suggestions about measuring it, serves, then, to emphasize the inevitable waiting-over-time element of production.

CHAPTER 8

Changes in Wants, Resources, and Technology

Often the question comes up of transferring goods or consumption (strictly, availability of or entitlements to consumption) from present-to-future or future-to-present. As Hirshleifer (1970, p. 130) puts it, the fundamental magnitudes of intertemporal choice are "dated consumptions." An individual or institution transfers consumption to the future by lending or otherwise acquiring financial claims or capital goods or human capital—in short, by waiting. Someone hastens consumption by borrowing, by liquidating financial claims or capital goods held, or by neglecting the repair of capital goods. Society as a whole transfers consumption possibilities toward the future by cutting back on current consumption and using the saved resources for future-oriented investment. It transfers consumption possibilities from future-to-present by cutting back investment and even by disinvesting through neglect of maintenance and replacement of existing capital goods. Time-transfers can also be accomplished by lending or borrowing abroad. The link between financial transactions and real activity shown in these examples justifies speaking simply, in the cases that follow, of present-to-future and future-to-present shifts of capacity to consume.

Since capital and intermediate goods and land raise the productivity of labor and other inputs working with them, their destruction and their magical appearance can serve as instructive, if extreme, examples of changes in resources.

L. B. Yeager and S. H. Hanke, *Capital, Interest, and Waiting*,
https://doi.org/10.1007/978-3-031-63398-0_8

Time enters in two ways into how an underlying change in thrift affects prices. The interest rate expresses the terms of exchange between present and future consumption in general. Also affected are the relative prices of goods of different waiting-intensities available at the same time, including intermediate goods still ripening into final goods and services.

Changes in time preference pose an easier challenge than changes in technology or resources. We postpone considering the latter types, since their effects are likelier to be ambiguous. Intermediate between changes in tastes and in technology are changes, as in law or social institutions, that lead people to act *as if* their tastes had changed.

8.1 A Change in Thrift

One of Böhm-Bawerk's grounds for interest is an expectation of rising incomes. Future goods will be more abundant than present goods; and in accordance with the principle of diminishing marginal utility, they have a lower marginal utility relative to present goods. Present goods command an agio.

Suppose that people become thriftier; their time preference weakens. An increased supply of waiting relative to demand reduces the interest rate and releases more resources for capital formation. Increased thrift makes future goods more abundant relative to present goods and so, one might think, reduces their relative marginal utility and raises the agio on present goods. This intuition is wrong. The change in relative quantities, marginal utilities, and values is the direct expression of increased thrift, which already means subjectively attributing reduced relative marginal utility to present goods. In a graph, the supply curve of waiting shifts rightward relative to demand.[1] The fall in the interest rate and the shift of goods toward the future merely moderate one another.

A person who becomes thriftier and cuts back on consumption does not necessarily reduce his demand for high-waiting-content goods in particular; however, such a cutback would also reduce the derived demand for waiting relative to the supply.

[1] The distinction between supply shift and demand shift can be fuzzy; what matters here is how the intersection of the curves moves. Sometimes it is stylistically convenient, but hardly more, to speak of supply of and demand for *saving* rather than *waiting*. Net saving means an increase, *dissaving* a decrease, in total waiting performed.

Apart, perhaps, from exceptions related to the paradoxes reviewed in Chapter 4 or to a backward-bending supply curve of waiting, increased thrift raises the stock of capital goods, whether through broadening or deepening. The reduced interest rate might even increase the average waiting content of goods produced, just as an increased supply of labor and reduced wage rate might increase the labor content of goods.

Because increased thrift supplies labor with more physical and human capital and intermediate goods to work with, labor's marginal productivity and real wage rise, as the sweep of economic history shows.[2] A more extended market becomes even more productive through increasing returns from a greater division of labor (Buchanan 1994, Chapter 2). Although thrift pushes the interest rate down, total interest income could go either way, depending on the elasticity of derived demand for waiting.

Such conclusions depend on normally functioning markets. Waiting is not being wasted as supposed by the Keynesian "paradox of thrift." The roughly equivalent disorder diagnosed as "oversaving" implies the discoordination of recession or depression, which is typically linked with a monetary disequilibrium.

Chapter 10 explores how monetary influences may modify the productivity-and-thrift determinants of the interest rate. The distinction between real and monetary factors explains why the term "relative," referring to intertemporal and intercommodity relative values, occurs so often in what follows.

8.2 Further Effects of Increased Thrift

When increased thrift reduces the interest rate, prices of bonds and other assets rise, and more so for durable and long-yielding assets than for ones quickly used up.[3] Rapidly growing young trees or livestock are longer-term assets than their already mature counterparts. They have a higher ratio of (undiscounted) future-to-present value than slow-growing

[2] Factors may be complementary or substitutable, depending on the magnitude of the changes involved. If the demand for restaurant meals increases, labor and equipment are complementary in responding to their derived demands; yet labor and equipment can substitute for one another in small adjustments.

[3] The following paragraphs draw inspiration from Alchian and Allen's (1972, Chapter 23) admirable exposition, which emphasizes the pervasiveness of interest in its more and less explicit guises.

things, and the reduced interest rate differentially raises their present value. Holding them becomes more profitable. Fewer yearling steers are slaughtered, raising veal's price relative to beef. Houses, like young steers, are relatively long-term assets; and the reduced interest rate raises their price and present value of their future housing services relative to their current rents.

The preferred period for allowing an asset's value to grow is the one at which its marginal growth rate no longer exceeds the interest rate. Marginal growth rates decline as growth periods lengthen. Like the general principle of diminishing marginal returns, this is not a logical truism but a well-supported empirical generalization.

A distinction between growth in value rather than physical amount may be important for investment in producing particular goods of changeable relative value, but it does not arise for trading present consumer goods and services in general for more of the same in the future. That tradeoff is the domain of interest theory. These conclusions are consistent with interpreting the interest rate both as the agio of present goods over future goods and as the ratio of values of services relative to their sources.

Besides a change in tastes, what might make bourbon whiskey rise in price relative to corn, wine relative to grapes, and consumer goods in general relative to their ingredients? Well, something may have raised the rate of physical transformation of goods in early stages of production into finished goods, like young cattle into beefsteak. If the interest rate has not yet risen much, funding these longer-term investments becomes more profitable, and arbitrage generalizes the rate change.

If people become thriftier and more willing to postpone consumption, would durable redwood or flimsy pine lumber—both intermediate rather than final goods—rise more in price, or, similarly, steel relative to wood? The answer is the more durable material, whose longer-lasting services make it a better vehicle for trading present for future consumption. Its price rise is analogous to that of long-term bonds. More generally, a decline in the interest rate means that future goods rise in price relative to present goods.

Suppose that two annuities have the same present value of $710 at an interest rate of 5 percent. One pays $100 a year for 9 years, the other $200 for 4 years. A shift of preferences toward longer annuities implies an increase in thrift and so a decline in the target interest rate. At say 3 percent, present values rise to $779 for the longer annuity and $743 for the shorter (Alchian and Allen 1967, p. 434; 1972, p. 462).

We distinguish between changes in relative price at a given time (veal and beef, wood and steel) and a change in relative values of present and future goods in general. Although future goods will not, when ready, have a higher waiting content than goods of physically the same type and method of production available now, present goods in general do command an agio over future goods corresponding to the interest paid or forgone.

8.3 A Decline in Thrift

Reduced thrift throws the conclusions about increased thrift into reverse. The marginal rate of time preference and the interest rate rise. So, accordingly, do target marginal rates of return on transforming present goods into future goods and of growth in value in transforming original factors into intermediate and capital goods and finally into consumer goods. Consumer goods rise in price relative to intermediate and capital goods, which in turn rise relative to primary, nonwaiting factors. Although future consumption has become cheaper in present consumption sacrificed, it is not true that, among goods available at the same time, ones produced by time-consuming processes fall in price relative to ones made by quick processes and relative to original factors. On the contrary, high-waiting-content goods (like matured wine and high-tech science-fiction movies) rise in price relative to lower-waiting-content goods (like vodka and poetry readings). All of this is consistent with increased impatience to consume.

Suppose that homeowners, becoming less thrifty, decide to sell, spend the money on consumption, and become renters. House prices fall and yields on rental housing rise. The price ratio of housing services to houses, one manifestation of the pervasive interest rate, rises. Or, in a similar example, landowners become less inclined to hold wealth and more eager for current consumption. Land prices fall and percentage yields on land rise. Generalized through substitution and arbitrage, higher interest rates restrain investment in manmade capital goods.

Such results with land suggest qualifying Hayek's remark (1936/1946, p. 369) that only in connection with nonpermanent resources do problems of capital arise—decisions whether or not to replace them. Decisions about whether or not to hold an asset affect the supply of waiting and the interest rate, whether or not the asset is permanent. An increase or decrease in thrift directed to landownership in particular still affects real capital formation positively or negatively.

8.4 Indirect Changes in Thrift

As already implied, much or most of the demand for waiting, as for other factors, derives from the demand for products embodying it. Suppose that tastes shift from goods of relatively low to goods of relatively high waiting content—from soft drinks or grapes to matured wine or aged brandy, for example, or from low-tech poetry readings to high-tech science-fiction movies or theme parks as entertainment. The derived demand for waiting increases; the interest rate rises. Compare how international trade in goods and services, not only in financial instruments, can tend to equalize interest rates among countries (recall Chapter 4). As usual, such effects may be too small to be noticeable in the large and complex real world.

8.5 Changes in Preferences among Financial Assets

Suppose that although thrift has not otherwise changed, liquidity preference intensifies: demand for assets shifts toward real cash balances and away from capital goods or from securities issued to finance them. With the nominal money supply unchanged, the price level falls, and the interest rate rises. As argued in Chapter 10, these effects could be mitigated by an increased volume of financial intermediation through near-moneys.

8.6 Changes as If in Tastes

In cases intermediate between changes in tastes and changes in resources or technology, tastes do not change exogenously. Instead, changed circumstances lead people to act "as if" their tastes had changed. Something—climate, law, insurance availability, social pressures, or whatever—reduces the perceived burdens and risks of owning a house, investing in rental property, or owning land. Nothing, however, has directly affected the supplies of and demands for waiting in other forms or for other purposes.

It would be wrong to suppose that since neither underlying thrift nor the productivity of waiting has changed, neither does the interest rate.

General interdependence rules out any one change alone. Options for carrying entitlements to consumption over into the future have expanded in one particular way. The nonpecuniary advantage of owning houses has increased. Even with underlying tastes unchanged, an expansion in the ways to exercise the willingness to wait depresses the explicit interest rate to some slight extent.

With rental property more attractive, its price rises. If more is constructed in response, rents tend to fall. Furthermore, because housing services are a relatively waiting-intensive good, their price responds to the eventually reduced cost of their waiting content. With rents down or property prices up or both, the services-to-sources value ratio, which is one manifestation of the interest rate, falls. Substitution and arbitrage generalize this fall to the price of waiting performed in other ways. Some people who might have performed waiting by owning their own homes now rent instead and seek some other outlet for their thrift.

Intuition might suggest that since neither the productivity of waiting nor the underlying propensity to supply it has changed, neither should its price. However, the overall reward for holding assets has two components (as wages and land rents frequently do also): an explicit pecuniary return and a positive or negative nonpecuniary return. Partial removal of the nonpecuniary burden, as supposed here, allows the explicit pecuniary return to fall.

If land ownership in particular becomes a more attractive outlet for thrift, Allais's reservations, explained in Chapter 3, become relevant (to theory if not to policy). Some owners, feeling richer from increased land values, may increase their consumption. Again, the analogy between land and collectibles is instructive. Increases or decreases in their prices constitute what is gain or loss from the private but not social point of view.

If saving and real capital formation were to push the marginal productivity of investment and the interest rate extremely low, capitalizing land rents at that rate would make land extremely valuable. This great landed wealth from the private point of view would encourage consumption and leave fewer resources for further capital construction. Already wealthy landowners would see little reason to restrain themselves from current enjoyments. Thus, the tentatively supposed saving and capital construction would not go so far as to push the marginal productivity of investment and the interest rate so low in the first place.

8.7 Changes in Resources or Technology

The effect of a change in technology or resources is harder to pin down than that of a well-specified change in tastes. Such a change requires considering not only itself but also the tastes on which it impinges. For this reason, the conclusions that follow are less definite than earlier ones. The point remains, however, that markets for waiting, as for other factors and products, do take account of changed conditions.

An increased subjective propensity to save to recoup destroyed wealth or income does not appear as a rightward shift of the supply curve of waiting in a diagram. An increased *propensity* need not mean an increased *volume* of saving supplied at a given interest rate, especially if the loss was concentrated on current income or wealth, leaving people less able to afford saving. Future relative enrichment might reduce people's propensity to save and raise the supply and demand determined interest rate. This increased agio on present goods would be consistent with their worsened relative or absolute scarcity. Besides efforts effectively to transfer resources from future-to-present, the increased interest rate or agio on scarce present goods would tighten the rationing of them.

As a spur to intuition, it can be useful to imagine magic (exogenous) endowments of additional goods or catastrophic destruction of goods. Similarly, it can be useful to suppose that some invention spurs heavy investment in new capital goods, promising an eventual payoff in greater consumption. Future goods will become more abundant, and present goods are scarcer because their inputs are diverted into making future goods. The agio on present goods, the alias of the interest rate, goes up.

One might object that a higher interest rate deters investment. Under full employment, however, an increased interest rate in response to strengthened demand for investment finance motivates more waiting to make resources for investment available; and the increased rate also rations the more heavily demanded waiting among investment projects.

Is this rise in the interest rate consistent with the appropriate resource shift from future-to-present? In an individual experiment, an arbitrary rise in the interest rate would deter any shift of resources toward the present and instead encourage waiting along its upsloping supply curve. Here, however, in the market experiment, the duly explained rise in the interest rate takes account of the reduced net supply of (or increased net demand for) waiting and appropriately rations it more strictly than before, moderating the shift of resources toward the present. By analogy, a disaster wiping out many beef cattle would directly motivate a shift of livestock-raising resources from hogs to cattle, and the rise in the price of beef would not only reduce beef consumption and increase pork production but also moderate the shift of livestock resources in view of their increased scarcity. In an individual experiment, however, an arbitrary rise in beef prices would not only reduce beef consumption but leave a shift of resources from hog- to beef-raising undampened.

How do the following cases differ: (1) miraculous gift of future consumption, (2) miraculous gift of capital goods for future production, and (3) confidently expected future increases in productivity growth? It is worth noting, and as previously argued, any sharp distinction between consumer durables and capital goods is elusive, since both kinds are sources of future services.

Case 1 is the simplest. With future goods miraculously more abundant, people want to transfer resources from future-to-present. The demand for waiting decreases relative to supply, reducing the interest rate. The prospectively increased future abundance, considered in itself, leaves people with less reason to save resources for investment in the future, also reducing the interest rate.

Case 2: The miraculous gift of capital goods for future production would be qualitatively equivalent to a gift of future consumption goods themselves.

Case 3: The future increase in productivity growth's effect on the interest rate is now explained.

Suppose that new technology makes investment for the future more productive than before. Should resources shift toward investment? Yes, it might seem, to take advantage of the new opportunity; but perhaps no, because future goods will be relatively more abundant. However, that increased future abundance depends on investment now. Any ambiguity here illustrates the point that "the devil is in the details" and that dealing with a resources or technology change is less straightforward than with a change in tastes.

Suppose that a change in managerial technique or other technology (or even in workers' tastes) allows factories and equipment to run two or three shifts a day instead of just one (Cassel 1903/1956, pp. 102-103). Capital goods then yield their total services over a shortened calendar time, so a smaller stock suffices for a given daily output. Industries absorb less waiting relative to labor and output than before, freeing it for other lines of production or for more intensive use ("capital deepening") in their own lines. The demand for waiting declines relative to supply, as does the interest rate. Similarly, peak-load pricing of electricity can even out fluctuations in demand over hours of day and night and over seasons of the year, reducing the amounts of generating equipment and embodied waiting needed for a given annual flow of electricity.

The changes considered next impinge on tastes whose details are crucial to outcomes. A technology-based increase in the productivity of labor specialized in a particular line of production could increase or reduce its employment and wage, depending on the elasticities of derived demand for it and on its supply elasticity. Much the same is true of a technology-based increase in the productivity of waiting specialized in a particular line, but a high degree of specialization is less plausible for waiting than for labor. Waiting is more versatile, and arbitrage in financial transactions eases its shift among uses.

Böhm-Bawerk listed expectations that goods would be more abundant in the future than in the present as one possible reason for interest. An expected uptrend in income reduces the relative marginal utility of the relatively more abundant future goods. A greater gain in their quantity is then required to compensate for a given marginal loss of present goods. Present goods command an increased subjective agio; the interest rate rises.

8.8 Examples of Changes in Resources or Technology

The cases considered next involve technologically improved investment opportunities and opportunities changed by magic donation or catastrophic destruction of present or future consumer or capital goods or land.

Exogenous Temporary Increase in Current Supplies of Consumer Goods (e.g., An Exceptionally Bountiful Harvest)

People want to save some of their brief abundance to augment their relatively poorer future. Their extra thrift works toward restoring the disrupted equality of marginal rates of transformation and substitution between present and future goods. The increased supply of waiting relative to demand reduces the interest rate.

Because waiting may be performed in many ways, as by holding a claim or capital asset or even a durable consumer good, transactions in waiting cannot be observed as readily as transactions in ordinary goods. The demand curve and supply curve, each taken individually, are rather fuzzy notions. For example, what is the difference between supplying waiting and refraining from demanding it, as an asset-holder might refrain from borrowing to finance his holding? Therefore, instead of pondering individual shifts of the supply and demand curves, we might better ponder how one curve shifts relative to the other and which way their intersection moves. Or, remembering arbitrage, we might think of how schedules of supply and demand for loans in particular suggest what happens to supply and demand and the price of waiting in the fuller sense.

Short-Run-Only Loss of Consumer Goods

A meager harvest worsens opportunities. In this case, people want to cushion the decline in present consumption by bringing some of their future prospects forward in time. A reduced capacity to save and an increased desire to borrow shifts the supply curve of waiting leftward relative to the demand curve. The physical counterpart of reduced net waiting is a cutback in investment for the future or even letting some capital goods deteriorate without repair or replacement. The shift of resources toward present consumption is moderated by the increased interest rate appropriate to ration the scarcer waiting. Quirky tastes could reverse this conclusion. Reasoning is more conjectural about changes in resources or technology than about well-specified changes in tastes.[4]

Confidently Expected Future Magic Donation of Consumer Goods

As just before, present goods have become scarcer relative to future goods. People want advanced access to their increased future wealth, so the demand for loans shifts rightward relative to supply. Again, the interest-rate rise moderates the future-to-present shift of resources.

[4] Admittedly, also, comparing total volumes of production and consumption, actual or potential, current or future, raises an index-number problem. Here that complication may be brushed aside.

Firmly Expected Destruction of Future Supplies of Consumer Goods

This is the opposite of the preceding case.

Change in General Factor Productivity

A new lubricant doubles the useful life of every machine,[5] whether already existing or still to be built. Replacement machines become a smaller fraction of the total stock, and fewer resources maintain any given stock. Production possibilities improve more in the added future years than immediately. It would be superficial to suppose that since resources formerly used to replace worn-out machines become available for consumption and net investment, demand for waiting declines relative to supply and reduces the interest rate. On the other hand, the lengthened life of existing capital equipment makes future goods potentially more abundant relative to present goods, which acquire an increased scarcity value and agio relative to future goods. This however is a short-run phenomenon of the transition to the long-run reduced ratio of capital goods to output. Furthermore, the increased future services of already existing capital equipment are additional wealth that someone must hold, so performing waiting. The machine-owners, who gain, could supply this service themselves but may prefer to sell some of their machines or borrow against them to finance additional consumption. In this way, the interest rate could rise. Again, the consequences are more conjectural for a change in technology or resources than in tastes.

New Investment Opportunities Created by New Technology

Investment opportunities imply increased consumption potential in the future; future goods are potentially more abundant relative to present goods, whose scarcity value and agio tend to rise in the short run. An increased demand for waiting to finance investment projects also tends to raise the interest rate, at least for the short tun.

[5] We thank Roger Garrison for this example. Michaelsen (1973, p. 68) imagines a cheap new method of desalinizing sea water, promising development in desert areas. The demand for investment finance strengthens, raising the interest rate and so encouraging the volume of waiting.

Magic Donation and Catastrophic Destruction of Capital Goods

Disasters and their imaginary opposites resemble changes in technology or resources. Even far-fetched examples may yield insight. If capital goods descending from Heaven are oriented definitely toward present or definitely toward future production, the cases resemble those of increased abundance of present or future consumer goods due to improved productivity.[6] Capital goods without a definite time orientation are effectively an increase in present and future productivity and offer a straddle between present and future increases in consumption. Anyway, the magical increase of capital goods reduces the demand for waiting to finance their construction and tends in that respect to reduce the interest rate.

The analysis goes approximately into reverse for the catastrophic destruction of capital goods. More specifically, however, such a disaster typically damages output, especially of goods relatively close to consumption, more than an economy's enduring productive powers, including human capital (or so Hirshleifer 1976, p. 431, conjectures); growing crops suffer more than basic agricultural resources. With fewer goods available currently, they command an increased agio over future goods. Demand for finance to rebuild destroyed capital goods also tends to raise the interest rate.

Magic Appearance or Destruction of Land

Like durable capital goods, new land adds to long-lasting means of production. Demand drops off for funds to finance new capital goods for which land is substitutable. Also, people made wealthier by the new land have an increased capacity to save, tending to depress the interest rate, unless they should sell that land or borrow against it to spend on consumption. Then, a fall in land's price would tend to raise the interest rate, considering that the services-to-sources value ratio is a form of the rate. Since new capital goods tend to increase potential consumption more in the future than immediately, people are more inclined to borrow against the future and less inclined to save, also tending to raise the interest rate in the short run. On balance, we have no conclusive

[6] If we have trouble with examples involving Menger's "orders" of remoteness from final consumption, that trouble counts against the "orders" framework and in favor of attention to the factor-embodiment of goods.

presumptions about the interest rate and resource allocation. Again, the result depends largely on the unspecified structure of tastes.

Lengthening life of houses beyond when they would otherwise have disintegrated is analogous to the magic appearance of new land. Carried to its extreme, the example would postulate that houses become indestructible and essentially just like land. Since waiting and land use are complementary factors, the demand for waiting and the interest rate should rise when houses come to resemble land more closely.

The foregoing doubtful analysis goes into reverse for the loss of land or capital goods. Production possibilities suffer in both present and future. While various effects pull in different directions, market processes do take them into account.

Further Technological Changes

Radio, cell phones, and satellite signals eliminate much of the cables, wires, digging, and associated apparatus. A taxi company or Uber can give the same service with fewer cabs if it dispatches them by radio or cell phone instead of having them either just cruise around or wait to be summoned. The Spanish fast-fashion firm Inditex and its subsidiary, Zara, are noted for constant monitoring and quick response to changing consumer tastes, just-in-time deliveries to its stores, and avoiding large inventories that would require clearance sales and meanwhile embody waiting (Crofton and Dopico 2007).[7] Also, arrangements to share durable goods, as by short stays in private residences and, again, Uber, reduce the demand for them. Such reductions in the demand for waiting may not reduce the interest rate perceptibly, but the direction of effect is plausible.

[7] J. C. Penney was also an example of just-in-time inventory management. Asian suppliers of its house-brand shirts received electronic reports about the sale of each individual shirt in each store and continuously adjusted production and deliveries accordingly. "This speedy process ... has put Penney at the forefront of the continuing revolution in U.S. retailing. In an industry where the goal is speedy turnaround of merchandise, Penney stores now hold almost no extra inventory of house-brand dress shirts. Less than a decade ago, Penney would have had thousands of them warehoused across the U.S., tying up capital and slowly going out of style" (Kahn 2003, p. A1). Penney's later troubles apparently trace not to this policy but to capricious marketing and online competition.

A Change in Factor Productivity

Suppose that one factor becomes more productive, and the labor supply effectively doubles. Labor hours demanded might rise or fall, depending on substitutability with other factors and on elasticities of demand for goods produced with labor. The wage rate and total labor income could conceivably even fall, just as a bumper crop of a particular farm product could reduce its growers' revenue.

Similar reasoning applies to land use and waiting and their prices. If waiting becomes more productive, the future payoff of present abstinence increases. Conceivably, if implausibly, the volume of waiting demanded, and its income, might go down. Technological improvements might be biased in favor of future over current production. The prospect of increased *relative* scarcity of present goods might then raise their agio as people became less willing to postpone consumption and perhaps more eager to borrow. Business firms would seek finance for the more productive time-consuming processes. If inventions raise the productivity of investment, an increased interest rate helps ration available savings (Alchian and Allen 1972, p. 463).

A factor's increased productivity affects its quantity demanded and total income, but less plausibly so for labor than for waiting. Labor works in many different specializations, many of slight substitutability for one another and receiving different wage rates. Waiting is used in multiple ways; it is a more nearly homogeneous factor; and its price expresses the terms of exchange between the broad categories of future and present goods. It is arguably more mobile than labor. True, much value is tied up in specialized capital goods that neither wear out quickly nor shift uses readily. Still, investment in their dollar value is more mobile than its physical embodiments. Arbitrage links the many different forms and payments of waiting, and the financial markets contribute to mobility.

A similar ambiguity can hold for waiting as for labor if the waiting is employed in a quite specific way. Perhaps some cheap new special fertilizer lets a tree grow for more years yet no more slowly than before. Owners find it profitable to postpone harvesting the timber; and forestry employs more waiting, tending to bid up the interest rate. Yet this conclusion, along with any assumption of an unchanged price of timber, must be qualified. The demand for timber (or future timber) might be so inelastic that an increased physical productivity of waiting in producing it might yield output of reduced value.[8] Depending on demand elasticities, the extended physical growth might so depress the price of timber as even to reduce the growth of trees in terms of their value. In turn, the lumber industry might reduce its demand for waiting, so tending, however slightly, to reduce the interest rate. The case would parallel that of specialized labor, but the difference is instructive.

Interest theory pertains to the terms of exchange between future and present goods in general, not for specific goods. Realistically, the interest-rate effect of a change in the productivity of waiting only in some specific industry could be swamped and masked by ongoing other changes in the economy. Examples of a specific technological change serve a heuristic purpose only.

An example of increased productivity of waiting in a specific use would be a new technology that makes houses and apartments more durable at little cost and with no additional maintenance. Keeping buildings serviceable beyond when they would otherwise have deteriorated raises the interest rate and probably changes the term structure of rates.

Another way in which waiting could become more productive is with widened choice, as from new production methods or new and more highly valued products. Waiting cannot just intrinsically, in itself, become more productive. Neither can land, barring some treatment to increase its fertility. Nor can labor; an increase in its productivity must be due to better nutrition, health care, education, specialized training, work ethic—whatever. The parallelism between waiting and other factors stands.

8.9 Conclusion: A Spatial Analogy

The topic of change, particularly in financial tastes, continues in Chapter 10. First, however, Chapter 9 attends to the multiplicity of interest rates. Analogies between time and space may help the transition to that topic.

A disaster destroys consumption goods in a city. Their rise in price restrains consumption at home and attracts replacements from elsewhere. Yet the laws of demand and supply still operate. The increase in price and

[8] The distinction between physical and value productivity, though important in specific lines of production, has become an almost obfuscatory slogan to support a theory denying any role to the productivity of waiting in interest-rate determination.

quantity of the goods attracted are smaller than if the price rose enough to fully ration the shrunken local quantity, and if the original loss were fully offset by inward shipments at the old price. In the intertemporal example of the destruction of existing goods but not goods in the future, efforts to shift some of them toward the present operate through an increased demand for and reduced supply of loans. The resulting rise in the interest rate does not so much accomplish as moderate the shift of goods in time.

In a different case, what happens to the price and destination of goods still en route from the point of production to an originally intended market bears an analogy with what happens if existing houses are somehow made more durable at negligible cost. The value of goods already partway to market is increased by redirecting them to a lucrative newly opened market beyond the original one. This new opportunity also increases the demand for and price of the further transportation, especially if it is of a rather different type from the transportation already used. As for the houses of increased durability, their prices rise because they yield additional services over their extended lives. Their increased durability increases the demand for waiting for their services and so the interest rate in the extended future—this on the plausible assumption that housebuilding is less waiting-intensive than reaping the services of houses once built.

To anticipate Chapter 9, the spatial analogy tends to support a presumption of a generally upward tilt to the yield curve.

CHAPTER 9

The Yield Curve

9.1 Nonhomogeneous Factors of Production

Interest rates range widely. Brooding over a "pure" or "true" price of waiting is fruitless, like brooding over the "pure" price of labor, considered apart from specific kinds and working conditions. Even for labor of similar qualifications, compensating differences in wages recognize nonpecuniary advantages and disadvantages of different jobs. Similarly, interest rates differ because of differences in the size of loans, liquidity, default and other risks, transaction costs, knowledge, expectations of future conditions, and differences in duration and calendar dates. They differ according to whether they are explicit, like interest on money loans, or implicit, like rental on machinery or a general agio of present over future goods.

This diversity no more discredits price theory than the diversity of wages. Even if there were such a thing as the "pure" interest rate, quoted rates would deviate from it.[1] Risk and liquidity elements tend to pull the

For details about bonds and arithmetic related to material in this chapter, readers are directed to the Bond and Interest Rate Appendix.

[1] Gustav Cassel recognizes that waiting is not a homogeneous service with a uniform price. Like other productive factors grouped together for convenience in theorizing, it appears in many forms and under different conditions and commands a wide variety of

L. B. Yeager and S. H. Hanke, *Capital, Interest, and Waiting*,
https://doi.org/10.1007/978-3-031-63398-0_9

explicit rate away, in opposite directions, from any hypothetical pure rate, at least on loans of low or intermediate maturity. In the one direction, the explicit yield exceeds the pure rate because it includes not only the price of waiting alone but also a premium for the risk of loss. In the other direction, the explicit yield is lower because it omits the part of the reward for waiting that takes the form of the quasi-monetary services of a liquid short-term claim.

9.2 Differences in Time

Units of waiting and interest rates paid differ according to maturities in calendar time and durations of loans.[2] Rates are not the same on loans of 3 months compared with those of 10 years. Nor is the rate for a loan starting now the same as the rate agreed on now—the *forward rate*—for a loan not starting until a specific future date. Similarly, prices for labor or property use depend partly on when those services will be supplied.

In a static and fully equilibrated economy in which all conditions and activities recur and are fully expected to recur unchanged year after year, the annualized interest rates for all calendar periods and loans of all maturities are the same (Rothbard 1962, pp. 321, 382–385). Such an economy, though imaginary and impossible, can be a useful contrast in reasoning.

The yield curve in Fig. 9.1 shows the term structure of interest rates on obligations of different periods remaining until they come due. Each rate shown is a bond's yield to maturity, the rate at which the total of the time-discounted future interest payments and repayment of principal equals the bond's present market price.

The particular curve drawn here shows an interest rate higher on 3-year loans than on shorter or longer loans. It is not necessarily typical. Curves

prices. Still, he says, "waiting for *long periods* is the real and principal form of waiting. Waiting for *short periods* is ... a secondary form" (1903/1956, pp. 135–137; cf. p. 85 and Cassel 1932/1967, pp. 208–209). Compare Homer and Sylla (1996, p. 566): "short rates far more than long rates are a function of monetary policy, officially organized market machinery, and the technical structure of each market. Long rates in large and relatively free markets over long periods probably better reflect the economic behavior and investment preferences of large numbers of people acting without guidance, compulsion, or organization."

[2] Duration, a technical term explained later, is generally shorter than time remaining until a loan comes due.

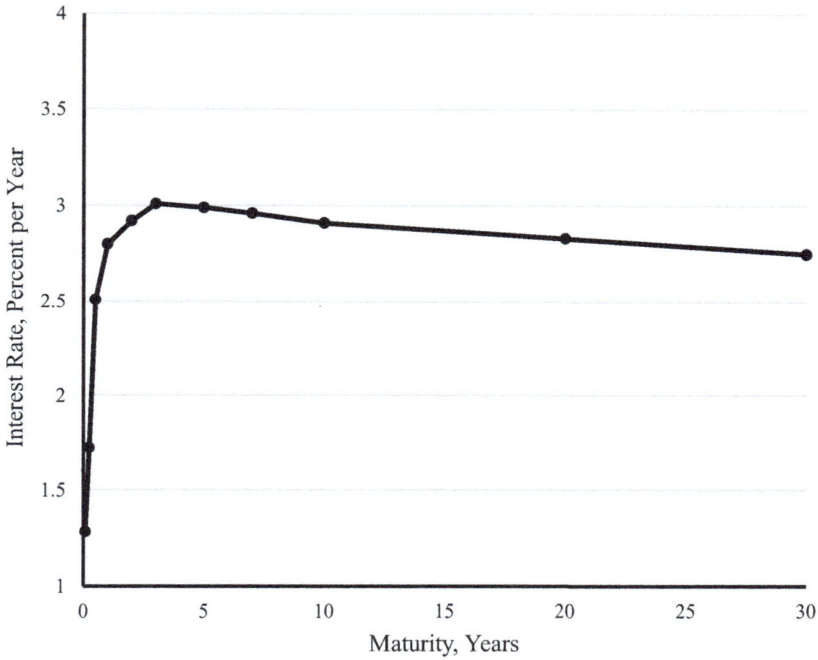

Fig. 9.1 Hypothetical yield curve at a definite date

sloping upward throughout are common. Less frequent are "inverted" curves that, after peaking very near the short end of the scale, slope downward and finally level off.

Ordinarily, however, the liquidity return on short-term instruments tends to hold down their explicit yields. A long-term instrument tends to yield higher explicit interest to compensate for its carrying fewer options than a short-term instrument, whose buyer will receive repayment sooner and so be sooner able to spend or reinvest his funds. Of course, the holder of a long bond, much like the owner of a durable physical asset, has the option of selling it before maturity at a price not yet known; but that option on a long bond or durable asset carries less weight than the option of receiving a specified early repayment. Actual cash carries the greatest options and so ordinarily pays little if any interest.

Interest rates in general, represented by the height of the whole yield curve, tend to fluctuate procyclically, moving up when good profit prospects for business and strong consumer confidence spur the demand for loans. Poor business tends to lower the locus of the curve. Short rates tend to fluctuate more widely than long rates[3] because long rates roughly average out ups and downs of actual and expected short rates. Averages of almost anything fluctuate less widely over time than the individual numbers.

The rough procyclicality of interest rates and the greater volatility of short than of long rates imply that the spread of long rates over short rates tends to rise in a slump and fall in prosperity (Hardouvelis, 1997, p. 676). Often a specific spread—say of the market rate on 10-year bonds over the rate on 3-month bills—summarizes a yield curve's steepness.[4]

During recessions or times of great uncertainty, the yield curve shifts downward and its slope becomes steeper as investors seek the relative security of short-term bonds and shy away from long-term bonds, pushing short yields down and long yields up, relatively. Later, as business recovery reduces perceived risk, the yield curve shifts upward and its slope flattens.[5]

The foregoing remarks describe tendencies, not hard-and-fast rules. Monetary policy, in particular, can modify tendencies that would prevail in loan markets left to themselves.

9.3 Theories of Term Structure: Expectations

The yield curve is sometimes summarized by its slope or by the spread of a long over a short rate. Three kinds of theory meant to explain it are partly rivals, partly complements. They focus on expectations, liquidity preference, and market segmentation or preferred-habitat. According to the expectations theory, the current term structure reflects expectations of future interest rates. The current long rate is higher or lower than the current short rate according to whether people confidently expect short rates to rise or fall. A rising or falling yield curve reflects expectations

[3] Homer and Sylla (1996, pp. 211–212, 317–322, 386, 393–394, 455–459, and 525) note "an interesting exception" in Switzerland from 1910 to 1920 "to the rule that short-term interest rates fluctuate more than long-term interest rates do."

[4] "[F]actor analysis reveals that most of the information in the yield curve is contained in two variables, the level of short rates and the spread between long and short rates" (Hardouvelis 1997, p. 676).

[5] On the possible predictive value of an inverted yield curve, see Sec. 9.12.

that the current short rate is only temporarily low or high, respectively. Furthermore, if future short rates do turn out as expected and if average rates over long time spans do not exhibit any definite uptrend or downtrend–which condition implies expectations, among others, of no change in price inflation–then long rates turn out to be averages of actual short rates.

Even nothing more definite than an idea of an enduring normal range of fluctuations implies something about the yield curve. An investor deciding whether to buy a short- or long-term bond is concerned whether rates are near the ceiling of the normal range and so less likely to rise than to fall or, on the contrary, are near the floor and likely to rise. When rates in general—the yield curve as a whole—seem high and likely to fall, investors are inclined to "lock in" an attractive long rate; but low rates thought likely to rise recommend making only short-term investments, if any. Such behavior tends to narrow or even reverse the familiar spread of long-over-short rates when rates are high and to widen it when rates are low. Particularly when the more volatile short rates lie toward the top of their normal range, implying an unusually small or even negative long-over-short spread, the yield curve rises less steeply than usual, or even falls. When short rates are unusually low, the curve tends to rise more steeply and have a large long-short spread.

Suppose that the Federal Reserve announces a program to lower short rates in 6 months. Before the announcement, yields on long bonds look attractive. Investors rush to buy bonds, reducing their yields and so the long-short spread. Later, if the expectations of lower short rates prove correct, the earlier spread would be revealed as a good predictor of the change in short rates (Hardouvelis 1997, p. 676). A downward-sloping yield curve suggests expectations that interest rates will fall, an upward-sloping curve that rates will rise.

The expectations hypothesis does not stand or fall on whether actual interest rates turn out equal to the implicit forward rates, for nothing guarantees that expectations will prove correct or even be definite. That excuse, however, makes a theory rather empty. A more meaningful theory would include some way of estimating what expectations actually are, some method beyond circularly trying to infer expectations from the yield curve itself.

An arithmetical curiosity about expectations may be worth notice. A bond's price expected to prevail at some future date depends not only on the future interest rate but also on whether the rate is expected as a definite figure or as the average of a probability distribution. In the latter case, the expected future bond price is an average of prices calculated from individual interest rates in the distribution; and that average slightly exceeds the price at a single definitely expected future rate.

An example illustrates this point.[6] A discount (coupon-free) bond having 2 years to run and paying $1000 at maturity currently sells at the competitively necessary 2-year yield of 10 percent a year, $1000/(1.1)^2 =$ $826.45. If the 1-year rate expected with certainty to prevail at the start of the second year is 10 percent also, so that 1- and 2-year rates are both 10 percent, then the bond's expected price 1 year from now, at the start of the second year, is 1000/1.1 = $909.09.

Suppose, now, that although the 1-year rate expected for the start of the second year is again 10 percent, the expectation is uncertain. The rate is expected to be somewhere between 8 and 12 percent. The bond's price at the beginning of the second year, 1 year before its payoff, is thus expected to be either 1000/1.08 or 1000/1.12 or more probably somewhere in between. If the probability distribution can be summarized by the average of the extreme rates (still 10 percent), the bond prices of $925.93 and $892.86 at those extremes average to $ 909.39, slightly higher than the 1000/1.1 = $909.09 price at a 10 percent rate expected with certainty.

Consider further the 10 percent initially prevailing 2-year rate. During the first year, the bond's value grows from $1000/(1.10)^2 =$ $826.45 to the price based on uncertain expectations of $909.39, that is, by 10.04 percent. The bond's price is expected to grow during the second year from that expected $909.39 to $1000, by 9.96 percent. Thus, the first-year rate of growth in value slightly exceeds both the second-year growth rate and the 10 percent rate over the whole 2-year period. In that perhaps peculiar sense, the yield curve slopes downward. This conclusion depends, to repeat, on a bond price at the beginning of the second year based on uncertain interest-rate expectations. By similar reasoning, the yield curve acquires a downward slope with multiple time periods and maturities also.

A short restatement may clinch the point. With uncertain expectations, the expected value of the 2-year bond at the beginning of its

[6] The example, although not all its details, comes from Litterman, et al. (1991, pp. 50–51). Increased uncertainty about future short rates, even apart from any change in their average expected level and apart from considerations of risk aversion, would tend to depress the current long rate and raise a long bond's price (Haubrich 1999, pp. 5–6).

second and final year, taken as the average of prices at the two 8- and 12 percent extremes of the possible second-year interest rate, is higher than the corresponding price with a certain expectation of 10 percent.[7] The higher future bond price with probabilistic rather than definite second-year expectations means that the growth in the bond's market value is slightly higher up to the start of the second year and slightly lower thereafter in the probabilistic than in the definite case; so part of the yield curve may slope downward. This contrast is stronger the greater the variability and wider the probability distributions of future interest rates (Haubrich 1999, Litterman, et al. 1991, Mark Fisher 2004).

The foregoing arithmetic pertains to uncertainty as such. Risk aversion is a distinct influence. Investors who want to keep their options open to sell their bonds and regain their money and who are averse to the risk of having to sell at higher interest rates—lower bond prices—"require" higher long-term rates than if future interest rates were not uncertain. They prefer liquidity and require extra compensation when they sacrifice it by holding long bonds.

9.4 Expectations Theory: Further Doubts and Alternatives

In contrast, some lenders have predictable long-term commitments and can forecast their long-term needs for cash. Life-insurance companies, some pension funds, and retirement savers have predictable long-term obligations or expenses in ordinary dollars. They are unlikely to sell well-chosen bonds before maturity. They shy away from short-term placements of funds for fear of having to roll them over at lower interest rates. To lock in their earnings, they might lend at long rates below the average rate that they thought they might earn on a series of short-term loans. These committed long-term investors show what might be called "solidity

[7] This result is an instance of Jensen's inequality, which says that the expected value of a function is in general not equal to the same function of the expected value of its uncertain argument. For a consumer whose marginal utility of wealth decreases with its amount, the expected utility of wealth is less than the utility of expected wealth. In a paradox described by Jeremy Siegel, the forward exchange rate between two currencies cannot be an unbiased indicator of the expected future spot rate because an expected increase in that euro/dollar rate (say) implies a smaller expected decrease in the dollar/euro rate (unless, presumably, all traders expect the same specific and unchanged rate).

preference" as opposed to liquidity preference.[8] Ordinarily, however, the liquidity preference of more typical lenders appears stronger in the markets.

Such considerations recommend weakening the expectations theory by recognizing that some lenders and borrowers have preferred positions on the scale of short to long rates. This *preferred-habitat* theory recognizes market segmentation. It is more inclusive than a theory emphasizing liquidity preference for fear of capital loss. Some lenders, like the just-mentioned insurance companies, worry more about having to renew their lending at lower short-term rates; they prefer to lock in the rates received on long-term loans. It is not clear a priori, then, that a passion for liquidity makes short-term bonds bear lower explicit interest rates than long-term bonds. From casual historical observation, however, the "solidity" of long-term loans does appear less appealing on the market as a whole than the liquidity of short-term loans.

Ideally, lenders and borrowers might want to match their expected inflows and outflows of funds perfectly date-by-date, but various conditions segment the loan market. Because of institutional factors, legal restrictions, and the nature of their business, some borrowers and lenders cannot readily shift between maturity sectors of the market to take advantage of interest-rate differences; substitution, hedging, and arbitrage are imperfect. As compensation for departing from their preferred habitats, borrowers and lenders settle for positive or negative term premia.[9]

One implication of expectations theories may seem counterintuitive. When rates are low in general, the typically more volatile short rates fall unusually far below long rates. Then, one might superficially expect a decline in long rates to erode their unusually large differential. On the contrary, long rates rise; the spread shrinks when short rates rise along with them, or even more (Campbell 1995, pp. 137–138; Campbell and coauthors 1997, p. 419, Eq. 11.2.14). Conformably with the expectations hypothesis, rising short rates exert some influence on long rates also.

[8] Michaelsen (1973, p. 91) refers to their "solidity premium" on lending long.

[9] Culbertson (1957) presents a version of this preferred-habitat theory, which, carried to an extreme, amounts to a market-segmentation theory; cf. Malkiel (1992, p. 652).

The notion of a historically suggested normal range of fluctuation helps dissolve any air of paradox. When rates in general appear abnormally low and likely to recover, possible capital losses loom larger than capital gains on long bonds and require, in compensation, a larger than usual illiquidity-premium spread in rates on long bonds (Malkiel 1966, Chapter 3).

Does this reasoning imply that long rates can never fall again? Surely not. On the assumptions made, short rates rise enough to equate their average level, minus whatever liquidity advantage short instruments yield, to the current long rates over the lifetimes of the current long bonds. Nothing rules out short and long rates declining again in the future.

Another case further helps dissolve any paradox about long rates moving counter to the way that would in itself tend to erode an unusual yield spread. Sometimes interest rates, especially the more volatile short rates, are unusually high, as in a classic money panic or when a tight-money policy attempts to protect a currency's exchange rate from bearish pressures. The familiar spread of long-over-short rates shrinks or even turns negative. Short rates are plausibly expected to recede from their unusual heights, and in such a way that their average over the lifetime of current long bonds equals the long rates (apart from any normal term premium). While rates in general are still unsustainably high, holders of long bonds have more reason to expect capital gains than to fear capital losses, in that respect, making long bonds more attractive than short ones. Mitigating this hope for capital gain, long interest yields are not as high as usual relative to short yields, with the long-short spread possibly even negative. Even so, as short rates recede from their abnormal heights, so do long rates, although more mildly.

The expectations theory is thus internally coherent. But coherence is not necessarily realism. For example, "the pure expectations hypothesis says that whenever a long bond yield exceeds a short yield, the yield on the long bond subsequently tends to rise over the life of the short bond" (Campbell 1995, p. 137). But, in the U.S. experience, "when the long-short yield spread is high, the long yield tends to fall, amplifying the yield differential between long and short bonds, rather than rising to offset the yield spread as required by the expectations hypothesis" (Campbell 1995, pp. 138–139).

9.5 The Long-Short Spread and Forecasts of Recession

When an inverted curve does occur, relatively rarely, it may reflect current or quite recent prosperity and may even presage a business downturn. Often it can be convenient to summarize an entire yield curve as a specific spread, say the spread between yields on 10-year bonds and 3-month Treasury bills. Anyway, this idea of an exceptional spread of short rates over long rates as a clue to impending recession enjoys some acceptance and historical support. Studies "have shown that the term structure forecasts real economic activity, since inverted yield curves tend to precede recessions and steeply upward-sloping yield curves tend to precede expansions" (Campbell, et al. 1997, p. 424; cf. Cwik 2004). One interpretation of the yield curve as a predictor is that unusually high short-term rates reflect tight monetary and credit policy that, although expected to be loosened later to fight recession, does meanwhile portend its familiar discouragement to business (Fig. 9.2).

The term spread can be analyzed into an expectations component and a term-premium or risk-allowance component. The former allows for the expectation of inflation and the real interest rate. The latter component allows not for definite expectations but for uncertainty and risk about the inflation and real interest rates. Using U.S. statistics from 1961 to 2007, Joshua V. Rosenberg and Samuel Maurer (2008) try to decompose

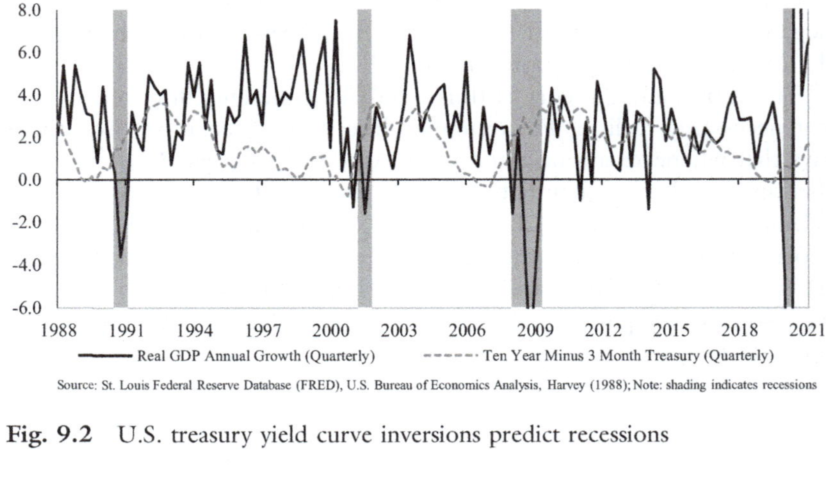

Source: St. Louis Federal Reserve Database (FRED), U.S. Bureau of Economics Analysis, Harvey (1988); Note: shading indicates recessions

Fig. 9.2 U.S. treasury yield curve inversions predict recessions

the term spread into these two components. They find the expectations component a better leading indicator of recession than the uncertainty-and-risk component and also better than the term spread combining both. This result gives perhaps some slight extra support to the expectations strand of yield-curve theory and to the idea of it as a recession predictor (for more on the predictive power of the yield curve, see Estrella 2003).

9.6 Liquidity and Preferred-Habitat Theories

A forward interest rate is one agreed on in advance for a loan at a specified future time. An exactly correct expectations theory would imply that a forward rate equals the corresponding expected future spot rate. But no dominant fraction of market participants (which could be far less than a majority) holds precise, firm, identical, and accurate expectations. Moreover, the arbitrage presupposed is impeded by transactions costs, credit rationing, and other so-called "market imperfections." Another strand of the story emphasizes an illiquidity or risk premium on the yields of longer-term securities. People may plausibly adjust rates subjectively upward or downward from their best but uncertain expectations.

Shiller (1990, p. 648) defines a *forward term premium* as "the difference between the forward rate and the [rational] expectation of the corresponding future spot rate."[10] It seems superficially plausible that term premia on longer loans would be positive, since most people and institutions prefer lending short (or holding bank deposits), leaving long loans in excess demand unless lenders received the extra inducement. If, plausibly, this premium rises with maturity, the yield curve slopes upward even when no rate changes are expected.

Savings accounts, treasury bills, and other short-term instruments provide part of their total yield in the nonpecuniary form of their liquidity services as quasi-money. On the other hand, part of the explicit pecuniary interest on long-term securities serves as compensation for the risk of capital loss from changes in market conditions, and this risk is an offset

[10] Shiller prefers the expression "term premium" to its approximate synonyms "risk premium" and "liquidity premium" because it does not imply any specific theory of the term structure. "Illiquidity premium" would seem a more exact term for the latter.

"Formally, the liquidity premium is typically expressed as an amount that is to be added to the expected future rate in arriving at the equilibrium-yield relationships described in [the equations for the pure-expectations theory]" (Malkiel 1992, p. 651).

to their total yield. Distinct from it is the risk of borrower default, an obvious reason why different securities and loans carry different interest rates.

One source of risk on a medium- or long-term bond is that price inflation may speed up, casting its shadow before it. A bondholder cannot preserve his purchasing power by selling when inflationary expectations have already developed, since they have by then become embodied in market interest rates. The price of the bond plunges, even in current money; and the holder bears the loss not only from inflation already experienced but also from inflation expected over the bond's remaining life. Scarcely any market in long bonds is said to exist in countries with a record of chronic high and variable inflation. A novel by Benjamin and Herbert Stein dramatizes the destruction of the bond market as the United States suffers extreme inflation (1977, esp. Chapters 5 and 6). Risks on bonds indexed for inflation are in one respect fewer than risks on ordinary nominal-value bonds.

Whether the observed historical variability of the term spread on long bonds primarily reflects the variability of perceived risk or variability of expected future rates is an empirical question. Hypotheses such as the *liquidity-premium hypothesis* or the *preferred-habitat hypothesis* emphasize fluctuations in the risk premium or other market imperfections (Hardouvelis 1997, p. 676).

9.7 Evidence on the Theories

Many econometric studies reject the theory of a long-term interest rate determined entirely by expectations of the short-term rate and also reject the idea of rational expectations. Still, "even if the theory is not strictly true, it may contain important elements of the truth." Many "practitioners of monetary policy continue to apply it as an admittedly imperfect yet useful benchmark" (King and Kurmann 2002, pp. 80, 49).

The chief obstacle to testing has been the lack of independent evidence on expectations. Theories of term structure and of how expectations are formed have been tested jointly. Inventive hypotheses have been tried. Studies have generally found expectations important, but the pure expectations hypothesis proves an exaggeration at best. Eclectic theories take account of expectations, risk preferences, characteristics of various investment alternatives, and individual preferences about segments of the market (Malkiel 1992). Eclecticism enters into explaining not only interest rate but also wage rate differences, which is yet another parallelism between the prices of waiting and of labor. Different interest rates on different securities cohere well with seeing interest rates as factor prices.

Hardouvelis judges that "short-run regressions such as the ones that uncover time-varying premia or find counterintuitive reactions of the long rate tend to emphasize tiny deviations from the expectations hypothesis and cloud its overall economic usefulness." Movements of the term-structure spread conform to the long-run predictions of the expectations hypothesis; discrepancies are economically small. Newer studies that allow for time trends in short and long rates contrast an older literature that consistently rejected the expectations hypothesis (Hardouvelis 1997, pp. 677–678).

In the United States since World War II, the term spread has been a good predictor of subsequent cumulative change in short-term rates. This prediction is a composite of predictions about the real interest rate and inflation. Over forecasting horizons longer than 1 year, the prediction is primarily about inflation. At long forecasting horizons, also, the expectations hypothesis is hard to reject (Hardouvelis, 1997, p. 676).

Of course, expectations are not the whole story of the yield curve. Traders do not act on definite, uniform, and confident expectations of future interest rates. Time-varying allowances for the riskiness and liquidity of various securities dilute the role of expectations. Diverse market participants have their own preferences for debt maturities, while transactions costs and other obstacles keep arbitrage and speculation from fully overcoming this partial segmentation of markets.

None of these points recommends squarely rejecting the expectations hypothesis. It is roughly correct, if less so than the quantity theory of money, the purchasing-power-parity theory of exchange rates, or the covered-interest-arbitrage theory of the relation between spot and forward exchange rates. Each of these theories focuses on one dominant factor. Each has been questioned because coefficients in econometrically fitted equations do not come significantly close enough to their theoretical values. The bare theoretical relation is indeed distorted by changeable miscellaneous factors hard to fit into a comprehensive theory. This is probably truer of the expectations theory than of the other three theories mentioned. Yet none of this justifies abandoning them with the almost empty remark that everything depends on "supply and demand."[11]

The expectations theory also finds support in episodes of extreme price inflation, especially inflation expected to persist or accelerate.

The intellectual challenge, rather than market transactions and advice, is what apparently and even laudably motivates many theorists' and econometricians' attention to the yield curve. This, though, is not our main concern.

9.8 Nonmonetary Circumstances Affecting the Yield Curve

Real conditions, both subjective and objective, including technology, influence the term structure of rates. What sort of nonmonetary development would raise the price of long waiting relative to short waiting, so tilting the yield curve upward (or lessening any downward tilt)? One might be a speed up in the rate of technological progress and so in the economic obsolescence of machinery, but with technological progress expected to slow down again in the longer run. Rapid short-run obsolescence reduces the value productivity of investment in the short run. Users tend to postpone buying machinery but expect to place big orders when the state of technology will have settled down at its new higher level. The demand for waiting to be tied up in owning new machinery is currently weak but will strengthen later. Other things being equal, the yield curve's upward tilt steepens.

What sort of development might raise the productivity of current or short waiting relative to future or long waiting, tending to tilt the yield curve downward? A disaster putting a premium on short-run reconstruction could do that.

What relation, if any, holds between the term structure of interest rates and the physical kinds and amounts of capital goods constructed? Some relation must almost surely exist. Suppose no finance was available for long-term projects like electric power plants, which take years to construct and then render their services over many further years. Unavailability of long-term finance would surely inhibit projects whose expected

[11] An Austrian message resonates: to look for numerical constants, or even for stable functional relations in the field of human action, is to chase a will o' the wisp.

payoffs came mostly in the distant future. Entrepreneurs might not totally abandon those projects, for they might bet on repeatedly getting new short-term loans when old ones come due. But the risk of being able to roll loans over either not at all or only on unfavorable terms would count with entrepreneurs as a nonpecuniary addition to the interest rate explicitly paid. Or long-term loans might be available, after all, from financial intermediaries acting as arbitrageurs or speculators, who might offer long-term loans and bet on being able to refinance themselves by a series of short-term borrowings. But arbitrageurs and speculators would surely allow for risk in the long-term interest rate they charged. This relatively high long-term rate might inhibit long-term projects as much as if the projects' promoters ran the risk of themselves piecing short-term loans together.

More generally, aversion to long-term financial commitments, whether as supplier or demander of waiting, has a physical counterpart in the construction of fewer durable (and specialized) projects with remote payoffs than if people were oriented toward long-term finance. High-cost or risky finance would inhibit long-term projects as much as would general turmoil and insecurity of property rights.

The foregoing points suggest that a downward-sloping or flat yield curve would tend to favor long-term projects and a steeply upward-sloping curve would discourage them, especially if something other than expected price inflation were the main reason for the upward slope. Very low interest rates only at short maturities would not favor long-term projects, particularly if, as seems likely, their very lowness suggested that they were available only temporarily.[12]

The yield on non-interest-bearing money is implicit in the form of convenience and liquidity and options kept open. It exhibits the general principle of diminishing marginal returns. The individual or firm holds a cash balance of such size that its subjectively appraised yield is equal at the margin to the yields on other assets. The general level of these other yields—loosely, the interest rate—affects the demand for cash balances. A rise in this level spells a rise in the opportunity cost of holding particular assets, including cash balances; so, the target marginal yield sought on them rises. A holder raises this implicit marginal yield on its cash balance

[12] This consideration speaks against the hard-core Austrian theory of the business cycle, which sees even only temporarily low interest rates caused by monetary expansion as an incentive for excessive investment in the so-called higher stages of production.

by reducing its size. Efforts to do so show up in the overall economy as a rise in the velocity of money. A fall in the interest rate, conversely, tends to increase individual cash balances demanded at not-yet-changed price and income levels. When some change in "wants, resources, or technology" or in the quantity of money causes an initial discrepancy between desired and actual money holdings, individual efforts to adjust the discrepancy away cause changes in price and income levels.[13]

Although the interest rate does affect the demand for cash balances, the theory itself says nothing about how sensitive that response is. Responsiveness would be low if the marginal implicit yields on cash balances, as subjectively appraised by their holders, rose and fell sharply with the size of the balances; for then just a slight change in the size of a balance would suffice to realign its yield with a changed interest rate.

9.9 Other Sources of Interest-Rate Differences

Interest rates differ according to lengths and calendar times of loans and according to perceived risk. Should these different rates be regarded as prices of different varieties of waiting, or even as prices of distinct factors? As this book has already insisted, what counts as a productive factor is not a question about objective reality. What matters is convenience in analysis and exposition. Something conveniently treated as a distinct factor in one piece of analysis may legitimately be treated otherwise in another context.

9.10 Risk-Bearing as a Factor of Production

The great diversity of interest rates, wage rates, and land rents does not rule out treating waiting, labor, and land use as factors of production. Interest rates differ according to a loan's time to maturity, calendar time, size, collateral, adjustability of the rate, guarantees, opinions of rating agencies, and innumerable other characteristics. Some loans are repayable at the option of the borrower, like home mortgage loans and callable bonds; others, like savings accounts, are repayable on demand if the depositor so desires; some loans carry the presumption but not the actual obligation by the lender to repeatedly roll them over.

[13] Greidanus (1932), Hutt (1956/1975), and Selgin (1987/1994) are fundamental contributions to understanding the implicit yield on money and its role in how the money supply influences the economy.

Should their different interest rates be regarded as prices of different varieties of waiting, as prices for a distinct factor of production? As this book has already insisted, what counts as a productive factor is not a question about objective reality alone. What matters is convenience in analysis and exposition. Something conveniently treated as a distinct factor in one piece of analysis may well be treated otherwise in another context.

How best to treat waiting and risk-bearing linked with it depends on context. Readiness to bear risk may sometimes be treated as a productive factor and even be subdivided by types and degrees. Risk-bearing is scarce: the more of it absorbed in some activities, the less remains for others. True enough, it is not generally priced explicitly, since its price is mixed up with factor prices of more straightforward kinds, like wage rates in risky occupations. But having only an elusive price does not keep risk-bearing from counting as a productive factor. Many projects could not be carried out unless the risks associated with them were borne, reallocated, or somehow canceled against opposite risks of other projects, perhaps through financial derivatives.

Like any ordinary factor, risk-bearing has an opportunity cost: employing it in one way forecloses its use in others. Economists are sometimes skeptical of *contrived* risks, as in gambling, casinos, and lotteries, on the grounds that they divert some of the willingness to bear risk away from more straightforwardly productive activities, either directly or through investment in securities. This objection weakens if government lotteries count as a taxation and reduce the need for other tax revenues, if the contrived risks produce harmless and pleasurable excitement, or if meddling with such pleasures is repulsive on philosophical grounds.

Should bearing risk or uncertainty[14] count as a distinct factor of production? A substantial literature, sympathetically reviewed by Braun (2003), argues that it should.[15] Cassel (1932, pp. 175–176) writes: "[u]nder economically advanced conditions this factor has a market of its own and a fairly definite price [insurance premiums, for example]. It

[14] Hirshleifer and Riley (1992, pp. 9–10) dismiss Frank Knight's distinction between the two concepts as sterile. Here the two words are practically synonyms.

[15] As supporters of this interpretation, Braun (Chapter 3, esp. Sect. 4) cites Hans von Mangoldt (1855), A. C. Pigou (1932/1950, appendix I, pp. 771–781), Frederick B. Hawley (1892, pp. 280–307; 1893, pp. 459–479), John Haynes (1895, pp. 409–449), J. R. Hicks (1931, pp. 170–189.), Hans-Werner Sinn (1986), Klaus Beckmann (1998, esp. Sects. 5.1 and 5.1.1), Dirk Meyer (1992), and Udo Martinsohn (2003).

may also be substituted for other factors of production, as always happens when, in order to reduce costs, a lower grade of security is tolerated." Willingness to bear risk is essential in any but an impossibly routinized economy and perhaps especially so for Schumpeter's "creative destruction." Without any risk-bearing, our world would have no doctors, no fire-fighters, no roofers. No one would explore for oil or other minerals; no entrepreneurs would make novel investments. No one would risk changing occupation or residence to earn higher income. Security fanatics would everywhere restrict themselves to administering and preserving existing routines. In reality, insurance promotes production by evening out and atomizing risks and shrinking mutually independent risks to a fraction of what they would otherwise be (Udo Martinsohn 2003; Sinn 1986).

Risk-bearing is both complementary with and substitutable for other productive factors. It could rarely be supplied and demanded totally apart from the time element–waiting. It can substitute at the margin for other factors. A product or service or production method might be made safer, but at the cost of employing more land use, labor, or waiting. Things might be produced in a more routinized and less risky way by using more of those factors. A close approach to whatever total safety might mean would be extremely uneconomic; and a less prosperous economy would itself be riskier, as to health. Just as the opportunity to choose more time-consuming methods broadens the range of choice within which the entrepreneur may find a more productive method—recall Böhm-Bawerk's argument—so the opportunity to choose riskier methods broadens the range of choice.

Another parallel between risk-bearing and other factors is that it can move internationally through capital movements, perhaps particularly in the form of equity and direct investment (Sinn 1986). Furthermore, risk-bearing, like waiting, can also be traded internationally through embodiment in imports and exports, as in medicines, whose discovery, development, marketing, and exposure to lawsuits can be risky. In such ways, differences in readiness to bear risk may figure in the comparative advantages or disadvantages of countries in world trade. A company might produce gizmos at home while paying labor handsomely for inherently risky work. Alternatively, it might import gizmos from a country whose desperately poor workers would gladly bear the risks of the work for a lower wage. Instead of exploiting those poor foreign workers, such a deal would arguably give them a welcome new opportunity (Heyne 1993/

2008). The home country would in effect be importing the risk-bearing embodied in the imported gizmos, freeing domestic risk-bearing for other purposes.

A detailed theory would exhibit the characteristics, such as diminishing marginal returns, that risk-bearing shares with other factors. It would describe the implausible conditions under which the rewards to risk-bearing and the other factors, each equaling their marginal value product, just exhaust the total value of the product. But could such a theory help us understand the real world? Elegance is counterproductive if the necessary assumptions, as for handling positive and negative rewards to entrepreneurship, are too far-fetched.

The tradeoff between elegance and relevance requires assessing each particular case and rejecting any all-purpose treatment. Treating risk-bearing as a distinct factor might work well in some contexts; in others, different types and degrees of risk might best be treated as associated with different varieties of waiting, labor, or land use. Again, Niels Bohr's principle of complementarity is relevant: different and even superficially rival frameworks of analysis can be useful. In some contexts, it matters much, in others little, that risk-bearing and entrepreneurship, unlike labor and waiting, both lack contractual prices expressed in money.

It is idle to inquire whether something "really" is a factor, just as to insist on specifying the mathematical form, arguments, and parameters in "the" production function of a firm, industry, or whole economy. Nothing laid down in objective reality answers such questions. Factors of production, production function, and related concepts are devices for observing and understanding how the world works; they are tools to use as best suits each particular context.

Saying so echoes this whole book's contention about waiting. Whether it counts as a factor and even whether the concept serves the analysis of capital and interest better than other formulations—all this is an issue not of hard-and-fast reality but of convenience in observation, analysis, and exposition.

9.11 Proposals for How to Handle Risk-Bearing

Besides counting waiting among the factors, A. C. Pigou (1932/1950, Appendix I) considers adding various sorts of uncertainty-bearing, as he calls it, to the list. This is not usually done, he continues, because it is not clear how to analytically separate uncertainty-bearing from waiting. True enough, it is possible to bear uncertainty apart from tying up much wealth over time, as when someone sells wheat 6 months forward, intending to buy it then for less than the agreed forward price. Unlike labor, land use, and waiting, uncertainty-bearing does seem to lack a straightforward time dimension, but Pigou devises a unit: "the exposure of a £ to a given scheme of uncertainty, in an act the consummation of which occupies a year" (p. 772).

This definition invites both attention and skepticism. Suppose you risk $1000 on the chance of winning $1500. What difference does it make if the result and settlement are to take place in four or in 8 months? The time difference affects little more than a small difference in interest received or forgone. Twice as much time does not mean twice as much risk borne.

A second difficulty is that while labor and waiting are relatively objective services, uncertainty-bearing is more subjective, depending largely on the bearer's temperament (p.773). Pigou distinguishes between projects of low risk with low expected return and high risk with high return. Labor, also, comes in many types. For both uncertainty-bearing and labor, a standardized grade might ideally somehow be devised for theorizing, along with corresponding supply and demand prices.

Pigou distinguishes payment for uncertainty-bearing from the exceptional profits of successful risky businesses. Payment for the former consists not in the above-normal profits of successful enterprises but only in the generally small part of this excess that is not canceled by the corresponding losses of other entrepreneurs (p. 776)—but why should the losses of some be set against the gains of others? Risks can be shifted onto the shoulders of specialists (p. 777). Pigou mentions indoor and outdoor entertainment businesses that bear risks of weather and exporters and importers who bear exchange-rate risks. The law of large numbers permits canceling uncertainties against one another, and the range over which this principle applies has been extended by improvements in transportation and communication, the limited liability of corporations, insurance, and markets for hedging and speculation (pp. 778–781).

Frederick B. Hawley (1892) thought that Böhm-Bawerk paid too little attention to the entrepreneur's demand for capital funds. The entrepreneur relieves others of risk (p. 283). Risk occurs in all industrial undertakings, and the consumer must pay for it (p. 285). Through insurance, a number of separate risks incurred by the same person can neutralize each other (p. 286). On Hawley's interpretation, Böhm throughout wrongly identified interest mixed with the reward for risk-bearing. But interest is really a composite of pure interest, the wages of management, and pure profit from risk-bearing (Hawley 1892, p. 289). Hawley foreshadows J. B. Clark's "dynamic theory" of profit (which Shailesh 2017 examines).

Hans-Werner Sinn (1986) explicitly counts risk-tolerance or risk-bearing as a factor. He wonders whether redistribution by the government might be partly an insurance scheme to cover risks of career choices, entrepreneurial ventures, and so forth. Such quasi-insurance might free human and other resources for use in risky projects and lines of work (pp. 566–567).

What would the world look like if no one were willing to bear risk (Sinn 1986; cf. Martinsohn 2003)? Sinn draws parallels between Böhm-Bawerk's capital and interest theory and his own theory of risk as a factor. In particular, the option of choosing riskier methods of production may well be more productive than less risky methods. Böhm-Bawerk's agio of present goods over future goods is not a matter of time alone, since the lapse of time also involves risk, compensation for which is part of what Böhm-Bawerk calls interest. The greater the prospective reward of overcoming risk-aversion and time preference alike, the stronger the incentive to do so.

Sinn (1986, pp. 557–562) suggests the variance of the probability distribution of prospective returns as a measure of the risk of a project. We can interpret the measure of risk "as the mathematical variance of the outcomes considered possible by the decisionmaker" ("als die mathematische Varianz der vom Entscheidungsträger für möglich gehaltenen Ergebnisausprägungen"). That measure takes no explicit account of the time during which money or resources are tied up, for Sinn regards time as the concern of capital and interest theory instead.

9.12 Conclusion

The great variety of interest rates might seem to discredit the concept of the interest rate as the price of a productive factor. Yet the prices of other factors also come in great variety. In theorizing, it is equally legitimate to speak of "the" interest rate, "the" wage rate, and "the" rent of land. Relations between short-term and longer-term interest rates and between currently quoted and forward rates pose challenges to theorists and econometricians. They want to offer explanations more definite than just "supply and demand." Concepts of duration in contrast with maturity come into the story, as do expectations and preferred-habitat or market-segmentation theories.

Should risk-bearing count as a distinct factor of production? The answer, like the answer about waiting, does not fit objective reality in a hard-and-fast way. It is a matter of convenience in theorizing and exposition, and it may legitimately vary from context to context and according to authors and readers.

The next chapter examines how money influences interest rates.

CHAPTER 10

Money and Interest

A chapter on money and interest should mention the quantity theory. The familiar tautology MV = PQ is not the theory itself; rather, it is a device for organizing attention to the theory. The theory postulates a rough proportionality between the quantity of money and the price level. Under some institutions, most clearly fiat money, the quantity determines the price level. Under others—like that of a country operating under a currency board system (Hanke 2002), or a small country on an international gold standard, or a single city in a unified monetary area—the externally determined price level, together with the local demand for money, determines the local quantity of money. In any case, the theory asserts the just-mentioned rough proportionality. The great inflations of history are evidence.

But what counts as money these days, when many kinds of media of exchange and their close substitutes proliferate? What is a quantity theory of something whose quantity cannot be measured? The theory must consider how the total mix of money and near-moneys relates to the quantities demanded by the public. When demand exceeds supply, business recession and price declines are likely; the opposite imbalance causes inflation. In between lies monetary equilibrium.

How might a monetary authority promote supply and demand equality between these scarcely measurable quantities? It cannot do so directly but it might try by responding to symptoms, easing policy on clues to

L. B. Yeager and S. H. Hanke, *Capital, Interest, and Waiting*,
https://doi.org/10.1007/978-3-031-63398-0_10

impending recession and price deflation and tightening policy on clues to inflation. This seems to be the rationale of the currently prevalent policy of lowering or raising some target interest rate to resist perceived signs of deflation or inflation.

Still, the logic of the quantity theory and "monetarism" (so named by Karl Brunner 1968, 1983, and Milton Friedman 1969) suggest trying to revive the quantity of money as a definite concept. A weighted total of various monetary instruments might suffice. The growth rate of the total would be the weighted average of the growth rates of its components. The weights would depend on how closely each component was judged to share the properties of the purest kind of money. This might be estimated from the interest rate paid on each type: media of exchange paying nothing are the purest types of money, while instruments paying the highest interest count as money minimally, if at all (W. H. Hutt 1956/1975). The result is a Divisia index, named for the French engineer-economist François Divisia. The quantity theory then asserts a proportionality between the Divisia total and the price level.[1] The idea of the quantity of money *driving* rather than *responding* to spending, prices, and employment is weaker for a Divisia total than for narrowly defined money like base money and perhaps bank demand deposits. The reason is that at least some near-moneys respond to economic conditions and regulations, for example, checkable money-market mutual funds. Although the money supply is not an unambiguous single figure, neither is the price level; both are weighted totals of many individual components.

10.1 The Real—Not Just Monetary—Character of Interest

After recognizing the actual multiplicity of interest rates, we return to their general level— "the" interest rate of theorizing. Interest is the price of a "real" factor. Its suppliers postpone using wealth over time for their own purposes and advance its use to its demanders. This factor has an obvious monetary aspect, since prices, wealth, saving, and credit are overwhelmingly measured in money and since the most explicit transactions

[1] The application of the quantity theory of money has most recently and thoroughly been evaluated by William A. Barnett (2011).

in it are loans of money. This role of money no more negates the fundamentally real character of what the interest rate is the price of than money prices negate the real character of goods and services.

David Hume insisted on this character. "Lowness of interest is generally ascribed to plenty of money. But money, however plentiful, has no other effect, *if fixed*, than to raise the price of labour" (1752/1970, p. 47).[2] High or low interest rates are due to great or small demand for borrowing, little or great wealth to meet that demand, and great or small profits in business (p. 49). Hume recognized that a sudden increase in money or gold and silver could depress the interest rate; but after the new money "has been digested, and has circulated through the whole state, [real economic magnitudes] will soon return to their former situation ..., and consequently the high interest returns" (pp. 57–58). These points parallel Hume's recognition that although increases or decreases in the quantity of money can temporarily stimulate or depress real activity, the steady *size* of the money supply determines the price level and leaves real activities and relations unaffected (pp. 33–46).

John Stuart Mill echoed Hume. The permanent amount of money affects only its purchasing power, not the interest rate. "The greater or smaller number of counters which must be used to express a given amount of real wealth, makes no difference... in the demand and supply of loans. There is the same amount of real capital lent and borrowed...." Depreciation of money in process and when it is expected to continue tends to raise the interest rate. On the other hand, putting new money into circulation by loans tends to lower the rate while the process continues. "The rate of interest, then, depends ... on the comparative amount of real capital offered and demanded in the way of loan; but is subject to temporary disturbances of various sorts from increase and diminution of the circulating medium" (1848/1929, pp. 645–647; note Mill's anticipation of the Fisher effect).

10.2 The Benefits of a Monetary Economy

Nevertheless, interest and money remain linked in popular thinking. The short-term rate in particular is often called the price or cost of money; and monetary policy is, or was until recently, interpreted, even by central

2 "Labour" here evidently includes goods also.

bankers, as interest-rate policy. This entanglement invites reviewing the benefits and complications of a monetary economy.

Money and money prices overcome the notorious difficulties of barter and facilitate complex multilateral transactions and a fine-grained division of labor. The system coordinates the activities of innumerable persons using their own localized and fleeting knowledge. Money simplifies keeping track of relative values and debts and credits. Estimating benefits, costs, profits, and losses in a common unit makes possible the economic calculation whose absence or incompleteness is the bane of a centrally planned economy. By receiving their incomes in generalized purchasing power rather than in specific goods, people enjoy wide options about what and when to consume; consumer sovereignty operates.[3] Money promotes the pooling and mobilization of savings through financial institutions and securities markets and so promotes capital goods construction and long-term-oriented projects.

The existence or nonexistence of money, as distinguished from its quantity, counts among the ultimate realities of an economic system. In Patinkin's formulation (1965, Chapter VIII), an economy's "real framework" comprises "wants, resources, and technology," broadly conceived. The resulting real outcomes include quantities of goods and services and relative prices, of which the interest rate is one. The "monetary framework" is the nominal quantity of money and the price level.

10.3 Financial Intermediation

Financial intermediation is the activity of financial institutions, including banks and the "shadow" banking system, other deposit-taking and loan-making firms, and life-insurance companies and other companies operating in the markets for stocks, bonds, and shorter-term credit instruments. The intermediaries acquire "primary securities," such as promissory notes, bonds, or stock, issued by ultimate borrowers, including both households and business firms financing real investment. The intermediaries issue their own securities, including banknotes and deposits, to the ultimate "surplus units," whose savings include money. Without intermediation, command over resources could be transferred from ultimate

[3] Also, worker sovereignty operates through workers' decisions on jobs and on what terms. Investor sovereignty operates through, for example, mutual funds designed to make only "social" investments.

savers to ultimate investors and other borrowers only by direct transactions between them. All would face the obstacles of transactions costs, imperfect and costly information, risks, and innumerable inconveniences. Such obstacles amount to a tax wedged between the effective interest rates received by lenders and those paid by borrowers, a quasi-tax yielding no revenue. That wedge would keep the real volumes of saving and loans and capital formation smaller than they would otherwise be.

Intermediation shrinks this wedge of disadvantages (Gurley and Shaw 1960, McKinnon 1973, Shaw 1973, and Short 1979). It exploits lenders' expertise and special knowledge of borrowers' creditworthiness, reaps economies of scale, diversifies risks, and tailors the characteristics of financial instruments to the different preferences of lenders and borrowers. Through "maturity transformation," savers ready to make only short-term loans, like bank depositors, can indirectly lend to borrowers who want long-term loans, like house buyers and business firms. Much risk-bearing can be transferred to willing bearers by the design of credit instruments and by such derivatives as credit-default swaps that insure against default on bonds. These benefits of intermediation are typically thrown into reverse during financial crises.

Not only specific financial institutions and instruments function as intermediaries; the entire money and banking system can function as a giant intermediary (McKinnon 1973, Shaw 1973, Fry 1988). Money is a vehicle of transferring command over resources from ultimate savers to ultimate borrowers. The benefits of money in facilitating transactions and in channeling savings into investment are most evident as an economy evolves further away from barter.

Intermediation operates paradigmatically, although not in the greatest volume, through banks and checking accounts. By holding bank deposits and other claims on wealth, people postpone consumption and make the saved resources available to business firms and other borrowers. As media of exchange and liquidity for their holders, demand deposits even provide a kind of subsidy to waiting and therefore to capital formation, so far as the bank loans go, for investment rather than consumption.

The demand for real cash balances ordinarily grows along with growth in population, labor force, productivity, and transactions. When people hold more money by spending less than they are currently taking in, they are postponing some command over resources and freeing it for private and public borrowers. If, now, the money and banking system puts additional money into circulation by expanding its loans, or if the government collects seigniorage on prudently issued new money, the system acts as a kind of super financial intermediary. Money itself becomes an "indirect security" in the terminology of Gurley and Shaw (1960).

Non-interest-bearing cash is sometimes called "the present good *par excellence*," "the dominant present good," as distinguished from future goods (Rothbard 1962, p. 375). It bears options to a greater degree than any other asset or claim: it can readily be spent at any time. Yet it sits awkwardly on any ordinary scale from present-to-future. As long as its holder continues to hold it—as holders *in the aggregate* normally do—he continues to perform waiting, compensated in the nonpecuniary form of liquidity, or options kept open.

Financial intermediation intertwines with what might be called "real intermediation." Not only financial transactions convey command over resources from some parties to others. Even if bakers borrow very little directly, the ingredients of their bread do contain much waiting performed by others. Farmers wait between planting and harvesting their grain. Farm machinery and baking consume electricity, which is the product of electric power plants requiring much waiting both to build and to render their services over many years. Labor and land use also move in many stages from their ultimate suppliers into ultimate consumer goods. Again, we find parallels between waiting and other factors.

10.4 Patinkin's System

Don Patinkin (1956/1965, Chapters IX–XI) presents a diagrammatic apparatus that, while not designed to treat waiting as a factor of production, can be useful for organizing thoughts about "wants, resources, and technology." Patinkin's main diagram measures the price level (p) on the horizontal axis, and the interest rate (r) on the vertical. The line CC, sloping downward from left to right, shows pairs of price levels and interest rates that equilibrate the market for "commodities," broadly interpreted to include consumer and capital goods and even labor. To the left of CC, commodities are in excess demand, to the right in excess supply (Fig. 10.1).

The line BB shows market equilibrium for bonds (inclusively understood). It is horizontal or slopes mildly upward. It may slope upward because bond-market equilibrium may not depend on the interest rate alone: an arbitrarily increased price level would leave money in excess demand, so decreasing demand for bonds relative to supply and requiring

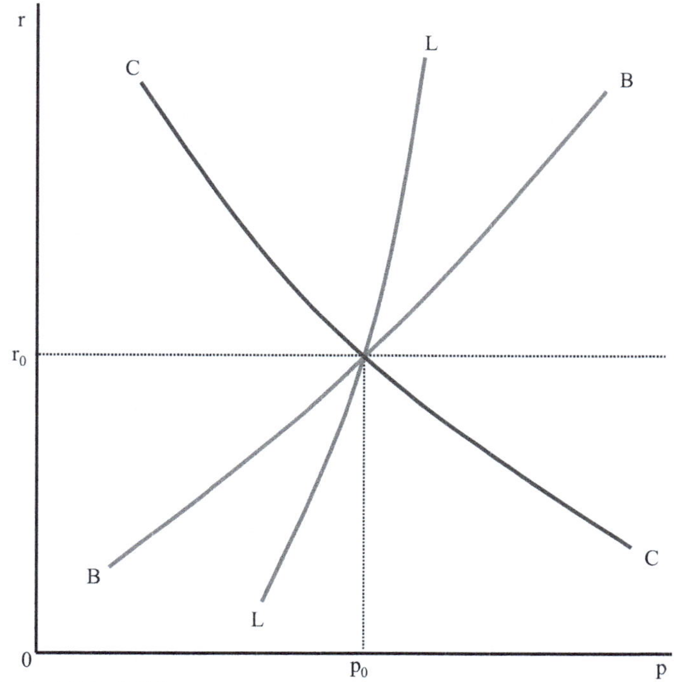

Source: Patinkin (1965)

Fig. 10.1 Patinkin's system

a higher interest rate to maintain partial equilibrium in the bond market. Anyway, bonds are in excess demand above BB and in excess supply below it.

The line LL shows supply and demand equilibrium for money. Money is in excess supply to the left of and above LL, in excess demand to the right and below it. Positions not lying on any of the three lines represent general disequilibrium. LL goes through the intersection of the CC and BB lines and slopes more steeply upward than BB; otherwise Walras's Law would be violated.

Walras's Law is a tautology emphasizing that no one thing or group of things can be in excess demand or excess supply by itself (Yeager and Rabin 1997). Since transactions are two-sided, frustration of desired transactions in one thing necessarily implies opposite frustration of transactions in one or more other things. The sum of the values at their prices of excess-demand quantities of all traded things, with excess supplies counting as negative excess demands, is tautologically zero.

All three of Patinkin's lines go through a common point of general equilibrium; other points on those lines represent *partial* equilibrium in their respective markets. It would be logically impossible and contrary to Walras's Law for one market to be in disequilibrium while the other two were in (partial) equilibrium, and also contrary if LL sloped less steeply than as described.

In Patinkin's apparatus (Fig. 10.2), increased thrift expressed as an increased demand for bonds and decreased demand for broadly defined "commodities" appears as a downward shift of the BB curve and a southwestward shift of the CC curve. A shift of one line alone, meaning a change in the requirements for equilibrium in one market, would violate Walras's Law. The new intersection of those two curves falls on the unshifted LL curves, showing a reduced interest rate. Within "commodities," the reduced rate stimulates investment in capital goods while the postulated increase in thrift reduces current consumption.

Patinkin's apparatus is useful for considering the effects of the quantity of money and of shifts of preferences among commodities, bonds, and money. Increased thrift directed toward bonds is represented by a leftward shift of CC, a downward shift of BB, and a common intersection with the unshifted LL curve. At this new general equilibrium, the price level and the interest rate have both declined.

In Fig. 10.3, increased thrift directed toward money is represented by leftward shifts of the CC and LL curves and a new general intersection on the unshifted BB curve; again, the price level declines and so does the interest rate (assuming some upward slope of BB). Declines in both prices and the interest rate are to be expected from a shift of tastes away from the consumption goods included in "commodities" and so of the CC curve and toward bonds or even money, which is one vehicle of waiting. A reduced general-equilibrium interest rate stimulates demand for investment goods, also included in "commodities."

In Patinkin's analysis, a strengthened demand for money is kept from impairing capital construction by the assumption that a decrease in demand for "commodities" applies to consumer goods in particular and allows demand for investment goods to increase, leaving the total CC line unshifted. Alternatively, impairment of real investment could be avoided

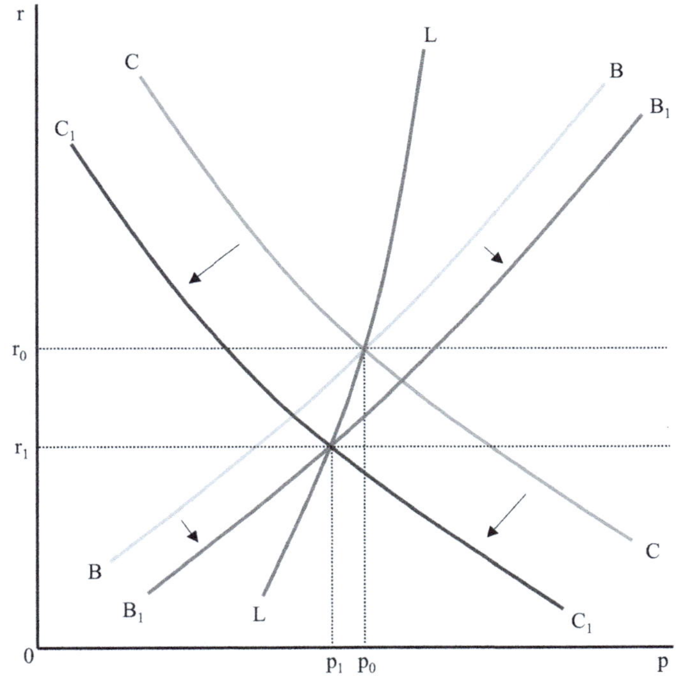

Source: Patinkin (1965)

Fig. 10.2 Patinkin's system: increased thrift toward bonds

by satisfying the strengthened demand for money through increasing the nominal money supply rather than through price deflation. Either way, the real value of monetary wealth, a vehicle of waiting, still increases. Furthermore, the very issue of money, depending on characteristics of the particular monetary system, could serve as financial intermediation, helping convey command over resources from savers to real investors.

A shift of tastes toward money and away not from commodities but from bonds is something that the Keynesian liquidity-preference theory of interest is meant to deal with. Patinkin's framework represents it by a leftward shift of the LL curve and an upward shift in the BB curve. The two shifted curves intersect at a new point on the unshifted CC curve. The price level falls, and the interest rate rises. This result is reasonable. A strengthened demand for an unchanged nominal money supply raises

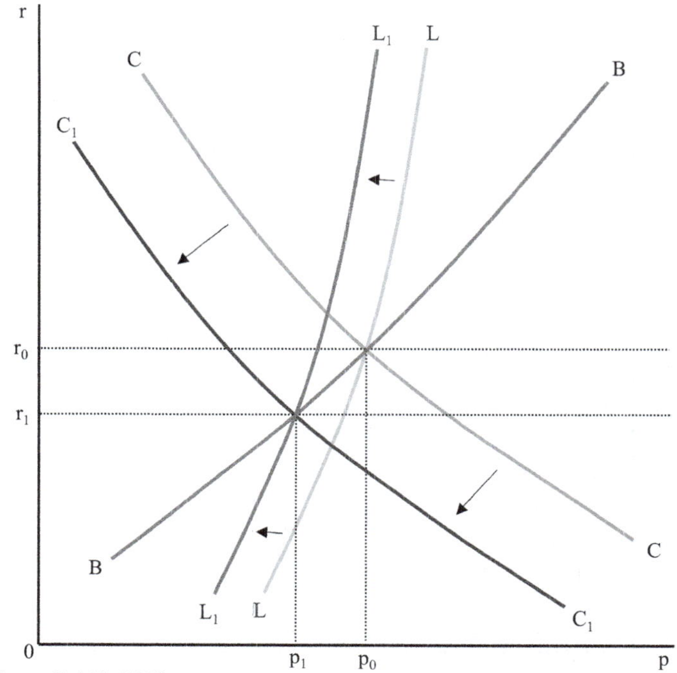

Source: Patinkin (1965)

Fig. 10.3 Patinkin's system: increased thrift toward money

its purchasing power. An increase in the interest rate compensates for a shift of demand away from bonds and toward a less direct instrument, money. Saying so does not deny that money is an instrument for carrying waiting from consumption into real capital formation; it merely recognizes that money does so less directly. An opposite shift of preferences, from money to bonds, shows a downshift of the three-curve intersection; and the reduced interest rate can motivate an increase in real investment at the expense of consumer goods within the "commodities" category (Fig. 10.4).

An overall increase in thrift, as shown in Fig. 10.5, would imply a shift of production from consumer goods to investment goods within the

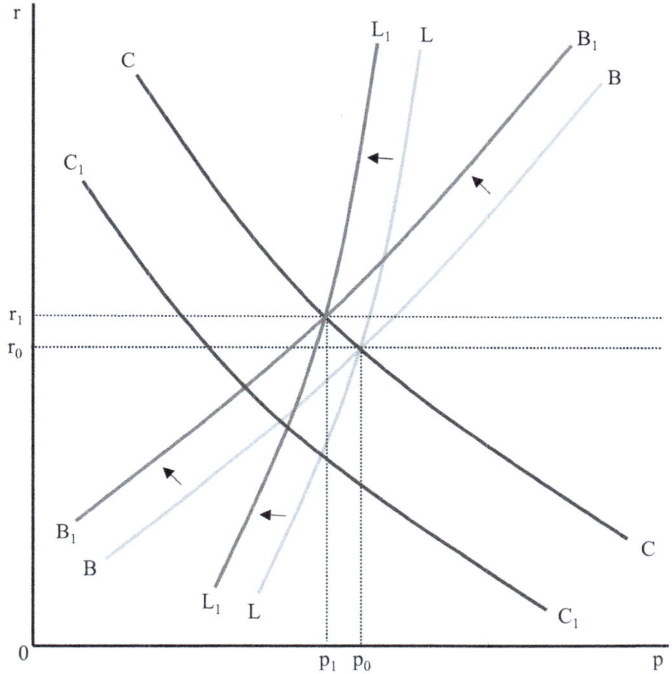

Source: Patinkin (1965)

Fig. 10.4 Patinkin's system: liquidity preference

"commodities" category, a leftward shift of the LL curve, and a downward shift of the BB curve. The new triple intersection shows a reduced interest rate.

In Fig. 10.6, with thrift unchanged but inventions stimulating the demand for investment finance and so for bonds, the BB curve shifts upward. A rightward shift of LL shows a reduced demand for liquidity. A plausible rightward shift of CC shows the increased exogenous demand for investment goods not being fully offset by a decrease in consumption. The new triple intersection shows an increased interest rate and an increased price level at an unchanged money supply with increased velocity.

These considerations seem to override Maurice Allais's worry that money represents wealth from the private but not the social point of

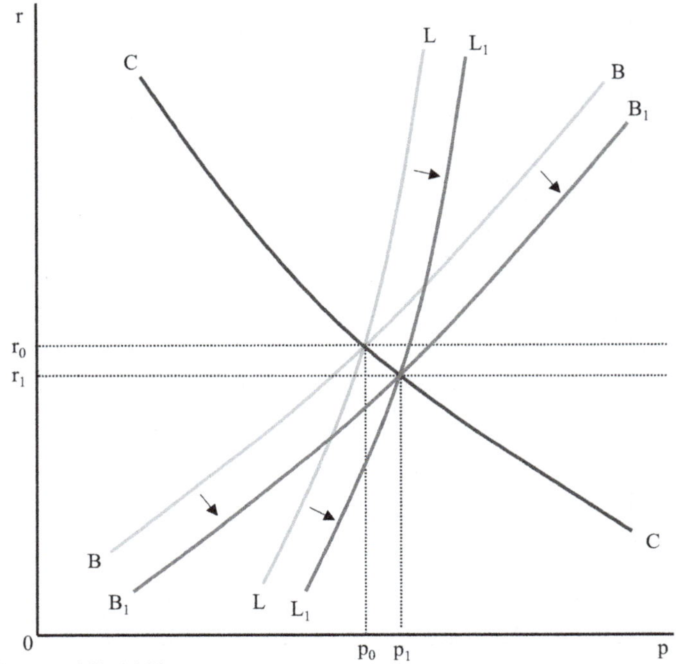

Source: Patinkin (1965)

Fig. 10.5 Patinkin's system: overall increased thrift

view and that the opportunity to hold it diverts the propensity to wait away from capital construction. Allais himself points out that the existence and growth of the demand for money provide opportunities for the banking system to create new money for business loans (1947, Chapter VIII), even without price inflation. His worry, properly narrowed and interpreted, applies only to commodity money, whose production uses up real resources; to money created to finance consumption (including government budget deficits); and to money whose real quantity expands by price-level deflation, which activates the wealth effect and so favors consumption. One reason why Allais's concern about money does not yield a persuasive policy proposal is that a penalty on holding money reduces the volume of real cash and their real services, particularly in facilitating transactions.

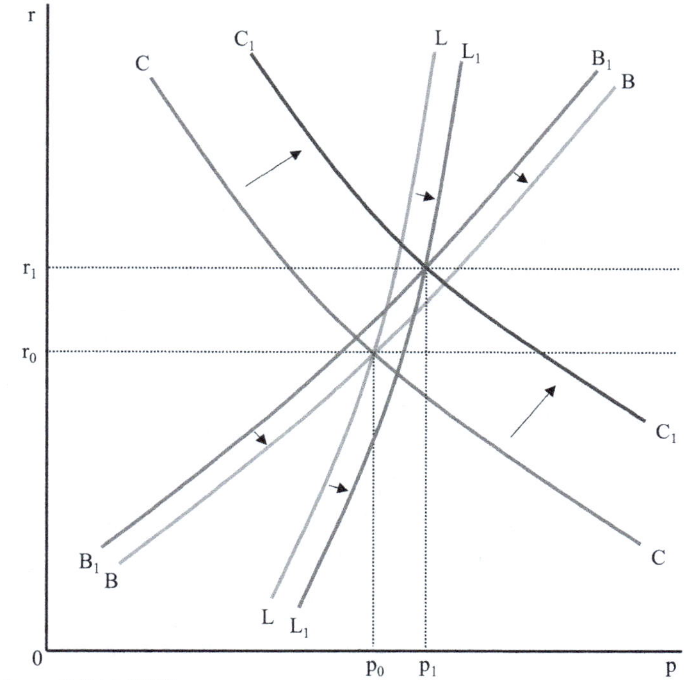

Source: Patinkin (1965)

Fig. 10.6 Patinkin's system: new inventions

The pro-investment countereffect, restricted to a noninflationary degree, is a mild version of "forced saving" (Hansson 1987): new money loaned to investors enables them to bid resources away from other people, who are "forced" to consume less as inflation shrinks the purchasing powers of their incomes, cash holdings, and other nominal assets. In this mild case, for which the term "forced saving" may not be appropriate after all, banks create new money merely in amounts meeting the growing demand for money at the existing price level in a growing economy. New real money created as nominal money in limited amount then does not appear through price deflation, which, accruing to money holders in general, would make them feel richer and promote consumption. Anyway, how additional real and nominal money comes into circulation can more or less correct for the consumption-promoting divergence between the private and social views of money as wealth. An increased willingness to wait, even by way of holding money, then does promote capital construction.

Does this offset to Allais's worry hinge on the *existence* or instead on the *expansion* of money issued to make investment loans? Money matched by loans to investors on the asset sides of its issuers' balance sheets serves as an instrument of intermediation and so facilitates saving or waiting and the construction or maintenance of capital goods. If new investment-related loans replace old ones being paid off, then, even with their total amount unchanged, the money matching them continues serving as a vehicle of intermediation. Even the continued existence of money matched by loans to investors, then, promotes rather than impedes waiting and the maintenance or replacement of capital goods. Like other obligations of nonbank financial intermediaries, and like bonds, money in such a system is an instrument of transferring resources from postponed consumption to capital formation and maintenance.

Once we recognize the intermediary roles of both bank demand deposits and claims on nonbank financial intermediaries, we may wonder whether a sharp distinction holds, after all, between deposit money and government fiat money. Doesn't the public's willingness to hold fiat money convey credit to the government (perhaps through its central bank), so that it need not issue as many bonds as it would issue if the public's demand for real-money balances were weaker? Perhaps one distinction between private and government money rests on the notion that the latter is less likely to finance capital formation and that if the government could issue only bonds but not money, it would compete resources away from capital formation even more effectively. Anyway, a sharper distinction seems to hold between credit money of banks and government alike and commodity money. Satisfying the demand for commodity money does consume real resources.

These remarks do not cancel out what was said previously about how people's willingness to acquire and hold land rather than spend the proceeds of its sale on current consumption does tend to hold down the interest rate and promote capital formation. Nor do they cancel Allais's point that, given the propensity to postpone current consumption, which is a function of income and wealth, the opportunity to accumulate private wealth in the form of land does tend to absorb the propensity to wait in such a way as to impede capital formation.

The entire foregoing discussion serves an analytical purpose only and conveys no policy recommendations. Inflation, for example, might be viewed as a near-equivalent of Allais's tax on money holdings.[4] As such, it would penalize the holding of wealth in that form and so cause a given propensity to wait to be gratified in ways more conducive, directly or indirectly, to capital formation. Yet, even if this argument were clearly correct, it would have to be weighed against the costs of inflation. One among several serious costs is the impairment of economic calculation and distortion of resource allocation through instability and unreliability of the unit of account and standard of deferred payments. Furthermore, inflation can obstruct some channels of financial intermediation.

[4] Actually, Allais does recommend inflation. Money would have two aspects, a constant-valued unit of account and a medium of exchange gradually losing purchasing power (1947, vol. II: pp. 579–585 and passim).

CHAPTER 11

Monetary Policy

Does a judgment about appropriate money supply growth hinge on a distinction between population-based and productivity-based economic growth? George Selgin, for one, thinks so. With the nominal money supply unchanged, growth that reduces real costs of production would depress affected prices and so satisfy an increased demand for real cash balances more or less painlessly (Selgin 1997). But even when nominal money growth in line with real economic growth keeps the price level from sinking, people wanting to hold the increased real balances restrain their spending; they genuinely save. The question arises whether the price-deflation method of real-money expansion would not frustrate, though possibly in lesser degree, the intermediation of saving when productivity grows, much as if the growth came in population instead.

A growth-accommodating increase in the nominal money supply does not misrepresent the availability of resources released by saving. People building up their cash balances really are relinquishing some of their current command over resources, and the intermediaries are transferring that command to borrowers financing real investment.

If the money and banking system did not accommodate the increased demand for real balances, command over the saved resources would have to be transferred in some other way, if at all. Would price and wage deflation transfer resources just as effectively?

L. B. Yeager and S. H. Hanke, *Capital, Interest, and Waiting*, https://doi.org/10.1007/978-3-031-63398-0_11

11.1 Demand and Supply of Real Cash Balances and Liquidity Preference

What happens, however, if the strengthened demand for money, instead of corresponding to the accumulators' underspending of their incomes, merely corresponds to strengthened liquidity preference? What if people want to shift from holding securities to holding more money without doing more saving or waiting? They are demanding more intermediation services. Wanting to hold fewer securities and more money, they are implicitly calling on intermediary institutions to take over some securities and provide money. People's reduced desire to hold securities depresses their prices—raises their interest and dividend yields—while their increased demand for money joins in reducing the interest rate, if any, paid on deposits and near-moneys. By hypothesis, people have become no less willing than before to set real resources free by holding financial assets; only their preferences among financial assets have changed. It seems appropriate, then, that the financial intermediaries accommodate that change in preferences and, so doing, mitigate upward pressure on interest rates.

11.2 Oversaving

Recessions and depressions bring worries about "oversaving"–more saving than real investment absorbs. Total demand is then inadequate to buy all the output of a fully employed economy. If the supply of waiting (not just of money loans) exceeds the demand at the prevailing or even at an attainable lower interest rate, a glut of labor and goods occurs.

The central issue of allocating resources between near-future and remoter-future consumption is distinct from the issue of oversaving or undersaving as the supposed cause of deficient demand and depression or excessive demand and inflation. The latter disorders are types of macroeconomic discoordination. In particular, it is perverse to seek a remedy for supposed oversaving in a pro-spending redistribution of income and wealth. Saving means consuming less than one's income, yes, but it also means trying to accumulate savings, that is, assets. Supposed oversaving involves in some sense excessive efforts to accumulate assets, i.e., an excess demand for them. The theorist must investigate what such assets might be and how they come to be in excess demand. Money turns out to play a key role in the disorder.

Deficient demand for some things necessarily implies excess demand for other things. Walras's Law follows from the fact that market transactions are two-sided. It shows that the positive and negative excess demand values for all marketable things necessarily add up to zero. If desired sales of goods, services, and securities in the aggregate should exceed desired purchases, then some remaining thing must be in matching excess demand. That remaining thing is money. People in the aggregate want to hold more than exists; they are frustratedly trying to build up their cash balances. Conversely, an aggregate excess demand for all things but money implies an excess supply of money. These propositions are tautologically true regardless of just where the line is drawn between money itself and near-moneys and securities, provided that money is defined consistently throughout the argument.

If oversaving (a deficiency of money) prevails, and unless the nominal money supply expands as a remedy, a deflationary gap pushes down prices and wages until the total purchasing power of money is enough to satisfy the demand for it at full employment. But relying on this automatic process as a policy, instead of increasing the nominal quantity of money, would be slow and painful. Letting the nominal money supply shrink would make matters even worse.

The familiar wealth or Pigou effect plays a role in the process (Pigou 1943, 1947; Haberler 1952; Patinkin 1956/1965). As the purchasing power of cash balances rises and people feel wealthier, they become more inclined to spend and less anxious to save. Strictly speaking, this wealth effect operates only on "outside" money. "Inside" money is matched mostly by private debt, like bank accounts before the peculiarities triggered by the 2008 crisis. (Sect. 11.4 defines "outside" and "inside" money.) An increase in the purchasing power of inside money means an increase in real debt burdens also.

11.3 Aspects of the Cash-Balance Effect

The cash-balance effect involves the principle of equal marginal returns on assets held. Holders demand money and other financial and real assets in such amounts that each yields the same rate of expected marginal total return (the sum of both pecuniary and nonpecuniary returns), subject to standard qualifications about imprecise estimation or guesses, risk, lumpiness, marketability, and so forth. If these marginal rates were not equal, holders would switch from relatively low-yielding assets into high-yielding ones. If, on this equal-yield criterion, the actual quantity of money exceeds the total cash balances desired, holders can try to unload their excess money in the markets for investment goods, consumer goods and services, and securities. They can try to replenish deficient cash balances by opposite actions.[1]

Three aspects of this comprehensive real-balance or cash-balance effect may be distinguished. Each potentially operates both directly in the markets for goods and services and indirectly through the financial markets, initially affecting interest rates and other assets and thereby affecting behavior in the nonfinancial markets.

The first, commonly called the *wealth effect*, is essentially what Patinkin (1956/1965) rather narrowly construed as his real-balance effect. An increase in the real quantity of money, accomplished through either nominal expansion or price deflation and considered in addition to other assets, may make holders feel that they are carrying too much portfolio wealth over into the future at the expense of currently enjoyed goods and services, perhaps including personal development. In other words, yields on money and other items of wealth, pecuniary plus subjective, fall short of rates of time preference. Holders will devote some of their perceived excess monetary wealth to current purposes. A shrinkage of real-money holdings works in the opposite direction. Strictly speaking, this wealth effect works not on the total quantity of money but only on what Gurley and Shaw (1960) called "outside" money, money not matched by private debt, such as commodity money or government fiat money; and by itself it is of empirically doubtful potency for other reasons as well.

A second aspect is the *portfolio-balance effect*: people are not indifferent to the composition of their asset and debt portfolios. They heed, perhaps only intuitively, the principle of equal marginal yields, and they will set about remedying a money share that they consider clearly too large or too small. Finding their portfolios unbalanced, holders unload excess money onto goods and services or repair deficient money holdings by opposite market behavior.

A third aspect may be called the *Cambridge effect* with reference to an actual Cambridge *k* (the demand for money, namely the inverse of velocity) higher or lower than desired *k* (Robertson 1963, pp. 443–444

[1] For a somewhat different formulation of these matters, partly rearranged, see Rabin (2004, pp. 126–128) (which we are not plagiarizing; see that book's Preface and Acknowledgments).

described this effect without naming it). People will set about remedying what they consider too large or too small a ratio of their money holdings to their periodic receipts and expenditures by suitably spending down or replenishing their cash balances.

Furthermore, as already noted, each of these three aspects may operate either directly in the markets for goods and services or indirectly through the financial markets, affecting interest rates and other yields. Money-holders may buy bonds because they consider their wealth including money excessive; because they consider money too large a portion of their portfolios; or because they consider their money holdings too large relative to their incomes and expenditures. Cheaper and more readily available loans then spur investment and consumption spending.

Still other slants on the indirect channels may be distinguished. One recognizes that the interest rate is an intertemporal price and that a decline in it means a rise in the price of future goods relative to present goods, which tends to hasten planned expenditures. We consider this point overstressed in recent writings on monetary policy. Furthermore, reduced interest rates raise the prices of existing securities, possibly making their holders feel wealthier and more inclined to spend. Banks tend to become more willing to accommodate credit-rationed borrowers, even judging that their creditworthiness may have improved. Interest rates reduced relative to rates abroad tend to deter imports and spur exports of financial capital, tending to weaken the home currency at a floating exchange rate. Domestic-currency prices of imports and exports then tend to rise and the current account of the balance of payments to move in the direction of a surplus. In all these ways, spending on domestic goods and services tends to increase. In the opposite direction, a policy of tightening the money supply and letting interest rates rise tends to restrain spending and dampen inflationary pressures.

Attention to these combined effects may draw the obvious objection that, as everybody supposedly knows, monetary policy works differently nowadays. But as long as monetary disequilibrium persists, changes keep happening that push the economy closer to equilibrium.

The direct and indirect aspects of the cash-balance effects, plus any subeffects, become deflationary when scarcity of money, perhaps tracing to tight-money policy, makes holders consider their money holdings deficient. This deficiency implies marginal total yields (pecuniary plus nonpecuniary or subjective yields) on their money holdings are higher than the marginal yields on other things that they might buy. A consequent eventual fall in the price and wage level would work toward a new equilibrium, but a policy of just waiting for this sluggish automaticity would be doing things the hard way.

The cash-balance effects are not distinct and separate channels through which the quantity of money affects economywide spending, prices, and real activity. They are aspects of—ways of viewing—a single but multifaceted process. They are like views of a statue from different angles that illuminate a single reality.[2] Distinguishing the various aspects of the cash-balance effect and so of monetary policy is an expository device.

Ample reasons warrant doubt that each of the aspects keeps the same importance always and everywhere. The so-called transmission mechanism of monetary policy scarcely always works in the same way despite changes in accumulated experience, accepted doctrines, policy procedures, technology, and financial institutions and instruments.

An account of how monetary policy bites on the economy should include more than what so much of the recent literature on interest-oriented monetary policy supposes, namely, how changes in the relative price of future and current goods make people hasten or postpone their spending. One central-bank economist who does duly emphasize the quantity of money is Robert Hetzel (2004). He shows how monetary policy can work even if many central-bank colleagues do not think in his own monetarist terms. However, nothing guarantees that changes in the money supply always work with the same potency. The demand for money relative to income (inversely, the velocity of money) will rise when economic distress, uncertainties, and increased caution make individuals and firms want to keep their options open by hanging onto their money.

11.4 "Outside" and "Inside" Money

Gurley and Shaw (1960) distinguished between two parts of the total money supply. "Inside money" is money matched by private debt, like deposits matched on the asset side of banks' balance sheets mostly by loans to borrowers. The narrow Pigou or wealth effect operates either

[2] "The world does not relapse into helpless confusion just because things have more than one aspect and can be correctly described in more than one way. On the contrary, overlapping pictures taken from different angles provide the right way to get a reasonably unified notion of an object" (Mary Midgley 1994/2002, p. 56).

feebly or not at all on inside money, since the increased wealth of its holders at a reduced price level is pretty much offset by the increased real debt burden of borrowers. "Outside money," nearly the same thing as base money, is not matched by private debt; examples are gold coins and irredeemable government fiat money. To the extent that bank money, instead of being matched by debt, is matched by outside money held as reserves, it too counts as outside money. But it would be double counting to count both those reserves and the bank money that they back.

Anyway, as long as saving exceeds intended investment and effective demand for goods and services remains deficient, downward pressure on prices and wages persists until the real value of monetary wealth eventually grows large enough to sufficiently affect propensities to save and invest. Some price and wage levels must be low enough, and some real value of the outside money supply high enough, to do the trick. Long before prices and wages had fallen low enough to raise the real value of money holdings fivefold, say, people's sense of being wealthy and of holding too much purchasing power in money relative to other assets and to income would override any otherwise prevailing tendencies to oversaving out of current income.[3] Saving and investment propensities—or, more broadly, the supply of and demand for waiting in real terms—would become such as to clear the market at a positive interest rate attainable in a monetary economy. The very operation of the monetary mechanism would make a negative or zero interest rate unnecessary to equilibrate the supply of and demand for waiting.

Relying on price and wage cuts to restore equilibrium automatically, however, would be a slow and painful process. Much the same remedy would operate if the monetary authorities expanded the nominal money supply at the existing price and wage level.

As this reasoning suggests, the existence of money does not keep the interest rate from being a price that tends to prevent or remedy oversaving. True, the interest rate is not the only magnitude that changes in an extreme adjustment process; most prices and wages do. But as for any factor of production and given general interdependence, the interest rate price is not the only magnitude that changes in correcting a supply/demand imbalance.

[3] This would happen unless, improbably, the increase in monetary wealth were somehow offset by declines in the purchasing power of other paper wealth.

11.5 Cash Balances and the Possible Diversion of Resources

Maurice Allais (1947) has questioned whether the monetary system performs financial intermediation as satisfactorily as just described. It might conceivably even impair capital formation. The option of holding money tends to divert people's propensity to save and accumulate wealth away from constructing capital goods.[4] This concern applies most straightforwardly to outside money, as Allais himself recognizes, not to the inside money created by financial intermediaries. This effect can hardly be quantitatively important, but it does relate to saving and real investment makes it relevant to a book on that topic.

Allais's concern about money parallels and is illuminated by his concern about land. The argument becomes clearer through comparison with collectibles also—Old Masters, antiques, rare coins, and so forth—demanded as a form of accumulating saved wealth.

Intensified bidding for collectibles, as for land, raises their prices. Their increased value—not merely nominal value but value relative to other goods and services—spells an increase in wealth for individual holders and helps satisfy their propensities to save. Yet the increased values of collectibles and land do not represent any overall increase in real wealth. Still, this increased total market value of wealth encourages consumption and discourages further saving. Holding more wealth of this privately genuine but socially spurious kind leads people to hold less of their savings in capital goods or securities issued to finance them, Allais would claim.

A similar effect can occur with outside money in particular. When strengthened demands for cash balances raise money's purchasing power, the gain in wealth seems genuine to money holders but is less so from the social point of view. Increased real balances of such money, like other privately held wealth, tend to promote consumption; and their growth through price-level deflation makes saving smaller than it would otherwise be. A socially spurious increase in monetary wealth makes real capital formation and purchases of securities to finance it smaller than otherwise.

This whole line of argument clearly regards saving and investment as a good thing, essential to economic growth. Oversaving is bad because it means that monetary disequilibrium leaves labor and other markets

[4] Much the same concern was later and independently expressed by James Tobin and Robert Mundell; Yeager 2003/2011 reviews these writings.

uncleared and frustrates the application of the propensity to save for real investment. Furthermore, nothing in Allais's analysis denies that money is social wealth. Its existence makes a market economy function much more efficiently than a barter economy.

Allais's proposed remedy provides further insight into his reasoning. He suggested stamped money, as Silvio Gesell (1934) did, but for a different purpose. A tax on cash balances would prod people to accumulate wealth in other forms, such as capital goods or securities. Almost equivalently, a policy of chronic mild price inflation would discourage money holding and channel propensities to save and accumulate wealth into socially more productive directions.

He even suggested splitting the unit of account and medium of exchange. The "franc," the unit, would be defined to have a stable purchasing power. The "circul," or medium of exchange, would continuously depreciate against the stable franc, discouraging holdings of circul-denominated money and motivating people to allocate their saving more toward real capital formation. The circul's use as a unit of account would somehow be "flatly forbidden" (Allais 1947, vol. II, pp. 579–585 and passim). The inflationary erosion of wealth held in circuls would also promote saving insofar as people tried to recoup their lost wealth (cf. Mundell 1963; 1971, Chapter 2). On the other hand, some loss of the services of real cash balances would be a drag on economic activity (cf. Short 1979).

It does not greatly matter whether the willingness to save is applied directly to productive projects or goes to buy stocks and bonds. Ultimately, securities can be bought only if they are issued; and, by and large, they are issued more to finance real investment than to finance consumption. If either Allais's tax or ongoing price inflation prods people away from cash balances, financing capital construction becomes cheaper and easier for companies. The resulting larger stock of capital goods tends to raise the productivity of complementary factors of production and tends to reduce the marginal productivities of capital goods and investment, all in line with a reduced interest rate.

Allais evidently assumed a given degree of overall thrift. An increase in overall thrift, even if initially directed toward acquiring larger real-money balances instead of toward securities that finance investment, does tend to promote capital formation, although less so than in the absence of the Allais effect.

Don Patinkin's apparatus of CC-BB-LL curves, explained in Chapter 10, illustrates the process. Although the apparatus, unsupplemented, does not distinguish between consumer goods and capital goods, it does indicate changes in the interest rate and price level that in turn imply effects on capital construction. A shift of preferences away from current consumption, within the category "commodities," toward holding money appears as a leftward shift of the LL curve and southwestward shift of CC, with a new intersection southwestward on the unchanged and slightly upward-sloping BB curve. The reduced interest rate shown by the new general intersection tends to promote capital construction at the expense of consumption within the broad category of "commodities." This result is weaker, however, than if the shift of preferences away from current consumption had been in favor of holding bonds (Fig. 11.1).

More interesting is a shift of preferences, within an unchanged degree of thrift, between two vehicles of thrift—from holding money toward holding bonds. The reduced demand for money appears as a rightward shift of LL, while the increased demand for bonds shifts BB downward. Their new common intersection on an unshifted CC curve shows an increased price level and reduced interest rate, the latter stimulating the demand for investment goods. Briefly, a shift of preferences from the more liquid to the less liquid financial asset—a decline in liquidity preference—has these consequences (Fig. 11.2).

These considerations scarcely rehabilitate the Keynesian liquidity-preference theory. According to Keynes (1936, Chapter 13), the interest rate is the reward for parting with liquidity and is determined by the supply and demand of cash balances. It is not a measure of time preference or of the greater productivity of well-chosen roundabout methods of production.

Relative desires for money and securities belong to "wants, resources, and technology," the ultimate real determinants of prices and quantities. No single price or quantity can change alone. Markets are two-sided. Interdependence is general: everything has some causal relation with everything else, even if of infinitesimal strength. It is no surprise, then, that the taste for cash balances, as one of the ultimate realities, has some influence on prices and quantities and even the interest rate.

It is a fact of experience that the interest rate has some influence on the amount of cash balances demanded. Rain affects how many umbrellas are demanded, but this does not mean that the supply and demand for

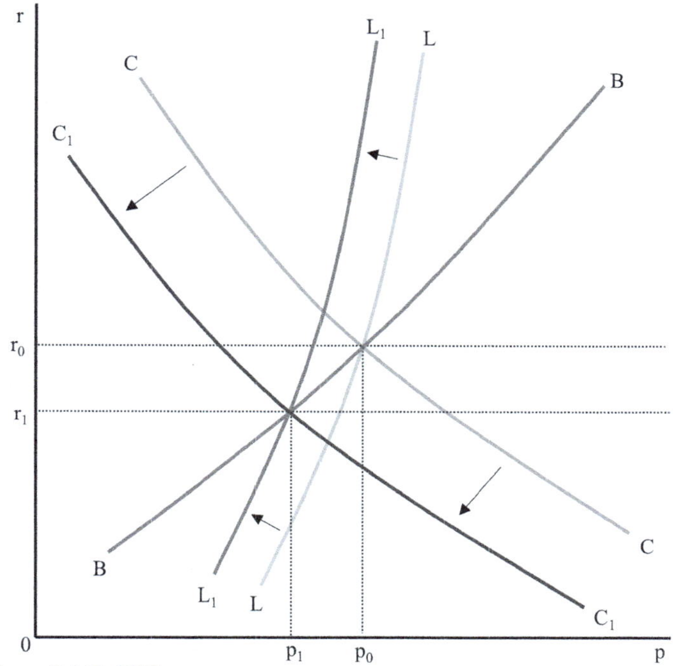

Source: Patinkin (1965)

Fig. 11.1 Patinkin's system: a shift in preferences from current consumption to money

umbrellas govern the volume of rainfall. Neglecting "productivity and thrift" as it does, the liquidity-preference theory does not explain interest rates.

Again, we see that money itself, especially inside money, can be a vehicle of financial intermediation, a means of conveying command over resources from savers to real investors (McKinnon 1973, Shaw 1973). Allais's objection to nontaxed and noninflationary money does not deny this intermediary function but suggests that some types of money perform it imperfectly. He himself recognized that creating new money in ways favoring real investment, as through bank loans, could more or less neutralize the anti-capital-formation effect (Allais 1947, vol. I, Chapter VIII, esp. pp. 338–340). Issuing new inside money to meet a strengthened demand for it, instead of letting price deflation increase the real value

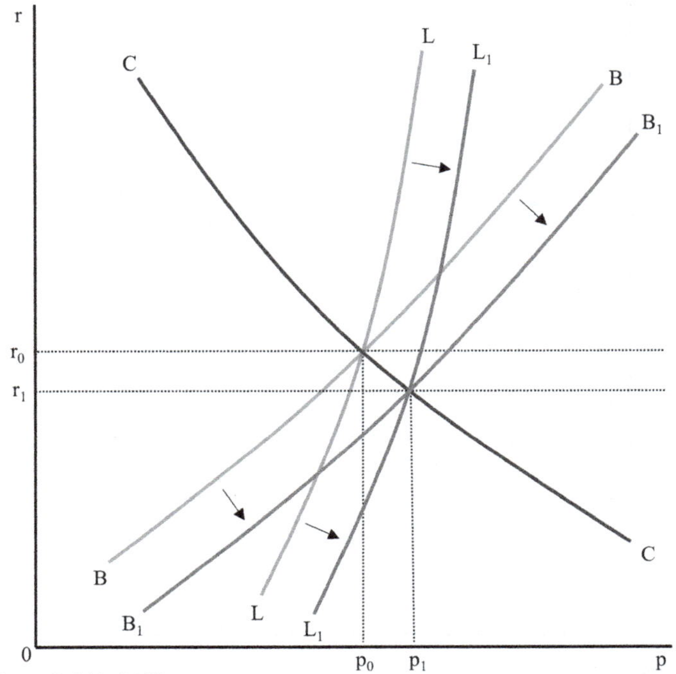

Source: Patinkin (1965)

Fig. 11.2 Patinkin's system: a shift in preferences from holding money to bonds

of the existing outside money, could help convey to real investors the command over resources released by savers who acquire the new money.

This effect of new money is a mild version of "forced saving" (cf. Hansson 1987), although the term is inexact in the mild and noninflationary case considered here. In the prototypical case, new money loaned to investors enables them to bid resources away from other people, who are forced to consume less as inflation shrinks the purchasing powers of their incomes, money holdings, and other nominal claims. In the present mild case, new money does not exploit other people; it appears merely in amounts that meet a growing demand for it at the existing price level. The way in which additional real and nominal money comes into circulation more or less corrects for the consumption-promoting divergence between the private and social views of money as wealth. An increased willingness to wait, even by way of holding money, does then promote capital construction.

This result can even arise from the mere existence and not just the expansion of money if it is inside money matched on the asset sides of its issuers' balance sheets by loans to real investors. As new investment-related loans replace old ones being paid off, even with their total amount unchanged, the money matching them continues serving as a vehicle of intermediation. Continuing to hold savings, even if only as money, promotes rather than deters the maintenance or replacement of capital goods.

The other way of meeting a growth-strengthened demand for real-money balances works through price deflation. Allais's worry does apply to that method and in particular to outside money: money based on a commodity, like gold, whose production uses up real resources; government fiat money of fixed nominal amount; and bank money backed by such kinds of base money. It also applies to money created to finance consumption, including government budget deficits.

Conceivably, outside money such as government fiat money could be partially a vehicle of financial intermediation after all. If the government issues additional fiat money, but no more than enough to avoid price deflation, and if it covers a prudent fraction of its spending with this money, taxes can be lower than otherwise, permitting more private saving and real investment as well as more consumption. Noninflationary new money might even gradually retire the government debt, leaving more funds available for investment, but saying so is somewhat of a fantasy these days. By issuing money in those ways, the government could function as an intermediary helping to channel saved resources into investment. The public-choice literature casts doubt, however, on the likelihood of such government prudence.

11.6 The Issue of a Stable Price Level

Relative to the saving, financial intermediation, and real investment routinely accomplished anyway, the additional volume of that activity accommodated by a nominal money supply growing in line with real economic growth might be modest. Even so, price-level deflation has disadvantages as the way to satisfying a growing demand for real cash balances. It rewards and strengthens the demand for holding money. Price and wage stickiness, although still reasonable from private points of view, then impair production and employment.[5]

Despite the persuasive case for accommodating a growing demand for money in a growing economy by nominal money expansion rather than by price deflation, some Austrian economists worry about "injection effects" of new money. New money does not flow into all sectors of the economy at the same pace, so not all real quantities and relative prices can remain the same as otherwise. But the very existence of money cannot—fortunately—leave all real quantities and prices the same as under barter. Even when price deflation rather than nominal monetary expansion accommodates economic growth, quantities and relative prices are bound to be affected. No monetary institutions, then, can avoid injection effects altogether.

Two opposite extremes are instructive. (1) Money consisting exclusively of a fixed stock of gold or of government fiat money. Its total real value can grow only through price deflation. (2) Monetary expansion and price inflation prodding people to keep their real balances small. Money's services as a quasi-factor of production suffer; getting along on scanty real cash balances wastes resources (Friedman 1969, Chapter 1). Total saving is discouraged by the unattractiveness of accumulating money and by disruptions of economic calculation and asset markets by rapid and unsteady inflation itself. If inflation and market disruption make saving for the future difficult and risky, as sometimes shown by resort to exotic inflation hedges like collectibles, land, and superfluous luxuries, why not live for today? Little financial intermediation can occur through a monetary system so shrunken in real size. Extreme inflation even yields the government less real seigniorage revenue than inflating at a more moderate rate.

No "optimum" behavior of money and prices can be specified precisely. One reason is that at least two dimensions are involved: (a) rates of nominal money growth and of price deflation or inflation, and (b) the degree to which money's "outside" character hampers or "inside" character facilitates monetary intermediation, and here bank reserve ratios are relevant.

[5] It is worth noting, however, that decades of mild price deflation in the United States in the late nineteenth century seem not to have conspicuously impaired real growth.

What arguments for steady mild inflation are available?[6]

1. Chronic inflation and the resulting higher nominal interest rates supposedly give expansionary monetary policy, when appropriate, more room to reduce nominal rates and even push real rates below zero. But interest-rate effects are hardly the essence of monetary policy. The quantity of money and the direct cash-balance effects remain important, even if forgotten. And anyway, would a sound monetary reform retain a central authority practicing discretionary monetary policy?
2. Charles Schultze (1959) argued that a background of rising prices makes it easier for relative price and wage adjustments to clear markets: necessary real cuts in wages or prices can be accomplished by their merely lagging behind the upward nominal trend. But isn't this a matter of fooling people in a way that they eventually catch onto? Persistent money illusion is hard to rationalize. With price-level stability achieved and expected, necessary wage and price cuts would seem more normal than under inflationary price uncertainty. In a dynamic economy, new sectors and occupations are always displacing old ones, and it seems reasonable that price and wage adjustments, not just plant closings and job losses, should ease the ongoing process. An uptrend in productivity and average wages already allows some relative wage cuts to occur without nominal cuts. Price-level uncertainty impairs the formation and adjustment of relative prices; it worsens the signal-extraction problem. Monetary policy is no real remedy for labor-market frictions.
3. Monetary expansion and the resulting price inflation, if at a sufficiently moderate rate, provides government revenue through seigniorage. This could be only a minor source of revenue for advanced countries.
4. One argument of theoretical interest turns out to have little practical importance. Inflation could discourage accumulating wealth as real-money balances and close near-moneys and so divert saving toward productive capital goods instead or securities to finance them. Or, new money might be created directly to finance investment. More capital goods would increase productivity and economic growth.

[6] Marty and Thornton (1995) review and criticize several of the arguments that follow.

> Allais presented this idea in detail. Later, more famously, and as far as we know, independently, it was rediscovered by James Tobin (1965) and Robert Mundell (1971). On the other hand, at least anecdotal evidence suggests that severe inflation diverts saving into bidding up the prices of land and collectibles and into buying ostentatiously expensive residences, cars, watches, and the like, as well as foreign assets. Inflation complicates transactions for the long run. It distorts the tax system. It may divert resources into coping with it through financial, legal, and consulting activities and away from more straightforwardly useful production. Yet such activities count as part of real GDP. Leijonhufvud (1981) describes several such ways in which inflation can impair output and growth.

Another point against inflation is that real-money balances are in effect a factor of production. Holding them economizes on costs of transactions, cash-balance management, and hedging against business fluctuations. Loss of purchasing power through inflation penalizes holding cash balances, causing holders to economize on them and lose some of their services. For this reason, Milton Friedman (1969) advocated an actually declining price level so that the gain in the purchasing power of cash balances would offset the opportunity cost of lost interest on alternative assets. Moreover, Friedman added, cash balances of fiat money are essentially costless to create.

One cannot prove that the ideal money growth rate or the ideal commodity definition of the unit of account is one that keeps the price level stable. However, a flat price-level trend, interrupted by only small and soon reversed oscillations around it, has intuitive appeal. The analogy between a stable money unit and fixed units of distance, weight, and so forth seems persuasive; something is special about zero change. Zero as the price-level trend is a kind of "Schelling point" (Schelling, 1960, pp. 56–59, 111ff.).[7]

Still, the case for a stable price level is inconclusive. Plausible arguments exist for chronic mild inflation and, alternatively, for the "productivity norm" (Selgin 1997). The latter, though ordinarily allowing the price level to drift mildly and painlessly downward in line with reduced real

[7] Schelling advanced the concept of a salient or focal point—a place, number, or whatever—that people desiring to cooperate would spontaneously tend to converge upon in the absence of specific agreement.

costs of production, would permit a rise when productivity deteriorates, or an adverse supply shock occurs.

The arguments for chronic mild inflation won out. Nowadays, it is commonplace for central banks to pursue a modest inflation rate of 2 percent. After being first implemented in New Zealand in 1989, the inflation target spread across the globe (Irwin 2014). Although, recently, Olivier Blanchard and other economists have made arguments to move the target to 4 percent (Blanchard 2022).

11.7 Money and Interest

Although Hume, Mill, and present-day economists recognize the real character of capital and interest, more attention seems to focus nowadays on how monetary conditions can influence and even "distort" market interest rates. Following changes in the money supply, there are three distinguishable stages of transmission. (1) *Injection effect*: new money, if it expands the supply of loans directly or early, pushes interest rates down. (2) *Income effect*: as the new money gets spent around, it raises nominal income and, given economic slack, real income also. Then, interest rates begin to recover from their previously depressed levels. (3) *Inflation-expectations effect*, which operates if monetary expansion and price inflation are expected to continue, further driving inflation and interest rates upward. Monetary expansion may thus affect the interest rate differently in the longer run than at first. As Irving Fisher himself recognized, however, his inflation-expectations effect does not usually take hold promptly and completely. Furthermore, an Allais-Tobin-Mundell effect may drive a wedge between nominal and real rates of interest, not only raising the nominal rate but somewhat depressing the real rate. Shrinkage of money throws these three effects into reverse.

11.8 Monetary Policy and Interest Rates

Monetary policy used to mean regulating the quantity of money to influence the price level, production, and employment. A full-fledged gold standard—if one ever existed—restricted the scope for active monetary policy. Unrestricted two-way convertibility between the dollar and a definite quantity of gold regulated the dollar's gold value and indirectly the money supply and price level. Under a fiat-money system, the central bank regulates the money supply more nearly directly, typically through open-market operations.

Yet, for several decades the public has interpreted monetary policy as manipulating a short-term interest rate to achieve price-level and employment goals. Many or most financial journalists, economists, and central bankers share this interpretation.

In the United States, the Federal Reserve sets or influences the federal funds rate, the rate that banks charge each other for overnight loans, by standing ready to conduct appropriate open-market operations. Almost equivalently, a central bank can dominate short-term interest rates by setting and varying the rate it pays on commercial banks' deposits, and the typically slightly higher rate at which it lends to those banks.

Financial innovations of the last several decades[8] have hopelessly blurred any clear line between just what does and what does not count as money. Since the Federal Reserve can no longer measure, regulate, or even separately conceptualize actual and desired total cash balances, it has given up trying to keep them nearly equal. Taking account of symptoms, it merely tries to correct or forestall major imbalances between money's supply and demand indirectly, by manipulating interest rates. However, this may be too sympathetic an interpretation of what the Federal Reserve is or should be doing; it is not the official story. The diversity of changing concepts and definitions of money may be awkward for policymakers, but it is no embarrassment for a theory of monetary equilibrium and disequilibrium.

In the United States, interpretations of the *Taylor rule* (named for John Taylor, a Stanford University economist) waver between describing interest-rate-oriented monetary policy during its apparently most successful years and actually recommending it as policy. The rule would have the Federal Reserve raise (or lower) its target interest rate if the actual or expected rate of price inflation exceeds (or falls short of) its target inflation rate. A second prong of the rule prescribes cutting (or raising) the target interest rate if the actual unemployment rate exceeds (or falls short of) its target, sometimes called "the full-employment rate of unemployment." Thus, the Taylor rule prescribes a straddle between fighting excessive inflation and fighting unemployment. Whether a central

[8] These arguably in large part represent efforts to wriggle around regulations. Money-market mutual funds, for example, were a response to a ban on interest on bank demand deposits.

bank should try to control both the purchasing power of money and the volume of real economic activity is a discussable issue.

The literature on interest-rate policy generally expects the targeted short-term rate to influence longer-term interest rates also through expectations and arbitrage among time sectors of the credit market. This intersectoral linkage is relatively plausible if the central bank can govern even long-run interest-rate expectations by clearly instructing the public on the rationale and consistency of its policy. The "ifs" involved are major ones. And how could the public confidently expect the target short-term rate to remain unchanged over months or years into the future if the policy works by setting and resetting the target (unless policy is so implausibly successful as to eliminate the business fluctuations that would otherwise call for adjusting the target)? It is no surprise that the connection between short-term and long-term rates in the United States has proved loose indeed.

The rationale of interest-rate-oriented monetary policy, whether generally recognized or not, must ultimately be control of the quantities of whatever instruments serve as money, especially when suitable control cannot be exercised directly. The policy role of interest rates was the theme of Knut Wicksell's influential *Interest and Prices* (1898/1936/1965). Even so, Wicksell considered himself an adherent of the quantity theory of money, and his pages 40–41 give an early and excellent exposition of the cash-balance effect central to that theory.[9]

Wicksell distinguished between *market* and *natural* rates of interest (1898/1936/1965, Chapter 8). The market rate, also called money rate or bank rate, is the observed actual rate, the one set by the banks under the prevailing policy. Of the two rates, Wicksell's natural rate more nearly corresponds to the fundamental price of waiting that mainly concerns this book. His natural rate has been variously interpreted as the rate that would prevail in a natural (barter) economy (which is implausible and almost meaningless), the rate that would equilibrate loanable funds demanded (notably for investment) with a supply of loanable funds from saving and not augmented by money creation or diminished by money shrinkage, or the rate conducive to a stable price level. In recent literature, the natural rate is often interpreted as the equilibrium real rate in a

[9] Humphrey (1975) discusses Wicksell's monetary doctrines briefly and sympathetically.

neoclassical model with perfectly flexible prices. In an alternative interpretation, the natural rate is more changeable; it is the quasi-equilibrium rate that would balance waiting supply and demand under actual conditions, apart from monetary policy. A duly vague summary of all these rival interpretations might be that it is the *appropriate* rate at a given time. Anyway, the actual interest rate may stand in contrast to it.

A clear-cut natural rate of interest no more and no less exists than a natural rate of wages. Both are analytical concepts rather than objectively observable realities. And both are changeable. In any case, setting the actual or market rate below (or above) the natural rate would involve expanding (or contracting) the quantity of money.[10] The main idea is that what makes the market rate below the natural rate is the supply of new money on the loan market, and what makes the market rate above the natural rate is the withdrawal of money.

If policy targets an interest rate rather than the quantity of money, keeping the rate steady would be questionable. The natural rate itself fluctuates over time. If inventions and profitable new investment opportunities should raise the demand for investable funds and so the natural rate necessary to clear the market for savings, keeping the market rate stable would then require pumping new money into the system. If this policy were to persist for a long time, the repercussions of the expanded money supply on nominal incomes and the nominal demand for loans would require even more injections of new money in efforts to keep the market rate stable. In the opposite direction, something, perhaps a decline in productivity or some other adverse shock, might push down the natural rate of interest; and to keep the market rate from falling would require ongoing withdrawals of money from the system.

[10] Whether the money expansion or contraction is associated with a market rate below or above the natural rate is not entirely clear in Wicksell's book. The reason is that he counted the bank-account money that expands or contracts not as *money* itself but as money substitutes affecting the velocity of actual money (base money). This difference between Wicksell and a modern formulation is terminological.

11.9 Austrian Business-Cycle Theory

Although a divergence between market and natural rates of interest cannot be measured precisely, it can sometimes be identified. This fact gives rise to the Austrian theory of the business cycle, originated by Ludwig von Mises and Friedrich Hayek and still cultivated by some present-day Austrian school economists.[11] When the central bank, perhaps under political pressure, drives market rates unduly low, business firms are lured into making interest-rate-sensitive investments. These are typically long-term-oriented projects whose construction and exploitation stretch over many years, like electric power stations, factories, and housing. Although responding alike to cheap finance, such investments are not well coordinated. On some occasions, it eventually becomes unprofitable to complete all the projects, either because the required labor and materials have become especially scarce, which is the usual scenario of the Austrian theorists, or because demand is deficient for the products of the over-optimistically undertaken investments. Austrians disagree about whether to describe the situation as general overinvestment or as malinvestment in particular projects. Anyway, entrepreneurs abandon or cut back on their failing projects, dismissing labor and buying fewer materials, less transportation, and so forth. A snowballing recession is under way. No easy way out is available; the best though belated advice is to avoid artificially cheap money in the first place.

Such an account is conceivable but scarcely supported by evidence. Each recession is a specific historical event. History, informed by theory, has the task of discovering what conditions or events blocked transactions and impaired the economic coordination. There is a scant warrant for supposing that one specific theory explains all episodes. Theory is no substitute for history.

Moreover, the Austrian theory is implausible, unless what counts as supporting evidence is widened into a reminder of miscellaneous troubles that artificially easy money might cause. Is it plausible that entrepreneurs should repeatedly take policy-depressed short-term interest rates as promising cheap finance for their long-run projects? Would they not understand that an interest rate used as a policy tool is meant to be

[11] Ebeling (1978) contains essays by Ludwig von Mises, F. A. Hayek, Gottfried Haberler, and Murray Rothbard.

changed and rechanged as central bankers recognize changed economic conditions?

11.10 Interest-Sensitivity and Wicksell's Cumulative Process

The interest-sensitivity of demand for loans was a favorite topic of questionnaires submitted to business firms decades ago. That sensitivity might well be slight, counting against the Austrian cycle theory, but emphasizing it would understate the power of monetary policy. If cutting the market interest rate can at first get some new money borrowed into existence and spent, even if only a small amount at first, more action follows, as Wicksell's cumulative process explains (Wicksell 1898/1936/1965, pp. 94–101; Patinkin 1965, pp. 368–369, 587–597; Humphrey 1975). Spending the first round of new money tends to raise real output and employment or prices or both, which improves business prospects and the perceived attractiveness of loan-financed projects. Even if the interest rate is not further reduced, the demand for loans grows and is met by further monetary expansion.

When prices rise, even apart from growing real activity, the nominal volume of loans demanded to accomplish definite real purposes, like buying a car or building a factory, increases and provides scope for further monetary expansion. If policy remains doggedly accommodative at the set interest rate, price increases might breed expectations of continuing or accelerating inflation. The nominal interest rate, though not further reduced, would then have become ridiculously low, triggering an ever-increasing volume of loans demanded and accommodated by still more monetary expansion. This story goes into reverse for a market interest rate set above the natural rate and maintained amidst cumulative contraction of loans and money.

Wicksell recognized that the expansionary process could not go on forever if a limited volume of bank reserves (or a responsible central bank) brought it to a halt. Our emphasis here is on the otherwise cumulative nature of the process. The supply of loans granted with newly created money feeds demands for more of the same. People want not only larger loans but also larger nominal cash balances at increased levels of prices and real activity.

This story can recognize that a low-interest-sensitivity of demand for loans and a slight willingness to spend borrowed money might make the expansion sluggish in its early rounds. But the process is self-reinforcing: *cumulative*. Contemplating a low interest-sensitivity of borrowing and spending understates the potency of a persistent policy. Even though it is described in terms of a target interest rate, the policy does involve changes in the quantity of money. The role of money should not be forgotten in discussions of interest-rate-oriented monetary policies.

The natural rate of interest is an elusive, hard-to-define concept, and the advice occasionally encountered to keep the market rate always equal to it verges on vacuity. Although it cannot be clearly defined, something loosely related to it, and likewise not directly observable, also varies over time. This quasi-natural rate also varies because of business-cycle conditions accompanying but distinguishable from monetary factors. This elusive rate is the partial-equilibrium rate that would temporarily balance supply and demand of loanable funds without money creation or contraction. It is relatively high in the boom, when good profit prospects encourage borrowing, and low on poor prospects in the slump. Apart from cyclical booms, a high productivity of waiting and bright investment prospects offered by technological progress should raise the natural rate. So should a strong demand for loans from consumers borrowing against bright future prospects.

A market rate of interest held constant despite changed conditions would contribute to economic instability by being sometimes below and sometimes above a changing natural or quasi-natural rate. A market rate held above a natural rate depressed by bad business conditions would worsen the recession. An interest-rate-oriented policy does affect the money supply; so, policymakers should arguably target some monetary aggregate or aggregates rather than count on interest-rate manipulations to do their job indirectly.

A changing theoretical rate, capable of being only roughly estimated, poses a challenge to interest-rate-oriented monetary policy. Sometimes, however, it is reasonable to hypothesize that this rate lies above the policy-driven market rate. This is true, for example, when the monetary authorities are responding to political pressure to keep interest rates low, when the money supply is growing rapidly, and when inflation is evident. Conversely, it is reasonable to hypothesize that the natural rate is below the policy rate when the latter has not been lowered despite business recession and falling market interest rates.

Moreover, it is not surprising that a gap between the natural and policy-driven actual rates should be variable. And a widely varying actual rate, however excusable or even recommendable as policy, does impede the formation of definite expectations that might otherwise govern longer-term rates.

Setting the market or money rate below the natural rate is possible because the banking system makes loans not only with their depositors' savings but with newly created money. In the opposite situation, the market rate exceeds the natural rate because money supply shrinkage withdraws part of the supply of loanable funds.

11.11 A Supposed Liquidity Trap and Wicksell's Cumulative Process

Many commentators worry that monetary policy becomes ineffective at very low interest rates because the target nominal rate cannot go below zero. A self-feeding deflationary spiral might even develop. But policy could prevent or stop deflation. Even if bad policy had allowed severe deflation, ways to increase the quantity of money would remain. The central bank could massively buy long-term bonds or other claims with newly created base money. It could even persuade holders to sell bonds by paying more than their maturity values, thereby receiving negative interest. The government might cut taxes and cover its budget deficit with newly created central-bank money. In the most stubborn imaginable case, the government could even drop freshly printed money from the proverbial "helicopters."

If even such extreme measures would not work, the economy would be in a so-called liquidity trap. Increases in the quantity of money would fail to stimulate spending because people add all the new money to their idle cash balances. Such a stubborn case is almost inconceivable. Even though a zero-interest yield might leave no incentive to switch from cash into bonds, some consumer goods and services would still provide some positive marginal utility. Massive increases in the quantity of money could make yields on money so low (even negative because of fear of inflation) that the subjective yields on residences, consumer durables, travel, and other luxuries would be almost irresistibly attractive for some consumers. Remember the principle of seeking equal marginal yields on all assets. It is almost inconceivable that the public would go on and on accumulating newly created money in idle hoards, never letting it inflate spending and prices. The several aspects of the cash-balance effect enter into explaining why not. Realistically, money supply expansion would sooner or later trigger Wicksell's cumulative process.

If, despite everything, an inconceivably stubborn liquidity trap was to develop and persist, the government could abolish taxes and finance itself painlessly by the printing press. *Reductio ad absurdum!*

These thoughts do not recommend complacency. Remarkable foresight and skill would be required to get the timing, dosage, and an eventual partial withdrawal of new money just right. A plausible worry about massive measures to forestall or stop deflation would be severe inflation later on.[12]

11.12 Forgetting the Money in Monetary Policy

Neglecting how interest-rate policy relates to the quantity of money, as so much recent literature does, neglects essential channels through which policy works. The currently prevailing account appeals to an intertemporal substitution effect. A reduced interest rate cheapens present goods relative to future goods, inducing people to hasten their purchases of investment and consumer goods. An increased rate cheapens future relative to present goods, inducing people to postpone purchases. Perhaps so, but by how much and with what effect are purchases hastened or postponed? Summers (2016, p. 108) questions this "pull forward" view, as he calls it. If reduced interest rates do persuade people to buy cars and capital goods sooner than otherwise, what happens to demand for such things in the later period, from which the demand has been pulled forward?

If monetary policy works, it must work in some way besides this effect of the relative prices of present and future goods. By the way, what determines general price levels? On Wicksell's quantity-theory view, policy works through additions to or withdrawals from the money supply as the market interest rate is set below or above the natural rate. Yet the current policy literature, although not flatly denying this money supply aspect, does neglect or downplay it and the three mutually complementary strands of the cash-balance effect.

Sellon (2004, p. 5) represents a remarkable example of this literature:

[12] For a "foolproof" way to avoid the Keynesian liquidity trap, see (Congdon 2011, pp. 70–72).

> In principle, the monetary policy transmission mechanism can be described rather simply. When the Federal Reserve raises its target for the federal funds rate, other interest rates also rise—reducing interest-sensitive spending and slowing the economy. Conversely, when the federal funds rate target is lowered, other interest rates tend to fall—stimulating spending and spurring economic activity.

While adequate for some purposes, this stylized description of the transmission mechanism is less helpful in explaining the complex relationship actually observed in financial markets.

The description is inadequate, Sellon himself continues, because it skims over the complex relations between the policy-determined interest rate and longer-term rates. He stresses expectations of future rates. The Federal Reserve can manipulate expectations not only by how it sets the current target rate but also by communicating with the financial markets in various ways.

So Sellon simply takes it for granted that interest rates affect total spending through people's decisions to accelerate or delay their purchases. Not once does he allude to the quantity of money or any monetary aggregate or any cash-balance effect.

Bennett McCallum entitles one of his articles "Monetary Policy Analysis in Models Without Money" (2001). While not outright endorsing or condemning that modeling style, he recognizes its prevalence in the literature. Michael Woodford's much-admired *Interest and Prices* (2003) is a prominent example. A Google search turns up several articles entitled something like "Monetary Policy Without Money." Quite a few economists who consider themselves researchers on the frontiers of knowledge apparently consider earlier contributions to understanding how money matters either so well incorporated into the current literature or else so out of fashion that reminding their readers of them would be condescending.

11.13 Dangling Puzzles

One puzzle concerns why interest rates fluctuate as they do; a second concerns the relation between government finance and interest rates. The third, a multifaceted puzzle, follows in a section of its own.

Why do market interest rates fluctuate sometimes so much and sometimes so little? Around 1980, short-term interest rates in the United States briefly reached almost 20 percent. Since the economic crisis struck in 2008 until early 2022, on the other hand, interest rates on high-quality short-term debt have been kept down to a small fraction of 1 percent.

The natural rate of interest has some influence on market rates. This is true, more particularly, of the *quasi*-natural rate. The rate of intertemporal transformability of resources, the marginal productivity or marginal efficiency of capital or investment, or whatever one may call it, is not something purely objective. It largely reflects subjective assessments of the prospective profitability of investment; Keynes spoke of "animal spirits." Business pessimism depresses and optimism stimulates the demand for investable funds. Those circumstances are partially real (nonmonetary) even though business fluctuations themselves often trace to monetary causes.

Sometimes a high market rate of interest reflects price inflation expected to continue—the Fisher effect. Sometimes a high rate is part of a tight monetary policy intended to resist inflation, as in the early 1980s.

On the other hand, a low market rate of interest may be largely because of "regime uncertainty." As Robert Higgs (1997) noted, during the Great Depression, confusion and fear surrounding the New Deal's overwhelming new set of expenditures, regulations, and government involvement in the economy severely depressed private sector economic activity and investment. The government's own heightened activity could not make up for the reduction in the private sector. As a result, "regime uncertainty" depressed the natural rate to very low levels.

The state of U.S. government finances seems to influence interest rates much less than one might plausibly expect. A deficit implies government borrowing, so one might expect interest rates to rise and fall with its size. Yet, statistics of recent decades show no clear relation. In years flanking 2010 or thereabouts, the U.S. government deficit and debt have zoomed, yet interest rates remained at historically low levels.

The distinction between saving and waiting is unimportant in some earlier contexts, but not here. Interest rates tend to reconcile the supply of and demand for total waiting, not just current saving. Saving is the part of current income withheld from current consumption and applied to building up *savings* (or paying down debt); *savings* are net financial and physical wealth that its owners continue holding over time. They *wait*, perhaps indefinitely, before cashing these assets to pay for consumption. The total volume of this waiting is vastly greater than any year's addition to or subtraction from it through saving or dissaving. The government's annual deficit absorbs only a small fraction of the waiting required to carry its already incurred and still growing debt and required, moreover, to meet the much larger total of other nationwide and worldwide demands for waiting. Given the many ways in which waiting is performed and given the worldwide integration of financial markets, one government's current deficit and accumulated debt are both small indeed in relation to the worldwide ongoing total volume of waiting.[13]

Whether reassuring or disturbing, this circumstance must explain why government deficits (and the occasional surplus) have little noticeable effect on interest rates. Damage can be slow and insidious. A deficit can avoid trenching on current consumption by allowing neglect of constructing new capital goods or of repairing or replacing old ones. Whether the method of financing a deficit might eventually cause inflation is a genuine but distinguishable issue.

11.14 Deficit Spending

Fiscal policy and monetary policy can be distinguished as ways of manipulating total spending toward macroeconomic goals, but the two overlap. They can even be tightly combined, most obviously as deficit spending financed by the issuance of money, or what is often termed the monetization of the deficit.

What is the relation between government finance and a shift of burdens between generations? It used to be widely thought, especially in the heyday of Keynesianism in the early years after World War II, and even among sophisticated economists, that government deficit spending could not shift the costs of government activities from the present generation to future generations—not, anyway, if the bonds to cover the deficit were sold at home rather than to foreigners. For them, "we owe the debt to ourselves." People in the future may have to pay to redeem the bonds, but future people will also collect the payments. Furthermore, resources are used when they are used: resources to fight a war, for example, are taken from the current generation, not resources somehow conjured out of the future.

It is a correct but superficial comment that taxpayers who will have to repay maturing bonds do not coincide with bondholders who will

[13] It doesn't much matter whether we regard the deficit and debt as a demand for waiting or as a subtraction from the total supply.

receive repayments. A fuller answer explores the subjective nature of "the burden." Persons who voluntarily buy government bonds do not suffer a burden merely because they thereby relinquish current use of their money; after all, they judge buying the bonds advantageous. James Buchanan (1958) developed this point. The burden comes later and falls on whatever people must pay taxes to service the bonds or on bondholders and others who may lose their wealth as irresponsible government expropriates it by default or, more probably, inflation.

Most importantly, although future generations cannot identify specific resources somehow physically conjured away from them by their ancestors, government debt finance can have much the same effect by altering resource allocation. Government deficits subtract from total national saving and so impair investment in material and human capital. To some extent, people buying government bonds divert savings that they might otherwise have put into stocks and bonds and so into real investment. They themselves do not suffer a burden from voluntarily placing their savings that way, but the changed allocation of resources leaves less physical and human capital for the future than would have been created without the government's deficit spending. Future generations inherit a less productive economy, unless the government borrowing went to finance truly productive projects, which only a small fraction of it does in the United States today. Future generations lose as if resources had actually been conjured away from them.

Furthermore, deficit spending has implications for the current account of the balance of payments and for foreign indebtedness. For example, the United States, largely as a result of its fiscal deficit, has had a savings deficiency every year since 1975, which is mirrored by the current account deficit (Hanke and Li 2019). Nevertheless, it does not call for blanket condemnation as sheer waste. It may create publicly owned capital goods—"infrastructure." Its rationale during a major war is obvious.

11.15 The Puzzle of Persistently Low Recent Rates

We might wonder how the Federal Reserve kept short-term and even long-term interest rates exceptionally low from the onset of the 2008 crisis through early 2022, although the ordinary money supply (M2) grew moderately. Federal Reserve purchases of securities greatly expanded the supply of base money, but banks kept most of this expansion idle as excess reserves instead of using it, as one might expect, to expand their loans and investments and so the system's deposits.

This unprecedented accumulation of excess reserves had something to do with keeping interest rates low. In effect, the Federal Reserve was supplying loans to the credit markets by buying securities. Banks passively, by default, collaborated in supplying credit by only very partially activating the resulting excess reserves into deposit money. Credit was created without much creation of ordinary money, and the persistent excess reserves cry out for explanation. The Federal Reserve's payment of interest on excess reserves enters into the story.

Interest rates were remarkably low during most of the twenty-first century until early 2022. Central-bank policies enter into the explanation but are not the whole story. Ben Bernanke (2015) explained persistently low rates largely by a "global savings glut." The absorption approach to the balance of payments shows how a country's surplus exports of goods and services may reflect saving not invested at home. Surplus-country purchases of financial assets do seem at times to have pushed down interest rates in reserve-currency countries like the United States.

Alvin Hansen put forth the theory of secular stagnation at the end of the 1930s, when it was wrong, but Lawrence Summers (2016) finds it applying nowadays. A long-term slowdown of economic growth and consequent loss of investment opportunities have left a relative glut of saving. Slower population growth has slowed building houses and making consumer durables for them. Technology has reduced the use of capital goods relative to GDP. Capital flight or reserve accumulation by China has been a factor. An increased global demand for safe assets has pushed down yields on government securities in particular. Various kinds of credit rationing constrain borrowing, while financial capital has access to world markets.

Researchers have brought demography into the story. One way to summarize this material is to list the factors tending to promote relatively high or low rates, other things being equal. These factors intertwine with each other and with non-demographic factors. We can agree that prosperity promotes high interest rates and depression, low rates.

Growth makes the standard life-cycle model work: dependency in childhood, borrowing in early working years (for education, family formation, and purchases of houses and furnishings), net saving in the peak earning years, and dissaving in retirement. Prospective borrowers would prevail over lenders, were not interest rates at ordinarily high levels.

Differential growth among segments of a population complicates matters. Growth promotes the supply of waiting as well as the demand for it, but less so if the growth occurs among young people, who tend not to be big savers. When the population grows faster among prime-age earner-savers than among borrower-dissavers, interest rates come under downward pressure, except that growth of the working-age population promotes high interest rates by creating opportunities for investment in capital goods, infrastructure, and human capital. Population is already declining in some advanced and middle-income countries, and in others, growth is expected to slow down. Working-age populations have begun to decline as a fraction of the total; the dependency ratio (nonworkers/workers) is expected to rise globally, with Africa the main exception (Wynne 2016). Because retirees in the aggregate do not save or in any case save less than workers, aggregate saving would fall, and the interest-rate rise.

Economic growth depends not only on population but on gains in productivity. These potential gains create investment opportunities to put them to use through machinery, for example, and human capital. On the other hand, technological advances may reduce demands for capital goods. But do investment opportunities depend more on the growth of the *total* or of the *working-age* population?

Expectations of longer life and more years of retirement should encourage people of prime working age to build up more savings, putting downward pressure on interest rates. Richard Fisher, former president of the Dallas Federal Reserve bank, suggested a self-reinforcing aspect: low interest rates press people to save more for their retirement needs (Hilsenrath 2016).

Slower population growth slows building houses and making consumer durables for them. It leaves more capital equipment per worker, reducing its marginal productivity and the demand for more of it (Carvalho, Ferrero, and Nechio 2016). Technology has apparently reduced the use of capital goods relative to GDP. Uncertainty and regulation may also have slowed real investment. An increased global demand for safe assets instead of investment assets has pushed down yields on government securities in particular (Summers 2016; cf. Higgs 1997 on "regime uncertainty").

Just as strong economic growth tends toward high interest rates, a slowdown tends toward lower rates. Slower growth in developed economies and fast growth in emerging markets give the higher household savings rates in the latter more worldwide weight. Especially, moreover, where incompletely developed financial institutions, imperfect knowledge, risk, and credit rationing constrain the demand for loans more than the supply, lenders are freer than borrowers in their financial activity. Interest rates are held down, and savers look for better opportunities to lend and invest abroad (Coeurdacier, Guibaud, and Jin 2015) Persistent surpluses of exports of goods and services and of financial capital suggest a kind of forced saving imposed, perhaps inadvertently, by policy. In advanced economies receiving these capital flows, interest rates are pushed down.

Coeurdacier, Guibaud, and Jin (2015), note that credit rationing puts would-be borrowers at a disadvantage. They cannot obtain all the loans they might want at the going interest rate because potential lenders must judge their creditworthiness, and with imperfect knowledge. Lenders, who bear or shun risk, are relatively free to choose among outlets for their money. This asymmetry is notable in developing market economies, where incomplete financial development disadvantages would-be borrowers more than lenders. Also, rapid growth favors saving, as in China and some other Asian countries. Paradoxically or not, then, rapid growth with still relatively credit-constrained domestic finance tends to promote capital outflows and export surpluses, with opposite balance of payments positions in the developed countries that receive these capital inflows and so experience downward pressure on interest rates.

Researchers find some demographic support for attributing the fall in interest rates to a supply of waiting that would exceed demand at the old rates to a changed balance between the supply of and demand for waiting. Michael A. Walker (2016, echoed by Jordan 2016) argued that in the 29 economies making up 90 percent of the world's GDP, the generations that save have come to overshadow the borrowers. Only in the middle years of peak earnings in a typical life-cycle do people, saving for retirement, have a net demand for financial assets. In recent years their supply of savings (waiting) has become exceptionally heavy.

For evidence, Walker constructs a population ratio of saver-lenders to borrower-dissavers. Plausibly, with other things equal, the higher (or lower) this ratio the lower (or higher) interest rates are. This lenders/borrowers ratio has been rising in major countries. It works as an explanatory variable in multiple regressions for interest rates.

However, Walker may have reached a correct conclusion but misinterpreted the evidence. He counts people aged 0 to 49 as borrowers and aged 50 to 75 as savers. But don't the middle years of net saving begin and end before those ages? Walker pays scant attention to the cohort that dissaves in retirement, which plausibly begins before age 75. Many households, he says, do not enter that phase and remain in surplus until death. Yet, a familiar complaint in the United States is that the percentage of the working-age population in the labor force has been shrinking and, furthermore, that the typical family does not save enough for retirement. Walker recognizes that the standard view about saving and dissaving would hold true if households behaved as in the familiar life-cycle story and if population growth were steady, which it no longer is.

Thus, whether growth tends to lower or raise interest rates depends on various distinctions. The current consensus seems to be that the slowdown in growth in developed countries has reduced interest rates. Carvalho, Ferrero, and Nechio (2016) estimate that demographics can account for a 1.5 percentage point decline in the equilibrium interest rate in developed countries between 1990 and 2014. Rachel and Smith (2015) argue that demographics account for close to 1 percentage point of the 4.5 percentage point decline in the global neutral interest rate[14] between 1980 and 2015, with the sharper decline since the crisis of 2008 possibly triggered by the consequent pessimism about growth.

Other economists have independently rediscovered the "regime uncertainty" already emphasized by Higgs (1997). Baker, Bloom, and Davis (2016), by exhaustive scrutiny of leading newspapers, have constructed an index of "economic-policy uncertainty" for the United States and other countries. Unsurprisingly, uncertainty was high in the 1930s, and recovery from the uncertainty triggered by the 2008 crisis has been slow. Ion and Gulen (2013) argue that such uncertainty discourages big investments. Akey and Lewellen (2015) add that uncertainty encourages defensive political activity by policy-sensitive firms. Weak demand for investment finance surely contributes to holding interest rates down.

Our survey of factors tending toward high or low interest rates is admittedly incomplete and inconclusive. The same is true of factors bearing on the price of an ordinary good. Again, considering the supply and demand for waiting and its price parallels the understanding of an ordinary factor price.

Do the very low interest rates persisting since about 2007 argue that interest is a purely monetary phenomenon and discredit the concept of waiting as a real factor of production? While Federal Reserve policy goes

[14] Evidently related to a long-term equilibrium rate and to Wicksell's rate.

far toward explaining the low rates, mere monetary policy cannot abolish their fundamentally real character and the scarcity of waiting. The yields on a variety of securities, loans, and investment projects, including credit-card rates, have not fallen fully in step with the federal funds rate (at which far fewer transactions take place than earlier) and other short rates. Nonprice rationing of credit seems to have been stricter than usual, but it is not the whole story.

If Wicksell's natural rate of interest were definitely higher than the prevailing low rates, keeping them so low would require the Federal Reserve to keep expanding the money supply. The Federal Reserve has indeed been buying securities (in "quantitative easing") and stands ready to buy as many as necessary to keep the federal funds rate near its low target level. Yet, although the Federal Reserve has expanded its balance sheet at an unprecedented level since the start of the recession in 2007, the ordinary total money supply (say M2) has grown nowhere nearly in step. Wicksell's theory has not been put to a recent test. Banks have so far accumulated vast excess reserves, which, if and when put to use, would greatly change the picture. Until 2021, price inflation had been mild. Indeed, central bankers had been worrying about actual deflation and even about supposedly inadequate—below 2 percent—price inflation. Plausibly, such complacency betrays a very short-run perspective.

In applying Wicksell's analysis of what interest rates below the natural rate do to the money supply, what counts in the short run is a shortfall from the quasi-natural rate, as explained previously. Sluggish recovery from the recession of 2007 on, with heavy unemployment persisting, perhaps promoted consumer and business caution and so supported a propensity to save or wait that held down this quasi-natural rate.

Also contributing to pessimism were persisting uncertainties and lack of confidence related to economic policies, notably in housing and mortgage finance, that contributed to the housing bubble and crash and its financial consequences. Many financiers and real-estate brokers took reckless and predatory advantage of the opportunities offered by perverse policies. Also belonging in the story is a background of cheap money that promoted debt and caused a search for yield through newfangled financial instruments that soon belied pervasive optimism about their soundness.[15]

[15] However, Robert Hetzel (2009, 2012) argues that a short episode of *tight* money also belongs in the story. Although a recession had begun at the end of 2007, as late as the summer of 2008, before the crisis turned dramatic in September, the Federal Reserve

Business suffers from uncertainties about policies regarding the ominous shape of government finances, taxes, health-insurance costs, and financial and environmental regulations. Often we hear, however, that the problem is not a lack of confidence but a lack of spending, or effective demand. But the issue is not one or the other. Lack of confidence and lack of demand reinforce each other. Questionable policies and pervasive uncertainties tempt households, firms, and banks to keep their options open by just holding onto their money.

And uncertainties may motivate a flight into supposedly safe assets, which may partly account for low rates on bank accounts, commercial paper, and U.S. government securities—despite the huge and growing government debt. Just as the high interest rates on junk bonds consist largely of an insurance premium collected as a reward for bearing the risk of default, so, in the opposite direction, the differential lowness of interest rates accepted on the reputedly safest securities may be interpreted as an insurance premium paid for avoiding the risk of the riskier securities.

And explicit interest is not the only reward for waiting. By and large and on average, rates of return on stock, consisting of dividends and price appreciation, have been higher than the puzzlingly low interest rates of recent years. Further psychological factors and sluggishness of responses might be dragged into an explanation–but rather lamely. Until early in 2022, the puzzle of persistently low rates persisted.

11.16 A General Theory of Recession?

Capital and interest and monetary theories enter into explaining business recessions, but they do not add up to a single detailed theory for all episodes. Each is a specific historical event. Historical research, guided by economic theory, has the task of identifying similarities and differences among them.

Broadly, a recession is a disruption of the intersectoral and intertemporal coordination explained in any good microeconomics course. People are unemployed and businesses are short of customers, even though people would gladly become better customers if they had jobs and incomes, and businesses would gladly hire more workers if they had more customers.

had not yet cut the federal funds rate to match the already declining quasi-natural interest rate.

The price system ordinarily accomplishes tolerably good coordination—almost miraculously, given the many billions of interdependent transactions, domestic and international, carried out or attempted every day. Almost all are multilateral transactions (rather than barter between two parties), and transactions are not only between households and business firms but among firms themselves. Firms deal with one another in innumerable basic resources, materials, semi-finished goods and parts, transport and other services, and consumer goods for inventories. Transactions in securities and consumer and business credit are vital. Furthermore, all these transactions (except barter) are indirect, requiring money or credit denominated in money, which leaves open the possibility that transactors might try to hold more money than exists. Transactors must take account not only of changes in technology and tastes but also in interest rates, foreign-exchange rates, taxes, and regulations and controls. Prices convey, in condensed form, information about consumer and worker preferences, current and potential production methods, scarcities and gluts, and innumerable local and changing conditions, including information that cannot be expressed in words or numbers. Transactions, whether accomplished or frustrated, also convey information, along with prices (Hayek 1945).

Again, this immensely complicated and decentralized system works almost miraculously well. Disruptions do occur, though, and become contagious. Since transactions are voluntary, the smaller of the demand and supply quantities is the actual quantity traded on a market. A fall of activity and income in one economic sector reduces its demands for the products of other sectors, where production, incomes, and capacity to pay for the outputs of still other sectors also fall. And so on cumulatively.

Clower (1967/1984) presents a "dual decision theory" distinguishing between the "notional" demands and supplies of general equilibrium and the "effective" supplies and demands expressed in the real world, where people must take account of their actual circumstances and incomes. For example, an unemployed person expresses a weaker demand for goods than he would if the market for his labor cleared (Clower 1967/1984).

Say's Law (Say 1836) is sometimes stated and criticized without due regard to money, but its central idea is essential. People produce particular goods to trade them away for other goods: they supply in order to demand. There cannot be a general excess of supply relative to demand except as impairment of transactions causes that appearance. If transactors cannot sell their own goods for money, they cannot make their demands for others' goods fully effective. Impaired transactions can thus worsen one another, as Clower, as well as W.H. Hutt (1974) describes.

Many employer/worker and buyer/supplier contacts are established, maintained, broken, or restored. Many prices are gotten right or wrong, and not only current prices relative to each other and to the quantity of money but also intertemporal prices, including interest rates. Business-cycle research investigates, or should, what worsens obstacles to transactions from time to time.

Many modern Austrian economists blame excessively easy monetary policy and artificially low interest rates. These lure business firms into "malinvestments," especially interest-sensitive, long-term oriented projects that cannot all be completed either for lack of resources voluntarily saved from consumption or else for lack of enough customers for the over-optimistic projects even to cover their costs. Reversal of the cheap-money policy lest inflation grow extreme may contribute to ending the boom. Production and employment fall off cumulatively. The recession is under way.

As abstract logic, such a scenario is coherent. But is it a general explanation of recessions? We know of no adequately documented recession for which it is plausibly the main explanation. Some other explanation applies to most episodes. Saying so is not to deny, however, that artificially cheap money and low interest rates have indeed sometimes caused bubbles and other troubles.

Clark Warburton, Milton Friedman, and others before them have focused on monetary obstacles. As they have shown, most recessions and depressions have involved disorders of money and of credits denominated in and ultimately to be settled in money. Does an economywide disruption of business trace instead to shocks to technology, tastes, or prices on particular markets, as supposed by the lately fashionable theory of "real" business cycles? Evidence for that idea is scarce. Even the few recessions appearing to be of basically nonmonetary origin have the monetary aspect of households and firms trying to hold more money than usual in relation to their incomes and transactions.

To insist that all recessions originate in a deficient (or conceivably excessive) supply of money would be dogmatism, but diagnosis must take money into account. Money is the one thing traded on all markets (apart from barter); and almost all prices and debts, even disequilibrium prices, are expressed in money. Unlike other things, money has no market of its own on which supplies and demands confront each other and achieve equilibrium through adjustment of money's own price—for money has no price of its own. The inverse of the general price level is not the same as a definite price directly pushed toward equilibrium on its own market.

"Real" factors sometimes do appear in economywide discoordination. Not all unsatisfactory realities can be remedied by manipulating money; that is one of the teachings of monetarism itself. Before and in the recession of 2007–2009 and during the unusually sluggish recovery that followed, transactions were disrupted by the consequences of questionable earlier policies, notably in housing and mortgage finance. A background of excessive monetary ease, promoting debt and a "search for yield" through new financial instruments, also belongs in the story. The shriveling of credit markets worsened conditions on themselves and on other markets.

Media reports at the time of the 2007–2009 recession were full of accounts of how existing policies and pervasive uncertainties caused households, firms, and banks to keep their options open by just holding onto their money. The uncertainties included the usual ones of recession but also concerned looming policies regarding government deficits and debt, taxes, health-insurance costs for businesses, and financial and environmental regulations. Ignorance of economics, even at the highest levels of government, was evident (as always). The business and consumer confidence necessary for recovery suffered.

Often, however, the problem was blamed not on a lack of confidence but lack of spending, of effective demand. But the issue is not one or the other. Lack of demand is a defining aspect of recession. Lack of confidence and lack of demand interact; each reinforces the other.

Even such a situation might be alleviated, temporarily, by still more government deficit spending and by flooding the markets with so much additional money that consumers, firms, and banks, despite obstacles and uncertainties, would venture some of their superabundant funds on increased lending, consumption, investment, and employment. But that would be only a short-run palliative, not a remedy.

Here we have another of the contrasts in economics between what is true or effective in the short run and in the long run. Extreme monetary/fiscal stimulus or the rescue of shaky banks have nowadays left an ominously overexpanded supply of bank reserves difficult to reverse. Increased government deficits and debt, furthermore, increase uncertainty about whether and when and what corrective measures might be taken.

Misdiagnosis of recession is evident in the pervasive call for "jobs," as if more jobs were the means to, rather than a happy result of, restored coordination. Calls are pervasive to provide jobs by fostering particular sectors like "green" (subsidized or mandated) energy. Such jobs-oriented arguments put micromanagement of resource allocation ahead of recognizing obstacles to economywide coordination. An analogy would be to recommend jogging for a wheelchair-bound accident victim. Being able to go jogging would be the happy result of the patient's recovery, not a means to it.

11.17 Conclusion

Interest rates fundamentally represent real phenomena such as time preferences and investment opportunities to trade potential current consumption for more later on, but monetary conditions can affect them. As Hume and Mill explained, the size of an unchanging money supply has nothing to do with the level of interest rates, but *changes* in the quantity of money have often had large, if temporary, effects. Wicksell's analysis of natural and market rates and the cumulative process goes far toward explaining how.

Keynes's theory of interest (1936) requires attention. It regards interest as the reward not for waiting but for the sacrifice of liquidity. Assets of slight liquidity do generally yield higher interest than highly liquid ones like cash or quickly cashable claims. Unsurprisingly, "the" interest rate, like "the" wage rate, takes on different levels, depending on the conditions under which the waiting or the labor is performed. The reward for holding any instrument less liquid than actual money is partly the nonpecuniary advantage of whatever liquidity the instrument may possess, along with explicit interest.

But this fact in no way justifies disregarding the supply of and demand for waiting as the fundamental determinant of interest rates. In principle, everything has some influence on everything else, however indirect and immeasurably small, and the interest rate and the demand for cash balances do have some detectable effect on each other. But to make the demand for and quantity of money the fundamental determinants of interest, as the liquidity-preference theory does, is just wrong. The volume of rain has an effect on the demand for umbrellas, but the supply of and demand for umbrellas does not determine rainfall.

Still, one aspect of liquidity-preference theory holds a grain of truth. Preferences are realities, and it is no surprise that they may influence other basically real variables, even the interest rate.[16]

This book has presented Allais's ideas about how the opportunity to hold savings in cash tends to divert thrift away from productive real investment, but so far it has not endorsed any policy proposal. A slight exception here turns back to financial intermediation. Intermediation can tailor financial instruments to the divergent requirements of both savers and borrowers. Readily cashable financial instruments can largely satisfy demands for liquidity, reducing demands for actual money. Intermediation can channel savers' funds even into long-term loans to and equity investment in companies that invest even in long-term projects. Saying so is not unqualified praise of intermediation, however. High degrees of leverage can pose risks to the whole financial system.

[16] Patinkin's diagrams (1956/1965, Chapters IX–XI) illustrate this effect. (On why the curves slope, shift, and intersect as shown, see Sect. 10.4 and Patinkin's Chapters IX–XI.).

CHAPTER 12

Conclusion

Capital and interest theory is part of general price theory. Time is indispensable for production and consumption. What would a world be like where labor and other factors of production converted themselves instantly into machinery and semi-finished goods, which in turn converted themselves into final consumer goods and their services, all instantly? For production in the real world, some people must be willing to tie up wealth over time, forgoing immediate consumption. If building a house is to be worthwhile, the contractor must expect someone to buy it and wait for its services over many years. If an owner or occupant is unwilling or unable to tie up wealth of his own, he must find somebody to take over that burden, as by lending money or renting the property to him. Waiting is required in both building and using a house or car or refrigerator.

Even in an imaginary world where everything repeats itself in the same old ruts, making production and consumption superficially look simultaneous, production takes time. Because semi-finished goods and capital goods intervene between ultimate factors of production and final consumer satisfactions, some people must tie up wealth in these forms and wait for ultimate payoffs. Waiting is necessary even to keep the imaginary steady state steady; without it, even the steady state would collapse into total poverty. Waiting for a payoff by holding value over time carries a price, the interest rate.

L. B. Yeager and S. H. Hanke, *Capital, Interest, and Waiting*,
https://doi.org/10.1007/978-3-031-63398-0_12

"Waiting" may be unsatisfactory as the name of a factor, but no one has succeeded in popularizing or, to our knowledge, even suggesting something better. The term "waiting" is more exact from a supplier's standpoint than from that of a demander, who pays someone else to perform it. Yet economists are content with the term "labor," referring both to its employer and to the actual laborer. Why not be similarly content with "waiting"?

Approaches to capital and interest different from this book's are not downright wrong. Böhm-Bawerk, Allais, Eucken, Irving Fisher, and others have made major contributions without recognizing waiting as a factor and interest as its price. However, the concept of waiting pulls different strands of price theory together. It bypasses useless argument over what goods are capital goods. It avoids quibbles over Carl Menger's successive stages of production. It develops analogies with other factors, such as labor.

12.1 Waiting as a Factor and Interest as Its Price

Waiting is an essential factor of production. Like land and labor and many other goods used in production, waiting can also be a consumer good, as in a consumer loan. Waiting has two dimensions: (1) the *value* of resources whose output is waited for (rather than devoted to current consumption) and (2) the duration of this waiting, *time*. Beyond the most immediate results, like eating a wild fruit found by accident, time is essential to production. Time-consuming processes of production, the productivity of waiting, and human time preference ("impatience") establish a rate of interest, which is positive in all but unusual circumstances. Waiting would be employed and explicit or implicit interest would exist even in the hypothetical evenly rotating or static economy. Innovation counts among innumerable influences on the interest rate, but it is by no means necessary for the very existence of interest. The concepts of period of production and degree of roundaboutness are devices for emphasizing these points.

To recognize waiting as a use of value, not as something physically measurable, dissolves the paradoxes examined in Chapter 4 which were thought in some circles to discredit mainstream interest theory and even mainstream price theory.

The demand for waiting comes from both productive enterprises and consumers. Its supply is scarce. The reasons why it is both demanded and scarce are, put briefly, "productivity and thrift," or, almost equivalently, "roundaboutness and time preference." Like other scarce things, waiting must be rationed somehow, most obviously by price.

In its strictest sense, interest is the price of a money loan; but it also appears in other guises, such as rent on real estate and other property, an agio of present over future goods, dividends on stock, expected appreciation of assets, and even in the relation between spot and forward currency exchange rates. Waiting is not unique in lacking a completely pure price. Employers and workers make job decisions on factors besides wage rates. Consumers often consider more than price in deciding whether and where to buy some product. Bank loan officers take account of more than how much interest an applicant is willing to pay.

Interest, so-called, may include compensation for other factors, like risk-bearing; and nonpecuniary benefits of holding some types of claims or property may hold down explicit interest rates.

Chapter 9 abandons the assumption, already suspended in some earlier chapters, that the interest rate is one single uniform price. The yield curve, showing the dependence of the interest rate on the duration of a loan or bond, is a standard example of multiple rates. The chapter considers several hypotheses about the relations between short-term and long-term rates. It also glances at the idea of risk-bearing as a factor of production.

Although appearing in several forms, not all of them explicit, the interest rate is a price conforming to the logic of a price system. A price system permits achieving a high level of productivity and innovation that presupposes a well-coordinated fine-grained division of labor. It activates knowledge scattered about in billions of minds, knowledge that simply could not be assembled for implementing a central plan. Prices convey information and incentives and perform a rationing function. Measuring opportunity costs and values paid for ultimately by consumers, prices permit comparing costs and prices and avoiding the waste of resources in ways that provide less value to consumers than an alternative mix of resources would provide.

Treating waiting as a productive factor and interest as its price has advantages. It avoids unnecessary distinctions. Worse than useless are brooding over the many meanings of "capital" and over which goods do and which do not count as "capital goods." Waiting resembles other factors in being a consumer good as well as a producer good, exhibiting diminishing marginal returns and complementarity and substitutability with other factors, and being embodied in internationally traded goods and having its price so affected. Theory conveniently deals with "the" interest rate but recognizes that it takes on many forms. In this way, interest parallels other factor prices: land rents depend on location and fertility and possible easements, and labor comes in many forms and receives wages conditioned by "compensating differences."

This book deals more with the economic system as a whole than with managing a business firm or investment portfolio, although some attention to those aspects is necessary. It exploits parallels between capital and interest and more familiar microeconomic topics. It portrays decisions about saving and investment as particular kinds of decisions about production and resource allocation. The interest rate appears as a factor price performing the familiar informational, incentive, and rationing functions. It comes within the purview of ordinary theories of supply and demand and functional income distribution. The theory shows how the principle of derived demand applies to the interest rate as well as other factor prices and shows what sort of opportunity cost the interest rate measures. Grappling with these matters tests and deepens one's understanding of the very logic of a price system as a device that transmits information and incentives and promotes coordination.

12.2 Productivity and Thrift

Chapter 8 examines responses to a changed interest rate and how the rate responds to underlying changes in "wants, resources, and technology." Supply and demand determine the interest rate, of course, but what determines supply and demand? "Productivity and thrift" is a frequent answer. Thrift refers to time preference. Despite an erroneous pure-time preference theory, it is not an economywide agio of present over future goods that pulls the interest rate into line with itself. Thrift refers, rather, to people's tradeoffs between present and future consumption, much as between wine and beer. Not all people have the same preferences and tradeoffs. "Thrift" means a willingness to postpone satisfactions, meanwhile tying up wealth in capital goods, securities, and the like.

Tradeoffs are marginal adjustments, not all-or-nothing alternatives: how much future consumption would just compensate you for the loss of one unit of present consumption? The interest rate and people's marginal tradeoffs tend to pull each other into equality on the market.

The "productivity" part of the slogan refers to the benefits of roundabout, time-consuming methods of production, or as Böhm-Bawerk duly emphasized "well-chosen" methods. Roundaboutness refers to the time required for production. Especially for a society's overall economic activity, the concept and attempts to measure it are almost pointless complications. Still, the attention they have received in abstract theorizing justifies the clarification presented in Chapter 7.

12.3 Opportunity Cost

Like product prices and other factor prices, the interest rate in its various forms expresses opportunity cost. The more of a good and ultimately of productive factors goes toward satisfying one's own or other persons' purposes, the less of it or its substitutes remains for other purposes. Scarcity poses a need for choice. The scarcity of waiting cannot be conjured away by loan guarantees or favorable terms, desirable as this diversion of resources may be for special reasons. Neglecting opportunity cost causes perverse decisions in private and public affairs when the casual thought prevails that something would be "nice to have." Neglecting opportunity cost is common when the people deciding on some expenditures are not those who actually pay. This is a classic problem when decisions are made by government bureaucrats. As put by Thomas Sowell, "It is hard to imagine a more stupid or more dangerous way of making decisions than by putting those decisions in the hands of people who pay no price for being wrong."

12.4 Financial Intermediation

The functioning and benefits (and occasional dangers) of intermediation through money and other financial instruments and institutions are well understood. Intimately related is intermediation in waiting and avoiding or offloading its burden. People who want housing but are unable or unwilling to tie up wealth of their own can shift this burden by buying houses with borrowed money or simply by renting. Airlines unwilling or unable to tie up wealth of their own in airplanes can buy them with borrowed money or can lease them and pay currently for their services. Banks and the stock and bond markets make savings even in small amounts and of limited or uncertain duration available to enterprises requiring large amounts with a dependable duration of waiting. Tastes in readiness to bear risk or shun it can be matched: someone ready to gamble on high gains can buy junk bonds or speculative stocks; cautious types can buy staid utility stocks or government bills and bonds.

12.5 Money and Interest

Don Patinkin distinguished between the real and monetary frameworks of an economy (Chapter 10). The real data are "wants, resources, and technology." Basically, interest is a real, not monetary, phenomenon. Hume and Mill insisted eloquently on this point. A minor clarification concerns liquidity preference, the degree of preference between holding actual money and holding near-money and nonmoney instruments. Like other tastes, it has some influence, however slight, on all variables in a world of general interdependence and so on the equilibrium interest rate. Keynes's liquidity-preference theory of interest is something different and is not saved by the just-mentioned clarification.

Transitionally and undependably, changes in the quantity of money can affect the interest rate; but, as per our analogy, the wage rate and land rate can also be affected. Knut Wicksell explained how. In the other direction, the interest rate, especially as determined by policy, can affect the quantity of money. Beyond equilibrium, monetary expansion can supply a kind of counterfeit waiting, not always with welcome consequences. Wicksell also explained a process whereby meeting a demand for loans with newly created money can intensify the demand for loans, and so on cumulatively. The process does not depend on a high interest-rate sensitivity in the demand for loans.

Like other prices, interest rates may be distorted by controls, taxes, and subsidies. Heavy bond purchases by the Federal Reserve subsidize credit; and before the crisis beginning in 2007–2008, several government programs were making housing or housing finance artificially available and cheap. The influence of monetary factors on interest rates can be great enough to challenge the understanding of how interest is a fundamentally real phenomenon. At the same time, the idea that monetary policy is interest-rate policy is incomplete and superficial to almost the degree of being outright wrong.

Chapter 11 distinguishes among three aspects of the cash-balance effect, which shows how interaction between the quantity of money and the demand for cash balances determines total nominal spending.

12.6 Irving Fisher's Instructive Error

Irving Fisher was instructively wrong in rejecting the interest rate as a factor price. Without the concept of waiting, one of the most eminent capital and interest theorists of all time blundered into denying that interest measures any genuine cost (Fisher 1930/1955, pp. 485–487, 534–541). He rejected the idea "that abstinence or waiting exists as an independent item in the cost of production, to be added to the other costs and to be treated in all ways like them" (p. 486).

If waiting or the interest that it earns were a true cost, he said, it should be discountable the same as any other cost; yet it is not. If Fisher were right and interest paid for waiting were not a true cost, then it and its rate would have nothing to do with the opportunity cost of a project—the forgone alternative uses of waiting and complementary resources.

Fisher offered the example of a tree planted some years earlier at an initial and unrepeated cost of labor alone. It has now, at the starting point of the analysis, grown to be worth \$2; and it is destined to grow in 11 more years to be worth \$3. The \$2 is the present discounted value of the future \$3. Yet if waiting were a cost, said Fisher, our discounting should recognize not only the \$3 positive item but also the negative items of annual waitings, much as if these were tree-pruning costs. Such arithmetic would produce an inapplicable figure, which Fisher failed to specify (pp. 486–487, 534–536).

But what is the problem? We can indeed discount the then-current values of the waiting performed in each of the subsequent 11 years. In each year, the owner continues to own the tree at its then-grown value rather than sell it, and his waiting is rewarded by the further growth in the tree's current value. The sum of those 11 discounted growths, which are the rewards of the further waiting, equals the likewise discounted total growth of \$1 over those final 11 years. A year's reward, divided by the tree's value at the time, is a form of the economywide pervasive interest rate.

The waiting and its current reward are presumably not quite the same in each of those years since the tree's value has grown from the year before. On the other hand, a slowdown in the growth rate is implied if the owner decides to sell the timber after 11 years because the tree's growth rate no longer exceeds the target rate of interest. Incidentally, the average annually compounded growth rate of \$2 to \$3 in 11 years is a plausible 3.8 percent.

Again, where is the problem? The current values of waiting performed and rewarded can indeed be discounted to any earlier year, much as if they had been pruning costs and contributions to value. Without a clear purpose, however, such arithmetic risks divert attention away from the central questions of capital and interest.

For another example, Fisher suggests a perpetual annuity paying $100 a year. Equivalently but more realistically, a perpetual bond pays the holder $100 a year. The present value of any future annual payment is the discounted value of the waiting to be performed in that year by continuing to hold the bond. Today's present value of the $100 payment to be made 30 years from now, say, is well below that year's actual payment of $100. Discounted at the going rate of interest, say 5 percent, the present value of that payment for the waiting then to be performed is $23.14. Lower still are the present values of $100 in the subsequent years. The sum to infinity of all such decreasing contributions to present value is today's actual present value of the bond: $2000 at a prevailing interest rate of 5 percent.

If the going and target rate of interest rises to 6 percent, the bond's price falls to $1666.67 so that it now yields 6 percent. If the interest rate is 4 percent, the price is $2500.

The arithmetic is trivial. The surprise is that Fisher counts not only the reward for waiting but also its cost to the bondholder as the full $100 a year, leaving the bondholder with a net income of zero. The theory that treats waiting or its remuneration as a cost, says Fisher, "has worked out its own absurdity" (pp. 537–538). Standard theory, however, does not neglect cost: maximizing the satisfaction or profit or whatever from some activity implies carrying it to the point where the reward no longer exceeds cost at the margin. The owner of the perpetual bond receives his $100 each year for continuing to wait during that year instead of selling it for immediately spendable funds. He incurs the cost of waiting in order to receive its reward.

On an unauthorized extension of Fisher's view, someone working for $50,000 a year receives no net income because he suffers an offset—the $50,000 worth of labor performed. What could be the point of such quibbling with the ordinary use of the word "income"? Why not recognize both the $50,000 and the $100 annual bond payment as items traded in transactions yielding gains from trade? Each party incurs costs to receive benefits.

Fisher continues with remarkable assertions. "For society as a whole, … even in the case of interest which is explicitly paid, it cannot be said that it constitutes a cost of production. In the case of a person who works with his own capital, the truth of this statement is even more evident." If interest is a cost of production to the independent capitalist, it is income also—and Fisher implies that the two cancel each other out. "Labor sacrifice is quite different. It is a real cost and in no time bookkeeping can it be canceled out" (p. 540).

Suppose an electric power company pays interest of $5 million a year. Is that not a cost? And have not its executives judged the project and its financing to pass the test of opportunity cost? Suppose an airline buys its planes with borrowed money; alternatively, it rents them. Would Fisher reject the interest payments but recognize the rentals as a cost?

If interest (and equivalent payments, like rentals) is not a cost of production, then waiting is not scarce. People are willing to tie up unlimited amounts of wealth over time. Waiting need not be rationed by price or otherwise; using it has no opportunity cost. Billions and billions of dollars of bond-financed labor and other resources could be drawn into building and owning dams and electric power plants without trenching in the least on the waiting required for theaters and superhighways.

Not all resources are free, of course, but waiting, which is what finance deals in, is free, if Fisher is correct. Realistically, because waiting is a scarce factor, using it in one way leaves less available for other ways. Artificially encouraging or burdening any particular uses of waiting twists its own and the allocations of substitute and complementary factors alike away from the pattern that would otherwise result from voluntary transactions. If mortgage guarantees or cheap credit encourage house building, they reduce the waiting available for producing other things. The same is true of loan guarantees to favored companies. Even if they do not turn out to require direct government payments, they still, as intended, encourage more use of waiting and complementary factors in the guaranteed activities at the expense of other production. This is not to say that such governmental favoritism is always bad policy; but, however allocated, waiting is not a free good.

Might Fisher's position be saved by interpreting it as a warning against some sort of double counting or verbal equivocation by his opponents? No such interpretation works. Fisher seems not to understand that ordinary resources like labor and land and their services are not the only ones both limited in supply and demanded for rival uses. The more of people's waiting that is allocated for hydroelectric power projects, the less remains for transportation systems.

Despite everything, Fisher does implicitly recognize, after all, that interest rations something wanted but scarce. He made the following remarks in a context of neither supporting nor challenging the status of waiting as a factor and interest as its price, but to explain market forces tending to resist wide fluctuations in the interest rate.

> Beyond the margin of choice there always lie untouched options ready to be exploited the instant the rate of interest falls. Among these, as Cassel [1903, p. 122] has pointed out, are waterworks of various kinds. Not only works of stupendous size but hundreds of less conspicuous improvements are subjects of possible investment as soon as the rate of interest falls low enough to make the return upon cost equal to the rate of interest. The same is true of improving, dredging, and deepening of harbors and rivers, the use of dikes and jetties, the construction of irrigation works for arid lands, and Boulder Dam projects (203–204).

Fisher's major contributions to price theory, monetary theory, and even capital and interest theory do not exclude his being instructively wrong on one main issue. True, he has "devoted considerable space to the refutation of the abstinence [waiting] theory so far as it is more than verbal, and collides with any workable theory of income, because its errors are so subtle and insidious as to beguile many of the best and most wary of economists" (p. 541). Have we too been beguiled?

Appendix 1: Mathematical Appendix

Definitions of Symbols

P = present value
F = future value
r = the interest rate per period (expressed as a decimal, i.e., percentage divided by 100)
ρ = the interest rate in the case of continuous compounding (expressed as a decimal)
t = the number of elapsed time periods (e.g., years)
m = the number of times interest is compounded per period t
n = the number of periods to the time horizon (or number of periods from the date of P to the date of F)
S = the size of future payments to be received either in a series of equal lumps or at a steady rate per period.

Future Value

The future value of a present lump sum (assuming compounding once per period):

$$F = P(1 + r)^t$$

L. B. Yeager and S. H. Hanke, *Capital, Interest, and Waiting*,
https://doi.org/10.1007/978-3-031-63398-0

For more frequent compounding, *m* times per period:

$$F = P\left(1 + \frac{r}{m}\right)^{mt}$$

To obtain the formula for compounding continuously, an infinite number of times per period, let $a = \frac{m}{r}$, so $\frac{r}{m} = \frac{1}{a}$ and $m = ra$.

$$F = P\left(1 + \frac{1}{a}\right)^{\text{rat}} = P\left[\left(1 + \frac{1}{a}\right)^{a}\right]^{rt}$$

Now, let $m \to \infty$, so that $a \to \infty$, also. The limit of $\left(1 + \frac{1}{a}\right)^{a}$ as $a \to \infty$ defines *e*, the base of natural logarithms. Thus, $F = Pe^{rt}$ (note the analogy between the discrete case and continuous case formulas, the correspondence between $1 + r$ and e^{r}).

Discounting

For the present value of a future lump sum, in the formula for *F* as a function of *P*, solve for *P*:

$$P = \frac{F}{(1 + r)^{t}} = F(1 + r)^{-t}$$

Discounting of a future lump sum with continuous compounding:

$$P = \frac{F}{e^{rt}} = Fe^{-rt}$$

Strictly, as Hirshleifer says, our symbols should distinguish among interest rates according to the frequency of compounding. Ordinary *r* per year is understood to mean compounding once a year. For continuous compounding, the symbol ρ (rho) is often used.

What is the relation between the ordinary *r* of once a year compounding and the ρ of continuous compounding? Suppose a given present value has the same future value compounded once per period at *r* for *n* periods and compounded continuously at ρ over the same time span.

$$F = P(1 + r)^{n}, \quad \text{where} \quad (1 + r)^{n} = e^{\rho n}$$

$$\text{therefore,} \quad F = Pe^{\rho n}$$

$$(1+r)^n = e^{\rho n} \text{ is equivalent to } n(\ln(1+r)) = \rho n$$
$$\text{therefore,} \quad \rho = \ln(1+r)$$

ρ is somewhat smaller than r because if compounding is continuous, a smaller interest rate is required to yield a specified increment in dollar value than if compounding occurs only at discrete intervals. For example, with $r = 0.10$, $\rho = 0.0953$.

What is the present value of a series of discrete payments, the first of which is to be received at time 0 and thus suffers no discounting? The first term of the formula below drops out if the first payment is received only after the lapse of one period.

$$P = \frac{F_0}{(1+r)^0} + \frac{F_1}{(1+r)^1} + \frac{F_2}{(1+r)^2} + \cdots + \frac{F_n}{(1+r)^n} = \sum_{t=0}^{n} F_t(1+r)^{-t}$$

We continue assuming the same interest rate r for the different lengths of time (a flat yield curve). For different interest rates, we would have to distinguish them as, for example, r_t.

Suppose F_o (if any) $= F_1 = F_2 = F_3 = \cdots = F_n = S$ (for the size of a steady stream). Then,

$$P = S\sum_{t=0}^{n}(1+r)^{-t}$$

This formulation still supposes that the initial payment S is received at time zero. If it is not received until after the lapse of 1 period, at time point 1, then,

$$P = S\sum_{t=1}^{n}(1+r)^{-t}$$

Through the use of the formula for the sum of the first n terms of a geometric progression–see forthcoming paragraphs–this last expression manipulates into:

$$P = \frac{S\left(1-(1+r)^{-n}\right)}{r}$$

Remember, we are now referring to discrete lumps of even-size S received for n periods starting with period 1 (i.e., after a lapse of 1 period from time zero).

When we talk about rates of flow rather than discrete lumps, we should perhaps use a symbol other than S. For simplicity, though, we keep S and reinterpret it as a steady rate of flow per period.

What is the present value of an annuity in this continuous-flow case? The annuity runs for n periods and is paid continuously, starting at time zero, at the rate S. Examples of applications concern the growth of a tree or of wine in value.

$$P = \int_{t=0}^{n} Se^{-rt}\mathrm{d}t = S\int_{t=0}^{n} e^{-rt}\mathrm{d}t$$

The various Se^{-rt} inside the integration symbols is the various infinitesimal bits of present value of the steady state rate of future payment. Remember, S is constant. For rates S that change with t, the corresponding formula does not admit of much simplification.

Performing the integration, we get:

$$P = S\left[\frac{1}{-r}e^{-rt}\right]_{t=0}^{n}$$

To check the integration, note that the time derivative of the expression in parentheses is indeed e^{-rt}. We omit the constant of integration because it would drop out anyway when we evaluate the expression in parentheses between 0 and n.

The value of the expression in parentheses at $t = n$ minus its value at $t = 0$ is:

$$-\frac{1}{r}e^{-rn} - \frac{1}{-r} = \frac{1}{r}\left(1 - e^{-rn}\right)$$

This value is multiplied by S, the steady rate of payment, so

$$P = \frac{S}{r}\left(1 - e^{-rn}\right)$$

This formula makes sense. For $n = \infty$, $P = \frac{S}{r}$, which is the familiar formula for capitalizing a perpetual stream of revenues. For $n = 0$, $P = 0$. For $n = 1$, $P = \frac{S}{r}\left(1 - e^{-r}\right) = \frac{S}{r}\left(\frac{e^{r}-1}{e^{r}}\right)$.

It is not obvious how further to simplify this formula for the $n = 1$ case, but numerical calculations show that for $r = 0.02$, $P = 0.99S$ approximately; for $r = 0.10$, $P = 0.95S$, and so on. That is, the discounting is by approximately half the rate of interest. Recall that the payments accrue at a steady rate of S per period over the time from $t = 0$ to $t = 1$. The earliest payments are exposed to discounting over practically none of that period, the latest to discounting over practically the full period. On average, the payments are discounted for half a period, or at half the full-period discount rate.

We now return to the case of future payments made in equal discrete lumps. Paradoxically, perhaps, although involving no calculus, the formula for this case at least looks more complicated than the formula for the continuous case. We suppose that lumps of equal size S are received for n periods, starting with $t = 1$.

$$P = \sum_{t=1}^{n} \frac{S}{(1+r)^t} = S \sum_{t=1}^{n} \frac{1}{(1+r)^t}$$

The summation sign introduces a geometric progression whose first term is $\frac{1}{1+r}$ and whose common ratio is also $\frac{1}{1+r}$. Applying the general formula for the sum of the n terms of such a geometric progression results in:

$$P = \frac{\frac{1}{1+r}\left(\left(\frac{1}{1+r}\right)^n - 1\right)}{\frac{1}{1+r} - 1} = \frac{1-(1+r)^{-n}}{r}$$

Remembering that S premultiplies this summation, we get

$$P = \frac{S}{r}(1-(1+r)^{-n})$$

Note the analogy with the continuous case formula already obtained. The e^{-rn} in that formula corresponds to the $(1 + r)^{-n}$ in this one. Again, perhaps we should be finicky and distinguish between interest rate r in the discrete case and ρ in the continuous case.

Like the continuous case formula, this discrete case formula makes intuitive sense. For $n = \infty$, $P = \frac{S}{r}$, which is the formula for capitalizing a perpetuity. For $n = 0$, $P = 0$. For $n = 1$, $P = \frac{S}{1+r}$.

Price Premium in the Interest Rate (Fisher Effect)

As before, rates are rates per year expressed as decimals.

r = the real interest rate
i = the nominal interest rate
p = the expected rate of price inflation

The nominal interest rate i "should" be such that $1 lent now is repaid in a year multiplied by $1 + p$ to allow for the rise in prices and also by $1 + r$ to allow for real interest.

$$1 + i = (1 + p)(1 + r) = 1 + p + r + pr$$

$$i = p + r + pr$$

If p and r are "small," as in the usual range, pr is negligible, and we are left with the usual approximate formula $i = p + r$. Suppose, however, that p and r are big, say $p = 0.50$ and $r = 0.10$. Then $p + r + pr = 0.65$, in contrast with the 0.6 given by the approximation.

In the context of *continuous compounding*, however, the theoretical nominal interest rate is simply the sum of the real interest rate and the expected rate of price increase. Greek letters corresponding to the Roman letters already introduced will stand, respectively, for the continuously compounded nominal interest rate, real interest rate, and expected rate of price increase. $1 at the start, increased by the real interest rate and the price-rise rate in 1 year becomes:

$$e^{1\iota} = e^{1\rho} e^{1\pi}$$

$$e^{\iota} = e^{\rho + \pi}.$$

Appendix 2: Bond and Interest Rate Appendix

Some Interest-Rate Arithmetic

Theories of term structure consider how expectations, transactions costs, and other factors condition the arbitrage and substitution that relate the different long, intermediate, and short interest rates to each other. According to a "pure" version of the term structure, if people already knew with complete confidence on January 1, 2023 what rates would prevail on 1-year loans beginning on January 1 of 2023, 2024, and 2025, then the relation depicted next would hold between these rates and the rate on a 3-year loan beginning now. The *if* is a huge one. A formula for what would be true if people agreed and acted on precise, firm, and correct expectations in no way implies that people do or could act that way. The *expectations theory*, along with its rivals, is the topic of Sect. 9.4.

In the next formula (and usually in others in this appendix unless otherwise indicated), interest rates are expressed as decimals (percentages divided by 100). The symbols i_3, i_4, and i_5 represent the interest rates on 1-year loans in 2023, 2024, and 2025. The rate per year on the 3-year loan is i_{345}. The formula assumes interest accruing on a one-dollar principal amount. The loans are discount bonds, whose interest is included in the final payoff at face value and none paid before then.

$$1 + i_{345} = ((1 + i_3)(1 + i_4)(1 + i_5))^{\frac{1}{3}}$$

L. B. Yeager and S. H. Hanke, *Capital, Interest, and Waiting*,
https://doi.org/10.1007/978-3-031-63398-0

That geometric mean, minus the 1 on the left, gives the rate for the 3-year loan. If the rates on 1-year loans for 2023, 2024, and 2025 were 3, 4, and 5 percent respectively, then the rate on a 3-year loan beginning on 1 January 2023 would be 4 (more precisely, 3.997) percent. If this relation did not hold, arbitrageurs could profit from transactions tending to establish it. If the actual rate on 3-year loans was 5 percent, arbitrageurs would make 3-year loans at that rate while obtaining the necessary funds at an average rate of only 4 percent (apart from transactions costs and the like). They would borrow for the first year at 3 percent and count on renewing their borrowing by obtaining successive 1-year loans at 4 and 5 percent. Their lending would tend to depress the rate on 3-year loans and their borrowing would tend to raise the rates on 1-year loans until the different rates were consistent with the formula.

In an opposite case, with the 3-year rate only 3 percent and the successive 1-year rates again 3, 4, and 5 percent, arbitrageurs would borrow for 3 years at 3 percent and relend at 1-year rates averaging 4 percent. Their activity would tend to raise the 3-year rate and lower the 1-year rates toward conformity with the formula.

As these examples illustrate, a yield curve implies forward interest rates on loans to be made in the future, as if the rates on them were already known. Suppose that the current market prices and payoff face values of the discount bonds maturing 2 years and 3 years from now are known, and thus also their yields to maturity are known. How can someone lock in today the interest rate on a 1-year loan to begin 2 years from now? A would-be future lender buys a discount bond today maturing at the end of 3 years, obtaining the money by selling a bond coming due 1 year earlier, when he wants the proposed loan to begin. With suitably chosen dollar amounts, he makes no net outlay today. When his bond comes due, he pays it off; when the longer bond comes due, he collects its face value. During the third year, meanwhile, he is in the desired position of being a net lender, and at an effectively predetermined interest rate.

A would-be future borrower makes opposite arrangements. He sells a discount bond that he will pay off at the end of 3 years and uses the money to buy a bond whose maturity value he will collect earlier, at the beginning of the desired loan period. During the third year, he is a net debtor. In each of these cases, the yield to maturity of the constructed synthetic bond running from the end of year 2 to the end of year 3 is the forward rate over that future period (cf. Campbell 1995, p. 134).

Assuming complete markets, no transactions costs, and so forth, multiple transactions can lock in the rate to be received or paid on the future loan. If expectations were precise and quite generally held, implicit forward rates as described would equal the expected future spot rates. However, the lender or borrower has no guarantee that he might not do better by simply waiting until the contemplated future period, receiving or paying the interest rate then prevailing. The logic behind forward transactions and their equivalent is to avoid gambling. In short, the transactor forgoes the chance of doing better to shed the risk of doing worse.

Strict arbitrage between short-run and long-run interest rates supposes that arbitrageurs borrow and lend in such a way as to avoid gambling. Their activity is analogous to covered interest arbitrage in international trade: borrowing in one currency and lending in another while hedging against the risk of loss from an exchange-rate move. By contrast, the so-called carry trade is when one borrows cheap and lends dear between currencies while accepting the exchange-rate risk. Something analogous quite probably occurs in short-term and long-term loan markets within a country: arbitragers speculate rather than protect themselves against the risk of adverse interest-rate changes. Therefore, the foregoing arithmetic of arbitrage is suggestive at best.

The interest rates portrayed in the usual yield curve are nominal, not real, rates. Price inflation affects them. One reason why nominal rates on intermediate and long-term bonds might exceed current short rates, causing or reinforcing the yield curve's upward slope, is expectations of future or increased inflation.

Irving Fisher explained the effect of price inflation (Fisher 1896/1961, Howitt 1992). Let r be the real interest rate and p the price inflation rate, both expressed as decimals. The nominal interest rate, i, is then $r + p$, approximately. To receive back the real purchasing power of one dollar lent for a year plus the real interest on it, a lender must receive $1 + i = (1 + r)(1 + p) = 1 + r + p + rp$. With r and p being small decimals, their product is negligible, and the \$1 loan is repaid in $1 + r + p$dollars. The nominal interest rate is the real rate plus the inflation rate.[1]

This approximate version of the formula is rough indeed for substantial interest and inflation rates. At a 10 percent real interest rate and 50

[1] The effects of inflation, the Fisher effect, on nominal rates are elaborated upon in Hanke, et al. (1975).

percent inflation rate, it implies a nominal interest rate of 60 percent. The formula retaining the term *rp* gives a nominal rate of 65 percent.

The contrast between approximate and exact formulations vanishes if the real interest and inflation rates are compounded not periodically but continuously. Greek letters now symbolize the rates: the inflation rate is π and the real interest rate is ρ, making the nominal rate $= \rho + \pi$. The natural logarithms of the sum of 1 plus each term are $\rho = \ln(1.1) = 0.095$ and $\pi = \ln(1.5) = 0.405$. Those logarithms add to 0.500, whose antilogarithm is $e^{0.500} = 1.65$, the same repayment amount as given by the exact formula for periodic compounding.

The contrast between the two mathematical formulations of the Fisher effect deserves little emphasis, since it shows itself in practice only incompletely, anyway, as Fisher himself recognized in connection with "money illusion" (1930, pp. 43, 415). Allowance for inflation is inexact because people cannot predict it correctly and do not give full attention to mild inflation over long periods; also, nominal interest income, although eroded by inflation, is ordinarily taxed (Howitt 1992). Inflation inserts a wedge between nominal and real interest rates that not only drives the nominal rate up but the real rate down. Robert Mundell explains this wedge by noting that when inflation cuts the real value of money balances, people's reduced wealth may cause them to save more (Mundell 1963, pp. 282–283). However, this effect operates more, if at all, through outside money, which is not matched by private debt, than through inside money, of which bank-account money is the prime example, being matched in normal times mostly by private borrowers' debt to the banks.[2]

Maurice Allais also considered the inflationary erosion of wealth and thought mild inflation beneficial.[3] What amounts to a tax on real cash balances motivates people to allocate a given volume of saving less to cash and more toward real capital formation or the securities that finance it.

[2] Chapter 10 further considers the outside/inside distinction.

[3] Overlooking the earlier work of Allais, Peter Abken (1993, p. 16) summarized the "Mundell-Tobin Theory" (Mundell 1963, 1971, Tobin 1965). With inflation raising the opportunity cost of holding money, people shift into bonds, depressing the real interest rate and so stimulating real investment.

Rates of Yield Defined

The *yields to maturity* shown in a yield curve are the annual rates of return on bonds coming due after different lapses of time. This yield on a bond is the rate of discount at which the sum of the present values of future interest-coupon payments (if any) plus the final payoff equals the bond's current price.

A bond's yield to maturity tends to equal the *competitively necessary interest rate* (a term introduced here), which is the rate that a bond must yield, taking account of its final payoff and intermediate interest payments, for it to be priced competitively with similarly attractive investments. It is "the interest rate" in general (when that term is applicable), the rate whose rise or fall makes outstanding bonds fall or rise in price.

A bond's *holding-period rate of return* resembles a yield to maturity except that it pertains to a bond whose holder sells it before it comes due. Since its price when sold cannot be known in advance, neither can its holding-period return. If its price falls by the time its holder sells it, he has received a holding-period return less than initially expected—if the price rises, a greater return. A bond's holding-period return thus depends on what affects bond prices, especially on the competitively necessary interest rate. If a bond's prices at two future dates were already firmly known in advance, its holding-period return over that future interval would be the forward rate on a loan over that interval.

A bond's *coupon yield* or *current yield* is the ratio of its annual interest payment to its current market price. It varies inversely to the bond's price. A bond's *coupon rate*, in contrast, is its periodic fixed interest payment expressed as a percentage of its par (face) value. Since both coupon rate and face value are specified from the start, so is the dollar amount of the periodic payment. It is usually convenient, therefore, to handle that payment in dollars rather than as an additional kind of percentage.

Bonds and Duration

Three types of bonds are:

1. The extreme case of a "discount bond", also called a zero-coupon, coupon-free, or stripped bond, paying interest only as included in its payoff at maturity, for example, a U.S. Treasury bill. An

outstanding bond with no intermediate interest payments remaining before maturity is effectively the same thing.

2. The opposite extreme is a "consol," "perpetuity," or "perpetual annuity," which pays interest periodically "forever," but never matures.
3. The intermediate case of a "plain vanilla" bond, so-called for being typical; it pays face value at maturity and also makes intermediate interest (coupon) payments.

Complicated cases defying generalizations include a bond or term loan with a periodically adjustable interest rate, one whose final payoff or intermediate interest payments or both are linked to a price index, a callable bond repayable before maturity at the option of the issuer, and a bond convertible into shares of common stock. Preferred stock has some characteristics of a bond. The classification also omits trivial cases, as of a bond never coming due and never paying interest, which would be a sheer gift from lender to borrower, and of one due in a few hours or minutes and so already having practically its full maturity value and practically no remaining duration.

A neat analysis requires setting complications aside for discussion elsewhere; these include different degrees of riskiness. On these assumptions, all bonds must be priced to have the same yield to maturity, which equals the prevailing market interest rate, here called the *competitively necessary rate of yield*.

Duration in this appendix is a technical term, distinct from calendar time. A bond's duration depends inversely on its periodic coupon payments, if any. The larger the share of present value of a bond comes from these payments rather than from its final payoff, the faster on average the bondholder gets paid. For a given dollar coupon, duration is also shorter the higher the bond's interest yield (equaling the market yield) because heavier time discounting reduces the contributions of the relatively remote payments to the bond's total present value. (Campbell 1995, p. 132; Campbell, et al. 1997, p. 401; cf. Bierwag 1992).

Only for a discount bond is duration identical with calendar time to maturity. Its yield to maturity is the compound rate at which its current market price grows to become its final and only payoff. Its price depends inversely on the competitively necessary interest rate, and that price is more sensitive to interest rate changes when the starting interest rate is low. This characteristic applies to other types of bonds also.

The discount bond is instructive because the plain vanilla bond may be analyzed as a package of discount bonds with staggered maturities, one for each interest payment and one for its final payoff. Absent transactions costs and the like, arbitrage would keep the vanilla bond's current price equal to the total of the prices of the discount bonds packaged into it. Each of those conceptual components has a term to maturity of the calendar time until its one-and-only payoff. The duration of the complete bond is a kind of average of these component maturities and so is less than its own calendar time to maturity.

A vanilla bond's duration, sometimes called "Macaulay duration," is a weighted average of the times elapsing until each of its interest payments and its final payoff; it is a weighted average of the maturities of its conceptual coupon-free components. The weights are each payment's share of contribution to the bond's total present value at the competitively necessary market interest rate. Time discounting gives the relatively remote payments smaller weights than earlier ones. Similarly, duration is time elapsing until the date before which and after which the total discounted values of payments are equal.[4]

At the opposite extreme of bond types, a coupon-only consol best dramatizes the difference between duration and calendar time. Paying a fixed dollar amount of interest periodically forever, say once a year, the consol never comes due and never repays any principal. It could be regarded as a series of discount bonds with longer and longer maturities stretching out over infinite time. A consol is rare indeed but not totally unknown to history. Its current or coupon yield is its annual interest payment divided by its current (and changeable) market price. That changeable yield is the competitively necessary discount rate that would make the present value of the perpetual stream of coupon payments equal to the consol's current price.

A consol's duration is far from infinite. The long intervals until its remote interest payments count for little in an overall average because their present values are so heavily time-discounted, while the short times until the early payments do count heavily because they are exposed to relatively little time discount. The times until payments increase year by year

[4] Macaulay (1938), Nickolas (2015). Jean Folger (n.d.) elegantly illustrates the reasoning with pictures.

arithmetically while the present values of the payments decrease geometrically, each being multiplied by a factor less than one, by $\frac{1}{(1+i)^n}$. The number of years until a payment, *n*, increases year by year.

Suppose that the market interest rate and competitively necessary yield on the consol's price is 5 percent, 0.05. The present value of its 75th annual \$100 interest payment is $\frac{100}{1.05^{75}} = \$2.58$ which is 0.13 percent of the consol's total present value of \$2000 (the value yielding \$100 a year at 5 percent). This minuscule percentage is the weight that the time until the 75th payment carries in the consol's overall average duration, and 0.0013 of 75 is 0.0966 years = 1.1588 months. The still longer periods until the more remote interest payments make even smaller contributions to the total duration. A higher interest rate would make those contributions even smaller. At a zero generally prevailing interest rate, however, the consol's value and duration *would* be infinite because no time-discounting at all of its yearly payments would enter the picture.

Is a consol's duration a weighted average or a weighted sum of time periods? The two approaches are equivalent. The weighted average of the full times elapsing from the start until each of the interest payments is the same as the weighted sum of each of its successive individual years, stretching to infinity and each weighted by the (reduced) contribution of that year's payment to the consol's present value.

The sum to infinity of a diminishing geometric progression–here, the sum of ever-more discounted years–is the starting value of the series divided by (1-*a*), where *a*, less than 1, is the ratio of each successive value to its predecessor.[5] For the consol, that common ratio *a* is $\frac{1}{1+r}$, where *r* is the discount rate. Substituting this ratio into the above formula and taking the initial value as 1 year gives $\frac{1+r}{r}$ years (Campbell, et al. 1997, p. 403; Jones 2004).

An alternative formula (e.g., Shiller 1990, pp. 637–638) gives duration as simply $\frac{1}{r}$, which looks like the intuitively appealing present-value formula. Apart from the dimensions, years, and dollars, the sum of the more and more effectively diminished time periods stretching to infinity equals the sum of the more and more discounted interest payments. Now, subtracting $\frac{1}{r}$ from the diminishing-series result $\frac{1+r}{r}$ gives just 1 year: duration is 1 year longer by the diminishing-series formula than by $\frac{1}{r}$.

[5] For example, think of the Keynesian and bank-reserve multipliers.

Which present value of the consol corresponds to each of those two durations? It is each calendar year's coupon payment of C dollars multiplied by the number of time-discounted years: C times duration. These alternative present values are $C\frac{1+r}{r}$ and $\frac{C}{r}$ dollars. The second and simpler expression makes intuitive sense since price times r is the coupon payment necessary for the consol to be priced at the competitive interest rate. The first expression for price exceeds the second by simply C, the undiscounted amount of one annual payment.

The first pair of expressions for time duration and present value tacitly assumes that payments begin at time 0, which is not preposterous for the purchase of an outstanding consol immediately before its next interest payment. Payment over the longer period means one more payment and therefore a greater value. In this immediate-payment case, the addition to the price may be interpreted as reimbursement to the seller of interest to be received at once but not yet earned by the buyer. The second pair of expressions assumes payments beginning at the end of the first year, when waiting has actually been performed.

The contrast between immediate and delayed first payment vanishes at the extreme interest rates of zero and infinity. With zero time-discounting, a consol has infinite price and duration both. With discounting at an infinite interest rate, only an immediate first payment consol—preposterous as such—has any present value at all. The contrast between earlier and later first payments also vanishes if payments and compounding are continuous rather than discrete.

The extreme cases of a consol and a discount bond illuminate some features of a coupon-bearing plain vanilla bond. For all three bonds, its price falls as the competitively necessary interest rate rises; but for each percentage point rise in that rate, these losses become smaller and smaller both in dollars and as a percentage of the bond's remaining price. The price approaches zero at a very high but finite interest rate but does not fall all the way to zero.

A bond's price depends not only on its coupon, final payment, and the competitively necessary interest rate but also on its time to final payoff. Is a 1 year longer but otherwise identical bond worth more or less? The question cannot arise for a consol, which never comes due. The answer is obvious for a discount bond: at any positive interest rate, delaying its final and only payment reduces present value. A coupon bond's price depends on coupon payments, final payoff, and the number of payment periods until maturity.

In what follows, P, C, M, and i are a vanilla bond's current price, periodic coupon payment, payment at maturity, and interest yield, taken as given; and n is the number of periods remaining until maturity.

$$P = \frac{C\left(1 - \frac{1}{(1+i)^n}\right)}{i} + \frac{M}{(1+i)^n}$$

With apologies for treating n as a continuous variable, the derivative is:

$$\frac{\ln(1+i)(C - iM)}{i(1+i)^n}$$

The sign of this derivative depends on the sign of $C - iM$ in the numerator. An extra coupon payment C is the marginal gain from lengthening the bond; iM is the lost opportunity of otherwise earning interest during the extended time until payoff. If $C > iM$, a one-period extension brings marginal gain exceeding marginal loss; if $C < iM$, marginal gain falls short of marginal loss. Gain and loss are measured in dollars current at the time of the extension. Both amounts refer to the same extension period and so need not be discounted to the present or any other particular time. The rest of the formula discounts that gain/loss comparison into present value.

For the bondholder, a 1-year extension costs the loss of interest that could have been earned on the amount paid at maturity: iM. The benefit is the additional coupon payment C. The bondholder would be indifferent to the extension if $iM = C$ (as would be true of a bond paying \$1000 at maturity and an annual coupon of \$50 with a 5 percent interest rate prevailing). The bondholder would reject it if $iM > C$ and prefer it if $iM < C$. Thus, favoring the extension is a relatively low interest rate or maturity payoff and a relatively large coupon.

While it is often convenient to theorize about "the" interest rate without worrying about bond maturities and rate changes, the interest rate in question here is the one in effect at the time of deciding on an extension; any different rate when the bond was originally priced and sold has become ancient history. Wise investment decisions try to take account of the rate to be earned on funds received when bonds come due. Some investors want to keep their options open by buying only short bonds; others, like a life-insurance company, want to delay making reinvestments at possibly fallen interest rates by holding long-term bonds.

Modified Duration, a Measure of Bond-Price Sensitivity

"Macaulay" duration is equivalently the weighted sum of the lengths of subperiods until a bond's maturity. The weights are the present values of the then-current contributions to value during each subperiod. Time duration is mainly of theoretical interest. It might, for example, illuminate Chapter 7s concepts of average period of production, investment, or degree of roundaboutness.

In practice, investors care less about time duration than how sensitively a bond's price responds to a change in the generally prevailing interest rate to which its own yield must conform. The straightforward but tedious way to an answer, amply illustrated, calculates the sum of the present values of the bond's final and intermediate payments at before-and-after interest rates.

"Modified duration" is a simplified report of such calculations. It is not a straightforward length of time. Rather, it is the ratio of a percentage change in a bond's price to a percentage point change of the prevailing interest rate in the opposite direction. It is not an elasticity in the ordinary sense of a dimensionless ratio of two proportionate changes. Still, as dimensions, the percentages in numerator and denominator cancel out, leaving years, rather irrelevantly, as the dimension of this ratio. The result could even be negative in weird cases mentioned later.[6]

A long bond has a larger modified duration than a short bond; a percentage point rise or fall in the prevailing interest rate causes a greater percentage fall or rise in its price. Investors fearful of an increased interest rate, perhaps from inflation, would shun long bonds for short

[6] Descriptions by two investment firms recognize the technicality of a time dimension in different but compatible ways. For one firm, modified duration is:

the approximate change in a bond's price for every 100 basis point (one single percentage point) change in market interest rate levels. Ordinarily, the longer the duration, the higher the risk that the bond's price will change as interest rates change. Duration of five, for example, means a bond's price should rise by approximately 5% for a one percentage point drop in interest rates and fall 5% for a one percentage point rise in interest rates" (*DWS Active Reports*, June 2011, p. 3).

In the words of another firm,

The [modified] duration of an instrument is different from the maturity of an instrument in that duration measures the average period remaining until the discounted value of the amounts due (principal and interest) under the instrument are to be paid, rather than the instrument's stated final maturity. In addition, portfolio duration of two years means that if interest rates increased by one percent, the value of the portfolio would decrease by approximately two percent (William Blair Funds 2013).

ones. By the sheer arithmetic of discounting, duration in years moves inversely to interest rates (except for the final-payment-only discount bond, whose duration just is its time to maturity). Furthermore, a bond's price responds more sensitively when the interest rate changes within a low range than within a high range (that is, when its price is high, not low) and at long rather than short durations.

Tables A.1, A.2, and A.3 illustrate these points. A bond's price sensitivity depends positively on its time to maturity, as is intuitively obvious, and inversely on the general level within which the market interest rate changes. A 1 point change is relatively larger in the 1–2 percent range than in the 11–12 percent range. The tables consider discount bonds, since a coupon-bearing "plain vanilla" bond may be analyzed as a package of discount bonds and shares their just-mentioned characteristics.

Complications assumed away for the sake of clean analysis in the tables that follow include default risk, convertibility and call and adjustable-rate provisions, preferential tax treatment, and other special features.

Table A.1 Present values of discount bonds by maturity and interest rate

Present value of a discount bond for $100 in 1 year	Present value of a discount bond for $100 in 3 years
At 1%: $99.01	At 1%: $97.06
At 2%: $98.04	At 2%: $94.23
Price drops 0.98% when the interest rate rises 1 point	Price drops 2.92% when the interest rate rises 1 point
At 11%: $90.09	At 11%: $73.12
At 12%: $89.29	At 12%: $71.18
Price drops 0.89% when the interest rate rises 1 point	Price drops 2.65% when the interest rate rises 1 point

Table A.2 Interest rates and price changes for a 5-year discount bond paying $1000 at maturity

Interest rate	*Price*	*Price rise in dollars*	*Price rise as % of first price shown (%)*	*% Rise by log method (%)*
0.15	$497.18	$22.19	4.46	4.37
0.14	$519.37			
0.03	$862.61	$43.12	5.00	4.88
0.02	$905.73			

Table A.3 Interest rates and price changes for a 10-year discount bond paying $1000 at maturity

Interest rate	*Price*	*Price rise in dollars*	*Price rise as % of first price shown (%)*	*% Rise by log method (%)*
0.15	$247.18	$22.56	9.13	8.73
0.14	$269.74			
0.03	$744.09	$76.25	10.25	9.76
0.02	$820.35			

Table A.4 Interest rates and price changes for a consol paying $100 a year forever

Interest rate	*Price*	*Price rise in dollars*	*Price rise as % of first price shown (%)*	*% Rise by log method (%)*
0.15	$666.67	$47.62	7.14	6.90
0.14	$714.29			
0.03	$3333.33	$1666.67	50.00	40.55
0.02	$5000.00			

Simplicity also recommends working with once-per-year compounding of interest (although we could work with a shorter period or continuous compounding and a correspondingly lower rate).

Table A.4 describes a consol paying $100 at the end of the first year and every year forever. Its price equals this annual payment divided by the interest rate. Again, as with a discount bond, the price is more sensitive to an interest-rate change in a low than in a high range of rates.

Analyzing a "plain vanilla" bond as a package of discount bonds yields the numbers in Tables A.5 and A.6. Again, the same characteristics of price sensitivity appear.

Convexity

Modified duration expresses a change along a nonlinear function as if it were linear. The precise relation between interest rates and bond prices is represented by the slopes at various positions on a curve bowed in toward the origin. The slope of a secant between any old and new points on the curve only approximates the interest-rate/bond-price relation within that

Table A.5 Interest rates and price changes for a coupon-bearing bond paying \$100 at the end of each of 5 years and \$1000 at maturity

Interest rate	*Price*	*Price rise in dollars*	*Price rise as % of first price shown (%)*	*% Rise by log method (%)*
0.15	\$832.39	\$30.28	3.64	3.57
0.14	\$862.68			
0.03	\$1320.58	\$56.50	4.28	4.19
0.02	\$1377.08			

Table A.6 Interest rates and price changes for a coupon-bearing bond paying \$100 at the end of each of 10 years and \$1000 at maturity

Interest rate	*Price*	*Price rise in dollars*	*Price rise as % of first price shown (%)*	*% Rise by log method (%)*
0.15	\$582.40	\$30.65	5.26	5.13
0.14	\$613.05			
0.03	\$1202.06	\$89.63	7.46	7.19
0.02	\$1291.69			

range. This approximation is inadequate for large interest-rate changes. The professional jargon calls this phenomenon "convexity."

The horizontal axis in Fig. A.1 measures the general, competitively necessary, interest rate. The vertical axis measures the dollar price of a specific bond with its payments schedule. Each bond has its own characteristics and curve; but the generic type drawn is widely descriptive. The curve hits the vertical axis at the bond's undiscounted full payoff value at zero interest. The curve slopes downward and is bowed in toward the origin. It shows price more sensitive to interest-rate changes in a low range of rates (in the upper left of the diagram) than in a high range. The curve's downslope becomes less and less steep—more and more flat—at higher and higher interest rates. The curve cannot remain straight throughout; for then it would hit the horizontal axis at some definite interest rate, meaning that the bond's price drops all the way to zero at some less-than-infinite rate. And that would be nonsensical for the mere arithmetic of bond prices (setting aside complications like the possibility of default).

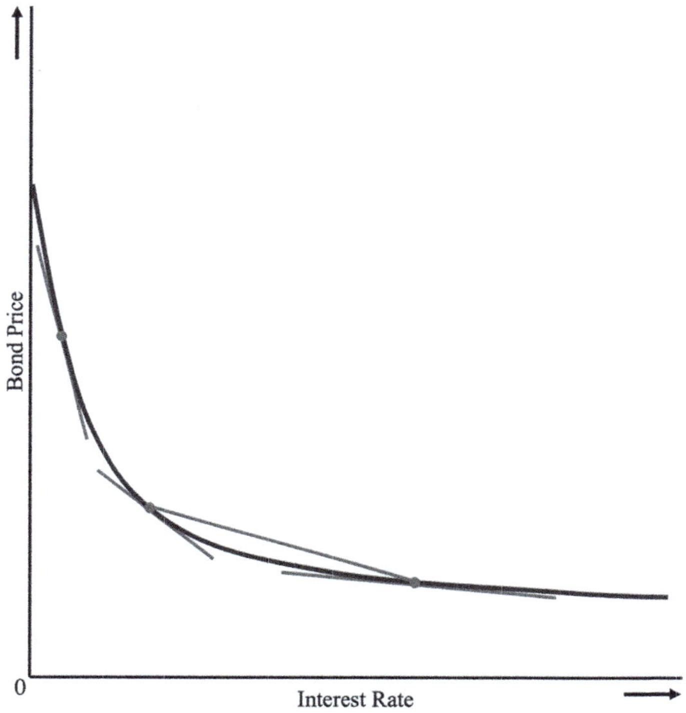

Fig. A.1 Changes in interest rates and bond prices

The bowed-in shape of the curve illustrates why the concept of modified duration is called "approximate." If the curve were straight over a certain range, the loss in the bond's value when the interest rate rises in that range from, say, 3 to 5 percent, would be twice as great as when it rises from 3 to only 4 percent. In fact, the loss is slightly less. A straight line simplification over a particular stretch of the bowed-in curve does not, then, precisely describe the interest-rate sensitivity over the entire range of interest rates. Still, as numerical examples show, the approximation is good for interest rates in a range that a bond expert has in mind when quoting a modified duration.

A Plain Vanilla Bond

So far, we have mostly considered a discount bond. A plain vanilla bond, paying interest periodically plus its face value at maturity, is more complicated. With A representing annual coupon payments, i the interest rate, and Z the bond's face value, the general formula for a plain vanilla bond's present value is:

$$P = \sum_{n=1}^{\text{end period}} \left(A(1+i)^{-n}\right) + Z(1+i)^{-\text{end period}}$$

A 3-year bond has a present value of:

$$P = A(1+i)^{-1} + A(1+i)^{-2} + A(1+i)^{-3} + Z(1+i)^{-3}$$

Or, equivalently:

$$P = \sum_{n=1}^{3}\left(A(1+i)^{-n}\right) + Z(1+i)^{-3}$$

The first derivative of this expression with respect to I is:

$$\frac{-Ai^2 - 4Ai - 6A - 3Z}{(1+i)^4} = -\frac{Ai^2 + 4Ai + 6A + 3Z}{(1+i)^4}$$

This derivative's negative sign means that price moves inversely to the interest rate.

The second derivative of this expression with respect to r is:

$$\frac{-2\left(-10A - 5Ai - Ai^2 - 6Z\right)}{(i+1)^5} = \frac{2\left(10A + 5Ai + Ai^2 + 6Z\right)}{(i+1)^5}$$

This second derivative's positive sign means that the price curve in Fig. A.25 slopes less steeply downward as the interest rate rises, which in turn means that each further increase in the interest rate brings a smaller further drop in the bond's already reduced dollar price.

Complications

One complication concerns the interest rate at which the proceeds of selling or cashing a bond could be reinvested. The issuer of a *callable* bond has the option of paying it off before maturity. If prevailing interest rates should fall, the issuer might exercise this option, pay off his debt, and borrow again at a lower rate. This commonly occurs with re-financeable mortgages. Creditors would be left to reinvest their money on less attractive terms. Since a decline in interest rates makes a call more likely, the bond's price falls. Furthermore, one might imagine an exceptional bond with amounts and times of interest payments flexibly adjusted so that the calculated duration turns out to be negative. That such a paradox is even conceivable emphasizes that modified duration is not straightforwardly a number of years.

References

Abken, Peter A. "Inflation and the Yield Curve." Federal Reserve Bank of Atlanta *Economic Review* 78, May/June 1993, pp. 13–31.

Adelman, Morris. *The World Petroleum Market*. Baltimore: Johns Hopkins University Press, 1972.

Akey, Pat and Stefan Lewellen. "Political Uncertainty, Political Capital and Firm Risk-Taking." Available at SSRN. March 22, 2017.

Alchian, Armen A. "Costs and Outputs." In Moses Abramowitz and others, *The Allocation of Economic Resources*. Stanford, CA: Stanford University Press, 1959, pp. 23–40. Reprinted in Armen A. Alchian. *Economic Forces at Work*. Indianapolis: LibertyPress, 1977, pp. 273–299.

Alchian, Armen A. "The Rate of Interest, Fisher's Rate of Return over Costs and Keynes' Internal Rate of Return." In Ezra Solomon, ed., *The Management of Corporate Capital*. New York: Free Press, 1959, pp. 67–71.

Alchian, Armen A. and William R. Allen. *University Economics*. 2d ed. Belmont, CA: Wadsworth, 1967, Chapter 22.

Alchian, Armen A. and William R. Allen. *University Economics*. 3d ed. Belmont, CA: Wadsworth, 1972, Chapter 23.

Allais, Maurice. *Économie et Intérêt*, 2 vols. Paris: Imprimerie Nationale, 1947.

Aristotle. *Nichomachean Ethics*. In *Introduction to Aristotle*. Trans. By W. D. Ross, ed. by Richard McKeon. New York: Modern Library, 1947, pp. 308–543.

Arnold, Frank S. "Issues in Interest." Manuscript, Menlo Park, CA: Institute for Humane Studies, Summer 1977.

Bailey, Martin J. *National Income and the Price Level*. 1st ed. New York: McGraw-Hill, 1962.

L. B. Yeager and S. H. Hanke, *Capital, Interest, and Waiting*,
https://doi.org/10.1007/978-3-031-63398-0

Baker, Scott R., Nicholas Bloom, and Steven J. Davis. "Measuring Economic Policy Uncertainty." *Quarterly Journal of Economics* 131, 4, November 2016, pp. 1593-1636.

Barnett, William A. *Getting It Wrong: How Faulty Monetary Statistics Undermine the Fed, the Financial System, and the Economy*. Cambridge, MA: MIT Press, 2011.

Barro, Robert J. and James W. Friedman. "On Uncertain Lifetimes." *Journal of Political Economy* 85, August 1977, pp. 843-849.

Beckmann, Klaus. *Analytische Grundlagen einer Finanzverfassung. Regelbegründungen und Regelbindungsprobleme aus finanzwissenschaftlicher Perspektive*, Passau: Peter Lang. 1998.

Bernanke, Ben. "Why Are Interest Rates So Low, Part 3: The Global Savings Glut." Brookings Institution, 1 Apr. 2015. https://www.brookings.edu/blog/ben-bernanke/2015/04/01/why-are-interest-rates-so-low-part-3-the-global-savings-glut/

Biddle, Frederic M. "Boeing Receives Order for 10 of Its 717 Jetliners." *Wall Street Journal*, 7 December 1998, p. A4.

Bierwag, Gerald O. "Duration and Immunization." In Peter Newman, Murray Milgate, and John Eatwell, eds., *The New Palgrave Dictionary of Money & Finance*, 1. New York: Stockton Press, 1992, pp. 708–710.

Blanchard, Olivier. "It Is Time to Revisit the 2% Inflation Target." *Financial Times*, 28 Nov. 2022.

Blaug, Mark. *Economic Theory in Retrospect*. 1st ed. Homewood, IL: Irwin, 1962. 4th ed. New York: Cambridge University Press, 1985, Chapter 12.

Bliss, C.J. *Capital Theory and the Distribution of Income*. Amsterdam, Netherlands: North Holland Publishign Company, 1975.

Blyth, C. A. "Wage Fund Doctrine." In Peter Newman, Murray Milgate, and John Eatwell, eds., *The New Palgrave Dictionary of Economics*, 4. New York: Stockton Press, 1987, pp. 835-837.

Böhm-Bawerk, Eugen von. *Capital and Interest*. In German, piecemeal, 1884–1912. Trans. by George D. Huncke and Hans F. Sennholz. 3 vols. South Holland, IL: Libertarian Press, 1959.

Bohr, Niels. *Atomic Physics and Human Knowledge*. New York: Wiley, 1958.

Bohr, Niels. *Essays 1958–1962 on Atomic Physics and Human Knowledge*. Bungay, England: Richard Clay and Company.

Boudry, Maarten and Johan Braeckman. "Immunizing Strategies & Epistemic Defense Mechanisms." *Philosophia* 39, 2011, pp. 145-161.

Boulding, Kenneth E. *The Economics of Peace*. New York: Prentice Hall, 1946.

Bowen, H. R. *Toward Social Economy*. New York: Rinehart, 1948.

Braun, Thomas. "Versicherungsprodukte für den Internetabsatz: Eine empirische Analyse des deutschen Direktversicherungsmarktes." Universität Passau doctoral dissertation, May 2003, Chapter 3, section 4.

Brown, Harry G. "The Marginal Productivity Versus the Impatience Theory of Interest." *Quarterly Journal of Economics* 27, August 1913, pp. 630–650.

Brunner, Karl. "The Role of Money and Monetary Policy." Federal Reserve Bank of St. Louis *Review,* July 1968.

Brunner, Karl. "Has Monetarism Failed?" *Cato Journal* 3, Spring 1983, pp. 23–62.

Buchanan, James M. *Public Principles of Public Debt.* Homewood, IL: Richard D. Irwin, 1958, reprinted Indianapolis: Liberty Fund, 1999.

Buchanan, James M. *Ethics and Economic Progress.* Norman, OK and London: University of Oklahoma Press, 1994, Chapter 2.

Burmeister, Edwin and Rodney A. Dobell. *Mathematical Theories of Economic Growth.* New York: Macmillan, 1970.

Caldwell, Bruce J., ed. *Carl Menger and his Legacy in Economics.* Durham, NC: Duke University Press, 1990.

Caldwell, Bruce J. "Clarifying Popper." *Journal of Economic Literature* 29, March 1991, pp.1- 33.

Campbell, John Y. "Some Lessons from the Yield Curve." *Journal of Economic Perspectives* 9, Summer 1995, pp. 129–152.

Campbell, John Y, Andrew W. Lo, and A.. Craig MacKinlay. *The Econometrics of Financial Markets.* Princeton, NJ: Princeton University Press, 1997.

Capra, Fritjof. *The Tao of Physics.* 3d ed. Boston: Shambala, 1991.

Carvalho, Carlos, Andrea Ferrero, and Fernanda Nechio. "Demographics and Real Interest Rates: Inspecting the Mechanism." Federal Reserve Bank of San Francisco Working Paper no. 2016–05, 2016.

Cass, David and Menahem E. Yaari, "A Re-examination of the Pure Consumption Loans Model." *Journal of Political Economy* 74, August 1966, pp. 353-367.

Cassel, Gustav. *The Nature and Necessity of Interest.* New York: Macmillan, 1903, reprinted New York: Augustus M. Kelley, 1956.

Cassel, Gustav. *The Theory of Social Economy.* Trans. by S. L. Barron from 5th German ed. New York: Harcourt, Brace, 1932. Reprinted New York: Augustus M. Kelley, 1967.

Cecchetti, Stephen G. "The Case of the Negative Nominal Interest Rates: New Estimates of the Term Structure of Interest Rates during the Great Depression." *Journal of Political Economy* 96, December 1988, pp. 1111–1141.

Champion, Rafe. "Essentialism and the Organic State." In *Reason and Imagination: Some Thoughts of Karl Popper and William W. Bartley,* CreateSpace Independent Publishing Platform; 2nd edition 2015.

Clower, Robert. "A Reconsideration of the Microfoundations of Monetary Theory," 1967. Reprinted in D. A. Walker, ed., *Money and Markets: Essays by Robert W. Clower.* Cambridge: Cambridge University Press, 1984, pp. 81-89.

Coeurdacier, Nicolas, Stéphane Guibaud, and Keyu Jin. "Credit Constraints and Growth in a Global Economy." *American Economic Review* 105 (9), September 2015, pp. 2838-81.

Cohen, Avi J. and G. C. Harcourt. "Whatever Happened to the Cambridge Capital Theory Controversies?" *Journal of Economic Perspectives* 17, Winter 2003, pp. 199–214.

"Commercial Aircraft Sales and Leasing." *Wikipedia*, 2008.

Conard, Joseph W. *An Introduction to the Theory of Interest*. Berkeley and Los Angeles: University of California Press, 1959.

Congdon, Tim. *Money in a Free Society*, New York: Encounter Books, first ed. 2011. Essay 4, "Keynes, Bernanke, and Krugman, and the Pathologies of Capitalism."

Crofton, Stephanie O. and Luis G. Dopico. "Zara-Inditex and the Growth of Fast Fashion." *Essays in Economic and Business History* 25, 2007, pp. 41-53.

Culbertson, J. M. "The Term Structure of Interest Rates." *Quarterly Journal of Economics* 71, November 1957, pp. 485-517.

Cwik, Paul F. "An Investigation of Inverted Yield Curves and Economic Downturns." Auburn University dissertation, 2004.

Dewey, Donald, *Modern Capital Theory.* New York: Columbia University Press, 1965.

Dorfman, Robert. "Waiting and the Period of Production." *Quarterly Journal of Economics* 73, August 1959, pp. 351-372.

Ebeling, Richard J., ed. *The Austrian Theory of the Trade Cycle and Other Essays*. New York: Center for Libertarian Studies, 1978. Reprinted Ludwig von Mises Institute.

Estrella, Arturo, Anthony R. Rodrigues, and Sebastian Schich. "How Stable is the Predictive Power of the Yield Curve? Evidence from Germany and the United States." *The Review of Economics and Statistics* 85, no. 3, August 2003, pp. 629-644.

Eucken, Walter. *Kapitaltheoretische Untersuchungen*. 2d edition. Tübingen: Mohr and Zurich: Polygraphischer Verlag, 1954.

Federal Reserve Bank of St. Louis, 10-Year Treasury Constant Maturity Minus 3-Month Treasury Constant Maturity [T10Y3M], retrieved from FRED, Federal Reserve Bank of St. Louis.

Fetter, Frank A. *Capital, Interest, and Rent*. Edited with an Introduction by Murray N. Rothbard. Kansas City, MO: Sheed Andrews and McMeel, 1977.

Fisher, Irving. "Appreciation and Interest." American Economic Association *Publications* 3 (11), August 1896, pp. 331–442; reprinted New York: Augustus M. Kelley, 1961.

Fisher, Irving. *The Theory of Interest*. New York: Macmillan, 1930, reprinted New York: Augustus M. Kelley, 1955–1970.

Fisher, Mark 2004. "Modeling the Term Structure of Interest Rates: An Introduction." Federal Reserve Bank of Atlanta *Economic Review* 89, no. 3, 2004.

Folger, Jean. "Duration." *Investopedia*, n.d.

Frederick, Shane, George Loewenstein, and Ted O'Donoghue. "Time Discounting and Time Preference: A Critical Review." *Journal of Economic Literature* 40, June 2002, pp. 351- 401.

Friedman, Milton. *The Optimum Quantity of Money and Other Essays*. Chicago: Aldine, 1969. Friedman, Milton. *Price Theory*. Chicago: Aldine, 1976.

Fry, Maxwell J. *Money, Interest, and Banking in Economic Development*. 1984. Baltimore: Johns Hopkins University Press, 1988.

Garrison, Roger W. "Austrian Capital Theory: The Early Controversies" in Bruce J. Caldwell, ed., *Carl Menger and His Legacy in Economics*. Durham: Duke University Press, 1990, pp. 133–154.

Garrison, Roger W. "Reflections on Reswitching and Roundaboutness" in Roger Koppl, ed., *Money and Markets: Essays in Honor of Leland B. Yeager.* London and New York: Routledge, 2006, pp. 186–206.

Garrison, Roger W. "Capital, Interest, and Professor Kirzner." *Journal des Economistes et des Etudes Humaines* 12, June/September 2002, pp. 343–356.

George, Henry. *Progress and Poverty*. 1879. Reprinted New York: Robert Schalkenbach Foundation, 1940, pp. 57-59.

George, Henry. *The Science of Political Economy*. 1897. Reprinted New York: Robert Schalkenbach Foundation, 1941.

Gesell, Silvio. *The Natural Economic Order*. San Antonio: Free Economy Publishing Co., 1934. Greidanus, Tjardus. *The Value of Money*. London: P. S. King and Son, 1932.

Green, David I., "Pain-Cost and Opportunity-Cost," *The Quarterly Journal of Economics*, Volume 8, Issue 2, January 1894, Pages 218–229.

Gulen, Huseyin and Mihai Ion. "Policy Uncertainty and Corporate Investment." *Review of Financial Studies*, 29, 3, March 2016, pp. 523-564.

Gurley, John G. and Edward S. Shaw. *Money in a Theory of Finance*. Washington, DC: Brookings Institution, 1960.

Hanke, Steve H. "Currency Boards." *Annals of the American Academy of Political and Social Science* 579, January 2002, pp. 87–105.

Hanke, Steve H. and Edward Li. "The Strange and Futile World of Trade Wars." *Journal of Applied Corporate Finance*, 31, 4, 2019, pp. 59-67.

Hanke, Steve H., P.H. Carver, and P. Bugg, "Project Evaluation During Inflation", *Water Resources* 11, 4, 1975, pp. 511–514.

Hansson, Björn. "Forced Saving." In Peter Newman, Murray Milgate, and John Eatwell, eds., *The New Palgrave Dictionary of Economics,* 2. New York: Stockton, 1987, pp. 398-399.

Hardouvelis, Gikas A. "Term Structure of Interest Rates." In David Glasner, ed., *Business Cycles and Depressions: An Encyclopedia*. New York: Garland Publishing, 1997, pp. 676–678.

Harsanyi, John C. *Essays on Ethics, Social Behavior, and Scientific Explanation*. Dordrecht and Boston: Reidel, 1976.

Harvey, Campbell R. "The Real Term Structure and Consumption Growth." *Journal of Financial Economics*, 22, 2, 1988, pp. 305-333.

Haubrich, Joseph G. "Term Structure from A to B." Federal Reserve Bank of Cleveland *Economic Review* 35, 1999 Quarter 3, pp. 2–9.

Hawley, Frederick B. "The Fundamental Error of *Kapital und Kapitalzins.*" *Quarterly Journal of Economics* 6, April 1892, pp. 280–307.

Hayek, Friedrich A. "The Mythology of Capital." *Quarterly Journal of Economics* 50, February 1936, pp. 199–228. Reprinted in American Economic Association, *Readings in the Theory of Income Distribution*. Philadelphia: Blakiston, 1946, pp. 355–383.

Hayek, Friedrich A. *The Pure Theory of Capital*. Chicago: University of Chicago Press, 1941, Midway reprint, 1975.

Hayek, Friedrich A. "The Use of Knowledge in Society." *American Economic Review* 35, 4, September 1945, pp. 519-530.

Haynes, John. "Risk as an Economic Factor." *Quarterly Journal of Economics* 9, July 1895, pp. 409-449.

Henderson, Hubert. *Supply and Demand*. Cambridge Economic Handbooks, 1921. Chicago: University of Chicago Press, 1958 (third impression 1963).

Hennings, Klaus H. "Waiting." In Peter Newman, Murray Milgate, and John Eatwell, eds., *The New Palgrave Dictionary of Economics* 4. New York: Stockton Press, 1987, pp. 846–848.

Hennings, Klaus H. *The Austrian Theory of Value and Capital*. Cheltenham, England, and Brookfield, VT: Edward Elgar, 1997.

Hetzel, Robert L. "How Do Central Banks Control Inflation?" Federal Reserve Bank of Richmond *Economic Quarterly* 90, Summer 2004, pp. 47–63.

Hetzel, Robert L. "Monetary Policy in the 2008–2009 Recession." Federal Reserve Bank of Richmond *Economic Quarterly* 95, no. 2, Spring 2009, pp. 201–233.

Hetzel, Robert L. *The Great Recession: Market Failure or Policy Failure?* New York: Cambridge University Press, 2012.

Heyne, Paul. "Are Economists Basically Immoral?" 1993. Chapter 1 in his *"Are Economists Basically Immoral?" and Other Essays in Economics, Ethics, and Religion*. Edited by Geoffrey Brennan and A. M. C. Waterman. Indianapolis: Liberty Fund, 2008.

Hicks, J. R. "The Theory of Uncertainty and Profit." *Economica*, old series no. 32, May 1931, pp. 170-189.

Hicks, J. R. "Is Interest the Price of a Factor of Production?" In Mario J. Rizzo, ed., *Time, Uncertainty, and Disequilibrium*. Lexington, MA: Lexington Books, 1979, pp. 51-63.

Higgs, Robert. "Regime Uncertainty: Why the Great Depression Lasted So Long and Why Prosperity Resumed after the War." *Independent Review* 1, 4, 1997, pp. 561-590.

Hilsenrath, Jon. "Years of Fed Missteps Fueled Disillusion with the Economy and Washington." *Wall Street Journal* online, 26 August 2016.

Hirshleifer, Jack. *Investment, Interest, and Capital*. Englewood Cliffs, NJ: Prentice-Hall, 1970.

Hirshleifer, Jack. "On the Theory of the Optimal Investment Decision." In Ezra Solomon, ed., *The Management of Corporate Capital*, New York: Free Press, 1959.

Hirshleifer, Jack. *Price Theory and Applications*. 1st ed., 2d ed. Englewood Cliffs, NJ: Prentice-Hall, 1976, 1980.

Hirshleifer, Jack and John G. Riley. *The Analytics of Uncertainty and Information*. Cambridge: Cambridge University Press, 1992.

Homer, Sidney and Richard Sylla. *A History of Interest Rates*. 3d ed. New Brunswick, NJ: Rutgers University Press, 1996.

Howitt, Peter. "Fisher Effect." In Peter Newman, Murray Milgate, and John Eatwell, eds., *New Palgrave Dictionary of Money & Finance* 2. New York: Stockton Press, 1992, pp. 123-124.

Hulten, Charles R. "Measuring the Economy of the 21st Century." *NBER Reporter* 2015, no. 4, pp. 1–7.

Hume, David. "Of Money" and "Of Interest." From *Political Discourses*, 1752. Reprinted in Hume's *Writings on Economics*, ed. Eugene Rotwein, 1955, pp. 33–46 and 47–59. 2d ed. Madison, WI: University of Wisconsin Press, 1970.

Humphrey, Thomas M. "Interest Rates, Expectations, and the Wicksellian Policy Rule." Federal Reserve Bank of Richmond Working Paper 75–2. July 1975.

Hutt, W. H. *Keynesianism—Retrospect and Prospect*. Chicago: Regnery, 1963.

Hutt, W. H. "The Yield from Money Held." In *Freedom and Free Enterprise*, ed. by Mary Sennholz, Van Nostrand, 1956. Reprinted in his *Individual Freedom*. Ed. by Svetozar Pejovich and David Klingaman. Westport, CT: Greenwood Press, 1975, pp. 207–229.

Hutt, W. H. *A Rehabilitation of Say's Law*. Columbus, OH: Ohio University Press, 1974.

Irwin, Neil. "Of Kiwis and Currencies: How a 2% Inflation Target Became Global Economic Gospel." *New York Times*, 19 December 2014.

Jones, Robert. "Notes on Duration", Simon Fraser University, Notes for Economics 811, Summer 2004.

Jordan, Jerry L. "The Age-Old Problem of Low Interest Rates." *Forbes Opinion*, June 16, 2016.

Kahn, Gabriel. "Invisible Supplier Has Penney's Shirts All Buttoned Up." *Wall Street Journal*, 11 September 2003, pp. A1, A9.

Kaldor, Nicholas. "Annual Survey of Economic Theory: The Recent Controversy on the Theory of Capital." *Econometrica* 5, July 1937, pp. 201-233.

Kenen, Peter B. "Nature, Capital, and Trade." *Journal of Political Economy* 73, October 1965, pp. 437–460.

Keynes, John Maynard. *The General Theory of Employment, Interest, and Money*. New York: Harcourt, Brace, 1936.

King, Robert G. and André Kurmann. "Expectations and the Term Structure of Interest Rates: Evidence and Implications." Federal Reserve Bank of Richmond *Economic Quarterly* 88, Fall 2002, pp. 49–95.

Kirzner, Israel M. *An Essay on Capital*. New York: Augustus M. Kelley, 1966.

Kirzner, Israel M. "Ludwig von Mises and The Theory of Capital and Interest." In Laurence S. Moss, ed., *The Economics of Ludwig von Mises*. Kansas City, MO: Sheed and Ward, 1974, pp. 51–65.

Kirzner, Israel M. "The Pure Time-Preference Theory of Interest: An Attempt at Clarification" in Jeffrey M. Herbener, ed., *The Meaning of Ludwig von Mises*. Auburn, AL: Mises Institute and Norwell, MA: Kluver, 1993, Chapter 6, pp. 166–192. Reprinted in Herbener, ed., 2011, pp. 99–126.

Knight, Frank H. "The Quantity of Capital and the Rate of Interest." Parts I & II. *Journal of Political Economy* 44, August 1936, pp. 433–463, and October 1936, pp. 612–642.

Knight, Frank H. "On the Theory of Capital: In Reply to Mr. Kaldor." *Econometrica* 6, January 1938, pp. 63–82.

Knight, Frank H. "Diminishing Returns from Investment." *Journal of Political Economy* 52, March 1944, pp. 26–47.

Koch Oil Company. "Did You Know?" In *At Your Service*, vol. 3, no. 2, April 1996.

Kuenne, Robert. *Eugen von Böhm-Bawerk*. New York: Columbia University Press, 1971.

Lachmann, Ludwig. *Capital and Its Structure*. Kansas City, MO: Sheed, Andrews and McMeel, 1956/1978.

Laibman, David and Edward J. Nell. "Reswitching, Wicksell Effects, and the Neoclassical Production Function." *American Economic Review* 67, December 1977, pp. 878-888.

Lassalle, Ferdinand. "What is Capital?" Freely translated by F. Keddell from chapter IV of *Herr Bastiat-Schulze von Delitzsch, der ökonomische Julian*. 1864. New York: New York Labor News, 1918.

Laudan, Larry. *Progress and Its Problems*. Berkeley: University of California Press, 1977.

Lerner, Abba P. *The Economics of Control*. New York: Macmillan, 1944, reprinted 1947.

Lerner, Abba P. "Capital." *International Encyclopedia of the Social Sciences* 2, New York: Macmillan and Free Press, 1968, pp. 270–278.

Lerner, Abba P. "Consumption-Loan Interest and Money," *Journal of Political Economy* 67, October 1959, pp. 512–518.

Levatter, Ross. "Von Mises and Time-Preference." *Reason Papers*, No. 5, Winter 1979, pp. 69–78.

Lewin, Peter. *Capital in Disequilibrium*. London and New York: Routledge, 1999.

Linebaugh, Kate. "The Math Changes on Bulbs." *Wall Street Journal*, 30 November 2011, pp. B1-B2.

Litterman, Robert, José Scheinkman, and Laurence Weiss. "Volatility and the Yield Curve." *Journal of Fixed Income* 1, June 1991, pp. 49-53.

Loewenstein, George and John Elster, eds. *Choice over Time*. New York: Russell Sage Foundation, 1992.

Lunsford, J. Lynn and Liam Pleven, "AIG Leasing Unit Mulls Split-Up", *Wall Street Journal*, 12 May 2008, pp. A1, A12.

Lutz, Friedrich A. *Zinstheorie*. 2d ed. Zurich: Polygraphischer Verlag and Tübingen: Mohr, 1967. Trans. by Claus Wittich as *The Theory of Interest*. Dordrecht: Reidel, 1968, pp. 96–99, 106–107.

Macaulay, Frederick R. *Some Theoretical Problems Suggested by the Movements of Interest Rates: Bond Yields, and Stock Prices in the United States Since 1856*. New York: National Bureau of Economic Research, 1938, no. 33.

MacVane, Silas Marcus. "Analysis of Cost of Production." *Quarterly Journal of Economics* 1, July 1887, pp. 481–487.

MacVane, Silas Marcus. "Boehm-Bawerk on Value and Wages." *Quarterly Journal of Economics* 5, October 1890, pp. 24–43.

MacVane, Silas Marcus. "Capital and Interest." *Quarterly Journal of Economics* 6, January 1892, pp. 129–150.

Malkiel, Burton G. *The Term Structure of Interest Rates*. Princeton, NJ: Princeton University Press, 1966, Chapter 3.

Malkiel, Burton G. "Term Structure of Interest Rates." In Peter Newman, Murray Milgate, and John Eatwell, eds., *The New Palgrave Dictionary of Money & Finance,* 3. New York: Stockton Press, 1992, pp. 650–653.

Marshall, Alfred. *Principles of Economics*. 8th ed. London: Macmillan, 1920, reprinted 1947.

Martinez, Barbara. "Why Own? Sell It and Then Lease Back the Space." *Wall Street Journal*, 20 April 1999, pp. A2, A6.

Martinsohn, Udo. "Kumulierte Unsicherheit—der Weg in die Rückversicherung." *Steirische Berichte*, nos. 2–3, 2003.

Marty, Alvin L. and Daniel L. Thornton. "Is There a Case for 'Moderate' Inflation?" Federal Reserve Bank of St. Louis *Review*, July/August 1995, pp. 27–37.

McCallum, Bennett T. "Monetary Policy Analysis in Models Without Money." Federal Reserve Bank of St. Louis *Review*, July/August 2001, pp. 145–160.

McKinnon, Ronald I. *Money and Capital in Economic Development*. Washington, DC: Brookings Institution, 1973.

Meckling, W. H. "An Exact Consumption-Loan Model of Interest: A Comment." *Journal of Political Economy* 68, February 1960, pp. 72-84.

Meigs, A. James. "Recent Innovations in the Functions of Banks." *American Economic Review* 56, May 1966, pp. 167–177.

Menger, Carl. *Principles of Economics*. German original 1871. Trans. and ed. by James Dingwall and Bert F. Hoselitz. Glencoe, IL: Free Press, 1950.

Meyer, Dirk. "Die Übernahme von Risiko als Produktionsfaktor am Beispiel von Versicherungen." *Zeitschrift für die gesamte Versicherungswissenschaft* 81, 4, 1992, pp. 597-615.

Michaelsen, Jacob B. *The Term Structure of Interest Rates*. New York: Intext, 1973.

Midgley, Mary. *The Ethical Primate*. London: Routledge, 1994/2002.

Mill, John Stuart. *Principles of Political Economy with some of their Applications to Social Philosophy*. 1848 and subsequent revisions. New edition edited by W. J. Ashley. London and New York: Longmans, Green, 1929.

Mises, Ludwig von. *Nationalökonomie*. Geneva: Editions Union, 1940. Reprinted by Mises Institute, Auburn, AL, 2007.

Mises, Ludwig von. *Human Action*. 2d ed. New Haven: Yale University Press, 1963. Third revised edition, Chicago: Regnery, 1966. Scholar's Edition, Auburn, AL: Mises Institute, 2008.

Mishan, E. J. *Cost-Benefit Analysis*. Revised new edition. London: Allen & Unwin, 1975.

Mundell, Robert. "Inflation and Real Interest." *Journal of Political Economy* 71, June 1963, pp. 280-283.

Mundell, Robert. *Monetary Theory*. Pacific Palisades, CA: Goodyear, 1971.

Nickolas, Steven. "What Is the Difference Between Macaulay Duration and Modified Duration?" *Investopedia*, 14 May 2015.

O'Hear, Anthony. *Karl Popper*. London: Routledge, 1980.

Patinkin, Don. *Money, Interest, and Prices*. Evanston, IL: Row, Peterson, 1956. 2nd ed. New York: Harper & Row, 1965.

Pigou, A. C. *The Economics of Welfare*. 4th ed. London: Macmillan, 1932, reprinted 1950.

Pigou, A. C. "The Classical Stationary State." *Economic Journal*, 53, December 1943, pp. 343-351.

Pigou, A. C. "Economic Progress in a Stable Environment." *Economica*, new series 14, August 1947, pp. 180-188.

Popper, Karl. *The Logic of Scientific Discovery*. New York: Basic Books, 1959.

Popper, Karl. *The Open Society and Its Enemies*. 5th ed. Princeton, NJ: Princeton University Press, 1966.

Popper, Karl. *Unended Quest*. Revised edition. LaSalle, IL and London: Open Court, 1982.

Rabin, Alan A. *Monetary Theory*. Cheltenham, UK, and Northampton MA: Elgar, 2004.

Rachel, Lukasz and Thomas D. Smith. "Secular Drivers of the Global Real Interest Rate." Bank of England Staff Working Paper no. 571, December 2015.

Ramsay, Frank P. "A Mathematical Theory of Saving." *Economic Journal* 38, December 1928, pp. 543–559.

Robertson, Dennis. *Lectures on Economic Principles*. London: Collins / Fontana Library, 1963.

Rosenberg, Joshua V. and Samuel Maurer. "Signal or Noise? Implications of the Term Premium for Recession Forecasting." Federal Reserve Bank of NY *Economic Policy Review* 14, July 2008, pp. 1–11.

Rosser Jr., J. Barkley. "Continuity and Capital-Reversal: Comment." *Economic Inquiry* 16, 1, January 1978, pp. 143–146.

Rothbard, Murray N. *Man, Economy, and State* (1962). Scholar's Edition, 2d ed., with *Power and Market* (1970). Auburn. AL: Ludwig von Mises Institute, 2009, pp. 319–330, 341, 375–386, 402, 414–423.

Rucker, Rudy. *Mind Tools: The Five Levels of Mathematical Reality.* Boston: Houghton Mifflin.

Samuelson, Paul A. "Equalization by Trade of the Interest Rate along with the Real Wage." In Robert E. Baldwin and others, eds., *Money, Growth, and the Balance of Payments.* Chicago: Rand McNally, 1965.

Samuelson, Paul A. "An Exact Consumption-Loan Model of Interest with or without the Social Contrivance of Money." *Journal of Political Economy* 66, December 1958, pp. 467–482.

Samuelson, Paul A. "A Summing Up." *Quarterly Journal of Economics* 80, November 1966, pp. 568–583.

Samuelson, Paul A. "Schumpeter as an Economic Theorist." In Helmut Frisch, ed., *Schumpeterian Economics.* New York: Praeger Publishers, 1981.

Samuelson, Paul A., Abba P. Lerner, W. H. Meckling, and David Cass and Menahem E. Yaari. Discussion in *Journal of Political Economy* 66, December 1958, pp. 467–482, vol. 67, October 1959, pp. 512–525, vol. 68, February 1960, pp. 72–84, and vol. 74, August 1966, pp. 353–367.

Say, J.-B. *A Treatise on Political Economy.* Translated by C. R. Prinsep. Philadelphia: Grigg & Elliot, 1836.

Schelling, Thomas C. *The Strategy of Conflict*. Cambridge: Harvard, University Press, 1960.
Schneider, Erich. *Wirtschaftlichkeitsrechnung*. 6th ed. Tübingen: Mohr and Zürich: Polygraphischer Verlag, 1966.
Schumpeter, Joseph A. *The Theory of Economic Development*. 1911. Trans. by Redvers Opie. Cambridge, MA: Harvard University Press, 1934, reprinted New Brunswick, NJ: Transaction, 1983.
Schumpeter, Joseph A. *History of Economic Analysis*. Edited from manuscript by Elizabeth Boody Schumpeter. New York: Oxford University Press, 1954.
Senior, Nassau W. *An Outline of the Science of Political Economy*. 1836, 6th ed. 1872. Reprinted New York: Augustus M. Kelley, 1965.
Scitovsky, Tibor. *Welfare and Competition*. Rev. ed. Homewood, IL: Irwin, 1971.
Scott, Anthony. *Natural Resources: The Economics of Conservation*. Toronto: University of Toronto Press, 1955.
Selgin, George. "The Yield on Money Held Revisited: Lessons for Today." *Market Process* [George Mason University] 5, no. 1, Spring 1987, pp. 18–24. Reprinted in Peter J. Boettke and David L. Prychitko, eds., *The Market Process: Essays in Contemporary Austrian Economics*. Aldershot, England and Brookfield, VT: Elgar, 1994, pp. 139–155.
Selgin, George. *Less Than Zero: The Case for a Falling Price Level in a Growing Economy*. London: Institute of Economic Affairs, 1997.
Sellon Jr., Gordon H. "Expectations and the Monetary Policy Transmission Mechanism." Federal Reserve Bank of Kansas City *Economic Review* 89, Fourth Quarter 2004, pp. 5–41.
Shackle, G. L. S. *Economics for Pleasure*. Cambridge: Cambridge University Press, 1962.
Shailesh, Kirti. "Top 7 Theories of Profit (With Criticisms)." *Economics Discussion*, 2017.
Shaw, Edward S. *Financial Deepening in Economic Development*. New York: Oxford University Press, 1973.
Shiller, Robert J. "The Term Structure of Interest Rates." In Benjamin M. Friedman and Frank H. Hahn, eds., *Handbook of Monetary Economics* I, with a data appendix by J. Huston McCulloch. Amsterdam and New York: North-Holland, 1990, pp. 627–722.
Sinn, Hans-Werner. "Risiko als Produktionsfaktor." *Jahrbücher für Nationalökonomie und Statistik* 201, no. 6, 1986, pp. 557-571.
Short, Eugenie Dudding. "A New Look at Real Money Balances as a Variable in the Production Function." *Journal of Money, Credit and Banking* 11, August 1979, pp. 326–339.
Skousen, Mark. *The Structure of Production: New Revised Edition*, New York: NYU Press, 2015

Smith, Barry. "Aristotelianism, Apriorism, Essentialism." In Peter J. Boettke, ed. *The Elgar Companion to Austrian Economics*. Aldershot, England, and Brookfield, VT: Elgar, 1994, pp. 33–37.

Solomon, Ezra. "Introduction", "The Arithmetic of Capital Budgeting Decisions," and "Measuring a Company's Cost of Capital." In Solomon, ed., *The Management of Corporate Capital*, New York: Free Press, 1959, pp. 13–20, 74–79, and 128–140.

Sowell, Thomas. *Knowledge and Decisions*. New York: Basic Books, 1980.

"The Spectrum of Bond Investing." *DWS Active Reports*, June 2011, p. 3.

Stein, Benjamin, with Herbert Stein. *On the Brink*. New York: Simon and Schuster, 1977.

Stigler, George J. *Production and Distribution Theories: The Formative Period*. New York: Macmillan, 1941.

Strigl, Richard von. *Capital and Production*. Trans. by Margaret and Hans-Hermann Hoppe, ed. by Jörg Guido Hülsmann. Auburn, AL: Mises Institute, 2000.

Taylor, Lester D. *Capital, Accumulation, and Money*. Boston, Dordrecht, and London: Kluwer, 2000.

Teller, Edward. *The Pursuit of Simplicity*. Malibu, CA: Pepperdine University Press, 1980.

Theimer, Otto H. *A Gentleman's Guide to Modern Physics*. Belmont, CA: Wadsworth, 1973.

Tobin, James. "Money and Economic Growth." *Econometrica* 33, October 1965, pp. 671-684.

Turgot, A. R. J. *Sur la Formation et la Distribution des Richesses*. 1766. Published in serial form in *Éphémérides*, 1769–70.

U.S. Bureau of Economic Analysis, Real Gross Domestic Product [GDPC1], retrieved from FRED database, Federal Reserve Bank of St. Louis.

Vickrey, William S. *Metastatics and Macroeconomics*. New York: Harcourt, Brace & World, 1964.

Walker, Michael A. "Why Are Interest Rates So Low? A Framework for Modeling Current Global Financial Developments." Vancouver: Fraser Institute, 2016.

Walras, Leon. *Elements of Pure Economics*. 1874/1926. Trans. by William Jaffé. Homewood, IL: Irwin, 1954.

Weil, Jonathan. "How Leases Play a Shadowy Role in Accounting." *Wall Street Journal*, 22 September 2004, pp. A1, A6.

Wicksell, Knut. *Interest and Prices*. 1936, Trans. by R. F. Kahn, from *Geldzins und Güterpreise*, 1898. Reprinted New York: Augustus M. Kelley, 1965.

Wicksell, Knut. *Lectures on Political Economy*. 1901, 1906. Trans. by E. Classen. London: Routledge & Kegan Paul; vol. I, 1934; vol. II, 1935.

William Blair Funds. *Prospectus*. Chicago, 1 May 2013.

Woodford, Michael. *Interest and Prices: Foundations of a Theory of Monetary Policy*. Princeton: Princeton University Press, 2003.

Wright, David McCord. "Professor Knight on Limits to the Use of Capital." *Quarterly Journal of Economics* 58, May 1944, pp. 331–358.

Wynne, Mark A. "Global Demographic Trends Shape Policy Environment." Federal Reserve Bank of Dallas *Economic Letter* 11, July 2016.

Yeager, Leland B. "Toward Understanding Some Paradoxes in Capital Theory." *Economic Inquiry* 14, September 1976, pp. 313–346.

Yeager, Leland B. *Ethics as Social Science*. Cheltenham, England and Northampton, MA: Edward Elgar, 2001.

Yeager, Leland B. "Land, Money, and Capital Formation." In J. G. Backhaus and others, eds., *Economic Policy in an Orderly Framework*, Liber Amicorum for Gerrit Meijer, Münster: Lit Verlag, 2003, pp. 455–469. Reprinted in Yeager, *Is the Market a Test of Truth and Beauty?* Auburn, AL: Ludwig von Mises Institute, 2011, Chapter 12.

Yeager, Leland B. and Edwin Burmeister. "Continuity and Capital-Reversal: Reply." *Economic Inquiry* 16, no. 1, January 1978, pp. 147-149.

Yeager, Leland B. and Alan A. Rabin. "Monetary Aspects of Walras's Law and the Stock-Flow Problem." *Atlantic Economic Journal*, March 1997, pp. 18–36.

Name Index

L. B. Yeager and S. H. Hanke, *Capital, Interest, and Waiting*,
https://doi.org/10.1007/978-3-031-63398-0

Subject Index

L. B. Yeager and S. H. Hanke, *Capital, Interest, and Waiting*, https://doi.org/10.1007/978-3-031-63398-0

D

E

M

N

S

T

GPSR Compliance

The European Union's (EU) General Product Safety Regulation (GPSR) is a set of rules that requires consumer products to be safe and our obligations to ensure this.

If you have any concerns about our products, you can contact us on ProductSafety@springernature.com

In case Publisher is established outside the EU, the EU authorized representative is:

Springer Nature Customer Service Center GmbH
Europaplatz 3
69115 Heidelberg, Germany

The manufacturer's authorised representative in the EU is Springer Nature Customer Service Centre GmbH, Europaplatz 3, 69115 Heidelberg, Germany. If you have any concerns regarding our products, please contact ProductSafety@springernature.com

Printed and bound by CPI Group (UK) Ltd, Croydon, CR0 4YY

30/09/2026

02225565-0018